Benjamin Krämer | Philipp Müller [Eds.]

Questions of Communicative Change and Continuity

In Memory of Wolfram Peiser

The book processing charge was funded by the Baden-Württemberg Ministry of Science, Research and Arts in the funding programme Open Access Publishing and the University of Mannheim.

The Deutsche Nationalbibliothek lists this publication in the Deutsche Nationalbibliografie; detailed bibliographic data are available on the Internet at http://dnb.d-nb.de

ISBN   978-3-8487-8402-8 (Print)
        978-3-7489-2823-2 (ePDF)

British Library Cataloguing-in-Publication Data
A catalogue record for this book is available from the British Library.

ISBN   978-3-8487-8402-8 (Print)
        978-3-7489-2823-2 (ePDF)

Library of Congress Cataloging-in-Publication Data
Krämer, Benjamin | Müller, Philipp
Questions of Communicative Change and Continuity
In Memory of Wolfram Peiser
Benjamin Krämer | Philipp Müller [Eds.]
316 pp.
Includes bibliographic references.

ISBN   978-3-8487-8402-8 (Print)
        978-3-7489-2823-2 (ePDF)

1st Edition 2022
© The Authors
Published by
Nomos Verlagsgesellschaft mbH & Co. KG
Waldseestraße 3 – 5 | 76530 Baden-Baden
www.nomos.de

Production of the printed version:
Nomos Verlagsgesellschaft mbH & Co. KG
Waldseestraße 3 – 5 | 76530 Baden-Baden

ISBN   978-3-8487-8402-8 (Print)
ISBN   978-3-7489-2823-2 (ePDF)
DOI   https://doi.org/10.5771/10.5771/9783748928232

Onlineversion
Nomos eLibrary

This work is licensed under the Creative Commons Attribution – ShareAlike 4.0 International License.

Table of Contents

Cycles and Coexistences, Comparisons and Catastrophes   7
An Introduction to the Volume
Benjamin Krämer & Philipp Müller

Why Are Most Published Research Findings Under-Theorized?   23
Or: Are We in an Interpretation Crisis?
Benjamin Krämer

Is Communication via the Internet *Public* Communication?   53
Hans-Bernd Brosius

How to Capture the Relations and Dynamics within the   67
Networked Public Sphere?
Modes of Interaction as a New Concept
Christoph Neuberger

How Does the Internet Change Group Processes?   96
Applying the Model of Collective Information Processing (MCIP)
to Online Environments
Johanna Schindler

Does Social Media Use Promote Political Mass Polarization?   118
A Structured Literature Review
Katharina Ludwig & Philipp Müller

Journalism or Public Relations?   167
Proposal for Conceptualizing a User-Oriented Research Program
on the Confounding of the Two Genres Online
Romy Fröhlich

Political Advertising – Good or Bad?   208
The Heterogeneity of U.S. Research Findings and Their Limited
Validity for Europe
Christina Holtz-Bacha

Table of Contents

Does the Media System Explain Individual Media Use
and Media Effects?
Findings From a Systematizing Literature Review
Cornelia Wallner

223

Do People Really Not Agree on What Can be Said?
Individual Differences in the Perception of Microaggressive, Derogatory and Hate Speech Against Women
Carsten Reinemann & Anna-Luisa Sacher

245

How Does One's Season of Birth Influence Television- and Music-Genre Preferences? And Why?
An Exploratory Analysis
Klaus Schönbach

274

Modes of Authentication
Realism Cues and Media Users' Assessment of Realism Across Media
and Genres
Felix Frey, Benjamin Krämer & Wolfram Peiser

294

Cycles and Coexistences, Comparisons and Catastrophes
An Introduction to the Volume

Benjamin Krämer & Philipp Müller

Modernity has a particular relationship with time and change. It has been characterized as the era in which the very idea of history as accelerating change toward the genuinely new has taken root in Occidental thought. Change is no longer restricted to a string of events to be chronicled, a more or less eternal cycle of life, or the inevitable course of decline toward the end time (on this view of modernity and these changing ideas of change, see, e.g., Koselleck, 1979). However, different philosophies of history and meta-narratives have since competed to capture the patterns and trends of change or the absence thereof (White, 1973). History and change have been described as moving, for example, in cycles, along generations of humans or other entities such as technologies coexisting or replacing each other, by catastrophes (to name some of the conceptions that will be taken up below), or in many other ways.

Mostly without any explicit reflection on the character of historicity in general and its own historicity, media and communication research has been strongly preoccupied with change—and much less so with continuities, although systematic theorizing would require to always consider the logical opposite of a term and to make a convincing argument for one side or for diverging tendencies. The development of the media (not only as merely technological artifacts but also as social institutions) has often been considered an agent of change (again, not necessarily in the sense of technological determinism but as a non-teleological social evolution catalyzed by, or interacting with the evolution of media technologies) or as reflective of social change. As mediated communication enables societies to self-monitor and come to a (collectively shared) understanding of itself and, therefore, fulfills a crucial function for their inner states, change (and continuities) in technologies, institutions, structures, and situations of communication can be decisive factors in further societal developments. This volume is dedicated to such patterns of communicative change and stability. It systematically explores different levels at which change and stability in communication can occur and be consequential.

Benjamin Krämer & Philipp Müller

This volume is dedicated to a scholar who has always been preoccupied with communicative change and continuities and the different scholarly and societal perspectives on these processes (which tend to overemphasize change over stability). In his research, he almost always dealt with different facets of the question whether different postulates of media and communication change can really be substantiated with hard empirical facts or whether they are based on specific or generalizable illusions of an ever-changing media landscape in which only seemingly nothing remains constant. This volume is dedicated to Wolfram Peiser who sadly passed away before his time in 2021.

It assembles contributions on communicative change and stability by a number of his academic companions, including his advisors, advisees, and peers. In one way or another all of these scholars' reasoning about communicative change has been influenced by Wolfram Peiser's thoughts on these questions which he shared with them, with us, widely. Even though coming from very different sub-fields of the communication discipline, all of the contributions in this book mirror Wolfram Peiser's influence, some very obvious and explicit, some in a more nuanced manner. Therefore, the contributions in this volume, despite touching upon very different aspects of communicative change and continuities resonate quite well with each other. It is Wolfram Peiser's intellectual legacy which lives on in his academic companions and binds their work together.

Wolfram Peiser was born in 1962 in the Bergisches Land, a wooded low mountain range in Northwestern Germany where he decided to study economics in the regional capital of Wuppertal. Soon drawn toward the social-scientific analysis of communication and the media, he completed his PhD at the Department of Journalism and Communication Research at Hanover University of Music and Drama under the supervision of Klaus Schönbach who also contributed to this volume. Peiser then worked and completed his habilitation at Johannes Gutenberg University Mainz at the chair of Christina Holtz-Bacha, who is also the author of one of the subsequent chapters. Thereafter, he served as interim professor and was then appointed as full professor at LMU Munich's Department of Media and Communication in 2006. Until his death, he supervised various PhD, habilitation, and other theses. Some of their authors and former members of his chair's academic staff are also among the contributors of this volume (Benjamin Krämer, Philipp Müller, Johanna Schindler, and Cornelia Wallner).

Among the different chairs at the department (several of Peiser's professorial colleagues are also present in this volume: Hans-Bernd Brosius, Romy Fröhlich, Christoph Neuberger, and Carsten Reinemann), Wolfram

Peiser specialized on media structures and media economics as well as media reception and effects—if this can still be termed "specialization" in today's highly differentiated academic landscape. The topics of the courses he taught ranged from a regular lecture on media economics to celebrity and stardom, media and acceleration, perceived realism of media content, or media and beauty.

Cycles and Continuities

The idea that history actually repeats itself is mostly seen as a simplistic or anachronistic concept. Popular sayings and quotes such as that we are doomed to repeat history if we do not learn from it or that history repeats itself as tragedy and farce demonstrate that we mostly do not really believe in the cyclical nature of history. Surely, cycles of, for instance, attention or scandalization are postulated in middle- to low-range theories of communicative phenomena, but only to discover and explore their exceptions or to contextualize assumptions of irreversible communicative change that structurally alters the conditions under which attention, moralization etc. function.

The seasons of the year are one of the last levels at which dominant Western thinking seems to accept cyclical conceptions of time in the stricter sense, if only to learn that due to global warming, the seasons 'are not longer what they used to be' in a given region. Googling information on the Bergisches Land, we can read from the local press that climate change raises hopes for more tourists in this region (reputed to be rather rainy), but that at the same time its forests are dying. This demonstrates that change can always be framed in different value-laden ways (or perceived and judged from different angles) and that the selection of a specific interpretation of change contributes to further change due to its impact on (other) actors' resulting (re-)actions—an argument which has been put forward with regard to media change by one of the PhD theses supervised by Wolfram Peiser (Müller, 2016).

Astrology, in contrast, is often derided by researchers as prototypically irrational folk belief based on anecdotal evidence, confirmation bias, and faulty causal reasoning. But what if, Wolfram Peiser and Klaus Schönbach thought in 1993, people actually differ in their character due to the season of birth, but for other reasons than the influence of the stars? As an academic side project, they analyzed data on seasons of birth and personality traits, found weak but significant effects, and published the results in a popular science journal (Schönbach & Peiser, 1994). Almost thirty years later, Klaus Schönbach (in this volume) now presents new evidence for such effects, this time on media use.

Actually, Schönbach's analysis does not only imply one but two levels of temporality: the cycles of the seasons and the continuing (albeit possibly weakening) influence of earlier experiences in later life. Wolfram Peiser also studied such continuing effects in other contexts, including his PhD thesis. The effects analyzed by Peiser, however, do not originate in cyclical phenomena but in irreversible historical media change that affects each cohort differently, leading to possible media generations such as the "television generation" he sought to distinguish from other cohorts (Peiser, 1996). Individuals passing through the different stages of life and historical changes intersect in the differential experiences and sometimes lasting differences of cohorts. Peiser addressed the "problem of generations" (Mannheim, 1970) in various ways. He discussed the analysis of effects of age, period, and cohort effects from a methodological perspective and its potential for strategic, i.e., future- and long-term oriented market research (Peiser, 1991) and applied cohort analysis in different empirical studies of media use (Peiser, 1996, 1999a, c, 2000a, c). One of the PhD theses supervised by Peiser throughout his career (three as main supervisor and six as second examiner) also discusses the temporal dimensions of media socialization along this logic (Krämer, 2012). In a short theoretical contribution going beyond media reception, Peiser discussed how not only generations that were socialized differently due to media change but also journalists with different generational experiences contribute to social change (Peiser, 2003).

The term "generation" also carries a second meaning, a genealogical and even more relational one where one person or entity, or one more or less contemporaneous group creates, or transforms into, a later one. In media history, we may ask whether and when evolutionary change can be periodized into generations of media and in academia, we can analyze the relations of power, transmission of institutional and cognitive resources, and (mutual) influence between academic generations of supervisors and the supervised. Here, the concept of generation is more strictly relational than categorical (as in the case of cohort analysis proper), a symbolic, social structure of corresponding roles and unequal conditions based on age (or career phase) (in analogy to the relationship between parents and children in the family, see Närvänen & Näsman, 2004). In this sense, this volume unites four academic generations: Peiser's supervisors, Wolfram Peiser himself and academic peers of his own age cohort, those he supervised, and his students' and staff's students.

Cycles and Coexistences, Comparisons and Catastrophes

Political history, it is typically assumed, does not repeat itself in the strict sense, but to get a chance of actually "changing things" in a democratic way (who is in government or the policies that they implement), we rely on election *cycles*. They come with election campaigns that may well be described as rituals which are repeated without much evidence of the desired effects. Christina Holtz-Bacha (in this volume) does not shy away from the question of whether political advertising is actually useless or even harmful. Reviewing the literature on US election advertising, she identifies many studies with minimal effects on persuasion and mobilization, except under favorable circumstances, and concludes that we know very little about the potentially detrimental effects of attack advertising. She concludes that it remains a mystery why political actors keep spending large amounts of money on communication measures whose effects are rather unsubstantiated. It may then be asked what history or histories campaigners have learned from to consider advertising effective.

Political communication is of course not limited to election campaigns and therefore calls for more literature reviews on important developments. One of the major trends discussed in the more recent literature is political polarization and the role of social media in the process. Ludwig and Müller (in this volume) synthesize the literature on this relationship, not only in terms of findings (that do not support any alarmism) but also in terms of conceptualizations and explanations.

In addition to the conceptual differences between polarization and the related concept of fragmentation that Ludwig and Müller discuss, a change in scholarly diagnoses is noteworthy: While Holtz-Bacha and Peiser (1999) asked: "Do the mass media lose their integrative function?," thus treating this function as formerly fulfilled, polarization research tends to treat (social) media as dysfunctional for social integration from the outset. A historical narrative of media-induced decline has been superseded by a narrative of media-caused threat. A certain cyclical model, however, seems once again confirmed by Ludwig and Müller's review: What starts out as a concept on which high hopes for diagnostic and explanatory values is placed in academia will become a vague catchword once it emerges as a trending research topic.

In comparison to another rather early publication by Wolfram Peiser (1999b), we can identify interesting shifts in communication researchers' concerns with the effects of digitization. Disintegration is already mentioned in his 1999 essay but described in terms that seem innocuous compared to today's fears of confrontation: He assumes that stronger audience fragmentation might lead to fewer common mediated experiences and topics for conversation, and more social contacts with like-minded people.

11

Similarly, problems of "credibility and quality" as identified by Peiser appear rather harmless compared to the threat of rampant disinformation discussed today. In addition to a very broad shift from television to the Internet or social media as the main media technologies scholars are discussing, today's research probably deals with social inequality somewhat less with regard to unequal resources and the provision of content that suits the interests of specific groups, as Peiser did in 1999, and more with a view to sociotechnical biases or discriminatory and offensive communication. Finally, while Peiser (1999) treated problems of information overload and the burdens of selection and judged them to be manageable by the users, today's discussion on selectivity on the one hand focuses more on how algorithmic filters already narrow down what recipients are confronted with in a biased and nontransparent way. On the other hand, it detects that an increasing number of users has given up on managing incoming information and has turned to (at least periodic) news avoidance.

Competitions and Coexistences

Communication is not only subject to change at the historical level, but creates irreversibilities at the micro level of each interaction. It transforms a contingent situation with two or more interdependent actors, each with their expectations and with a horizon of possible choices, into a new situation that then has its history and a new, differently pre-structured horizon (as Luhmann's, 1987, theory of communication suggests). Theories and methods that only consider a static constellation or only one actor's perspective fail to see the whole picture. This is the topic of two contributions in this volume by Christoph Neuberger and Johanna Schindler.

Neuberger discusses possible dynamic constellations in the public sphere, distinguishing different modes of interaction, namely diffusion, mobilization, conflict, cooperation, competition, and scandal. Going beyond the often rather static approach of social network analysis and public sphere theory, Neuberger describes how constellations of two or three actors with one-way or two-way communication, direct and indirect interactions, and shared or antagonistic interests create different fundamental courses of interaction. The interactions are always oriented both toward the past and the future: Actors pursue their interests (for example, they compete for a common but exclusive goal to be reached in the future), but also react to past communication (for example, to counter the accusations of scandalous behavior).

Cycles and Coexistences, Comparisons and Catastrophes

Johanna Schindler (in this volume) theorizes communication in groups as a process in which individual contributions are combined or transformed and that makes systems of interaction information processors not unlike, but distinct from individual cognitive systems. Group processes can either be oriented toward an open future if they process information in an open-ended mode or toward a predetermined common goal that, of course, may or may not be reached. This depends on the group members' individual and shared histories and the history in the making that is the interaction. Both orientations may be pursued in more automatic or systematic ways, adding a second dimension of processing modes.

Again, both articles imply more than one level of temporality. Interactions are not simply eternal structures deduced formally, but subject to social change and changes in media environments in particular. Christoph Neuberger thus also analyzes the shifts in different social fields in terms of the modes of interaction, such as the increasing reliance on competition in many areas or the increased potential for cooperation in online as opposed to mass media communication. Johanna Schindler also does not only aim for an abstract theory of information processing but relates the modes of processing to key technical possibilities of the Internet, namely participation, selectivity, interaction, interconnectedness, and automatization.

When new media environments are compared to older ones, an important topos in the analysis of social change comes into play: the idea of displacement, whether as complete substitution or coexistence, either on an equal footing or with certain entities persisting in niches (often framed metaphorically in terms of "death" or "survival"). Wolfram Peiser was well aware that theses on the displacement of media are highly contingent on the definition of the competing entities and of their former and possibly new functions, as well as the criteria for substitution. Furthermore, as he argues in his discussion of the so-called "Riepl's law" (see Riepl, 1913), such a "law"—according to which new media never completely replace older ones but push them into niches—entails difficult-to-test counterfactual assumptions on the development that would have occurred without the new competitor (Peiser, 2008). Such new structures cannot only substitute or complement older ones at the level of overall media technologies (however defined) but also at the level of organizational structures. A dissertation co-supervised by Peiser (see Engesser, 2013) analyzed whether participatory journalism the quality criteria of traditional journalism and what factors make this more likely.

Benjamin Krämer & Philipp Müller

Crises and Comparisons

Another recurring topos in historical descriptions is that of the crisis, a unique and deciding moment of danger, decline, or decision that, however, implies a chance of recovery or radical renewal (on the conceptual history of the term that also includes the possibility of recurring or chronic crises, see Koselleck & Richter, 2006). In the social sciences, crises have a double character: as a scholarly diagnosis and as social perception or construction to be reconstructed by the researcher.

Communication research itself may be said to be in a crisis—due to the dissolution of its disciplinary and methodological boundaries that recent media change has brought about but also due to its shortcomings in terms of theorizing science and scientific practices.

Hans-Bernd Brosius (in this volume) discusses whether the discipline is about to lose its former focus of analysis, public communication, and whether it should turn to all forms of mediated communication as its object. Brosius disagrees, warning of a crisis of identity in which the discipline would become indistinguishable from neighboring ones. However, the solution cannot be a return to the theories and methods of the disciplinary mainstream of the "golden age of mass communication," he argues. Although golden ages are a recurring theme in narratives of crisis, Brosius does not choose the completely nostalgic or restorative solution, but proposes a renewed concept of mass communication 2.0 that includes publicly visible interpersonal communication.

Wolfram Peiser also engaged with the question of mainstream and heterodox views, and of different paradigms more broadly, within a changing discipline, surveying the members of the German Communication Association (DGPuK) together with Matthias Hastall and Wolfgang Donsbach (Peiser, Hastall & Donsbach, 2003). Later, he also co-supervised a thesis on the scholarly identity and habitus of German-speaking communication professors (Huber, 2010) and speculated on the effects of changing media environments, theoretical fads, interests, or the generational socialization and media use of communication researchers on their conceptions of media effects (Peiser, 2009). In the 2003 survey, one third of respondents already agreed that the association's topics and divisions had differentiated too much while a third also felt that they are biased toward certain paradigms or that researchers with specific profiles do not really feel represented by the association. 60% of the participants responded that research on interpersonal communication should be represented in the DGPuK, but compared to 96% for mass communication and (only?) 82% for research on the Internet. The authors describe the identity of the discipline as both "pluralist" and "diffuse," but refuse to diagnose a crisis and also to takes sides, laconically concluding that the findings "are what they are" (p. 333). This is, however, not so say that Peiser rejected critical and normative perspectives, in particular on the discipline itself. For example, former member of his chair Cornelia Wallner typically adopts normative perspectives on the public sphere and other phenomena, including on the discipline itself, for now culminating in a special issue on criticism of, in, and through communication and media studies (Gentzel, Kannengießer, Wallner, & Wimmer, 2021).

Benjamin Krämer (in this volume) sees the discipline in a crisis not so much in terms of substantial objects and concepts, but due to a general lack of sufficiently systematic theoretical conceptualizations and of an awareness of the different functions of theory. In addition to, or maybe even as an underlying cause of the replication crisis diagnosed in several disciplines, unsystematic theorizing is an obstacle to fruitful research. Krämer identifies several types of shortcomings and argues that they do not only lead to unnecessary tests of badly justified hypotheses or arbitrary postulates of relationships and mechanisms, but, more broadly, to a lack of understanding of what objects of study, operationalizations, and research findings mean.

One of the problems identified by Krämer goes back to a frequent criticism raised by Peiser: One cannot reasonably make claims about what is new or what is specific to a phenomenon by studying only the novelty or the phenomenon in isolation. Wolfram Peiser therefore always encouraged his students and staff to conduct systematic comparisons, not necessarily based on original data on all eras or sides—which would often be uneconomical or impossible—but using either existing datasets or existing literature, at least for one side of the comparison. And compare they did!

One recent example that not only uses existing literature effectively but also connects different domains of communication research comparatively is the contribution by Cornelia Wallner (in this volume) who discusses relationships between structural features of media systems and media effects. While one might not necessarily expect media systems to exhibit a detectable effect at the individual level (yet, the literature reviewed by Wallner indicates such effects!), one would maybe expect the analysis of media systems to deal with some of the most stable structures in society. However, the logic of relating features of the media system to media use can also be applied to structural change, for example analyzing the effects of media use on democratization, as literature synthesized by Wallner does.

Benjamin Krämer & Philipp Müller

Two of Peiser's former PhD students also contributed to the—predominantly synchronic—comparative literature on media systems and their relationship with political systems, however considering tradition as one dimension of comparison, i.e., the time frame in which political and media institutions (the first newspaper, commercial TV station etc.) were established (Engesser & Franzetti, 2001). During her time at Peiser's chair in Munich, another colleague, Karin Knop, compared mediated constructions of reality in a variety of popular media genres. She went beyond the usual range of genres investigated in mainstream communication research, critically turning to advertising, comedy, or reality TV (Knop, 2012a, 2012b; Knop & Petsch, 2010). And to further highlight the diversity of topics addressed at the chair, we may also mention that during his short time in Munich, Felix Frey published an article on the changing historic media use of the lower classes in the German empire (Frey, 2016).

While the theory or interpretation crisis diagnosed by some (including Krämer in this volume) is one crisis that goes unnoted by many, Carsten Reinemann and Anna-Luisa Sacher (also in this volume) refer to a widely discussed alleged crisis: that free speech is supposedly increasingly restricted—or that people no longer agree about what can be said. Research may ask survey respondents whether they think opinions can be freely expressed and compare answers over time, or it may ask them for their perception of change. Both measurements, when interpreted with caution, will inform researchers about different perceptions that will probably be based on different experiences or individual interpretations of different discourses. Wolfram Peiser would probably have asked: What do people have in mind when they hear about "freedom of expression" or "what can be said"? And this is the kind of answer that Reinemann and Sacher are also seeking with their analysis. Subsequently, they also ask: Do people really disagree about what can be said and what statements do they think are acceptable? Empirically, their research indicates people seem to agree that certain statements towards women are unacceptable. In addition to this rather broad consensus, the authors find more complex and often unexpected patterns of small influences, not of gender but of experiences with discrimination and media trust, on the occurrence of specific perceptions of opinion expression. In terms of change, they also identify generational differences that, however, do not lend themselves to narratives according to which younger generations are simply more sensitive or critical toward discrimination.

Wolfram Peiser was always interested in media users' perceptions of reality, and their conditions and limitations. It is therefore no coincidence that among the different theories of media uses and effects, he published predominantly on the third-person effect (Peiser & Peter, 2000, 2001). He was also a most dedicated mentor and supervisor, but never pushed himself to the fore in this role. Consequently, to our knowledge, he only co-authored a single conference presentation with researchers at his chair. The contribution was successfully presented at an ICA conference but unfortunately never appeared as a published article during Wolfram Peiser's lifetime. Therefore, his co-authors decided to publish an article that aims to reconstruct the main ideas and findings of the study (Frey, Peiser & Krämer, in this volume). It is also not surprising that this text deals with perception, namely with the criteria media users employ to assess the degree of realism of media content. Very much in line with Peiser's exhortations not to focus on the most trendy, yet often narrow and short-lived, research interests, the contribution goes beyond the current preoccupations with disinformation and media skepticism, and considers media content more broadly, considering a wide range of cues of authenticity, and distinguishes different types of media users. In our modern understanding, time is irreversible and unrepeatable but Felix Frey and Benjamin Krämer tried to turn back the clock by returning to the old slides, notes, abstracts, and datasets to reconstruct what could have been one of the last publications co-authored by Wolfram Peiser.

Gender differences in communication professions are a topic dear to his long-time colleague Romy Fröhlich who, however, focuses on genre differences and their perception in her contribution to this volume. Her chapter is diagnostic as well as programmatic. Fröhlich observes that in today's media environment, users are more than ever confronted with "particular-interest oriented persuasive simulations of journalism" or PR texts by strategic communicators imitating journalism with a persuasive intention. She then asks what criteria could serve to distinguish this genre from actual journalistic coverage in content analyses and how recipients would process both types of texts. Symptoms of crises abound: Traditional advertising is less credible than ever, which is why communicators turn to PR genres that imitate journalism. Users migrating from traditional media to the Internet are increasingly likely to encounter such content—either by chance or because they deliberately avoid traditional journalism which, further weakened by economic crises, is decreasingly able to scrutinize and control what enters the public sphere. However, Fröhlich's argument does not stop at this general diagnosis but spells out its implications at both the levels of content and reception, as well as specific subsequent research questions and indicators. Following Wolfram Peiser's persistent strive for conceptual and methodological rigor, the outlined research program con-

Catastrophes and Choices

If large parts of the modern population do not share a specific understanding of an end time but only of mundane catastrophes, it is in this vein that we leave the otherworldly to individual meditation but express our great sadness about the—in a sense, "catastrophic"—loss that has been the early death of Wolfram Peiser (on the sometimes surprising conceptual history of the notion of "catastrophe" that includes dying or any quick change to the negative or positive, see Briese & Günter, 2009). We will conclude this introduction by summarizing some of the advice and strategies of doing research that, as one of his gifts to his students and colleagues, he often conveyed in courses, colloquiums, and individual conversations. They help avoid catastrophic failures of research as well as small and often unnoticed shortcomings.

The first step of each research endeavor has to be to *collect* systematically. Peiser usually recommended to *consider* a broad range of theoretical approaches, concepts, factors, and actors with their respective perspectives. This is to make sure to systematically contemplate as many alternatives as possible (and reasonably justifiable) in terms of research questions or hypotheses, forms of models, designs, and methods before choosing the ultimate research interest and framework for a study. As indicated above, Peiser emphasized systematic *comparison* in order to identify what is actually specific about a phenomenon and its causes or background. He also advised to try and *connect* all aspects of a research object or area among each other, even if the result is that some are more or less unrelated. For example, in his lecture on media economics, he provided a long list of key terms and suggested that students pick two or three at random and think about their relationship. This way, they could test whether they had actually understood the concepts and were able to apply them.

In order to understand a phenomenon, it is also useful to work by means of abstraction and analogy, finding one or more general categories it belongs to or similarities to other phenomena with similar properties. This opens up new strands of literature and conceptualizations that lead to new perspectives on the phenomena, whether they are under-researched or require new, original approaches.

Visual aides such as tables and diagrams can help to be systematic when selecting and connecting aspects, always considering all logical alternatives. Yet, they should not be used excessively and should always be prepared with greatest care as they always bear the risk of suggesting misleading or under-complex interpretations. Older literature can considerably broaden the horizon and avoid reinventing the wheel while including newer publications helps to find the actually remaining research gaps and to connect a study to the field and one's potential audience.

For example, when planning a study that deals with media and social change, a researcher should try to keep in mind the different kinds of models or narratives of developments: continuous evolution, crisis, catastrophic or revolutionary breaks, cycles or waves (whether actually repetitive or as regular patterns of innovation), complete or partial displacement, phase and genealogical models, etc.

The most important step is of course to *choose* wisely between all the alternatives considered: what to include in a study, how to theoretically frame and empirically investigate it, how to present the theoretical and methodological considerations and the results, and most importantly: how to justify the choices. Decisions create a before and after; they entail consequences, both logical and practical, and can be reasonable with regard to what has been done previously or the ends to be achieved. They come with costs for switching paths and neglecting aspects, come with risks of errors, failures, and criticism (which should be anticipated as systematically as possible). However, they are also liberating, reduce complexity, and pre-structure what is coming. And decisions can only be made between what has been considered before: they are themselves pre-structured by the question and the alternatives.

Once a project has been conducted and documented, with all the large and small decisions, the resulting documentation has to be *correct* and can be *corrected*. In this regard, time is not irreversible. Things can be made more understandable, better reasons can be provided, the order of presentation can be changed. The history one tells is not the history that happened, the text is not simply a chronological narrative or thought protocol, Peiser reminded us, but a logical flow that abstracts from many details and decisions. Yet, of course, it has to be true to what one has done.

Benjamin Krämer & Philipp Müller

References

Briese, O. & Günther, T. (2009). Katastrophe: Terminologische Vergangenheit, Gegenwart und Zukunft. *Archiv für Begriffsgeschichte, 51*, 155-195.

Engesser, S. (2012). *Die Qualität des Partizipativen Journalismus im Web. Bausteine für ein integratives theoretisches Konzept und eine explanative empirische Analyse.* Springer.

Engesser, S. & Franzetti, A. (2011). Media systems and political systems: Dimensions of comparison. *International Communication Gazette, 73*(4), 273-301.

Frey, F. (2016). Einflussfaktoren auf die Mediennutzung der Unterschichten im deutschen Kaiserreich (1871–1918). *Studies in Communication and Media, 5*(3), 241-306.

Gentzel, P., Kannengießer, S., Wallner, C., & Wimmer, J. (2021). Kritik an, in und durch Kommunikations-und Medienwissenschaft. Editorial zum Sonderheft. *Studies in Communication and Media, 10*(2), 131-145.

Holtz-Bacha, C. & Peiser, W. (1999). Verlieren die Massenmedien ihre Integrationsfunktion? Eine empirische Analyse zu den Folgen der Fragmentierung des Medienpublikums. In U. Hasebrink, P. Rössler (Eds.), *Publikumsbindungen. Medienrezeption zwischen Individualisierung und Integration* (pp. 41-53). Reinhard Fischer.

Huber, N. (2010). *Kommunikationswissenschaft als Beruf. Zum Selbstverständnis von Professoren des Faches im deutschsprachigen Raum.* Halem.

Knop, K. (2012a). Reality TV und Arbeitswelten: Inhalte und Rezeptionsweisen von Docu Soaps zum Thema Jobvermittlung. In C. Stegbauer (Ed.), *Ungleichheit. Medien- und kommunikationssoziologische Perspektiven* (pp. 121-149). VS.

Knop, K. (2012b). Zielgruppenstars im Fernsehen – Die medialen Starimages der Comedians Harald Schmidt und Stefan Raab im Wandel der Zeit. In C. Winter & M. Karmasin (Eds.), *Analyse, Theorie, und Geschichte der Medien. Festschrift für Werner Faulstich* (pp. 49-61). Fink.

Knop, K. & Petsch, T. (2010). „Initiative für wahre Schönheit" – Die Rückkehr des Alltagskörpers in die idealisierte Körperwelt der Werbung. In J. Röser, T. Thomas, & C. Peil (Eds.), *Alltag in den Medien – Medien im Alltag* (pp. 119-137). VS.

Koselleck, R. (1979). *Vergangene Zukunft. Zur Semantik geschichtlicher Zeiten.* Suhrkamp.

Koselleck, R. & Richter, M. W. (2006). Crisis. *Journal of the History of Ideas, 67*(2), 357–400.

Krämer, B. (2012). *Mediensozialisation. Theorie und Empirie zum Erwerb medienbezogener Dispositionen.* Springer.

Luhmann, N. (1987). *Soziale Systeme. Grundriß einer allgemeinen Theorie.* Suhrkamp.

Mannheim, K. (1970). The problem of generations. *Psychoanalytic Review, 57*(3), 378-404.

Müller, P. (2016). *Die Wahrnehmung des Medienwandels. Eine Exploration ihrer Dimensionen, Entstehungsbedingungen und Folgen.* Springer.

Närvänen, A.-L. & Näsman, E. (2004). Childhood as generation or life phase? *Young, 12*(1), 71–91

Peiser, W. (1991). *Kohortenanalyse in der Konsumentenforschung.* Deutscher Universitäts-Verlag.

Peiser, W. (1996). *Die Fernsehgeneration. Eine empirische Untersuchung ihrer Mediennutzung und Medienbewertung.* Westdeutscher Verlag.

Peiser, W. (1999a). Die Verbreitung von Medien in der Gesellschaft: Langfristiger Wandel durch Kohortensukzession. *Rundfunk und Fernsehen, 47*, 485-498.

Peiser, W. (1999b). Folgen der Digitalisierung aus kommunikationswissenschaftlicher Sicht. In M. Schumann & T. Hess (Eds.), *Medienunternehmen im digitalen Zeitalter. Neue Technologien — Neue Märkte — Neue Geschäftsansätze* (pp 123–136). Gabler.

Peiser, W. (1999c). The television generation's relation to the mass media in Germany: Accounting for the impact of private television. *Journal of Broadcasting & Electronic Media, 43*(3), 364-385.

Peiser, W. (2000a). Cohort replacement and the downward trend in newspaper readership. *Newspaper Research Journal, 21*(2), 11-22.

Peiser, W. (2000b). Cohort trends in media use in the United States. *Mass Communication & Society, 3*(2-3), 185-205.

Peiser, W. (2003). Gesellschaftswandel — Generationen — Medienwandel. In M. Behmer, F. Krotz, R. Stöber, & C. Winter (Eds.), *Medienentwicklung und gesellschaftlicher Wandel. Beiträge zu einer theoretischen und empirischen Herausforderung* (pp. 197-207). VS.

Peiser, W. (2008). Riepls "Gesetz" von der Komplementarität alter und neuer Medien. In K. Arnold, M. Behmer, & B. Semrad (Eds.), *Kommunikationsgeschichte. Positionen und Werkzeuge. Ein diskursives Hand- und Lehrbuch* (pp. 155-183). Lit.

Peiser, W. (2009). Allgemeine Vorstellungen über Medienwirkungen. In C. Holtz-Bacha, G. Reus, & L. Becker (Eds.), *Wissenschaft mit Wirkung. Beiträge zu Journalismus- und Medienwirkungsforschung. Festschrift für Klaus Schönbach* (pp. 143-159). VS.

Peiser, W., Hastall, M., & Donsbach, W. (2003). Zur Lage der Kommunikationswissenschaft und ihrer fachgesellschaft. Ergebnisse der DGPuK-Mitgliederbefragung 2003. *Publizistik, 48*(3), 310-339.

Peiser, W. & Peter, J. (2000). Third-person perception of television-viewing behavior. *Journal of Communication, 50*(1), 25-45.

Peiser, W. & Peter, J. (2001). Explaining individual differences in third-person perception: A limits/possibilities perspective. *Communication Research, 28*(2), 156-180.

Reinemann, C. (2022). Wahrnehmungen von Meinungsfreiheit und ihre Ursachen. Presentation at the memorial event in honour of Wolfram Peiser. 15 July 2022, Munich.

Benjamin Krämer & Philipp Müller

Riepl, W. (1913). *Das Nachrichtenwesen des Altertums mit besonderer Rücksicht auf die Römer*. Teubner.

Schönbach, K. & Peiser, W. (1994). Die Sterne lügen nicht. *Bild der Wissenschaft, 1994*(6), 70-73.

White, H. (1973). *Metahistory. The historical imagination in nineteenth-century Europe*. John Hopkins University Press.

Why Are Most Published Research Findings Under-Theorized?

Or: Are We in an Interpretation Crisis?

Benjamin Krämer

Abstract

While the so-called replication crisis is increasingly discussed and addressed through reformed research practices and institutional structures, this contribution diagnoses a theory or interpretation crisis and argues that the current emphasis on transparency, reproducibility, and reliability should be complemented by stronger efforts in terms of theory and validity. The article identifies different types of unsystematic (e.g., ad hoc, asymmetric, or trivial) theory building. Furthermore, objects of investigation, measurements, and findings are not interpreted carefully in the light of sufficiently elaborate and well-justified theoretical concepts or frameworks. Different consequences of such shortcomings are discussed—whether unfruitful or implausible hypotheses are tested or the implications of findings are remain poorly understood or are not critically reflected. Readers are invited to engage not only with methodological literature and previous research, but also with theoretical works and particularly with literature on methods or strategies of theorizing, and to practice theory building based on a clearer understanding of the multiple meanings and functions of theory.

John P. A. Ioannidis is probably most known for his article provocatively entitled "Why Most Published Research Findings Are False" (Ioannidis, 2005). He not only provides a strictly statistical argument that, all other things being equal, only a certain proportion of significant results can actually be true if a given Type I and II error rates are accepted (i.e., if the limit for p values and the power of a test are set at a certain level). He also mentions a number of corollaries that, somewhat contrary to his claims, cannot directly be deduced from his main argument. I will criticize one of them later.

I consider John Ioannidis a bit of a tragic figure of science and his story as a cautionary tale: He became famous by fighting for more trustworthy science through sufficient sample sizes, systematic reviews and meta-analyses, replication, the avoidance of data dredging, and other means that increase the probability that a positive finding is indeed true. But he later became a hero of those who wished to downplay the seriousness of Covid-19, thus effectively undermining trust in other scientists and public policy (that are, of course, never above criticism, but his conclusions were considered problematic based on the best epidemiological evidence, methodological principles, and normative arguments). This was possible because abstract methodological rigor cannot substitute substantial ideas about the object of inquiry, the reflection of ideological biases, or a clear conception of potential distortions of a study that cannot easily be corrected statistically or by means of replication in other contexts. Such biases can only be discovered by theorizing the object of inquiry and arguing about the validity of the methodology.

Fittingly, the article that Ioannidis co-authored and that demonstrates this lack of proper argumentation involved social media (Bendavid, Mulaney, Sood, Shah et al., 2021). The paper arrived at an unusually low infection fatality rate of Covid-19 in comparison to other studies, was widely publicized as an argument against strict containment measures, and was criticized for all kinds of reasons, ranging from details of the statistical analysis to potential undisclosed conflicts of interest (Lee, 2020). Most importantly in our context, the authors devote a lot of space and the most complex meta-analytical procedures to the calculation of the sensitivity and specificity of the antibody test. However, they only shortly comment on the bias due to participant self-selection in a revised version of their manuscript and initially only weighted their data along selected sociodemographic categories. Only in the later versions, they present some back-of-the-envelope calculations based on reported symptoms that are meant to address self-selection. However, a thorough discussion of who will probably respond to a Facebook ad inviting users to be tested after a drive to a test center would have shown that the bias of estimates based on such a curious, mobile, flexible etc. population is essentially incalculable. One does not have to call such a discussion a "theory" of recruitment via Facebook or of voluntary antibody testing (but why not? Let's not put the bar of what constitutes theory too high… However, a lot of research on social media and current media change *could* indeed profit from more elaborate theory in order to better assess how new developments affect all kinds of fields and activities, such as health or social research). But the total lack of such a reflection in the initial version of the paper shows that substantial ideas on an object of investigation or on participant behavior

Why Are Most Published Research Findings Under-Theorized?

cannot be replaced by the most sophisticated methods from the toolkit Ioannidis rightly recommends.

Over the years, I have reviewed and otherwise read many manuscripts in different areas of quantitative communication research with elaborate designs and sophisticated data analysis but with a number of recurring problems: Sometimes, the setting of the study, the wording of certain items, the style and content of a stimulus etc. did not really correspond to any real-world setting (even with some concessions that would be necessary for methodological reasons). In other cases, it was not clear whether the researchers had successfully manipulated or measured certain constructs given the ambiguity of certain concepts or of certain wordings in questionnaires. Or it was unclear whether they had successfully demonstrated a causal link because important confounding factors or biases had been overlooked.

These different cases constitute problems of validity—either external validity or the validity of causal inference and measurements. In both cases, this is not a problem of methodology as such but of the specific conceptualizations and theories of the object of investigation. Whether a study can claim to model or mimic a real-world situation can only be determined if we have a sufficiently clear idea about this type of situation. Whether a study can claim to have measured or manipulated a given construct or to have demonstrated a causal link without being misled by spurious correlations or biases can only be determined by a clear idea about what constructs and words or phrases mean and how phenomena are related.

I have also often noticed further problems beyond validity proper. Sometimes, the postulated causal order seemed arbitrary, or the explanation of hypotheses careless and unsystematic. I felt that instead of A causing B, it could easily be the other way round (or there could be no real causal relationship), or that instead of the explanation that more A causes more B, it may as well cause less, or instead of A being the main cause of B, it may be C, but A was picked for no particular reason.

Finally, I have also often found the interpretations of the results, the discussion of potential implications, and the reflection on limitations rather trivial or only loosely connected to the specific study—either extremely generic or overly narrow, without regard to the overall social context or scholarly discourse.

Of course, readers may brush this broad criticism of the field aside and assume that I only want to look down on some supposedly narrow-minded colleagues or that I am disappointed because my idiosyncratic pet theories are not reflected in current research. On the contrary, I would argue that there is number of specific reasons why theory building (including epistemological and methodological reflection beyond the technicalities of specific methods) is not always satisfactorily systematic and elaborate in mainstream communication research (see also Hagen, Frey & Koch, 2015, for similar observations). And I would further argue that this has a number of specific implications.

In sum, the argument will be that we are not only in a replication but an interpretation crisis, a crisis of theory building, and that the (legitimate) focus on transparency, reproducibility, and reliability (e.g., with open science, replications, meta-analyses etc.; Dienlin et al., 2021; Rains, Levine & Weber, 2018) should be complemented by stronger efforts in terms of theory and validity. To put it provocatively: If we do not know what our findings mean, there is no use reproducing them (or we do not even know what would count as an actual replication—see below). In psychology, it has even been argued that a theory crisis is one of the factors explaining the replication crisis because hypotheses that are not well-justified theoretically are more likely to result in false-positive findings and because the less explicitly and precisely a theory is spelt out (or the less it is clear what would actually count as valid measurement of the relevant constructs), the more difficult it is not decide what would count as an (un-)successful replication or what would even count as a test of a theory versus discovery-oriented research around a loose theoretical framework (see Eronen & Bringmann, 2021; Gigerenzer, 2010; Oberauer & Lewandowsky, 2019).

And the development or application of increasingly elaborate methods is not always matched by highly sophisticated or even sufficiently elaborate theories. Again provocatively: If we do not know what we are looking for or what our results mean, there is no need for complex methods (actually, no need for data collection and analysis of any kind). Ultimately, confronted with several planetary crises and threats to democracy, this is not the time to accumulate data without a clear idea what is or could be going on.

What Kind of Theory?

It should have become clear that this contribution focuses on quantitative research and its logic (usually variable-based and often focused on causal relationships). This is not to say that the state of theory building around qualitative research is beyond criticism. Even though there is also rather atheoretical qualitative research, some approaches to qualitative research explicitly focus on theory building, such as grounded theory. Due to the potentially complex interplay between theory and empirical studies, qualitative research has been discussed as "Theoretische Empirie" (Kalthoff, Hirschauer & Lindemann, 2008), 'theoretical *Empirie*,' the latter being a mass noun with no exact equivalent in the English language referring to everything empirical or the totality of empirical activities or findings in a given context. However, the role of theory in qualitative research is simply beyond the scope of the present article. It is an invitation to avoid bad theory and to do good theory, addressed at quantitative researchers in communication science. Although the focus on theory building as the crafting of sets of interrelated testable propositions can be criticized (see below), there is a considerable number of publications on how to establish such and related theories (e.g., Abbott, 2004; Bell, 2009; Elster, 2007; Jaccard & Jacoby, 2020; Runciman, 1983; Shoemaker, Tankard & Larsorsa, 2004; Sohlberg & Leiulfsrud, 2017; Swedberg, 2014b; Stinchcombe, 1986) and on other ways of stimulating theoretical thinking in the social sciences (the "sociological imagination," Mills, 1959, the "tricks" of social-scientific thinking, Becker, 1998, or the conditions for "intuitive theorizing," Knorr-Cetina, 2014). Therefore, the conditions for building theories of this type are relatively good and the need for it should have already become clear and will be substantiated in the following.

However, testable hypotheses cannot easily be separated from other types of theoretical statements.[1] Those include interpretive, conceptual, ontological, epistemological, and methodological statements—sometimes combined into whole "worldviews" and sometimes as solutions to specific problems—as well as normative theories of society and exegeses of classical works (Abend, 2008; Büttner, 2021; Merton, 1945). In other fields, one may debate whether certain exegetical exercises and esoteric analyses of minutiae of certain meta-theories are still fruitful for the understanding of social phenomena—or for the discussion of current challenges of representation and perspectivity (Krause, 2016). The challenge in communication research is probably different: to develop *better* explanations (and better concepts), but also to develop a greater sensibility for other types of theories that are closely connected with explanations (such as conceptualizations and epistemological frameworks) and that fulfill important other func-

---

1 Certain authors such as Abend (2008) emphasize that they are distinguishing *meanings* of the word "theory," not *types* of theories, because it is difficult or impossible to provide a single definition of the unitary concept of "theory" of which there could be different types. However, what is identified as the different meanings of "theory" in such semantic analyses, can at least be combined into a single "theory" or theoretical work and there are often necessary connections between the different types of statements.

tions (such as the justification of normative judgments or the reflections of judgments that are already unintentionally implied in seemingly value-free explanations).

Theoretical statements form continua or systems where one type of statement cannot easily be separated from another or where no single line can be drawn between "theory" and "non-theory" on the spectrum ranging from general presuppositions and specific observations (Alexander, 1982, p. 2f.). Even if one part is not spelled out, one can still ask what the parts that are not explicated may be (i.e., the more abstract presuppositions of single hypothesis or the empirical fruitfulness of a general theory). Thus, it makes sense to systematically reflect on the whole range of implications of one's explanations or hypotheses instead of developing them *ad hoc* and without any broader theoretical context.

For example, many arguments around newer online media or practices do not only involve individual hypotheses but are embedded into a set of postulates of historical trends and normative judgements (both often used to establish relevance, for example: Social media were once hoped to democratize X, but they did not), a set of ideas about the structure of society and social or psychological ontology (for example, a worldview in which there can be political *systems* and media *organizations* that can somehow respond to *technological* change, *actors* with *attitudes* that are *influenced* by new types of messages such as comments, etc.), epistemological assumption (e.g., about the validity of self-reports or the feasibility of automated analysis of meaning), a set of individual interpretations of entities and observations in terms of concepts (e.g., that Facebook and Google are both important new *intermediaries* in today's media environment), etc. If all of these types of conceptions are not carefully reflected, contradictions and confusion may arise (e.g., from category errors such as equating organizations with the sum of their members), problematic myths about society and history risk to be perpetuated (e.g., that there once must have been an era when everyone was ready to compromise, trusted the established media, and always sticked to facts in political discourse), and research designs may fail due to faulty assumptions.

The Problems with Bad Theory

Atheoretical research is easy to criticize, because "letting data speak for itself" means to rely on theory-like preconceptions and ad-hoc interpretations—or not to understand certain findings at all. One can sometimes see people put off a thorough discussion of the possible relationship between variables until the statistical results are in, only to realize that they still do not know why the relationship they found should exist and what to make of it.

In some cases, it can be acceptable to keep it simple, to rely on a number of everyday categories, and investigate how certain things are related. One simply needs to make sure to avoid the most blatant misconceptions and biases. In this case, our everyday understanding is already a sufficiently good "theory." However, I have observed certain styles of explicit and *ex ante* theorizing that does break with everyday conceptions in favor of more scientific terminology and concepts but that can nevertheless be dangerously biased or simply much less fruitful for our understanding of the social world than it could be. Thus, I will argue that theory building is not only a way of developing new ideas for research and something that we can dispense with if we can still come up with new studies. Nor is it something that we only need if we do not immediately understand our object of study or that only needs to be "just good enough" to make everything somewhat plausible. Instead, good theories (or at least thoroughly checked everyday conceptions) are a general prerequisite for the validity and usefulness of findings. However, a number of problematic strategies of theorizing in quantitative communication research (discussed below) sometimes prevent scholars from developing good explanations and understanding their phenomena well.

One might argue that bad theory work is harmless because it only concerns the "context of discovery" which is irrelevant to the actual research process, the testing of hypotheses, in which bad hypotheses are thrown out anyway. In a somewhat more nuanced manner, Popper (1935) held that the discovery of hypotheses is an irrational process that may be analyzed psychologically but is not completely open to rational reconstruction or justification, and his systematization did not include the process of theoretical justification of hypotheses (for an even more nuanced discussion of the different views on the distinction between the "context of discovery" and "justification," see Hoyningen-Huene, 1987). He only saw room for four types of tests: 1. for consistency, 2. for tautology (or falsifiability), 3. whether a theory postulates something new in comparison to older ones, and 4. testing through empirical application (Popper, 1935, p. 6).[2]

---

2 If this view were taken absolutely seriously by researchers claiming to be critical rationalists in the tradition of Popper, "theoretical" sections of manuscript in the social sciences would look quite differently or may not even exist in the current form. They would merely mention the hypotheses, maybe dispel any doubts that they are inconsistent internally or among each other, or argue that their

Benjamin Krämer

However, there are still theories that pass the first three tests that I would consider bad theories, for example because they are implausible, even if they are not strictly incompatible with well-established findings.

The view that bad theory development is harmless because of the fourth test would be naive for two reasons (that are of interest here, being only two of many reasons why the strict separation between discovery and testing is problematic). First, testing bad theories is a waste of resources. Although according to a Popperian logic, improbable hypotheses are very informative if they are not immediately and convincingly refuted, testing theories that are most probably doomed from the outset is to set problematic priorities. Certainly, science is about curiosity, even personal and collective fulfillment, and about the pursuit of knowledge without any foreseeable practical applications. And as problematic as populist criticisms of scientists "wasting taxpayers' money" are—science is practiced with limited resources and there is a certain obligation to focus on fruitful avenues (not necessarily the ones that promise the highest return on investment in the strict sense, but those that have a sufficient chance to produce actual insights). Furthermore, a seeming confirmation of a hypothesis that is *a priori* very likely to be false is more likely to be a false positive, as Ioannidis (2005) demonstrated. Thus, time for theorizing and developing and selecting the most plausible hypotheses is time well spent.

But more importantly, second, bad theories actually lead to bad interpretations of findings, with actual problematic consequences. Indeed, more or less naive falsificationism does not have a problem with bad theory because it is assumed to be in risk of being refuted by empirical findings. However, hypotheses cannot be considered in isolation. They are interwoven in a network of meanings, assumptions, logical rules, etc. According to more elaborate theories of "holist underdetermination" (Stanford, 2021)[3], such a network cannot be discarded at once by empirical findings. If findings seem to contradict one statement in such a network

---

testing will yield any important insight in comparison to previous research. Strictly speaking, there would be no need to justify or "deduce" the hypotheses, for example by drawing analogies with findings on similar phenomena, as is often done. The papers would then focus on the demonstration that they hypotheses have been tested rigorously, and on the results.

3 "Underdetermination" refers to the idea that theory is underdetermined by data, i.e., that available evidence never completely determines which theory or modifications thereof we should commit ourselves to, never allows us to pick exactly one (new) theory that would be the only one to match the data. "Holist" underdetermination refers to the argument that statements in theories are related and that therefore, evidence alone cannot determine what modifications in a theory should

Why Are Most Published Research Findings Under-Theorized?

(and even if there is no such contradiction), there are always multiple alternative arrangements that can in principle be accepted as consistent with the data (and a contradiction can only be asserted based on other parts of the network that convey meaning to the statement and that connect it to the data). If a mismatch is identified, we can always question the method of data collection, the deduction of specific testable prediction from general relationships, the meaning of statements implied in all steps of the research process (from definitions to items in questionnaires) etc. Therefore, bad theory can persist if it is protected by related, (seemingly) consistent, equally bad assumptions that make it seem in line with (seemingly) good evidence (that may actually be based on problematic methodological or epistemological premises).

But can there be such a thing as "good" and "bad theory" in the light of holistic underdetermination? Without entering the philosophical argument on how serious what kind of underdetermination is and how to legitimately respond to it, the history of science teaches us that we should always worry about the "unconceived alternatives" in science (Stanford, 2006) and even the small, useful, but unconceived modifications in existing theories. Still, even if we should never assume that we have already developed the optimal theory in a given area, there are theories we would be more inclined to (temporarily) accept or refute upon systematic reflection in the light of presently existing or new arguments or data. We can indeed conclude that certain theories, for example, rely on ill-defined concepts or contradict cherished assumptions or large amounts of evidence whose methodological basis we do not want to call into question, and those would be considered "bad" theories in comparison to those without such obvious problems.

And, maybe most importantly in the present context, we should be concerned about "bad theory" that is confined to seemingly self-explanatory "falsifiable" hypotheses and that does not make the wider elements and the structure of the network explicit—or at least, does not reflect on them even if large parts of the network cannot be presented in a single publication. In this case, it remains unclear what results mean and how concepts, methods, and findings are related. We cannot be certain about the validity of measurements or the (plausible) causal mechanisms, and may thus also be unaware of potential biases introduced by unsuitable methods and instruments or by neglected aspects.

---

be made in response to contrary evidence (or arguments) (see Stanford, 2021, with reference to classical theorists of underdetermination such as Duhem and Quine).

This can also lead to problematic conclusions. Methods are enshrined or dismissed for the wrong reasons, conceptions and explanations are questioned or left unquestioned based on insufficient arguments. And practical implications (in terms of instrumental usefulness or critical potential) of (supposed) findings may be missed or misrepresented because we lack adequate explanations for our results or because we do not have the right theoretical tools to derive such implications in the first place. Without good theory, we risk to mislead not only ourselves and other researchers, but also the public on what our research means, or to disappoint everyone waiting for our findings to make sense.

Based on a certain philosophy of history or social change, a caricaturesque researcher may be tempted to judge everything either in terms of progress, or, according to their biases, more likely in terms of decline, and hypothesize that the quality of argumentation has decreased with the advent of social media (without explaining whether "quality" is meant normatively or in terms of persuasion). Based on their idea of a universal, essential quality of arguments, they train a classifier to recognize good and bad arguments, using a sample of texts somehow collected online. They then apply this classifier to old newspaper editorials and recent social media comments, ignoring the different functions, stylistic conventions, linguistic features etc. associated with the two genres, and indeed find that comments contain many more bad arguments. The researcher may be convinced to have tested the hypothesis and proudly explain their results to an audience thirsty for this confirmation of their prejudices—that may however, be surprised to learn that arguments must be somewhat better on Instagram than on Twitter, whatever that means (the researcher has no clue).

Merton (1945, p. 462) once summarized the "radical empiricist motto" as follow: "This is demonstrably so, but we cannot indicate its [social and theoretical] significance." I would also add that without a certain theoretical context establishing the validity of the findings, we cannot even convincingly demonstrate that it is so—neither in a single study, nor by "replicating" certain findings. Without a clear conception of what is essential to the phenomenon under analysis and to the methodology of its investigation, it remains unclear what can count as a replication and what to make of seemingly contradictory evidence. Replication should therefore not be defined as the simple repetition of the original procedures, which may only mask a poor theoretical conceptualization of the relevant effects. Only good theory will allow to make a convincing argument that a new study with its specific conditions and its old or new methods, can actually produce new evidence both in favor of, or against an existing claim (Nossek & Errington, 2020). In the following, I distinguish different more specific problems in theorizing, grouped into a number of types, together with a somewhat catchy terminology that would be suited for critical discussions and reviews of all kinds.

Some Types of Insufficiently Systematic Theorizing

I would call the first interrelated patterns of problematic theorizing "associative asymmetry" and "theoretical cherry-picking." Usually, pairs of constructs are hypothesized to stand in some relationship, and the hypotheses are developed rather associatively. For example, the effect is assumed to mirror the stimulus (e.g., seeing violence leads to violent behavior). Or a type of behavior is explained by a tendency (such as a personality trait) to exhibit behavior from a broader category that includes the type of behavior to be explained (e.g., people with an "aggressive personality"—if we ignore whether this makes sense as a construct—will abuse others online because that is a type of aggression). Or if A has been found to cause B, it may also cause C' that is seen as similar to B (e.g., if reduced revenues of media organizations lead to less diverse coverage in terms of issues, it will also lead to less diversity in terms of actors being covered). Or if A leads to B and B leads to C (at least according to somewhat uncertain earlier research), A will lead to C.

These are of course potentially fruitful ways to arrive at new hypotheses (albeit sometimes rather trivial ones). The problems start when alternatives are not considered systematically ("asymmetry"), and existing theoretical and empirical literature is cited selectively to justify the hypotheses instead of considering a wide range of publications and arguments to arrive at the most plausible hypotheses ("cherry-picking"). While cherry-picking is considered a major issue when it comes to conclusions from empirical findings, it often seems to be considered perfectly acceptable when hypotheses have to be justified (although the literature is usually cited before mentioning the hypothesis, it often seems that it has been searched *ex post* based on the previously established hypothesis).

Systematic theorizing should therefore thoroughly consider arguments in favor of alternative causal orders (e.g., $B \rightarrow A$ instead of $A \rightarrow B$, or C being a mediator instead of a moderator of this relationship), inverse directions of relationships (i.e., a positive versus a negative effect), and alternative forms of relationship (e.g., curvilinear instead of linear). Graphs, cross-tabulation, and other tools can of course help to systematically go

Benjamin Krämer

through all the relationships between a set of concepts and to check, modify, and extend models.

Researchers cannot only switch the direction and form of a relationship and check for forgotten factors, but should always consider alternative types of explanations, whether they are immediately tested or only serve to justify a relationship under investigation. Other forms of explanations can also lead to new considerations on the direction and form of relationships and on the inclusion of factors. A number of authors have proposed typologies of explanations—not predictions pertaining to specific observable phenomena or classes thereof, but general "theoretical orientations" that propose certain causal mechanisms involving abstract concepts (e.g., actors who act according to their rational interests or according to social norms, or organizations that tend to legitimize their existence and their control of resources) (see e.g., Bell, 2009; Elster, 2007; Rueschemeyer, 2009; Stinchcombe, 1986).

It may be argued that debatable associations and cherry-picked types, directions, and forms of causal relationships are harmless because non-cherry-picked empirical evidence will weed out the false hypotheses and the potentially right ones can be discovered during data analysis (e.g., when, contrary to the initial hypothesis, a correlation turns out to be negative). However, not all correct relationships will necessarily be identified while testing false hypotheses (e.g., U-shaped forms of relationships in a linear regression or that the unmeasured factor D instead of A is the most important predictor of B). At best, to test the better hypotheses—if they finally come to mind—can require an unnecessary additional round of data analysis of even data collection. Or much space is unnecessarily spent to frame results as surprising and to go on about how they are still inexplicable and how further research is needed to explain them—which will fail unless the new studies are either exploratory and suited to identify the new explanation, or unless such an explanation is finally identified through new efforts of theory building and tested in new studies. At worst, better explanations and interpretations remain undiscovered and untested because data seems to fit the existing ones sufficiently well. Or new empirical research still produces "inexplicable" results because the findings do not speak for themselves, as one may have hoped, and no new explanations have been developed.

Systematic reviews and meta-analyses before or in between empirical studies can help to make sure that one does not cherry-pick from existing research and that the most relevant research gaps and, in particular, the effects that are most in need of further explanation or the most promising theoretical explanations can be addressed (Cooper & Hedges, 1994).

However, this does not prevent cases in which new but *a priori* implausible hypotheses are unnecessarily established and tested on the basis of a one-sided argumentation that is not yet grounded in empirical evidence or not yet made plausible by existing strong theoretical arguments that could be systematically reviewed beforehand.

Asymmetrical theorizing and cherry-picking lead researchers to neglect certain factors or to wrong assumptions about their relationship. In other cases, too many factors are added, also based on problematic assumptions about relationships. I would call these patterns "unstructured listing," and, as a particular subtype, "conventionalized controls." Instead of thinking in terms of processes and causal and temporal order, factors at different levels of abstraction and at different steps of a process are simply added to an unstructured list and to statistical models. In particular, some variables are sometimes only included because they belong to a group of usual control variables (such as age, gender, and formal education).

Assume that in a simultaneous test of the relationships *Attitude A* → *Behavior B* and *Education* → *Behavior B*, we do not find a (strong or significant) influence of education. But in reality, the causal order is *Education* → *A* → *B*, the attitude being the more proximate explanation of the behavior than "education" (or often more correctly, the social background which is approximated by formal education). If one is mainly interested in the attitudinal precursors of some behavior, controlling for education is unnecessary or even dangerous because the influence of A may be underestimated if education is a predictor of the relevant attitudes. But if one were interested in an analysis of socio-demographic or social-structural causes instead of effects of sometimes almost redundant dispositions (B being explained by the tendency to do something like B, what I would call "explanatory triviality"), one would find "education" to be a relevant factor and one should omit A from the theory and analysis. Of course, one can also postulate and test an overall multi-step causal order by means of a path model or it can of course be justified to include "education" as a control variable in order to account for other attitudes that are correlated with both formal education and A but that are difficult to include directly (but education then still remains a potential cause—or a proxy of the causes—of the attitudes). However, such decisions should be made based on good theoretical arguments, not on conventions about what control variables to routinely include. Otherwise, we may come to problematic conclusions, for example that social structure is irrelevant and everything is a matter of attitude, or that almost everything is related to social structure (which is not very surprising and informative in many cases) but that we still not know much about the more specific causes (because the effect of all more specific causes is "controlled away" by including all kinds of social-structural variables).

A final issue of asymmetric and thus unsystematic thinking is the "fallacy of studying the new to see what's new" instead of systematically comparing it to previous phenomena, both theoretically and empirically, in order to identify actual change. A lot of research on media change and social trends (with all kinds of theses on "-izations") lacks historical depth and appropriate theoretical criteria of comparison with earlier phenomena. This leads to illusions of change based on the wrong levels or dimensions of presumed change or an inadequate picture of a "primitive" past when certain things supposedly did not exist, a "nostalgic" past when current evils did not yet prevail, or a "simple" or "static" past when all the complexity, dynamics, and contradictions that make an analysis of current society challenging were not yet relevant. For example, a supposedly unitary era of the mass media with its corresponding political landscape may easily be idealized as being relatively harmonious, simple to understand, and developing only slowly, as opposed to the turbulence and confusion of the current era.

Problems with the Validity of Theories and Measurements

It has been argued above that the validity of causal inference relies on an adequate theory that helps to specify, among other things, what constructs are to be included, their relationships, the context in which a relationship can be expected, and a design that is consistent with these assumptions. To this question of the validity of causal inference comes the problem of the validity of measurements.

Theorists of validity do not agree on a single conceptualization of validity and the aim of this section is not to provide one but only to point to certain problems that will probably be detrimental to validity under different relevant theories. These problems concern the neglect of theory and interpretation in judgments of validity, or the restriction to "validity by correlation" and the "distant reading of definitions and items," as the problems may be called.

If we accept that to measure means to systematically assign values that we claim to stand in a systematic relationship to something (such as an existing phenomenon or a purpose), validity can be defined as the existence or justifiability of that systematic relationship (the measure is actually caused by that existing phenomenon, see Borsboom, Mellenbergh

& van Herden, 2004, or it is actually justifiable to use the measure for the intended purpose, see Messick, 1989).

In this sense, validity cannot in itself be demonstrated solely statistically but ultimately only interpretively and argumentatively, by relying on a theory about meanings and relationships that can only be tested empirically in parts, if at all.

Unfortunately, certain cues for the validity of measurements have come to more or less replace the originally fruitful and relevant core idea of the concept. For example, the correlation between the construct to be measured and other constructs has been called a type of validity ("criterion validity") instead of being a cue that could alert researchers to certain problems of validity (Messick, 1989).[4]

The problem of validity is then only shifted to the validity of the correlated construct (Messick, 1989). Correlations can vary according to the sample; and a high correlation cannot mean that two measures should be considered as measures of the same thing (otherwise, to the degree that almost everything correlates somewhat with almost everything else, everything would be a measure for everything, albeit a very imperfect one most of the times) (Borsboom, Mellenbergh & van Herden, 2004). The classical proposal by Cronbach and Meehl (1955) also does not go far enough. They assume that potentially complex "nomological nets" are built and rebuilt over time that connect constructs and tie them to observations and thus ensure the validity of a construct in question. They also emphasize that these networks of relationships have to be theoretically interpreted. However, the main issue for the validity of constructs cannot be to establish a network of theoretically interpreted but most importantly, empirically substantiated relationships, but a network of relationships made of assumptions about how the measurement can refer to what is claimed to be measured, and how the measurement is produced (thus, 1. a theory of meaning as reference to an existing phenomenon and its pro-

---

4 Of course, it is possible to define "validity" as on wishes to. However, if statistical tests dominate the evaluation of measurements (regardless of whether they are considered an assessment of "validity"), an important aspect of this evaluation would be lost. For example, overviews on the concept of validity aimed at communication researchers classify validity into different forms, such as "construct," "content," "face," "convergent," "discriminant" etc. and do in fact mention the role of theory or that an *argument* has to be made for the validity of a measurement (see, e.g., Dilbeck, 2017; Fink, 2017; Martinez, 2017). However, the logical relationship between what is mostly called "types" of validity (instead of strictly considering it as cues for validity) and validity proper is not always clear and statistical cues feature more or less prominently in such overviews.

perties and 2., in the case of questionnaire-based instruments, a theory of response behavior, see Borsboom, Mellenbergh & van Herden, 2004). Or if we do not subscribe to a realist ontology and theory of meaning in which a measurement refers to something that actually exists in the most direct sense of the word (which would then cause the measurement, Borsboom, Mellenbergh & van Herden, 2004), we need a theory of meaning that ties the measurement to a description of what it is supposed to do or represent, and an explanation of how it can achieve that.

Here, we are again faced with a challenge of holism: We need a theoretical network of interconnected definitions and semantic, causal, and other relationships that we consider consistent and—as far as some of the parts involve truth claims—to be true (but individual assumptions again cannot be falsified in isolation. In particular, a weak or counter-intuitive correlation cannot decide about the validity of a construct but must be considered in the context of the whole network). This network makes sure that we can systematically connect to measurement to its meaning.

Apart from the other theoretical considerations involved in the assessment of validity, I would like to emphasize the role of interpretation, in particular the careful and informed reading of definitions and of questionnaires (if we restrict ourselves to standardized interviews as an example). I often have the impression that the interpretive work and the work of logical deduction and argumentation in the context of measurement is not as careful as it could be (even if it concerns definitions established by the researchers themselves). For a measurement to be valid, we first have to ask ourselves whether we really include all aspects and nothing else than what is covered by the definition of a concept—which is of course a standard requirement for validity. However, this means to carefully apply the criteria in the definition to different candidate cases. Furthermore, we have to ask whether questions and items mean what we think they mean in the ordinary language of all relevant social groups that are to be included in a study. This requires interpretive skills, a particular sense for everyday language, or almost ethnographic experience and knowledge, as well as argumentative and logical rigor, and systematic "testing" of the scope of concepts (by discussing whether diverse and systematically selected examples fall into the definition and whether this is intended or fruitful. We should thus ask: "Can we reliably decide whether this is included in the definition?" and: "Do you really want that to be included in your definition?"). Only based on careful and well-substantiated interpretations, we can then disentangle the whole network of theoretical of assumptions that is supposed to guarantee the validity of some measurement.

For example, we have to assume, argue, or empirically demonstrate that ordinary speakers of the English language would interpret the word "politicians" in the statement "I trust politicians to work in the interest of ordinary people" to refer to political actors at all levels of government, from local to supranational, if that is our definition of "politicians" and our measurement of trust of politicians in a questionnaire. One may well doubt that respondents mostly think about mayors and EU Commissioners when they read this statement. Ultimately, if the validity of this measurement in relation to the above definition is questioned, what counts will be arguments or evidence on the typical interpretation of the word "politicians" (and not in general but if used in a statement such as the above). Maybe, the definition of "politician" may also turn out to be problematic—for example whether "government" refers to "government" as in "all branches of government" or "government" as the executive branch (whatever that means at the local level, depending on the system of "government"). And these are rather simple questions compared to the ontology of trust and its potential objects, and to a theory whether and how it can actually manifest itself in responses to such an item. Therefore, the more atheoretical and methodologically or epistemologically less elaborate among the studies on changes in political or media trust should be taken with a grain of salt, in particular as the interpretation of concepts and measures does not only refer to a single point in time.

If only "face validity" (e.g., the items make sense and one simply hopes that everyone will agree on the meaning and relation to the construct, and once a measurement is established, its meaning seems self-evident to those working in the field and it is no longer questioned) and statistical tests for convergent and discriminant validity are required, it is relatively easy to establish new constructs and easy for them and their measurements to persist. We are then subject to the "dictate of cumulativity" and can walk into a "reification trap."

We witness a trend toward standardization in communication research, from the canonization of methods (e.g., in introductory textbooks) to well-documented and reusable scales and other measurements. One of Ioannidis' (2005, p. 698) corollaries states that "flexibility increases the potential for transforming what would be 'negative' results into 'positive' results'" and that "adherence to common standards is likely to increase the proportion of true findings." According to his explanations of this corollary, he seems to have thought of two factors affecting the validity of measurements and data analyses and thus of the results: new versus time-tested methods and room for selectivity and manipulation. However, his reasoning seems to be biased toward standardization—as many communication researchers obviously seem to value fixed methods and measurements, and established constructs in general, for different reasons. The general belief is that science progresses if studies with a comparable basis accumulate.

Theories (!) of standardization suggest that the reduction in complexity, the gains in compatibility or comparability can come at the price of problematic lock-ins: A norm is perpetuated not because it is the best solution but because a break would come at certain costs (in the case of research, data can no longer be fused and time series cannot be extended, reviewers may reject divergent methodologies, etc.; see, e.g., David, 1985, for a famous explanation of lock-ins due to technological standardization which has also been subsequently applied to institutional path-dependencies).

In many fields, a convention is all that is needed to fulfill the functions and realize the gains of standardization. It is often more important that a standard exists than what the actual standard is, as long as it is in the range of sufficiently functional alternatives. However, if we believe that certain methods and measurements are superior to others, a well-justified choice cannot be replaced by convention, and has to be grounded in substantial conceptions of the object of study and the procedure. And we did not even enter the discussion on paradigm shifts and similar breaks that, according to different theories of science, lead to progress or new incommensurable but acceptable perspectives. Anyway, the idea that research is additive and progresses as long as its building blocks (new studies or new elements of theories that do not change the whole) are compatible, is a rather strong assumption both globally and with regard to specific objects of study, and the requirement that when in doubt, they should remain compatible (the dictate of cumulativity) has to be questioned in each individual case.

In terms of methodological and substantial theory, the opposite problem of "reinventing the wheel" can of course also be observed, and the systematic review and use of existing theories, concepts, and measurements is a potential solution. As another remedy, we should routinely and systematically identify superordinate categories, functional equivalents, or otherwise similar phenomena to the ones under investigation and check whether there are already theories, findings, and measurements pertaining to them. There is no need to theorize or operationalize a phenomenon *ad hoc* if we already have a convincing more general theory that applies to it, and we do not have to start from scratch if similar phenomena have already been theorized and investigated, risking to fall back behind existing approaches. Research do not have to repeat the same mistakes of schematic *ad hoc* theorizing for each new media technology, genre of content, application, organizational innovation, or social trend.

Why Are Most Published Research Findings Under-Theorized?

If we uncritically stick to existing conceptualizations or keep postulating new concepts *en passant,* and do not reflect on the broader context of our concepts and the underlying assumptions, we risk to commit ourselves to messy and contradictory ontologies or discredited epistemologies—which puts the validity of empirical findings into question on a much more fundamental level. Not only can there be a simple mismatch between some concept and some measurement, but we risk potentially fundamental category mistakes, for example by confusing statements on meaning with statements of facts (*A means B for actor C* with *A is B*), the perspective of observers with that of actors, or normative with factual claims.

For example, if we were to define "disinformation" as statements or sets of statements that we know to be false and that the communicator knows to be false, what does it mean for someone to be exposed to disinformation? The only thing that person is exposed to is the statements, so research on consequences of disinformation has to discuss whether "disinformation" can really be category of reception and effects research, because some of the defining features, such as the knowledge and intention of the communicator, are not really present in the situation of reception. It is easy to propose a number of hypotheses using the concept of "disinformation," either *ad hoc* or based on a number of known principles of persuasion, but it is important to reflect on the ontological and epistemological foundations of research that involves multiple perspectives on the truth of statements. Otherwise, the scope, meaning, and implications of empirical findings remain unclear: What kinds of statements do the results apply to, what were the actual mechanisms of persuasion (or resistance), and what kind of competence would recipients need in the present information environment or in the light of potential new types of disinformation (Krämer, 2021)?

In sum, it is problematic to postulate concepts by virtue of an existing measurement with certain statistical properties and to perpetuate them by virtue of their existence in the literature and of the continued use of the measurement. We should not unreflectedly reify concepts and uncritically "blackbox" constructs by routinely applying some operationalization without discussing the underlying assumptions and processes.

One aspect of such uncritical postulates of conceptualizations is what has been termed the "scholastic fallacy": "To place the models that the scientist must construct to account for practices into the consciousness of agents, to operate as if the constructions that the scientist must produce to understand practices, to account for them, were the main determinants, the actual cause of practices" (Bourdieu, 1990, p. 384). If we ignore the difference between the logic of "theoretical practice" and everyday "practical practice," we can establish all kinds of explanations and operationalizations that project a model into some subjects without checking whether it actually grasps their thinking and doing. Furthermore, the scholastic fallacy tends to take concepts outside the context where they are adequate and to assume that a given theory or the perspective of researchers from a given epoch, social class etc. are universally valid.

Carleheden (2016) criticizes the rather naive assumptions of a protagonist of the discourse on systematic theorizing, Richard Swedberg, who seems to imply that theorizing becomes more realistic and less out of touch if efforts of theorizing are preceded by some observations in the field. Such quick and dirty pilot studies, if done unsystematically, cannot be very fruitful (Tavory, 2016) and theorizing cannot be based on supposedly atheoretical creative and open-minded empirical research that is later turned into more formalized hypotheses (Carleheden, 2016).

However, it still seems important to find a third alternative to the naive realism of a belief in pre-theoretical data or experience, and the sterile modeling and operationalizing without any close contact to a field or corpus. The alternative would be theoretically informed and systematic but open qualitative research that reflects and continually adapts its theoretical basis, methodology, sampling etc., and systematic theorizing that critically draws on existing research and is accompanied by an ongoing engagement with the corresponding social fields. Often, this not only means to be present on the latest platforms, follow the latest trends, and talk to people about them instead of only plugging together constructs, but also to bury oneself in old newspaper articles, interviews, or other sources to really get a sense of past political, popular, or intellectual culture.

Problems with Critical Reflection of Studies and with Conclusions

Beyond the explanations a study can offer (often narrowly referred to as *the* "theoretical contribution" it makes), theory should also inform methodological reflection. This can range from a few simple thoughts on the behavior of (potential) participants (as in the example in the introduction) to fundamental methodological questions. Otherwise, concluding section of publications are often restricted to what I would call "ritualistic limitations" instead of actual reflection. The usual restrictions of the respective type of study are reiterated because it is custom to do so or maybe because one wants to preempt obvious criticism: cross-sectional designs do not allow for causal inferences based on temporal order, a convenience sample is not representative, self-reports may be biased by social desirability, etc.

More elaborate conceptions of the design and measurement process and of potential biases can render this discussion much more informative and instructive: What is the process that generates the data and are there any biases (in relation to what exactly?), does it apply to other phenomena and methods as well, is it possible to argue for a specific type and direction of bias, etc.?

Theory cannot only provide the framework for empirical research but if theory is defined as more than testable hypotheses, it can also serve as an interpretive framework or guide through *praxis* and through society. However, due to a restrictive concept of theory and the lack of familiarity with theories of society and normative theories, scholarly works in communication research often suffer from what may be called "diagnostic" and "normative triviality."

If the social sciences wish to offer more than isolated findings (some of which may of course be highly critical in a given historical situation), they should also embrace their function of making sense of the times and world we are living in (*Zeitdiagnose*, i.e., diagnosis of the times; Junge, 2016) and not leave this task to other commentators (who are of course entitled to their judgments and to participate in open debates, but who may be less familiar with current research and less skilled in conceptualizing certain phenomena).

Scholarship can then offer meaning or concepts to think or argue with in the public sphere and in conversations outside the scientific field instead of only taking up the debates and buzzwords of the day. Often, certain concepts of metaphors shape public discourse much more strongly than empirical findings as such that may or may not be in line with those concepts (think of "filter bubbles," "cancel culture," "information society," or "fake news"). While researchers should of course make sure that the ideas they offer to public discourse are not in direct contradiction to empirical research or other established standards of evaluation, such concepts are not necessarily just repackaged or (over-)generalized results, but more often schemata that group similar phenomena or descriptions and that highlight certain features of a phenomenon or a whole era, often with a critical tone.

C. Wright Mills emphasized the role of sociology—or, one might say, the social sciences in the broadest sense—to offer orientation beyond mere factual information (while also describing his "craftsmanship" and how he thinks "sociological imagination" can be methodologically stimulated, providing early but still useful insight into strategies of theorizing and conceptualization and the development of research interests):

Benjamin Krämer

> "The very shaping of history now outpaces the ability of people to orient themselves in accordance with cherished values. [...] Is it any wonder that ordinary people feel they cannot cope with the larger worlds with which they are so suddenly confronted? That they cannot understand the meaning of their epoch for their own lives? [...] It is not only information that they need – in this Age of Fact, information often dominates their attention and overwhelms their capacities to assimilate it. [...] What they need, and what they feel they need, is a quality of mind that will help them to use information and to develop reason in order to achieve lucid summations of what is going on in the world and of what may be happening within themselves. It is this quality, I am going to contend, that journalists and scholars, artists and publics, scientists and editors are coming to expect of what may be called the sociological imagination."
>
> (Mills, 1959, p. 4f.)

One might object that today, we do not live in an "Age of Fact" but an age of disinformation—but is that the case and what would be the theory that would provide clear criteria to decide? Be that as it may—if information from generally trustworthy sources is available more abundantly and more easily than ever, can even more information (in particular coming from researchers) be the solution? Certainly, specific kinds of knowledge can and should always be made more accessible to the public. But will it be understood and trusted without more general frames of interpretation that help us to make sense of social relationships and of social fields such as science, the media, or politics, and society?

Of course, such interpretations should not be thought of as authoritative guidelines conveyed by scientific eminences, but something that everyone should be able to challenge and adapt in open discourses. However, facticity in public discourse is not only about single statements and small pieces of evidence, but also about well-justified general frames of interpretations and worldviews in which individual claims about reality do or do not make sense and do or do not appear plausible or correct.

To offer this kind of interpretations, and to offer better ones than those already circulating, does not only require a certain amount of creativity, but also the readiness to transgress the boundaries of a scientistic habitus, i.e., a deep-seated sense of what is good and "real" science: only the most rigorous empirical research based on the most arid terminology, avoiding anything that could come close to speculation or editorializing.

While many empirically oriented researchers will be rather unfamiliar with, but aware of theories of society and more abstract and interpretive

Why Are Most Published Research Findings Under-Theorized?

social theory, they probably are even more "unmusical" when it comes to normative theories (to start with a catchy metaphor, which is one of many techniques in theory building!). Almost anyone can hum a simple melody they have heard or invented, and many publications in communication research mention at least some critical or normative implications. However, many publications and also many personal conversations seem to suggest that normative statements are either equated with references to commonsense social problems and dominant norms (such as professional norms in some field or basic norms of liberal democracy), or they are lumped together with personal "opinion" or ideology, and thus something "subjective" that is to be avoided in serious research—something like expressing one's musical taste, which can be interesting, but nothing interlocutors will be able to agree on based on the better arguments. As a piece of music (whether it is composed or even improvised) is not a random invention or intuition but something that relates its elements following or ostentatiously breaking certain rules, a normative theory is also a structured whole with basic concepts, logical or argumentative relations, presuppositions and implications, criteria of consistency or contradiction and tensions, etc.

As in all processes of theorizing based on metaphors, we have to decide how far we are willing to follow them. In the present case, it is questionable whether "good" music and "good" theory can be fruitfully compared. Be that as it may, normative and other interpretations, conclusions, and contextualization of research findings should strive for the same argumentative rigor and systematicity as empirical research or the development of those more specific statements that immediately guide data collection and analysis.

For example, a lot of interest in media change is ultimately motivated by the question of whether new developments have brought progress or decline (even if those emphatic terms themselves are rarely used) with regard to democracy, health or wellbeing, equality etc. However, what can count as positive and negative developments is often left to commonsense and rarely explicated in terms of a consistent and well-justified normative theory. It is taken for granted that readers will agree that increasing "fragmentation" is a bad thing, that people should assume responsibility for their health or the environment and should be persuaded to do so by the most effective messages in new media formats, that high levels of trust in the institutions and actors of liberal democracy are desirable and social media companies should help to achieve this goal, or that science communication should more than ever be based on randomized studies, meta-analysis, and similar types of "high quality" evidence. However, I would suggest that in each of these cases, elaborate normative reasoning

Benjamin Krämer

would lead us to answer with a "Yes, but…" or a "It depends what is exactly is meant by…"

Conclusion

Bad theory can lead to a waste of resources, biased analyses, and to a lack of understanding of an object of study and the social world, so that critical and practical implications of our research remain undiscussed and we can neither offer sound evidence nor interpretations and diagnoses to the public. Good theory leads to focused research efforts, appropriate methodologies, and valid measurements and analyses, and allows us to offer the public not only isolated findings, but concepts to think and discuss with and to understand society. It leads us out of an interpretation crisis that does not only concern individual results but also calls into question whether larger fields of research can really contribute to our understanding of our current social world and era. We should not restrict ourselves to the replicability of certain methodological aspects while testing isolated hypotheses (as important as this is), but aim for the transparency and critical reflection of interpretations and theoretical assumptions in the broadest sense. Without this attention to theory, it does not make much sense to retrace, repeat, and accumulate research—no replication without interpretation, no validity without theory, but also no true originality without reality checks. The first step toward better theory is to recognize potential causes for shortcomings, such as unsystematic theorizing and the lack of fruitful interpretive frameworks, resulting in questionable validity and a superficial reflection of implications.

Systematic theory building is thus a necessity in all projects, not a hobby of a few thinkers or a closed field that is separate from empirical research. Of course, a certain specialization is inevitable and functional, and methodological experts can always collaborate with good theorists, but they also need certain theoretical knowledge and competences in order to reflect their work beyond the methodological technicalities and to identify points of contact when working together.

When it comes to competences of theory building, I would bet that most graduates in communication have read a book or attended a course on methods of data collection, but most of them have never looked into a book on theorizing or even taken a course on the subject (i.e., courses on theorizing, not merely courses on theory), and might even rarely read explicitly theoretical contributions in the strict sense.

Still, one should not stand in awe of theorizing and see it as an irrational process that only geniuses master intuitively. Learning to theorize requires two kinds of practice:

1. reading actual theory, in particular genuinely theoretical contributions, and paying close attention on the theoretical sections of the theoretically most sophisticated empirical publications (with many concepts and approaches thus stored somewhere in long-term memory, we can also partly rely on intuitive theorizing, i.e. establish associations through heuristic processing even if we are not focusing on the specific topic of research or on the task of systematic theory building, see Knorr-Cetina, 2014), and

2. practicing theory building based on publications that codify the process, that specifically turn to the "context of discovery" (Swedberg, 2012), focusing on theorizing as opposed to theory—although existing overviews are often rather restrictive or idiosyncratic in their understanding of theory, and the procedures they propose remain rather abstract. This more general instruction therefore needs to be complemented by teaching or collaborative learning based on specific examples and a broader range of problems. This also allows theorizing to become more intuitive and maybe less painstaking over time, although we should always check its results for its systematicity (avoiding, for example, asymmetries or category mistakes).

The idea of systematic theorizing has been met with enthusiasm, sobering qualifications, pragmatism, and constructive criticism. After an initial optimism in the 1950s and 60s that the main social "laws" might soon be discovered, and the more modest proposal of grounded theory to build theory inductively from empirical material, a newer "pragmatic" wave of literature seeks to stimulate theory building based on heuristics and tricks for creativity (Tavory, 2016). However, this newer approach has also been criticized as overly narrow: It tends reduce the necessarily cyclical interplay between theorizing and empirical research to a strict distinction between the context of discovery and the context of justification that is reproduced uncritically, and it tends to reduce theory to causal explanations (Büttner, 2021; Tavory, 2016).

German-speaking scholars in particular seem to have increasingly turned toward different methods and aspects of building social theory that go beyond a narrow conception of theory as set of falsifiable propositions (e.g., Anicker, 2020; Büttner, 2021; Beregow, 2021; Farzin & Laux, 2014; Farzin & Laux, 2016; Krämer, 2015). Furthermore, the practice of doing theory has to be reflected as a social activity (not only the activity of an individual genius or craftsperson) that needs a sound basis in experience and existing thought, but that is not automatically without biases because it is done systematically, and that always requires a critically distance to previous approaches. We need to be aware of how contexts shape the production and circulation of theory and how doing theory always risks to shift from making, teaching, and critical analysis of theories to the consumption of ready-made, hegemonic, commonsense ideas (Chaudhuri & Thakur, 2018).

Unfortunately, teaching on theorizing is still often limited to some basics of Popperian philosophy of science, a few remarks on criteria for good theory (consistency, falsifiability, etc.), or some ways of coding qualitative material in methodology courses and textbooks. The "imbalance between methods and theory" (Swedberg, 2014a, p. 8) and between teaching theory and teaching theorizing needs to be overcome by more explicit teaching of the practice of theory building (Silver, 2019; Swedberg, 2014a, 2014b, ch. 7; Swedberg, 2016) at all levels of scientific qualification. It should be based on literature that conveys the methods of theorizing that is not restricted to specific types of theories or particular problems and aspects of theory building, and that includes the critical reflection on the contexts and biases of theorizing.

I think that it would also be a good idea to remember a number of teachings by a researcher who, unlike Ioannidis, did not put his approach to science in writing, let alone in such pithy words. Wolfram Peiser, whom the present volume is dedicated to, always advised me and his other students and collaborators to consider a broad range of explanations and factors, to systematically think about inverse relationships, and only thereafter focus on a range of concepts to be included in a study (and when in doubt, to include more instead of fewer as long as everything can be measured parsimoniously but validly and reliably). Instead of focusing on the next best idea, he always reminded everyone to think broadly, choose wisely, and explain their choices. He also urged everyone not to be narrow-minded due to a single preferred and closed theoretical framework but to check for alternatives and possible additions, to use common sense in order to find the most fruitful questions and adequate explanations, and to connect one's research to broader concerns and debates inside and outside the scientific field. Finally, he insisted that what is specific to a phenomenon or what is new can only be identified by systematic comparison. In particular, he always reminded us that claims of social or media change must be based on a systematic comparison with the past (whether based on original or existing research and data), not only on the study of the most recent phenomena. In this sense, much of the present argument is not that new but inspired by what he taught us.

References

Abbott, Andrew (2004). *Methods of discovery. Heuristics for the social sciences*. New York: W. W. Norton.

Abend, Gabriel (2008). The meaning of 'theory'. *Sociological Theory, 26*, 173-199.

Alexander, Jeffrey C. (1982). *Positivism, presuppositions, and current controversies [Theoretical logic in sociology, vol. 1]*. Berkeley: University of California Press.

Anicker, Fabian (2020). Theoriekonstruktion durch Theorienvergleich – eine soziologische Theorietechnik. *Kölner Zeitschrift für Soziologie und Sozialpsychologie, 72*, 567-596.

Becker, Howard S. (1998). *Tricks of the trade. How to think about your research while you're doing it*. Chicago: University of Chicago Press.

Bell, David C. (2009). *Constructing social theory*. Lanham: Rowman & Littlefield.

Bendavid, E., Mulaney, B., Sood, N., Shah, S., Bromley-Dulfano, R., Lai, C., ... & Bhattacharya, J. (2021). COVID-19 antibody seroprevalence in Santa Clara County, California. *International Journal of Epidemiology, 50*, 410-419.

Beregow, Elena (2021). Theorieatmosphären. Soziologische Denkstile als affektive Praxis. *Berliner Journal für Soziologie, 31*, 189-217.

Borsboom, Denny, Mellenbergh, Gideon J. & van Herden, Jaap (2004). The concept of validity. *Psychological Review, 4*, 1061-1071.

Bourdieu, Pierre (1990). The scholastic point of view. *Cultural Anthropology, 5*, 380-391.

Büttner, Alexander (2021). Theoretisieren in der Soziologie. Bezugskontexte und Modi soziologischer Theoriebildung. Available online: https://doi.org/10.31235/osf.io/bj42k

Carleheden, Mikael (2016). What conception of the theoretical does 'theorizing' presuppose? Comment on Richard Swedberg's 'Before theory comes theorizing or how to make social science more interesting.' *British Journal of Sociology, 67*(1), 36-42.

Chaudhuri, Maitrayee & Thakur, Manish (Eds.) (2018). *Doing theory. Locations, hierarchies and disjunctions*. Hyderabad: Orient Black Swan.

Cooper, Harris & Hedges, Larry V. (1994). Using research syntheses to plan future research. In Cooper, Harris & Hedges, Larry V. (Eds.), *The handbook of research synthesis* (pp. 485-500). New York: Russell Sage Foundation.

Cronbach, Lee J. & Meehl, Paul E. (1955). Construct validity in psychological tests. *Psychological Bulletin, 52*, 281-302.

David, Paul A. (1985). Clio and the Economics of QWERTY. *American Economic Review, 75*, 332-337.

Dienlin, Tobias, Johannes, Niklas, Bowman, Nicholas D., Masur, Philipp K., Engesser, Sven, Kümpel, Anna S., ... & De Vreese, Claes (2021). An agenda for open science in communication. *Journal of Communication, 71*, 1-26.

Dilbeck, Keith A. (2017). Validity, construct. In Allen: Mike (Eds.), *The SAGE Encyclopedia of Communication Research methods (vol. 4)* (pp. 1820-1822). Thousand Oaks: Sage.

Eronen, Markus I., & Bringmann, Laura F. (2021). The theory crisis in psychology: How to move forward. *Perspectives on Psychological Science, 16*(4), 779–788.

Elster, John (2007). *Explaining social behavior. More nuts and bolts for the social sciences.* Cambridge: Cambridge University Press.

Farzin, Sina & Laux, Henning (2016). Gründungsszenen – Eröffnungszüge des Theoretisierens am Beispiel von Heinrich Popitz' Machtsoziologie. *Zeitschrift für Soziologie, 45*, 241-260.

Farzin, Sina & Laux, Henning (Eds.) (2014). *Gründungsszenen soziologischer Theorie.* Wiesbaden: Springer VS.

Fink, Edward L. (2017). Validity, measurement of. In Allen: Mike (Eds.), *The SAGE Encyclopedia of Communication Research methods (vol. 4)* (pp. 1828-1833). Thousand Oaks: Sage.

Gigerenzer, Gerd (2010). Personal Reflections on Theory and Psychology. *Theory & Psychology, 20*(6), 733–743.

Hagen, Sebastian, Frey, Felix & Koch, Sebastian (2015). Theoriebildung in der Kommunikationswissenschaft. Eine Bestandsaufnahme zu Bedeutung, Arten und Verfahren der Theorieentwicklung. *Publizistik, 60*, 123-146.

Hoyningen-Huene, Paul (1987). Context of discovery and context of justification. *Studies in History and Philosophy of Science, 18*, 501-515.

Ioannidis, John P. A. (2005). Why most published research findings are false. *PLoS Medicine, 2*(8), e124.

Jaccard, James & Jacoby, Jacob (2020). *Theory construction and model-building skills. A practical guide for social scientists [2nd ed.].* New York: Guilford Press.

Junge, Matthias (2016). Zeitdiagnose als Chance der Soziologie. In Junge, Matthias (Eds.), *Metaphern soziologischer Zeitdiagnosen* (pp. 51-60). Wiesbaden: Springer VS.

Kalthoff, Herbert, Hirschauer, Stefan, Lindemann, Gesa (Eds.) (2008). *Theoretische Empirie. Zur Relevanz qualitativer Forschung.* Frankfurt a. M.: Suhrkamp.

Knorr-Cetina, Karin (2014). Intuitionist theorizing. In Swedberg, Richard (Eds.), *Theorizing in social science. The context of discovery* (pp. 29-60). Redwood City: Stanford University Press.

Krämer, Benjamin (2015). Luhmanns Operationen: Analyse einiger Wendungen der soziologischen Theoriebildung. Available online: https://nbn-resolving.org/u rn:nbn:de:0168-ssoar-438008

Krämer, Benjamin (2021). Stop studying "fake news" (we can still fight against disinformation in the media). *Studies in Communication and Media, 10*, 6-30.

Krause, Monika (2016). The meanings of theorizing. *British Journal of Sociology, 67*, 23-29.

Lee, Stephanie M. (2020). JetBlue's founder helped fund a Stanford study that said the Coronavirus wasn't that deadly. Buzzfeed News. Available online: https://www.buzzfeednews.com/article/stephaniemlee/stanford-coronavirus-neeleman-ioannidis-whistleblower

Martinez, Lourdes S. (2017). Validity, face and content. In Allen: Mike (Eds.), *The SAGE Encyclopedia of Communication Research methods (vol. 4)* (pp. 1823-1824). Thousand Oaks: Sage.

Merton, Robert K. (1945). Sociological theory. *American Journal of Sociology, 60*, 462-473.

Messick, Samuel (1989). Meaning and values in test validation: The science and ethics of assessment. *Educational Researcher, 18*, 5-11.

Mills, C. Wright (1959). *The sociological imagination.* Oxford: Oxford University Press.

Nossek, Brian A. & Errington, Timothy A. (2020). What is replication? *PLOS Biology, 18(3)*, e3000691.

Oberauer, Klaus & Lewandowsky, Stephan (2019). Addressing the theory crisis in psychology. *Psychonomic Bulletin & Review, 26(5)*, 1596-1618.

Popper, Karl (1935). *Logik der Forschung. Zur Erkenntnistheorie der modernen Naturwissenschaft.* Wien: Springer.

Rains, Stephen A., Levine, Timothy R. & Weber, Rene (2018). Sixty years of quantitative communication research summarized: Lessons from 149 meta-analyses. *Annals of the International Communication Association, 42*, 105-124.

Rueschemeyer, Dietrich (2009). *Usable theory. Analytic tools for social and political research.* Princeton: Princeton University Press.

Runciman, W. G. (1983). *A treatise on social theory. Vol. I: The methodology of social theory.* Cambridge: Cambridge University Press.

Shoemaker, Pamela J., Tankard, James William Jr. & Lasorsa, Dominic L. (2004). *How to build social science theories.* Thousand Oaks: Sage.

Silver, Daniel (2019). Theorizing is a practice, you can teach it. *Canadian Review of Sociology, 56*, 130-133.

Sohlberg, Peter & Leiulfsrud, Håkon (Eds.) (2017). *Theory in action. Theoretical constructionism.* Leiden: Brill.

Stanford, Kyle (2021). Underdetermination of scientific theory. In Zalta, Edward N. (Eds.), *The Stanford Encyclopedia of Philosophy.* Available online: https://plato.stanford.edu/archives/win2021/entries/scientific-underdetermination/

Stanford, Kyle S. (2006). *Exceeding our grasp: Science, history, and the problem of unconceived alternatives.* New York: Oxford University Press.

Stinchcombe, Arthur L. (1986). *Constructing social theories.* Chicago: University of Chicago Press.

Swedberg, Richard (2012). Theorizing in sociology and social science: Turning to the context of discovery. *Theory and Society, 41*, 1-40.

Swedberg, Richard (2014a). How to teach theorizing: Exercises and more. *Perspectives. Newsletter of the ASA Theory Section, 36(1)*, 1-10.

Swedberg, Richard (2014b). *The art of social theory*. Princeton: Princeton University Press.

Swedberg, Richard (2016). Reply to the commentators. *British Journal of Sociology, 67*, 57-70.

Tavory, Iddo (2016). The pragmatist wave of theory construction. *British Journal of Sociology, 67*, 50-56.

Benjamin Krämer *(Dr. rer. pol., LMU Munich, 2012) is Akademischer Rat auf Zeit and Privatdozent at LMU Munich's Department of Media Communication. His research focuses on political communication (with an emphasis on populist communication), media use and reception, and online communication as well as on the development and adaptation of new empirical methods and strategies of systematic theory building. Wolfram Peiser supervised his PhD and was a member of the supervision committee of his habilitation in Munich. Benjamin worked as research and teaching associate at his chair from 2006 to 2021.*

Is Communication via the Internet *Public* Communication?

Hans-Bernd Brosius

Abstract

The ongoing digitalization of almost all aspects of society also affects communication research as a scientific field. Recent years have witnessed an ongoing discussion of what exactly is communication research, how can our field be defined. In Germany, over the last decades communication scholars often define "mass communication" as their core research interest. In digitalized communication worlds, the boundaries between interpersonal and public communication have become more and more blurred. As a consequence, several authors have argued that we should study any kind of "mediated communication". This paper argues that communication scholars should rather study what I call public communication 2.0.

Recent years have witnessed a recurrent debate on the scope and the focus of Communication as an academic discipline (Vorderer, 2015; Brosius, 2003a, 2016; Hepp, 2016; Jarren, 2016, 2019; Theis-Berglmair, 2016; Strippel et al., 2018). Some authors (e.g., Hepp, 2016) argue for making the entire breadth of mediated communication the subject of our discipline, rather than making restrictions, for example, in the direction of a focus on "public communication" (Brosius, 2016; Jaren, 2008). In a world of digitalization with its infinite number of very different communication offerings and with blurring meaning of the terms "public communication" and "mass communication" and the emergence of several intermediate forms (e.g., interpersonal-public communication), it seems obvious to expand communication studies thematically to include all forms of mediated communication. This chapter argues that a more narrow and contoured conception of communication sensu "public" communication is necessary in order to show the unique contribution of communication as an academic discipline. I would like to take up these impulses and discussions and argue for the second standpoint. This chapter is an updated and extended version of my initial contribution to this debate (Brosius, 2016). It is a reaction to the (ongoing) German debate (and most of the examples refer to the German situation. However, this situation is far from being unique.

And, it can serve as a perspective in a broader international discussion on the future of communication research

The debate about the self-conception of Communication as an academic discipline has been going on for decades. Its fundamental question asks for the adequate description of what communication research should investigate. Some argue that „communication research is what communication researchers make it" (Schulz, 2006, S. 96). This rather descriptive approach has been contrasted with more normative ideas. These have become manifest in the two self-conception papers of the German Association of Communication Research (DGPuK) from 2001 and 2008. The 2001 version still states:

> "At the center of the subject is indirect public communication mediated by mass media. The associated production, processing, and reception processes are the focus of the subject's interest. In addition to mass media, however, other organizations such as political parties, associations, or companies increasingly function as corporate communicators." (DGPuK, 2001, p. 3)

In 2008, on the other hand, the respective passage reads:

> "Communication and media studies deals with the social conditions, consequences and meanings of media, public and interpersonal communication. The outstanding importance that communication and media have in society justifies the relevance of the subject. Communication and Media Studies sees itself as a theoretically and empirically working social science with interdisciplinary references. It conducts basic research to enlighten society, contributes to solving problems of communication practice through applied research, and provides educational services for a media and communication industry that has been growing dynamically for years." (DGPuK, 2008, p. 1)

The media change that took place in the meantime and can be subsumed using keywords such as digitalization, medialization/mediatization, web 2.0, or social media is certainly the driver for this change in the definition of the subject area from a narrow view as in "public communication" to a broad view as in "communication is mediated communication in general". The "field" and many of its prominent representatives have - in some cases decades ago - also repeatedly presented further definitions of the object and concepts of communication, some of which differ considerably (e.g., the Munich "Zeitungswissenschaft" or the Essen version of "Kommunikationswissenschaft"). Expansions of the field beyond the study of public communication are manifold, for example Klaus Beck's work on the telephone (Beck & Lange, 1989) or, even earlier, Winfried Lerg's habilitation on conversation (Lerg, 1970). If one reviews the abundance of definitions and approaches, the question arises whether it is not ultimately futile to establish definitions at all, if we essentially do what we want to do, and no one resents that. In the end, it will always be controversial to define the subject of a subject normatively. Is it not more fruitful to determine its meaning empirically? However, this does not leave us feeling happy either. As communication scholars, we are certainly asked more frequently than colleagues from other academic disciplines what we actually do. A clear self-conception gives the individual researcher self-confidence and provides the field with recognizability value and a unique selling point.

Changes in the Media Landscape

The technical digitization of communication channels has undoubtedly had (and still has) an outstanding impact on the constitution of our societies (regional, national, global). The multiplication of communication offers, the facilitated possibilities to react to communication of others, the chance to find new communication partners and to observe the communication of others has changed all our lives. This has certainly also changed our subject, our self-image as researchers as well as our theories and methods (cf. Brosius, 2013). However, I would like to add one aspect that seems important to me. Digitalization makes communication directly visible to all participants, including, but not limited to, communication scientists. Communication of others is abundantly observed by website owners and users and is registered, collected, sorted, and distributed by software, such as bots and algorithms. Thus traditional ways of communicating "offline" (bidirectional talk, group discussions, etc.) are resembled by different types of online communication, such as chats, blogs fora, and social media in general. These types of online communication are not per se public. However, they become public because they can be observed by a principally infinite number of others thus leaving the framework of private, interpersonal communication. We see other people playing, buying, talking, doing business, etc. Most types of communication are not new, but are now visible online. And this is true not only synchronously, but also diachronically due to the seemingly infinite memory of the Internet. The synchronous and diachronic observation of the communication of others expands our horizons of experience enormously and also provides the basis for the communication science study of the manifestations of the Internet. We react to the communication of others with our own communication and thus in turn expand the experiential space of others. The main effect of communication is thus primarily communication again.

The basic observability of the communication of others makes much that was previously private and interpersonal public, even though not many other people may actually observe a particular course of communication. But: Algorithms already do that, they aggregate, categorize and combine their observations of our communication. This result is in turn taken up by humans or other algorithms and made usable, also ultimately implemented again in further communication activities on the Internet. One example may suffice. If we search for web content on Google, this would certainly not be public communication at first, but because Google records and counts our search queries, it becomes part of public communication, becomes indirectly observable for others. This explains, for example, why Google can use the frequency of the search term "flu" as an early warning system for the occurrence of flu-like infections (Ginsberg et al., 2009) - and why the classical mass media take this up and report on it (Unkel, 2019).

Of course, there will still be private communication, which may not even be eavesdropped on by anyone (in the forest while walking, for example, hopefully!); but a large part of digitally mediated interpersonal communication will not be private, in the sense that no one else "hears" it, records it or evaluates it. This also becomes manifest, for example, in the fact that one talks about hiking boots with a conversation partner on an email platform, and the next day one receives corresponding advertisements on Amazon or Ebay. Communication that takes place on the Internet, whether interpersonal, in groups or social networks, initiated by private individuals or classic mass media, is public communication in the true sense of the word due to its basic observability and permanent storage and availability. Public communication is thus no longer bound to mass media dissemination, but it also manifests itself in social networks and in other forms of communication that were initially and actually meant to be interpersonal. We have elsewhere referred to this melange as "interpersonal-public communication (cf. Haas & Brosius, 2011; Haas, Keyling & Brosius, 2010) to emphasize the blurring boundaries between interpersonal and mass communication. A similar approach has been proposed by O'Sullivan & Carr (2018) with their introduction of the term "masspersonal communication".

Is Communication via the Internet Public Communication?

Mediated Communication as a Key Concept?

Hepp (2016) and others suggest, as a reaction to digitization, that the subject of the discipline should be expanded to include "mediated communication in its entire breadth" (p. 226). Outside of Germany, this is the typical approach (in line with what Schulz, 2006, suggested). What communication scholars do defines the field and its borders. In fact, in the American tradition, communication is – to a large degree – interpersonal communication. The German tradition is different in this respect (see Brosius, 2003b; Löblich, 2010). "Communication research in the public interest"[1] might be regarded as the key normative perspective. This can be regarded as the reason for a strong German focus on mass communication as the major vehicle of public communication. So why not shift to a broader definition of our field as mediated communication? I decidedly disagree with this option. Mainly, without a precisely defined concept of "media", the concept seems like an empty formula. What, after all, would be non-mediated communication? Isn't all communication somehow mediated by a medium of some kind (air, cable, waves, sound, internet, etc.)? Wouldn't the corollary necessarily be that we are studying "communication" (period!)? I have similar concerns with terms like technically mediated communication or social communication. What, then, would be non-social communication? In addition to the conceptual vagueness, there is also the question of whether such whether such definition are actually serving the purpose of a definition, which is to grant delineation from phenomena outside of its realms.

I want to delve into two aspects here: First, at least the concept of media would have to be clarified. In the lay understanding media stand for some type of technical devices that convey interesting information to the public (such as television). In a broader sense a medium also includes things like air, cable, paper, etc.) Is Facebook the medium? Or the embedded Youtube video? Or the browser that enables both applications? Or the Internet protocol that supports the browser? Or is it the screen on which communication content is presented? Is every kind of technical mediation of communication also mediated, so that the term "mediated" is ultimately used like other broad terms such as "social"? Can there be "non-mediated" communication? Such a de-limitation of the field's subject seems presumptuous to me. This is also the point of departure for my second

---

1 The title of the ICA-conference in 2004, most tellingly organized by the German ICA president Wolfgang Donsbach.

argument, which is of a more strategic nature: Of course, communication scholars can study self-presentation strategies and impression management of Facebook users, but psychologists can do that just as well and probably better. Of course, we can also survey learning success on various textbook platforms, but education researchers can probably do that better, too. Of course, we can also describe the use of communication technologies in digital value chains, but economists can do that just as well and probably better. This is not to exclude interdisciplinary research, which has always existed in the offline world. But our discipline needs a recognizable USP if it is to survive in the competition between disciplines for resources. Otherwise, we will become even more of a purely teaching-oriented discipline that defines itself in terms of professional fields and the training of students.

This does not necessarily mean that we should stick to the "old" concept of public communication as communication mediated by traditional mass media. Therefore, I would like to explain in the following how a modified and expanded concept of public communication could look like. For lack of a better term, I call it public communication 2.0.

Public Communication 2.0 as the Subject of the Field

A central feature of online communication is the disjunction between public and mass communication on the one hand and private and interpersonal communication on the other. In the "golden age of mass media," mass communication and public communication were largely congruent in our theoretical conceptions. Mass media coverage was seen as an indicator or even equivalent of public communication. Private and interpersonal communication were almost completely excluded, presumably mainly because of the difficulties in methodologically capturing them. When mass conversations of individuals take up current topics, deepen them, and derive conclusions from them, this has always constituted a part of public communication that is socially relevant. We have simply overlooked this for methodological reasons. As stated earlier, in the online world, communication activities of individuals exist in a variety of forms, are publicly observable, can be aggregated, stored, and forwarded. I therefore propose a modified model that suggests the vast amount of all communication activities we can observe constitutes public communication. For this model to be fruitful, however, it requires some additional assumptions:

a) The theme/the topic/the issue should act as the central feature of online communication acitvities. Communication is arranged around themes, themes structure communication. Theme/topic/issue has always play-ed a central role in communication research, even beyond agenda-setting research. Content analyses and media impact studies are usually based on one or more themes. Themes structure the totality of communication activities. Themes are socially constructed and can be classified according to various characteristics. Without structuring by themes, public commu-nication is difficult to imagine. It is one of the miracles of contemporary communication research how vague, blurred and ill-defined the concepts of themes/topics/issues are used.

b) Themes differ in terms of their relevance. Relevance is one of several criteria for quality of reporting. In the model I have outlined, relevance is determined on the one hand by the intensity of communication about a theme and can thus be counted and operationalized in online communica-tion through automated observations. On the other hand, the prominence of communicators generates different levels of relevance: One message from the German Chancellor makes a topic more relevant than one messa-ge of a a blogger, although both messages are distributed equally often (which is unlikely).

c) The intensity of communication on themes can be determined by the sum of all observable messages on that theme. The sum is of course not equally distributed among communicators. Communicators with a high reach (classic mass media, Spiegel online) have a greater influence on public communication than communicators with a lower reach (for example, individuals, most bloggers), simply because they create different numbers of recipients for their message.

d) Liking, commenting and sharing strengthen the intensity and articu-lation function of communication (Noelle-Neumann, 1980). At the same time, forming one's own opinion is presumably made more difficult.

e) The previous concept of interpersonal communication breaks down into interpersonal-public communication) and interpersonal private com-munication. The observability of a large share of interpersonal communi-cation in the online sphere makes it part of public communication 2.0; due to the multiplicity of communicators. Small reaches of individual communicators can sum up via networks of social media and makes themes more visible. Interpersonal public communication interacts and ingtermingles with mass media communication, for example via user com-ments under journalistic articles.

Hans-Bernd Brosius

Data Specification and Adaptation of Methods

Above, I have already explained that algorithms and software not only collect and aggregate and distribute data about our behavior and our communication, but that through further processing the algorithms themselves become part of the communication events on the Internet. Algorithms take on genuinely journalistic functions of agenda-setting and gate-keeping on the one hand. But they also take on intra- and interpersonal functions by giving us feedback on our behavior (e.g., in fitness apps) or influencing our buying behavior (e.g., on Amazon), to give just two examples. Algorithms and bots in particular, have become powerful communication agents. They are, for example, supposed to influence elections in foreign countries, manipulate public opinion on candidates and issues or create wrong impressions of products using fake user comments.

As communication scientists, we should also take advantage of datafication by developing and using data collection methods ourselves in the digitalized media world. The German Association of Communication Research (DGPuk) has established a working group on this topic. The results of their work have been presented to the German community (cf. Hepp et al., 2021). However, we are not alone and are competing with other disciplines – as I have mentioned before – , the platform operators, the private media sector and intelligence agencies, which have disproportionately larger budgets for the development of observation software of any kind. And almost logically, communication researchers are usually lagging behind, dependent on the good will of platform owners. This situation reminds me very much of the early days of survey research, when we were grateful, for example, that Gallup and other polling organizations provided us with survey data on the public agenda that we could not have collected ourselves to the same extent and quality. The fascinating possibilities of jumping on the bandwagon of datafication and even surveying people's behavior on the Net flash up every now and then in communication science publications, but are certainly not yet sufficiently exploited. One fundamental problem will presumably remain for some time to come, namely that others have much better and broader access to behavioral and communication activities than we scientists do. For example, Facebook can record and evaluate all communication activities of all users on their platform, while we can only look at the public pages, as long as the respective platform operators let us do so. And Facebook certainly has little interest in providing us with the complete data picture so we can do theory work. The relationship between platforms and communication research has been discussed in a paper by Bruns (2019).

Is Communication via the Internet Public Communication?

This also quickly leads to an imbalance in that we can collect vast amounts of behavioral and communication data on the one hand, but know comparatively little about the original communicators (public or private, organizational or individual) and the situation in which their messages were originated. Without knowledge of the communicator and/or recipient side, however, our findings often lack depth of focus, and ecological fallacies loom. Möller et al. (2020) have made a promising proposal of how to integrate observational with survey data. Unfortunately, we cannot approach the problem as unconcernedly as the media or advertisers, who often quite pragmatically infer personal characteristics from communication behavior. For example, if someone clicks on a sports website such as www.kicker.de from a computer with an identifiable IP address and later on purchases an aftershave on www.amazon.com, algorithms identify the person behind the IP address as male. This might be a good guess, but could also be woefully wrong. Inferences about other personal characteristics such as age or income are certainly even more difficult to make. Anyway, such procedures certainly do not score under "good research practice".

Method adaptations are not only necessary in data collection, but above all in data analysis. Datafication makes it necessary to move away from a pure regression logic with strictly separated independent and dependent variables. The interconnectedness of media messages and their communication in online media environments ultimately makes it impossible to distinguish unequivocally between the independent variable (media message) and the dependent variable (media impact). Media messages diffuse hence and forth in the cosmos of different online communicators (human or bot). Every "use" of a message changes it and alters its relevance and visibility on the web. For example, algorithms count the frequency with which an article is clicked on a news site, thereby extending or shortening its life on the site. Forwards, shares, and likes change the way the next user sees an article (cf. Kümpel, 2021). User comments following an article add information to the article that was not originally intended by its author. As a consequence, the article is possibly perceived differently by subsequent readers. So it is also no longer the journalists or the actual communicators alone who shape the appearance and meaning of a message, but the users through acts of actively using it. This means that the news situation and the relationship between the news items are changing almost continuously.

Messages therefore do not remain constant, but become variables themselves. This ultimately makes traditional pre-/post-designs which are intended to identify which message influenced which recipients superfluous.

Whereas in a periodically printed newspaper, for example, every piece of content could be assigned to exactly one and only this date and could thus be placed in a before-and-after relationship with the date of a survey, this is no longer possible in the online world. On the one hand, contributions are available online for longer and may change several times in the course of a publication period; on the other hand, communication is so fast that even intervals shorter than one day are no longer sufficient to determine a before and after of two time series (cf. Haim, Weimann & Brosius, 2016). In any case, conventional time series analyses with fixed intervals are rendered impossible.

However, datafication also means that we need to make theoretical adjustments. The close interplay between journalists and recipients requires to modify classical approaches such as agenda-setting or gate-keeping (cf. Weimann & Brosius, 2016; Friedrich, Keyling & Brosius, 2016). For example, the clear distinction between a media agenda and a public agenda is disappearing in favor of a shared online agenda that is developing with rapid dynamics and whose composition can be changed by every act of use.

Conclusion

Several aspects can be stated as a conclusion:

1. Digitization is challenging the self-conception of the discipline and its actors more than it ever did before. We need to rethink and adapt our approach to the manifestations of communication theoretically and methodologically.

2. The often drawn dichotomy between "mediated" and "public" communication cannot be resolved by giving up "public communication" as the USP of our discipline. "Mediated communication" is arbitrary, its methodological and theoretical implications make our research indistinguishable from that of neighboring disciplines.

3. All those involved in online communication (i.e. including scientists) observe each other and mutually influence each other. Through the synchronous and diachronic observation of the actors and their behavior, online communication becomes " public communication in principle" or, as I would like to call it, public communication 2.0.

4. Communication scholars are thus concerned with public communication in the broadest sense, but in a different sense than the classic "public communication" mediated by mass media and oriented toward ideas of democratic theory.

Is Communication via the Internet Public Communication?

5. Public communication 2.0 is the totality of all online communication activities that take place in a society. Communication creates messages that are classified by its recipients into themes, topics and/or issues. These identified themes are constituted by communicators and influences their further communication behavior. Depending on the number of communication partners, a distinction can be made between influential (e.g., traditional mass media) and less influential communicators (e.g., bloggers).

6. The relevance of a theme is thus determined by the intensity of communication, which can be operationalized as the sum of all communication activities originated by participants in online communication.

7. The consequences and effects of communication are primarily further communication activities.

8. In this way, the field can keep its raison d'être and can distinguish itself from other fields that also deal with the manifestations of digitization.

References

Beck, K. & Lange, U. (1989). Mensch und Telefon - Gedanken zu einer Soziologie der Telefonkommunikation. *Hessische Blätter für Volks- und Kulturforschung, 24*, 139–154.

Brosius, H.-B. (2003a). Aufgeregtheiten durch Technikfaszination. Trotzdem und gerade deshalb: Die neue ist die alte Kommunikationswissenschaft. In: M. Löffelholz & T. Quandt (eds.), *Die neue Kommunikationswissenschaft. Theorien, Themen und Berufsfelder im Internet-Zeitalter. Eine Einführung.* Wiesbaden: Westdeutscher Verlag, p. 43–48.

Brosius, H.-B. (2003b). Kommunikationswissenschaft als empirisch normative Sozialwissenschaft. In: H. Richter & H. W. Schmitz (eds.), *Kommunikation - ein Schlüsselbegriff der Humanwissenschaften?* Münster: Nodus Publikationen, pp. 401-420.

Brosius, H.-B. (2013). Neue Medienumgebungen: Theoretische und methodische Herausforderungen. In: O. Jandura, A. Fahr & H.-B. Brosius (eds.), *Theorieanpassungen in der digitalen Medienwelt.* Baden-Baden: Nomos, pp. 13–30.

Brosius, H.-B. (2016). Warum Kommunikation im Internet öffentlich ist. Zu Andreas Hepps Beitrag „Kommunikations- und Medienwissenschaft in datengetriebenen Zeiten. *Publizistik, 61*, 363-372.

Bruns, A. (2019). After the 'APIcalypse': Social media platforms and their fight against critical scholarly research. *Information, Communication & Society, 22*, 1544–1566.

DGPuK (2001). *Die Mediengesellschaft und ihre Wissenschaft. Herausforderungen für die Kommunikations- und Medienwissenschaft als akademische Disziplin.* München: Deutsche Gesellschaft für Publizistik- und Kommunikationswissenschaft.

Hans-Bernd Brosius

DGPuK (2008). *Kommunikation und Medien in der Gesellschaft: Leistungen und Perspektiven der Kommunikations- und Medienwissenschaft. Eckpunkte für das Selbstverständnis der Kommunikations- und Medienwissenschaft.* http://www.dgpuk.de/wp-c ontent/uploads/2012/01/DGPuK_Selbstverstaendnispapier-1.pdf

Friedrich, K., Keyling, T. & Brosius, H.-B. (2016). Gatekeeping revisited. In: G. Vowe & P. Henn (eds.), *Political Communication in the Online World Theoretical Approaches and Research Designs.* New York: Routledge, pp. 59–72.

Ginsberg, J., Mohebbi, M. H., Patel, R. S., Brammer, L., Smolinski, M. S. & Brilliant, L. (2009). Detecting influenza epidemics using search engine query data. *Nature, 457*(7232), 1012–1014.

Haas, A. & Brosius, H.-B. (2011). Interpersonal-öffentliche Kommunikation in Diskussionsforen: Strukturelle Äquivalenz mit der Alltagskommunikation? In: J. Wolling, A.Will & C. Schumann (eds.), *Medieninnovationen. Wie Medienentwicklungen die Kommunikation in der Gesellschaft verändern.* Konstanz: UVK, pp. 103–119.

Haas, A., Keyling, T. & Brosius, H.-B. (2010) Online-Diskussionsforen als Indikator für interpersonale (Offline-) Kommunikation? Methodische Ansätze und Probleme. In: N. Jackob, T. Zerback, O. Jandura & M. Maurer (eds.), *Das Internet als Forschungsinstrument und –gegenstand in der Kommunikationswissenschaft.* Köln: von Halem, pp. 246–267.

Haim, M., Weimann, G., & Brosius, H.-B. (2018). Who sets the cyber agenda? Intermedia agenda-setting online: the case of Edward Snowden's NSA revelations. *Journal of Computational Social Science, 1*(2), 277–294.

Hepp, A. (2016). Kommunikations- und Medienwissenschaft in datengetriebenen Zeiten. *Publizistik, 61,* 225-246.

Hepp, A., Hohmann, F., Belli, A., Boczek, K., Haim, M., Heft, A., Jünger, J., Jürgens, P., Koenen, E., von Nordheim, G., Rinsdorf, L., Rothenberger, L., Schatto-Eckrodt, T., & Unkel, J. (2021). *Forschungssoftware in der Kommunikations- und Medienwissenschaft: Stand, Herausforderungen und Perspektiven. Positionspapier der DGPuK-Arbeitsgruppe Forschungssoftware.* https://www.dgpuk.de/sites/default/files/DGPuK%20Positionspapier%20-%20Fo rschungssoftware%20in%20der%20Kommunikations-%20und%20Medienwisse nschaft_0.pdf

Jarren, O. (2008). Massenmedien als Intermediäre. Zur anhaltenden Relevanz der Massenmedien für die öffentliche Kommunikation. *Medien & Kommunikationswissenschaft, 56,* 329–346.

Jarren, O. (2016). Nicht Daten, sondern Institutionen fordern die Publizistik- und Kommunikationswissenschaft heraus. Zu Andreas Hepps Beitrag „Kommunikations- und Medienwissenschaft in datengetriebenen Zeiten. *Publizistik, 61,* 373-383.

Jarren, O. (2019). Fundamentale Institutionalisierung: Social Media als neue globale Kommunikationsinfrastruktur. Der Beitrag der Kommunikationswissenschaft zur Analyse medialer Institutionalisierungsprozesse. *Publizistik, 2,* 163–179.

Krotz, F. (2007). *Mediatisierung. Fallstudien zum Wandel von Kommunikation.* Wiesbaden: VS Verlag für Sozialwissenschaften.

Is Communication via the Internet Public Communication?

Kümpel, A. S. (2021). Social media information environments and their implications for the uses and effects of news: The PINGS framework. *Communication Theory*. Advance Online Publication.

Lerg, W. B. (1970). *Das Gespräch. Theorie und Praxis der unvermittelten Kommunikation*. Düsseldorf: Bertelsmann Universitätsverlag.

Löblich, M. (2010). *Die empirisch-sozialwissenschaftliche Wende in der Publizistik- und Zeitungswissenschaft*. Köln: Halem.

Möller, J., van de Velde, R. N., Merten, L., & Puschmann, C. (2020). Explaining online news engagement based on browsing behavior: Creatures of habit? *Social Science Computer Review, 38*, 616–632.

Noelle-Neumann, E. (1980). *Die Schweigespirale. Öffentliche Meinung – unsere soziale Haut*. München: Piper.

O'Sullivan, P. B., & Carr, C. T. (2018). Masspersonal communication: A model bridging the mass-interpersonal divide. *New Media & Society, 20*, 1161–1180.

Schulz, W. (2006). Communication Research in the Past Half Century. A Personal Account of what has been Typical, Striking, Important, and Deplorable in German-Speaking Countries. *Publizistik, 51*, 92–96.

Strippel, C., Bock, A., Katzenbach, C., Mahrt, M., Merten, L., Nuernbergk, C., Pentzold, C., Puschmann, C. & Waldherr, A. (2018). Die Zukunft der Kommunikationswissenschaft ist schon da, sie ist nur ungleich verteilt. Eine Kollektivreplik auf Beiträge im „Forum". *Publizistik, 63*, 11–27.

Theis-Berglmair, A. (2016). Auf dem Weg zu einer Kommunikationswissenschaft. Zu Andreas Hepps Beitrag „Kommunikations- und Medienwissenschaft in datengetriebenen Zeiten. *Publizistik, 61*, 385-391.

Unkel, J. (2019). *Informationsselektion mit Suchmaschinen. Wahrnehmung und Auswahl von Suchresultaten*. Baden-Baden: Nomos.

Vorderer, P. (2015) Der mediatisierte Lebenswandel. *Publizistik, 60,* 259–276.

Weimann, G. & Brosius, H.-B. (2016). A new agenda for agenda-setting research in the digital era. In: G. Vowe & P. Henn (eds.), *Political Communication in the Online World Theoretical Approaches and Research Designs*. New York: Routledge, pp. 26–44.

Hans-Bernd Brosius

Hans-Bernd Brosius (* 1957) *studied psychology and medicine at the Westfälische-Wilhelms-Universität in Münster. He received his doctoral degree there in 1983. From 1983 to 1995 he was a postdoctoral fellow and – later on – assistant professor for communication studies at the Universität of Mainz. He received his secondary doctoral degree (Habilitation) in 1994. Since 1996, he is professor of communication at the Institut für Kommunikationswissenschaft und Medienforschung, Ludwig-Maximilians-Universität München. From 1998 till 2002 he was chairman of the German Communication Association. From 2001 to 2021 he was dean of the faculty of social sciences. His research interests include media use, media effects, digitalization of mass media, and methodology. The overlap of our research interests led to many fruitful discussions between Wolfram and myself.*

How to Capture the Relations and Dynamics within the Networked Public Sphere?

Modes of Interaction as a New Concept

Christoph Neuberger

Abstract

The aim of this chapter is to suggest ways to better capture the diversity of constellations and the dynamics of interactions in the public sphere, triggered by the digital transformation. The starting point is the question of why relations and dynamics should be considered more in communication studies and how they have been researched so far. In this respect, the limits of public sphere theory and social network analysis (SNA) are discussed. To overcome these limits, I propose a theoretical framework that combines public sphere theory and SNA with – as a third and new concept – modes of interaction. Such modes of interaction are ideal-typical patterns of interaction between actors in different constellations – namely, diffusion, mobilization, conflict, cooperation, competition, and scandal. Afterwards, I discuss these modes of interaction in the context of different societal subsystems and phases of media change in order to demonstrate their heuristic value. Traditional mass media foster the universalization of competition in several dimensions because competition requires only one-way relations of observation and influence. The Internet supports the interactive, multi-stage, and sequential communication that is characteristic of conflict and cooperation.

Current analysis of the digitalized public sphere partly indicates a dissolution of the established order of the mass media era. Diagnoses state a "new crisis of public communication" (Chadwick, 2018) or a "disinformation order" (Bennett & Livingston, 2018). What we are faced with, however, is not only a crisis of the public sphere itself (symptoms are, e.g., fake news, hate speech, polarization, and the digital divide), but also a crisis of its scientific observation and interpretation.

How has the digital transformation changed the public sphere? Mass media constitute a comparatively simple and rigid structured public sphere with dominant one-way, single-step, and one-to-many communication, based on a strong hierarchy (professional monopoly of gatekeeping) and a clear separation of roles (journalists, audience, spokespeople). The technical affordances of digital media give more opportunities for more actors to shape public communication (van Dijk, 2012, pp. 14–18). As a result of the digital transformation, the expanded possibilities have led to a greater complexity of the public sphere (Benkler, 2006), characterized by a high diversity of different constellations between actors and patterns of interaction. Here, it would be wrong to make a strict distinction between an old and a new public sphere. Rather, we are confronted with a hybrid mixture of old and new media logic (Chadwick, 2013).

The changing media landscape confronts communication studies with the task of getting a grasp on the tremendous complexity of the digitalized public sphere. The aim of this chapter is to suggest ways to better capture the diversity of constellations and the dynamics of interactions, triggered by the digital transformation. This chapter is organized as follows: The starting point is the question of why relations and dynamics should be considered more in communication studies and how they have been researched so far. In this respect, the limits of public sphere theory and social network analysis (SNA) are discussed. To overcome these limits, I propose a theoretical framework that combines public sphere theory and SNA with – as a third and new concept – modes of interaction. Such modes of interaction are specific relations of observation and influence in specific constellations of actors – namely, diffusion, mobilization, conflict, cooperation, competition, and scandal. Afterwards, I discuss these modes of interaction in the context of different societal subsystems and phases of media change in order to demonstrate their heuristic value. The chapter revisits, updates, and develops an earlier paper on modes of interaction that I published several years ago (Neuberger, 2014).

Concepts for Analyzing the Public Sphere

I distinguish between two closely interrelated concepts to capture the public sphere: (1) the *relations* between actors in terms of quantity and quality, and (2) the *dynamics* of public communication.

How to Capture the Relations and Dynamics within the Networked Public Sphere?

Relations

In the mass media public sphere, the constellation can be depicted as a triangle of journalism, spokespeople (representing particular interests), and audience. Therefore, the dominant approaches in the field of communication studies are preoccupied with one-way, single-step mass communication. Their primary focus is on analyzing the effects resulting from immediate contact between media and recipients, and they consider messages (like news) as isolated items without relations to other messages. Furthermore, communication studies mostly look at communicators and recipients separately in different areas of research. This limits the opportunities to capture interaction from the outset, as participants must switch between roles for both phenomena to occur.

Whereas traditional mass media are limited to a one-way relationship, starting from spokespeople and leading via journalism to the audience, the Internet brings all three relationships into the limelight of the public sphere, with direct communication being technically feasible among all actors and in both directions (two-way communication). An immediate relationship between spokespeople and audience has become possible, as journalistic gatekeepers can be circumvented ("bypassing"); so has audience feedback to journalism (Lee & Tandoc, 2017). Online, not only is the number of possible communication partners growing, but so is the variety of types of communicative and receptive action (Friemel & Neuberger, 2021, pp. 79–81), such as linking, sharing, voting, recommending, and commenting (Costera Meijer & Kormelink, 2014; Krämer, 2020, pp. 230–235).

For this "context of expanded opportunities" (Bimber, 2017, p. 8), a network model of the public sphere is more suitable than the traditional gatekeeper model for grasping the higher complexity and dynamics. In such a network view, nodes represent actors and link the connective actions between them. The opportunities for networking are mainly provided by platforms. Parker, Van Alstyne, and Choudary (2016, pp. 6–12) have described the "platform revolution" as a transition from the traditional pipeline model of the fixed, linear, closed value chain to a model of interactive, open platforms. On the one hand, platforms enable broad participation, but on the other hand, they also have the power to define structures of networks (Castells, 2009, pp. 42–47) and influence the course of communication through algorithmic selection and aggregation (Just & Latzer, 2017; Krämer & Conrad, 2017). Several suggestions can be found in the communication studies literature to capture this new actor constellation in the public sphere in a renewed model, like the "cascading

Christoph Neuberger

network activation model" from Entman and Usher (2018, p. 288; see also Benkler et al., 2018, pp. 75–82; Shah et al., 2017, pp. 496–498).

Dynamics

The dynamics of communication must now be considered in wider temporal, spatial, and social contexts (Cappella, 2017, pp. 546–549). On the Internet, the multi-step dissemination of messages (diffusion), for instance, through retweets or the mutual exchange of messages between two or more actors in online discussions (conflict), are more prevalent than in traditional mass media. Mass-media-induced communication among audience members, as analyzed, for instance, by the two-step-flow approach (Maurer, 2008), occurs mostly outside of the public sphere. The same applies to interaction between spokespeople and journalists. Mass media do offer interactive formats that feature face-to-face communication, such as talk shows and interviews, but the number of participants is very small. Apart from the one-way flow of published information, the periodicity of traditional mass media is another obstacle to interaction, as temporal gaps are inevitable and references to earlier messages that are no longer present need to be made explicit. In the press and broadcasting, many instances of communication remain isolated acts lacking any connection to a wider web of messages.

The situation is different online because it favors longer interaction sequences by providing techniques for connecting messages (such as hyperlinking and retweeting) and the conservation of earlier messages. As follow-up communication online is often public, we can expect responses to be more frequent and related than in traditional mass media. The task then is to describe and explain these dynamics, which are often triggered unexpectedly, unfold rapidly, and are far reaching (González-Bailón, 2017; Margetts et al., 2016; Vasterman, 2018). Digitalization reinforces the general societal trend towards dynamization and the acceleration of processes (Rosa, 2013, pp. 153–154).

Empirical studies on the dynamics of public communication have mostly addressed patterns of diffusion (Rogers, 2003) and mobilization (Bennett & Segerberg, 2013). These are rather simple modes of interaction because they consist dominantly of one-way communication with one or several steps. This kind of unidirectional (linear) communication is successful if recipients transfer the received message to other people or become motivated to perform follow-up actions, such as a protest, boycott, or donation. The goal of this paper is to extend the analysis to other modes.

Towards a Theory of the Dynamic Networked Public Sphere

Theory development in communication studies has not been able to keep up with the rapid pace of media change (see, as alternative ways to address this theory deficit, Keinert et al., 2021; Waldherr et al., 2021). In order to meet this challenge, I suggest combining the theory of the public sphere, SNA, and – as a third and new component – modes of interaction as building blocks for a theory of the dynamic networked public sphere. Such a systematization of interactions is missing in the discussion of the theory so far (e.g., Benkler, 2006; boyd, 2011; Friedland et al., 2006; Friemel & Neuberger, 2021; González-Bailón, 2017; Kaiser et al., 2017; Meraz & Papacharissi, 2013; Simone, 2010; Waldherr et al., 2021).

In the next two paragraphs, I briefly discuss the limitations of public sphere theory and SNA. Afterwards, I introduce modes of interaction as a new theoretical component and show how it can compensate for their weaknesses.

Limitations of Public Sphere Theory

The theory of the public sphere can be applied to overcome the outdated division of communication studies into separate research areas, in which journalism, audience, and spokespeople are analyzed in separate fields of research. The theory of the public sphere considers the whole triangle of journalism, audience, and spokespeople as an interrelated constellation (Neuberger, 2014, p. 571). When thinking about the Internet in these terms, we must bear in mind that all actors can switch between the roles of communicator and recipient, and, furthermore, all actors can relate to each other. Instead of a uniform space, the public sphere is divided horizontally into multiple publics of different groups (counterpublics, enclave publics, satellite publics, dominant publics; e.g., Squires, 2002) and vertically into publics of different sizes (mass media, special interest media, gatherings, encounters).

However, so far, the theory of the public sphere has been limited by two restrictions (e.g., Wessler, 2018, pp. 82–108): It has largely remained a theory of political conflict and has neglected other modes of interaction and other subsystems. Furthermore, the perspective that it adopts is primarily of a static and normative nature, which is to say that its primary interest is in the affordances of different contexts and the criteria of deliberative quality. By contrast, little attention has been paid to interaction between actors and the dynamics thereof in the course of public deliberation (Bächtiger & Parkinson, 2019, pp. 87–93). For this, it is necessary to understand the public sphere not as a uniform space with sharp boundaries (e.g., "forum", "arena"), but relationally as a network (Friemel & Neuberger, 2021, pp. 88–91; Keinert et al., 2021).

Limitations of Social Network Analysis

A relational analysis of public communication leads to the concept of the network and the methods of SNA (Friemel, 2017; Foucault Welles & González-Bailón, 2020). SNA has the advantage that it can be used to map all conceivable constellations of actors and interaction relationships. Actors in different roles are the nodes of the network. The links between these nodes are established through the communicative and receptive acts of the participants. Although a network view seems especially pertinent when considering the Internet, it also lends itself to analyzing traditional mass media (van Dijk, 2012, p. 27). However, SNA has three often stated shortcomings.

First, SNA adopts a mostly static view of networks (Granovetter, 1973, p. 1366), which is therefore limited to describing network structures but not explaining their genesis, for example, with the help of evolutionary theory (Monge et al., 2008, pp. 468–469; on dynamic SNA, see Watts, 2004, pp. 256–261). Secondly, the quality of the communicative relations is largely not taken into account. Only a content analysis of exchanged messages can unearth the underlying "meaning structure of social networks" (Fuhse, 2009, p. 53). For this purpose, SNA needs to be combined with content analyses. However, doing so requires further development of both methods, as the units of analysis are typically analyzed without considering the quality of relations between texts or actors (Wellman, 1988, pp. 31–35). Content analysis must be designed so as to incorporate relational variables in order to capture the connections between messages (Nuernbergk, 2014). It must also be able to grasp the numerous steps of interaction sequences. A third weakness of SNA is that it is often used without much theoretical grounding (Fried, 2020; Monge & Contractor, 2003). By contrast, macro-theories of networked society (e.g., Castells, 2010) and theories of the public sphere (e.g., Habermas, 2006, p. 415) tend

How to Capture the Relations and Dynamics within the Networked Public Sphere?

to use the term "network" only in a metaphorical sense. What is needed is a description and explanation of the public sphere as a dynamic network (Friemel & Neuberger, 2021; Neuberger, 2017).

Modes of Interaction as Constellations of Actors

To overcome the weaknesses of public sphere theory and SNA, I suggest introducing modes of interaction as a further element of the theory of the dynamic networked public sphere (Neuberger, 2014). Modes of interaction are, in short, ideal-typical patterns of interaction between actors in different constellations. In recent years, there has been an intense discussion in German-speaking sociology about modes of interaction, referring to Georg Simmel's (1858–1918) formal sociology and his distinction between social forms. SNA also has its roots in Simmel's work (e.g., Burt, 1993; Granovetter, 1973; Wellman, 1988).

An actor constellation arises the moment the intentions of at least two actors interfere and this interference is perceived by those involved (Schimank, 2016, p. 202), that is, as soon as the action of one actor affects that of another and "several individuals are in a reciprocal relationship" (Simmel, 1909, p. 296). Such actor constellations can be determined either deductively, that is, as theory-driven ideal types, or inductively, that is, as real types through empirical exploration (as in the communicative figurations approach; Hepp & Hasebrink, 2014). The approach suggested here pursues the deductive path. Simmel distinguished "social forms" like conflict (Simmel, 1908/2009, pp. 227–305) and competition (Simmel, 1903/2008), which he saw as the core subject matter of sociology. However, Simmel – according to a criticism raised by Kieserling (2011, p. 196) – never went beyond merely listing forms, and his definition of the term "social form" remained vague (Kieserling, 2011, p. 193). Cederman (2005, p. 871) has defined social forms as "configurations of social interactions and actors that together constitute the structures in which they are embedded".

Modes of Interaction – A Literature Review

Which types of interaction modes can be discerned? Scholars in sociology have made several suggestions for systematization. For example, Scharpf (1997) developed a complex classification by combining game-theoretical constellations (pure conflict, pure coordination, and mixed-motive games), interaction orientations (individualism, solidarity, competition, altruism, hostility), modes of interaction (unilateral action, negotiated agreement, majority vote, hierarchical direction), and institutional contexts (anarchic fields, networks, associations, organizations). Game theory typically focuses on two players whose strategic decisions depend on the expected outcomes, and whose modes of interactions can lie anywhere between mutual gain (pure cooperation) and a gain for one player at the expense of the other (pure competition) (e.g., Weise, 1997). However, these typologies from game theory – used in laboratory experiments and computer simulations (Nowak & Highfield, 2011) to explore the conditions in which rational actors can be expected to cooperate and are able to form reliable expectations – are too simple and too abstract to be applied in empirical settings (Schimank, 2016, p. 209; Wellman, 1988, pp. 35–37). Public communication in networks, by contrast, involves a much larger number of participants, and the rationality assumption is questionable.

The concept of "interaction modes" suggested by Rosa (2006, pp. 84–85) is much better suited for analyzing interaction in public communication, as it draws on broad sociological categories. In addition to competition, he has mentioned (antagonistic) conflict, (associative) cooperation, (traditionalist, status-based) allotment, and (authoritarian-hierarchical) regulation. His main interest has been the concept of competition, which, so far, has been neglected in sociological analyses (Rosa, 2006, p. 83). The distinction between competition and conflict has not yet played a prominent role in sociology, as Werron has noted (2010, p. 303). Usually, he has claimed, there is a rather loose understanding of both forms (Werron, 2010, p. 303). However, sociology is not the only discipline that has concerned itself with modes of interaction.

From a linguistic perspective, Allwood (2007) drew the dividing line between cooperation and competition with reference to the attitude of participants. Cooperation is marked by actors taking each other into cognitive and ethical consideration, having a joint purpose, and trusting that the other will act according to these requirements. In the case of competition, the participants pursue the same goal but cannot all achieve it. In the event of conflict, there is no shared goal at all.

In political science, Bartolini (1999, pp. 439–441) distinguished competition from other types of interaction – namely, cooperation, negotiation, and conflict, which he systematized using the criteria of principles of action, goals, perceived interests, means, prizes, and unintended consequences. According to this reasoning, competition and conflict are individualistic modes of action, and cooperation and negotiation operate along lines of solidarity. Whereas in conflict and negotiation the goals are different, in the two other types they are similar. Whilst conflict involves using means against one another, this is not so for competitors. Other typologies can be found, for instance, in economics and biology (e.g., Hirshleifer, 1978). It becomes apparent that there is no common understanding of interaction modes and no elaborated typology.

Proposal for a Typology of Modes of Interaction within the Public Sphere

Modes of interaction represent patterns of related communication acts in different constellations of actors, which observe and influence each other. The term "interaction" is defined differently in the literature (Neuberger, 2007). Here, the term is not restricted to two-way (reciprocal) communication, which requires the continuous switching between the communicator and recipient role, but is defined more broadly and also considers one-way (linear) communication. Modes of interaction are not only categories applied by academic observers but are also relevant to those actors involved in a situation. Modes of interaction function as mental models to define typical situations (frames) and to select typical sequences of action (scripts) (Esser & Kroneberg, 2015).

In the following, only interactions in the context of public communication will be considered. The public sphere is a special context for communicative interaction, characterized by a high grade of openness, dynamic, and unpredictability, which is even further increased on the Internet (Bimber, 2017; Dolata & Schrape, 2016; Dolata & Schrape, 2018; Neuberger, 2017).

The aim of this chapter is to systematize modes of interaction, which often take place in public. Compared to the first systematization of modes of interaction, which was limited to conflict, competition, and cooperation (Neuberger, 2014, pp. 573–575), I add diffusion, mobilization, and scandal as further modes. This results in a list of six modes (see Table 1), which is not exhaustive, but is open to further additions. Such dynamic modes of interaction are traditionally studied in the fields of collective action (Flanagin et al., 2006) and collective behavior (van Ginneken, 2003). In the following, modes are excluded that are not based on communication primarily like violent conflicts or establish interactions stably through regulation.

I use the following criteria to distinguish modes of interaction as ideal types: They differ in terms of actor constellation (dyad, triad) and forms of communication (one-way or two-way, direct or indirect interaction). In the case of competition and scandal, the audience is essential as a third party because the members of the audience observe what is happening and their subsequent reaction is crucial to success in competition and scandal. In contrast, conflict and cooperation are also conceivable without an audience and in non-public contexts. When an observing audience is added, this can change the situation decisively. In democracy, communicative conflicts are also fought out in public in order to win over voters. Here, conflict and competition overlap.

Another distinguishing criterion are the shared or antagonistic interests of the parties involved. It is a basic sociological insight that people are dependent on one another because there is often a gap between their interest in the use of scarce resources and their control thereof (Esser, 1996, p. 342). Actors can either attempt to assert their interests jointly or against one another. In the first case – cooperation – they pursue their interests collectively and support one another. In the second case, rival actors engage in fighting one another to assert their interests even against resistance. Such antagonistic modes of interaction can be distinguished by whether the actors interact directly (conflict) or indirectly (competition, scandal) (see, as a typology of antagonistic structures on the Internet, Krämer & Springer, 2020). The result of the fight depends on the soft power of the antagonists to gain attention and persuade the audience. The course and outcome of these modes of interaction can also be considered normatively. Favorable conditions can be established for this, for instance, by mediating third parties such as journalism.

In the next sections, I will characterize the modes in more detail.

Table 1: Typology of Modes of Interaction

Characteristics	Diffusion	Mobilization	Conflict	Cooperation	Competition	Scandal
Actor constellation, forms of communication	*Dyad:* – One-way communication with one or multiple steps – Direct interaction	*Dyad:* – One-way communication with one or multiple steps – Direct interaction	*Dyad:* – Two-way communication between opponents – Direct interaction	*Dyad:* – Two-way communication between cooperation partners – Direct interaction	*Triad:* – Competitors engage in one-way communication with the audience to win its favor – Audience as "laughing" third party – Indirect interaction between competitors, mediated through the audience	*Triad:* – Culprit and denouncer engage in one-way communication to convince the audience that the allegations are correct or to rebut them – Audience as "indignant" third party – Indirect interaction between culprit and denouncer through the audience
Interests of the participants	Sharing of messages	Dissemination of a call to action to achieve a common goal	Antagonistic interests	Shared interest or cooperation in pursuing individual interests	Antagonistic interests (win the audience's favor)	Antagonistic interests (win the audience's favor)
Favorable conditions	Willingness to share messages correctly with other people	Willingness to share a message and to perform a collective/connective follow-up action	Rules of rational discourse free of coercion (deliberation)	Willingness to participate (problem of free-riding); productive form of cooperation (wisdom of crowds)	Equal opportunity for competitors; transparent and valid comparisons of performance for the audience	Equal opportunity for both sides; transparent and valid comparisons of the arguments from both sides for the audience

Christoph Neuberger

Dyadic Modes of One-Way Communication

Diffusion can be defined as dyadic, one-way communication. At least one sender and one receiver of the message are involved. The spread of the message can be limited to one step – as in the case of mass communication, in which simultaneously numerous recipients are reached (one-to-many communication). Or the message may be passed on through several steps, as in the case of rumors. Accordingly, a distinction can be drawn between a co-present and an additive audience being reached by the message (Neuberger, 2017, pp. 554–556). For example, the spread of topics, news, innovations, disinformation (like fake news), misinformation (like rumors), advertising (viral marketing), recommendations, insults (firestorms), and emotions (like fear and anger) can be analyzed. So far, there is no encompassing understanding of diffusion (Cohen, 2017; Rogers, 2003).

Mobilization extends the mode "diffusion" by a collective/connective follow-up action like protest, to which the recipients are encouraged in the distributed message. Mobilization can be the result of a centrally organized or crowd-enabled campaign (Bennett & Segerberg, 2013, pp. 45–48).

Dyadic Modes of Two-Way Communication

Conflicts are antagonistic, direct, interactive, and ongoing sequences of communicative acts between the counterparts, which demands high coordination efforts (Kieserling, 1999, pp. 37–44). According to Hug (1997, p. 207), conflict exists as soon as a proposal (first sequence) is rejected (second sequence). Messmer (2007, p. 104) did not speak of conflict until the third sequence, because the actual incompatibility of two expectations needs to be verified in communication and should not simply be assumed. Only once the initial objection is objected to does a shared definition of the situation exist.

Cooperation is characterized by the same forms of communication as conflict, and it too requires at least two participants (dyad). What they differ in is the goal of the interaction. Cooperation can be understood as communicative interaction serving a joint purpose and/or mutual support for achieving individual goals (Lewis, 2006, pp. 201–204). There have been studies addressing the motives underlying the willingness to cooperate (Benkler, 2011; Nowak & Highfield, 2011) and the question of how a certain quality of outcomes can be assured (McIntosh, 2008; Sunstein,

2006). Communication itself can be interpreted as cooperation (Bormann et al., 2021, pp. 6–11).

Triadic Modes of Indirect Communication

The constellation becomes more complicated when a third party is involved (Fischer, 2013). *Competition* is such a triadic constellation. In his article "Sociology of Competition", first published in 1903, Simmel (1903/2008, p. 959) defined competition as an indirect form of fighting in which one "proceed[s] as if there were no adversary present [...] but merely the goal". The situation is defined by two parties competing to attain something from a third party (Simmel, 1903/2008, p. 961). Actors like companies or political parties employ communicative "means of persuading and convincing" (Simmel, 1903/2008, p. 963) in order to win the public's favor.

The relationship between competitors is an indirect one that is mediated via the audience: Whoever gains greater attention and acceptance reduces the possible success of their competitors without having to have met or even having to know them. The audience is the third party that is courted and thus the beneficiary (Brankovic et al., 2018, pp. 272–273; Werron, 2014, pp. 62–66). Members of the audience observe, compare, assess, and choose from among competing offers.

The performances of providers are honored by means of attention, approval, payments, and other forms of follow-up action. To do so, members of the audience need to communicate neither with one another nor with the competitors. So while the audience members remain in a rather passive position of being mere recipients and the ones to choose from the different offers, the competitors engage in communication to court the public in order to gain an edge when services are being compared, and to coax it into making the desired choices, for instance, electing one's party or buying one's products. This kind of influence can operate effectively in a one-way fashion as well, that is, without interacting with the audience.

Besides competition, *scandal* is another example of a triadic actor constellation – with the culprit, allegedly responsible for breaching a moral norm, the denouncer, who exposes this offence and frames it in terms of a "scandal", and the audience as the indignant third party (Esser & Hartung, 2004, pp. 1043–1044; Neckel, 1989, p. 58), "for whose attention, affection, and compliance the scandal is performed" (Esser & Hartung, 2004, p. 1044). In the case of a scandal, a widespread agreement on the validity of the accusation of guilt must be reached, whereas culpability is

Christoph Neuberger

disputed in the case of a conflict (Kepplinger, 2018, p. 3156). A scandal is successful when the allegations are immediately convincing and cause outrage. Scandalized people must strive to transform the scandal into a conflict by denying the accusations and making the arguments for their falsity the subject of the dispute. Similar to the case of competition, culprit and denouncer want to win the favor of the audience. Whether a politician resigns depends crucially on how the audience's response is assessed, for example, with regard to the next election.

Systematization

Let us sum up the argument so far. Modes of interaction can be defined as constellations in which two or three actors directly or indirectly observe and influence one another. In the case of conflict or cooperation, acts of communication are rich in information, are direct, interactive, sequential, explicitly related to one another, expensive, time-intensive, and therefore sluggish; this is why the capacity of the media for the number of participants and the number of topics to be discussed is limited (Kieserling, 1999, pp. 32–47; Werron, 2010, p. 312). They differ in regard to the antagonistic and cooperative intentions of those involved. In contrast, competition and scandal are an indirect, one-way, isolated, implicit, anonymous, individual, efficient, and therefore light form of fighting (Werron, 2010, p. 312). The one-way observation of media offers by the audience and one-way influence on the public from media providers requires no role changes and little coordination.

Communication in its simplest form involves two people (dyad). In observing and reacting to one another, *alter* and *ego* form an interaction system. The presence of third parties introduces the viewpoint of an external observer, such as the audience in the case of competition and scandal. The dyad becomes an object to this third party (Werron, 2014, p. 64); interactions can thereby be objectified and their rules institutionalized (Fischer, 2013, p. 94; Pyythinen, 2009, pp. 116–117). There are a multitude of different triadic actor constellations and roles of third parties (Fischer, 2013; Pyythinen, 2009, p. 118). In public communication, two roles of third parties are of particular importance and have already been mentioned by Simmel (1903/2008, pp. 101–115): the audience, which derives gratification from the services of media providers ("*tertius gaudens*", translated as "the laughing third"), and intermediaries (mediators, brokers, gatekeepers), such as journalists, that shape actor constellations and create more favorable conditions for interactions, for example, as moderators of conflicts (Brankovic et al., 2018, p. 273; Burt, 1993, pp. 72–79; Granovetter, 1973, pp. 1370–1371; Werron, 2014, p. 66).

The basic dyadic and triadic constellations can expand to larger networks (van Dijk, 2012, p. 27). Media contribute to such a universalization of modes of interaction in the social, temporal, and spatial dimensions. Accordingly, there is an increase in the number of actors involved, the duration, and the spatial scope of relationships (Werron, 2014, pp. 66–67). As relationships of observation and exerting influence of a one-way nature are sufficient for competition, the latter can, in principle, fully participate in the universalization and globalization dynamics (Werron, 2010, p. 311). As a result, engaging in global competition is much more plausible than engaging in conflict in a global public sphere (Wessler, 2004).

The ideal-typical modes distinguished above can overlap, or one can change into another (Werron, 2010, p. 312–316). For example, conflicts waged in public expand from a dyad to a triad, because the audience is watching and judging (Schimank, 2016, pp. 291–292). In this case, conflict overlaps with competition as adversaries court the audience's favor (Hug, 1997, pp. 121–122).

In the next two sections, I apply modes of interaction in a *synchronic* perspective (subsystems) and a *diachronic* perspective (media change) in order to demonstrate their heuristic value (following Neuberger, 2014, pp. 577–580).

Modes of Interaction in Subsystems of Society

This section focuses on the macro-level and looks at the modes of interaction in subsystems of a functionally differentiated society (e.g., politics, economy, sports, art; Schimank, 2015). The basic constellation in such systems is pre-structured by the division into the roles of performance providers on the one hand, and the audience as performance recipients on the other (Stichweh, 2005). The providers of these subsystems (companies, political parties, sports clubs, artists, etc.) compete for the favor of the audience (consumers, citizens, sports fans, art recipients, etc.). In all subsystems, third parties mediate between actors in performance roles and audience roles. In politics, such intermediaries are parties, associations, and social movements; in business, merchants, unions, and consumer organizations; in sports, leagues and referees; and in art, museums, galleries, and critics. As a sort of meta-intermediary, journalism creates relationships of observation and influence between providers, recipients, and these system-specific intermediaries via the public sphere (Neuberger, 2022). Journalists act as intermediaries, which determine the rules according to which conflict, competition, scandal, and other modes of interaction unfold and contribute to enforcing them. They also mediate directly between service providers and the public. For example, journalists collect, validate, and distribute news, mobilize citizens, moderates conflicts, help citizens solve problems together, investigate scandals, and provide transparency about competing offers. Journalism is itself a societal subsystem that imposes its own logic on other subsystems through mediation in and between them – a process known as "medialization". As a general principle, modes of interaction are not tied to any particular subsystem (Rosa, 2006, p. 85). Conflict is not exclusive to politics, nor is competition a characteristic feature of the economy only (Simmel, 1908/2009, p. 24). This has already been shown by Hirschman (1970) in his famous distinction between "exit" and "voice": In circumstances defined by competition, the audience sanctions poor services by means of exit, that is, by switching to a competitor, whereas in the event of conflict, the audience publicly voices its criticism, which contains more information than just selecting another offer. The audience's role in a subsystem can be viewed as being either of a more active-critical (voice) or more passive-selective (exit) nature. For example, in democratic political systems, conflict and competition are combined, because citizens debate issues and elect politicians (Bartolini, 1999; McCombs & Poindexter, 1983). The relation between subsystems and modes of interaction is therefore variable in principle, and the relevance of each mode can shift. A growing dominance of competition is being witnessed in many subsystems (Rosa, 2006, p. 82). Competition is based on several practices: categorizing, comparing, evaluating, quantifying, and publishing (Heintz, 2021). These practices have expanded in all sectors of society (Mau, 2019; Ringel & Werron, 2020). This raises the question as to what degree traditional mass media have contributed to this development by enhancing the means of one-way observation and influence, which play a particularly important role in competitive relationships.

Media Change and Modes of Interaction

The Context of Mass Media

Traditional mass media has primarily enabled one-way, single-step relationships of observation and influence in society and thus has foremost favored diffusion, mobilization, competition, and scandal as modes of interaction. With the aid of transmission technology, the great reach of mass media, and professional journalism, the categorizing, comparing, evaluating, and quantifying has become a public endeavor, visible to a mass audience (Heintz, 2021; Ringel & Werron, 2020; Wehner et al., 2012, pp. 59–66; Werron, 2015). As Werron (2009) has shown, it was as early as the second half of the 19th century that the press and telegraphy furthered the multi-dimensional universalization dynamics of competition. In the case of sports, telegraphy not only enabled up-to-the-minute reports on athletic competitions held in different places, but also helped to assess and compare these events in journalism. Thus, traditional mass media have played a pioneering role in the temporal, spatial, and social universalization of competition in the system of sports.

- In the *temporal dimension*, a series of contests have led to a high frequency and continuity of comparisons in order to satisfy growing media demand. By means of their periodic publication, the media have been a driving force in establishing the continuity of performance comparisons; their high topicality has fueled the simultaneity of comparison; and their memory function has expanded the business of comparing by extending it into the past. All of this is reflected in rankings, for instance (Werron, 2009, pp. 27–29).
- In the *spatial dimension*, the ever-growing scope of media coverage and increasing dissemination has advanced the globalization of comparisons. In sports, differentiated levels of comparison have evolved that extend from the regional and national levels to the global level (Werron, 2009, p. 29).
- In the *social dimension*, mass media have expanded the circle of observers from an immediately present audience of assessable size to a mass media public of innumerable size (Werron, 2010, pp. 309–310; Werron, 2014, p. 70).

There is also evidence of such co-evolution of competition in other subsystems. In the 19th-century economy, for instance, the introduction of the telegraph, news agencies, and financial journalism accelerated and widened the distribution of stock information and business news (Stäheli, 2004). In the arts, the dissemination of creative works and hence the opportunities for their comparison underwent considerable expansion through developments in conservation, for example, of music performances, which are transient in nature, with the aid of audio-visual recording media as well as through broadcasting. This was accompanied by the development of cultural journalism. As a consequence, "the work of art in the age of its technological reproducibility" (Benjamin, 2008) and the producing artists came under competitive pressure (Sennett, 1992, p. 289). In education,

Christoph Neuberger

university rankings are another example of growing competition, initiated and organized by media (Brankovic et al., 2018).

By contrast, press and broadcasting are much more limited in their compatibility for conflict and cooperation because of the lack of opportunities for participation and interaction. Sequential interactions are only possible among a small circle of elite actors, for instance, on talk shows. Their periodic publication and the lack of access to archives impede linking messages.

The Internet as Context

The Internet is much more suitable for conflict and cooperation, as its technical potential facilitates two-way and sequential communication that these modes of interaction call for, while it also enables a broad public to participate. The structural affordances (persistence, replicability, scalability, searchability) foster the variability, speed, and range of the other modes of interaction as well (boyd, 2011, pp. 45–48). Interpersonal and mass communication merge online (Walther, 2017; Walther & Valkenburg, 2017). In contrast to the mass media, interactions are often not journalistically mediated, but can unfold unhindered, uncontrolled, and algorithmically amplified.

Diffusion and mobilization can unfold quickly and achieve broad reach under certain conditions. Research distinguishes several forms of online *diffusion* (Cha et al., 2020), which are labeled as "virality" (Nahon & Hemsley, 2013), "word-of-mouth" (Sun et al., 2006), "cascade" (Bollenbacher et al., 2021), "contagion" (Kramer et al., 2014), "firestorm" (Johnen et al., 2018), and "meme" (Shifman, 2013). What is still lacking is a systematization of such diffusion processes (González-Bailón, 2017, pp. 71–98; Nahon & Hemsley, 2013, pp. 35–40; Shifman, 2013, pp. 55–63). Empirical research has also devoted a lot of attention to new forms of online *mobilization* for collective/connective action, like protests (Bennett & Segerberg, 2013; Jungherr et al., 2020, pp. 132–144).

The Internet has significantly improved the opportunity to participate in *conflicts*: Consumers and citizens can now articulate their criticism publicly in a fairly unrestrained manner. However, empirical research shows weaknesses in deliberation quality with regard to civility, justification, and responsiveness in online contexts (Esau et al., 2020; Wessler, 2018, pp. 82–108).

In the pre-Internet era, *cooperation* was of little relevance in public communication, as neither was it feasible to involve a large number

How to Capture the Relations and Dynamics within the Networked Public Sphere?

of participants nor was such communication independent of time or space. The question of how cooperation via social media can function has been discussed with great, partly naive optimism under vague headings such as "peer production" (Tapscott & Williams, 2007), "wisdom of crowds" (Surowiecki, 2005), and "crowdsourcing" (Howe, 2009). Encouraging cooperativeness and assuring quality requires finding suitable formats and rules for the Internet (e.g., Bos et al., 2007; Walther & Bunz, 2005). The most successful and debated case of cooperative knowledge collection, validation, and dissemination is the online encyclopedia Wikipedia (Frost-Arnold, 2019). In future analysis, forms of cooperation should be distinguished more precisely (Krämer, 2020, pp. 200–201).

The Internet has also opened up new opportunities for *competition*. The audience, on the one hand, has become more transparent to performance providers. User behavior (data traces) and comments provide information that make the audience more legible. On the other hand, consumers can create transparency themselves by making their ratings of competing offers available to other consumers. Data-rich markets "help market participants to find better matches" (Mayer-Schönberger & Ramge, 2018, p. 63). Algorithms overtake the competition practices of categorizing, comparing, evaluating, quantifying, and even selecting options (Heintz, 2021, pp. 33–42; Mennicken & Kornberger, 2021). At the same time, however, algorithmic data processing also opens up possibilities for manipulating market actors.

Finally, *scandals* can no longer be triggered only by the media, but now can be, in principle, by anyone. On the one hand, this empowers citizens to allege norm violations, as in cases like the #metoo and #blacklivesmatter movements; on the other hand, it opens up opportunities for false accusations (Pörksen & Detel, 2014).

Conclusion

The starting point for the considerations presented here was the question of how relations and dynamics might be better taken into account in communication studies. I have proposed incorporating modes of interaction as an additional concept into the theory of the dynamic networked public sphere. Here, the goal is pursued in order to break the dominance of approaches in communication studies once designed for the analysis of one-way, single-step mass communication, which considers diffusion and mobilization as rather simple modes of interaction.

A more differentiated typology of modes of interaction can open new perspectives for research. They represent patterns of related communication acts, which can develop in different ways. Conflict can escalate and polarize, or it can lead to consensus. Accusations in a scandal can be confirmed and lead to a great deal of public pressure, resulting in the resignation of a politician, for example. Or the accusations may be refuted. To describe such dynamics of interactions, processual accounts in social analysis should be given greater attention (Abbott, 2016; Neuberger, 2017; Tilly, 2008, p. 27). As in the sociology of violence (Hoebel & Knöbl, 2019), processual accounts capture sequences as chains of events, and they prefer explanations that use endogenous factors coming out of the process instead of exogenous factors. Accordingly, communication networks can be understood as self-organizing complex systems, steered by generative mechanisms, which aggregate micro-behavior to macro-effects (Monge & Contractor, 2003, pp. 79–98; Neuberger, 2017, pp. 558–564; Schelling, 2006; Waldherr, 2017; Waldherr et al., 2021, pp. 158–161).

Empirically, modes of interaction should be analyzed at all three societal levels: Studies at the *micro-level* involve individual acts of communication and sequential patterns of one-way and two-way communication in dyadic and triadic constellations. Here, the question is how one act of communication initiates the next, and how they are interlinked (e.g., Cederman, 2005). SNA as a method would have to be developed further for the analysis of modes of interaction. Here, we can draw on, for example, work in sequence analysis (Abbott, 1995), network analysis of discourses (Leifeld, 2017; Song, 2015), mergers between content analysis and network analysis (Nuernbergk, 2014), and agent-based simulation studies (Waldherr, 2014). In social media, the commonly used techniques of linking, such as hyperlinks, retweets, mentions, and followers, make it easy to trace relations. Moreover, it is possible to continuously record communication threads online. Such relational analysis can help to explain how follow-up communication is triggered (Shugars & Beauchamp, 2019).

At the *meso-level*, the task would be to examine how media and platform affordances structure, for example, diffusion processes (Goel et al., 2012), and deliberation as a form of conflict resolution (Esau et al., 2020). There are special formats that favor certain modes of interaction. For instance, discussion forums have a structural affinity for conflict, "virtual communities" for cooperation, and consumer portals with testimonials for competition (Krämer & Springer, 2020).

At the *macro-level*, research would have to focus on larger patterns of communication, analyzed as dynamic networks. Here, the entire course of a conflict or scandal must be tracked in various contexts. Among the issues to be addressed by such analyses are vertical top-down and bottom-up dynamics (concentration of power vs. participation; Friedland et al., 2006,

How to Capture the Relations and Dynamics within the Networked Public Sphere?

pp. 8–9, 21–22), the horizontal dynamics of relations between actors (fragmentation vs. integration) and in the course of public opinion formation (polarization vs. consensus building; Friedland et al., 2006, pp. 22–23; Simone, 2010, pp. 123–126), and the intermediation of such processes by network gatekeepers (Meraz & Papacharissi, 2013), influentials (González-Bailón et al., 2013) or discussion catalysts (Himelboim et al., 2009).

These are some succinct suggestions of how modes of interaction can be studied empirically. In future research, the suggested modes of interaction need further theoretical elaboration and methodological operationalization.

References

Abbott, A. (1995). Sequence analysis: New methods for old ideas. *Annual Review of Sociology*, *21*, 93–113. https://www.jstor.org/stable/2083405

Abbott, A. (2016). *Processual sociology*. University of Chicago Press.

Allwood, J. (2007). *Cooperation, competition, conflict and communication*. Department of Linguistics, Göteborg University. http://sskkii.gu.se/jens/publications/docs101-150/107a.pdf

Bächtiger, A., & Parkinson, J. (2019). *Mapping and measuring deliberation: Towards a new deliberative quality*. Oxford University Press.

Bartolini, S. (1999). Collusion, competition and democracy. Part I. *Journal of Theoretical Politics*, *11*, 435–470. https://doi.org/10.1177/0951692899011004001

Benjamin, W. (2008). *The work of art in the age of its technological reproducibility, and other writings on media*. Belknap Press.

Benkler, Y. (2006). *The wealth of networks*. Yale University Press.

Benkler, Y. (2011). *The penguin and the Leviathan*. Crown Business.

Benkler, Y., Faris, R., & Roberts, H. (2018). *Network propaganda*. Oxford University Press.

Bennett, W. L., & Livingston, S. (2018). The disinformation order: Disruptive communication and the decline of democratic institutions. *European Journal of Communication*, *33*, 122–139. https://doi.org/10.1177/0267323118760317

Bennett, W. L., & Segerberg, A. (2013). *The logic of connective action*. Cambridge University Press.

Bimber, B. (2017). Three prompts for collective action in the context of digital media. *Political Communication*, *34*, 6–20. https://doi.org/10.1080/10584609.2016.1223772

Bollenbacher, J., Pacheco, D., Hui, P.-M., Ahn, Y.-Y., Flammini, A., & Menczer, F. (2021). On the challenges of predicting microscopic dynamics of online conversations. *Applied Network Science*, *6*, 1–21. https://doi.org/10.1007/s41109-021-00357-8

Bormann, M., Tranow, U., Vowe, G., & Ziegele, M. (2021). Incivility as a violation of communication norms – A typology based on normative expectations toward political communication. *Communication Theory*. Advance online publication. https://doi.org/10.1093/ct/qtab018

Bos, N., Zimmerman, A., Olson, J., Yew, J., Yerkie, J., Dahl, E., & Olson, G. (2007). From shared databases to communities of practice: A taxonomy of collaboratories. *Journal of Computer-Mediated Communication*, 12, 652–672. https://doi.org/10.1111/j.1083-6101.2007.00343.x

boyd, d. (2011). Social network sites as networked publics: Affordances, dynamics, and implications. In Z. Papacharissi (Ed.), *A networked self: Identity, community, and culture on social network sites* (pp. 39–58). Routledge.

Brankovic, J., Ringel, L., & Werron, T. (2018). How rankings produce competition: The case of global university rankings. *Zeitschrift für Soziologie*, 47, 270–288. https://doi.org/10.1515/zfsoz-2018-0118

Burt, R. S. (1993). The social structure of competition. In N. Nohria & R. G. Eccles (Eds.), *Networks and organizations* (pp. 57–91). Harvard Business School Press.

Cappella, J. N. (2017). Vectors into the future of mass and interpersonal communication research: Big data, social media, and computational social science. *Human Communication Research*, 43, 545–558. https://doi.org/10.1111/hcre.12114

Castells, M. (2009). *Communication power*. Oxford University Press.

Castells, M. (2010). *The Information Age. Volume 1: The rise of the network society* (2nd ed.). Wiley Blackwell.

Cederman, L.-E. (2005). Computational models of social forms: Advancing generative process theory. *American Journal of Sociology*, 110, 864–893. https://doi.org/10.1086/426412

Cha, M., Benevenuto, F., Ghosh, S., & Gummadi, K. (2020). Propagation phenomena in social media. In B. Foucault, B. Welles, & S. González-Bailón (Eds.), *The Oxford handbook of networked communication* (pp. 739–740). Oxford University Press. https://doi.org/10.1093/oxfordhb/9780190460518.013.6

Chadwick, A. (2013). *The hybrid media system*. Oxford University Press.

Chadwick, A. (2018). *The new crisis of public communication*. Loughborough University.

Cohen, Y. (2017). Diffusion theories: News diffusion. In P. Rössler, C. A. Hoffner, & L. van Zoonen (Eds.), *The international encyclopedia of media effects*. Wiley & Sons. http://doi.org/10.1002/9781118783764.wbieme0060

Costera Meijer, I., & Kormelink, T.G. (2014). Checking, sharing, clicking and linking. Changing patterns of news use between 2004 and 2014. *Digital Journalism*, 3, 664–679. https://doi.org/10.1080/21670811.2014.937149

Dolata, U., & Schrape, J.-F. (2016). Masses, crowds, communities, movements: Collective action in the Internet Age. *Social Movement Studies*, 15, 1–18. https://doi.org/10.1080/14742837.2015.1055722

How to Capture the Relations and Dynamics within the Networked Public Sphere?

Dolata, U., & Schrape, J.-F. (2018). Collective action in the Digital Age: An actor-based typology. In U. Dolata & J.-F. Schrape (Eds.), *Collectivity and power on the Internet. A sociological perspective* (pp. 7–29). Springer.

Entman, R. E., & Usher, N. (2018). Framing in a fractured democracy: Impacts of digital technology on ideology, power and cascading network activation. *Journal of Communication, 68*, 298–308. https://doi.org/10.1093/joc/jqy028

Esau, K., Fleuß, D., & Nienhaus, S. (2020). Different arenas, different deliberative quality? Using a systemic framework to evaluate online deliberation on immigration policy in Germany. *Policy & Internet, 4*(1), 86–112. https://doi.org/10.100 2/poi3.232

Esser, F., & Hartung, U. (2004). Nazis, pollution, and no sex: Political scandals as a reflection of political culture in Germany. *American Behavioral Scientist, 47*, 1040–1071. https://doi.org/10.1177/0002764203262277

Esser, H. (1996). *Soziologie. Allgemeine Grundlagen* [Sociology. General basics] (2nd ed.). Campus.

Esser, H., & Kroneberg, C. (2015). An integrative theory of action: The model of frame selection. In E. J. Lawler, S. R. Thye, & J. Yoon (Eds.), *Order on the edge of chaos: Social psychology and the problem of social order.* (pp. 63–85). Cambridge University Press.

Fischer, J. (2013). Turn to the third: A systematic consideration of an innovation in social theory. In B. Malkmus & I. Cooper (Eds.), *Dialectic and paradox: Configurations of the third in modernity* (pp. 81–102). Peter Lang.

Flanagin, A., Stohl, C., & Bimber, B. (2006). Modeling the structure of collective action. *Communication Monographs, 73*, 29–54. https://doi.org/10.1080/03637750 600557099

Foucault Welles, B., & González-Bailón, S. (Eds.). (2020). *The Oxford handbook of networked communication.* Oxford University Press.

Fried, E. I. (2020). Lack of theory building and testing impedes progress in the factor and network literature. *Psychological Inquiry, 32*, 271–288. https://doi.org/1 0.1080/1047840X.2020.1853461

Friedland, L. A., Hove, T., & Rojas, H. (2006). The networked public sphere. *Javnost – The Public, 13*, 5–26. https://javnost-thepublic.org/article/2006/4/1/

Friemel, T. (2017). Social network analysis. In J. Matthes, C. S. Davis, & R. Potter (Eds.), *The international encyclopedia of communication research methods* (pp. 1769–1782). Wiley & Sons. https://doi.org/10.1002/9781118901731.iecrm0235

Friemel, T., & Neuberger, C. (2021). Öffentlichkeit als dynamisches Netzwerk [The public as a dynamic network]. In M. Eisenegger, M. Prinzing, P. Ettinger, & R. Blum (Eds.), *Digitaler Strukturwandel der Öffentlichkeit* [Digital structural change of the public] (pp. 77–92). Springer VS.

Frost-Arnold, K. (2019). Wikipedia. In D. Coady & J. Chase (Eds.), *The Routledge handbook of applied epistemology* (pp. 28–40). Routledge.

Fuhse, J. A. (2009). The meaning structure of social networks. *Sociological Theory, 27*, 51–73.

Goel, S., Watts, D. J., & Goldstein, D. G. (2012, June). The structure of online diffusion networks. In *Proceedings of the 13th ACM Conference on Electronic Commerce* (pp. 623–638). https://doi.org/10.1145/2229012.2229058

Gonzáles-Bailón, S. (2017). *Decoding the social world.* MIT Press.

González-Bailón, S., Borge-Holthoefer, J., & Moreno, Y. (2013). Broadcasters and hidden influentials in online protest diffusion. *American Behavioral Scientist, 57,* 943–965. https://doi.org/10.1177/0002764213479371

Granovetter, M. S. (1973). The strength of weak ties. *The American Journal of Sociology, 78,* 1360–1380. https://doi.org/10.1086/225469

Habermas, J. (2006). Political communication in media society: Does democracy still enjoy an epistemic dimension? The impact of normative theory on empirical research. *Communication Theory, 16,* 411–426. https://doi.org/10.1111/j.1468-2885.2006.00280.x

Heintz, B. (2021). Kategorisieren, Vergleichen, Bewerten und Quantifizieren im Spiegel sozialer Beobachtungsformate [Categorizing, comparing, evaluating, and quantifying in the mirror of social observation formats]. *Kölner Zeitschrift für Soziologie und Sozialpsychologie, 73,* Supplement 61, 5–47. https://doi.org/10.1007/s11577-021-00741-3

Hepp, A., & Hasebrink, U. (2014). Human interaction and communicative figurations: The transformation of mediatized cultures and societies. In K. Lundby (Ed.), *Mediatization of communication* (pp. 249–271). de Gruyter.

Himelboim I., Gleave, E., & Smith, M. (2009). Discussion catalysts in online political discussions: Content importers and conversation starters. *Journal of Computer-Mediated Communication, 14,* 771–789. https://doi.org/10.1111/j.1083-6101.2009.01470.x

Hirschman, A. O. (1970). *Exit, voice, and loyalty.* Harvard University Press.

Hirshleifer, J. (1978). Competition, cooperation, and conflict in economics and biology. *The American Economic Review. Papers and Proceedings of the Ninetieth Annual Meeting of the American Economic Association (May, 1978), 68,* 238–243. https://EconPapers.repec.org/RePEc:aea:aecrev:v:68:y:1978:i:2:p:238-43

Hoebel, T., & Knöbl, W. (2019). *Gewalt erklären!* [Explaining violence!]. Hamburger Edition.

Howe, J. (2009). *Crowdsourcing.* Business Books.

Hug, D. M. (1997). *Konflikte und Öffentlichkeit* [Conflicts and the public sphere]. Westdeutscher Verlag.

Johnen, M., Jungblut, M., & Ziegele, M. (2018). The digital outcry: What incites participation behavior in an online firestorm? *New Media & Society, 20,* 3140–3160. https://doi.org/10.1177/1461444817741883

Jungherr A., Rivero, G., & Gayo-Avello, D. (2020). *Retooling politics: How digital media are shaping democracy.* Cambridge University Press.

Just, N., & Latzer, M. (2017). Governance by algorithms: Reality construction by algorithmic selection on the Internet. *Media, Culture & Society, 39,* 238–258. https://doi.org/10.1177/0163443716643157

Kaiser, J., Fähnrich, B., Rhomberg, M., & Filzmaier, P. (2017). What happened to the public sphere? The networked public sphere and public opinion formation. In E. G. Carayannis, D. F. J. Campbell, & M. P. Efthymiopoulos (Eds.), *Handbook of cyber-development, cyber-democracy, and cyber-defense* (pp. 433–459). Springer.

Keinert, A., Sayman, V., & Maier, D. (2021). Relational communication spaces: Infrastructures and discursive Practices. *Media and Communication, 9*(3), 86–96. https://doi.org/10.17645/mac.v9i3.3988

Kieserling, A. (1999). *Kommunikation unter Anwesenden* [Communication among attendants]. Suhrkamp.

Kieserling, A. (2011). Simmels Sozialformenlehre: Probleme eines Theorieprogramms [Simmel's theory of social forms: Problems of a theoretical program]. In H. Tyrell, O. Rammstedt, & I. Meyer (Eds.), *Georg Simmels große „Soziologie"* [Georg Simmel's great "Sociology"] (pp. 181–208). transcript.

Kramer, A. D. I., Guillory, J. E., & Hancock, J. T. (2014). Experimental evidence of massive-scale emotional contagion through social networks. *PNAS, 111*(24), 8788–8790. https://doi.org/10.1073/pnas.1320040111

Krämer, B. (2020). *How to do things with the Internet. Handlungstheorie online* [Action theory online]. Herbert von Halem.

Krämer, B., & Conrad, J. (2017). Social ontologies online: The representation of social structures on the Internet. *Social Media + Society, 3*(1), 1–11. https://doi.or g/10.1177/2056305117693648

Krämer, B., & Springer, N. (2020). Ontology of opposition online: Representing antagonistic structures on the Internet. *Studies in Communication and Media, 9*, 35–61. https://doi.org/10.5771/2192-4007-2020-1-35

Lee, E.-J., & Tandoc, E. C. Jr. (2017). When news meets the audience: How audience feedback online affects news production and consumption. *Human Communication Research, 43*, 436–449. https://doi.org/10.1111/hcre.12123

Leifeld, P. (2017). Discourse network analysis: Policy debates as dynamic networks. In J. N. Victor, A. H. Montgomery, & M. Lubell (Eds.), *The Oxford handbook of political networks*. Oxford University Press. https://doi.org/10.1093/oxfordhb/978 0190228217.013.25

Lewis, L. K. (2006). Collaborative interaction: Review of communication scholarship and a research agenda. In C. S. Beck (Ed.), *Communication Yearbook 30* (pp. 197–247). Lawrence Erlbaum.

Margetts, H., John, P., Hale, S., & Yasseri, T. (2016). *Political turbulence: How social media shape collective action*. Princeton University Press.

Mau, S. (2019). *The metric society: On the quantification of the social*. Polity.

Maurer, M. (2008). Two-step flow of communication. In W. Donsbach (Ed.), *The International Encyclopedia of Communication* (pp. 1–5). John Wiley & Sons. https://doi.org/10.1002/9781405186407.wbiect063

Mayer-Schönberger, V., & Ramge, T. (2018). *Reinventing capitalism in the age of big data*. John Murray.

McCombs, M., & Poindexter, P. (1983). The duty to keep informed: News exposure and civic obligation. *Journal of Communication*, *33*(2), 88–96. https://doi.org/10.1111/j.1460-2466.1983.tb02391.x

McIntosh, S. (2008). Collaboration, consensus, and conflict: Negotiating news the Wiki way. *Journalism Practice*, *2*, 197–211. https://doi.org/10.1080/17512780801999360

Mennicken, A., & Kornberger, M. (2021). Von Performativität zu Generativität: Bewertung und ihre Folgen im Kontext der Digitalisierung [From performativity to generativity: Valuation and its consequences in the context of digitization]. *Kölner Zeitschrift für Soziologie und Sozialpsychologie*, *73*, Supplement 61, 451–478. https://doi.org/10.1007/s11577-021-00755-x

Meraz, S., & Papacharissi, Z. (2013). Networked gatekeeping and networked framing on #Egypt. *The International Journal of Press/Politics*, *18*, 138–166. https://doi.org/10.1177/1940161212474472

Messmer, H. (2007). Contradiction, conflict and question of borders. In S. Stetter (Ed.), *Territorial conflicts in world society* (pp. 101–124). Routledge.

Monge, P., Heiss, B. M., & Margolin, D. B. (2008). Communication network evolution in organizational communities. *Communication Theory*, *18*, 449–477. https://doi.org/10.1111/j.1468-2885.2008.00330.x

Monge, Peter R., & Contractor, N. S. (2003). *Theories of communication networks.* Oxford University Press.

Nahon, K., & Hemsley, J. (2013). *Going viral.* Polity Press.

Neckel, S. (1989). Das Stellhölzchen der Macht. Zur Soziologie des politischen Skandals [The stick of power. On the sociology of political scandal]. In R. Ebbighausen & S. Neckel (Eds.), *Anatomie des politischen Skandals* [Anatomy of political scandals] (pp. 55–80). Suhrkamp.

Neuberger, C. (2007). Interaktivität, Interaktion, Internet. Eine Begriffsanalyse [Interactivity, interaction, Internet. An analysis of concepts]. *Publizistik*, *52*, 33–50. https://doi.org/10.1007/s11616-007-0004-3

Neuberger, C. (2014). Konflikt, Konkurrenz und Kooperation. Interaktionsmodi in einer Theorie der dynamischen Netzwerköffentlichkeit [Conflict, competition and cooperation. Modes of interaction in a theory of dynamic networked public sphere]. *Medien & Kommunikationswissenschaft*, *62*, 567–587. https://doi.org/10.5771/1615-634x-2014-4-567

Neuberger, C. (2017). Die Rückkehr der Masse. Kollektivphänomene im Internet aus Sicht der Massen- und Komplexitätstheorie [The return of the mass. Collective phenomena on the Internet from the perspective of mass and complexity theory]. *Medien & Kommunikationswissenschaft*, *65*, 550–572. https://doi.org/10.5771/1615-634X-2017-3-550

Neuberger, C. (2022). Journalismus und Plattformen als vermittelnde Dritte in der digitalen Öffentlichkeit [Journalism and platforms as mediating third parties in the digital public sphere]. *Kölner Zeitschrift für Soziologie und Sozialpsychologie*, *74*, Supplement 62, 159–181. https://doi.org/10.1007/s11577-022-00832-9

Nowak, M., & Highfield, R. (2011). *Super cooperators.* Canongate.

Nuernbergk, C. (2014). Follow-up communication in the blogosphere: A comparative study of bloggers' linking to professional and participatory media. *Digital Journalism*, 2, 434–445. https://doi.org/10.1080/21670811.2014.895520

Parker, G. G., Van Alstyne, M. W., & Choudary, S. P. (2016). *Platform revolution*. Norton.

Pörksen, B., & Detel, H. (2014). *The unleashed scandal: The end of control in the Digital Age*. Andrews.

Pyythinen, O. (2009). Being-with. Georg Simmel's sociology of association. *Theory, Culture & Society*, 26, 108–128. https://doi.org/10.1177/0263276409106353

Reich, Z. (2012). Journalism as bipolar interactional expertise. *Communication Theory*, 22, 339–358. https://doi.org/10.1111/j.1468-2885.2012.01411.x

Ringel, L., & Werron, T. (2020). Where do rankings come from? A historical-sociological perspective on the history of modern rankings. In A. Epple, W. Erhart, & J. Grave (Eds.), *Practices of comparing. Towards a new understanding of a fundamental human practice* (pp. 137–170). Bielefeld University Press

Rogers, E. M. (2003). *Diffusion of innovations* (5th ed.). Free Press.

Rosa, H. (2006). Wettbewerb als Interaktionsmodus. Kulturelle und sozialstrukturelle Konsequenzen der Konkurrenzgesellschaft [Competition as a mode of interaction. Cultural and social structural consequences of the competitive society]. *Leviathan*, 34, 82–104. https://doi.org/10.1007/s11578-006-0005-z

Rosa, H. (2013). *Social acceleration*. Columbia University Press.

Scharpf, F. W. (1997). *Games real actors play*. Westview Press.

Schelling, T. C. (2006). *Micromotives and macrobehavior*. W. W. Norton.

Schimank, U. (2015). Modernity as a functionally differentiated capitalist society: A general theoretical model. *European Journal of Social Theory*, 18, 413–430. https://doi.org/10.1177/1368431014543618

Schimank, U. (2016). *Handeln und Strukturen* [Action and structures] (5th ed.). Juventa.

Sennett, R. (1992). *The fall of public man*. W. W. Norton.

Shah, D. V., McLeod, D. M., Rojas, H., Cho, J., Wagner, M. W., & Friedland, L. A. (2017). Revising the communication mediation model for a new political communication ecology. *Human Communication Research*, 43, 491–504. https://doi.org/10.1111/hcre.12115

Shifman, L. (2013). *Memes in digital culture*. MIT Press.

Shugars, S., & Beauchamp, N. (2019). Why keep arguing? Predicting engagement in political conversations online. *Sage Open*, 9(1). https://doi.org/10.1177/2158244019828850

Simmel, G. (1909). The problem of sociology. *American Journal of Sociology*, 15, 289–320. https://doi.org/10.1086/211783

Simmel, G. (2008). Sociology of competition. *The Canadian Journal of Sociology / Cahiers canadiens de sociologie*, 33, 957–978. (Original work published 1903)

Christoph Neuberger

Simmel, G. (2009). *Sociology. Volume 1.* Brill. (Original work published 1908)

Simone, M. A. (2010). Deliberative democracy online: Bridging networks with digital technologies. *The Communication Review, 13*, 120–139. https://doi.org/10.1080/10714421003795527

Song, H. (2015). Uncovering the structural underpinnings of political discussion networks: Evidence from an exponential random graph model. *Journal of Communication, 65*, 146–169. https://doi.org/10.1111/jcom.12140

Squires, C. R. (2002). Rethinking the Black public sphere: An alternative vocabulary for multiple public spheres. *Communication Theory, 12*, 446–468. https://doi.org/10.1111/j.1468-2885.2002.tb00278.x

Stäheli, U. (2004). Der Takt der Börse. Inklusionseffekte von Verbreitungsmedien am Beispiel des Börsen-Tickers [The beat of the stock exchange. Inclusion effects of dissemination media using the example of the stock exchange ticker]. *Zeitschrift für Soziologie, 33*, 245–263. https://doi.org/10.1515/zfsoz-2004-0304

Stichweh, R. (2005). Inklusion in Funktionssysteme der modernen Gesellschaft [Inclusion in functional systems of modern society]. In R. Mayntz, B. Rosewitz, U. Schimank, & R. Stichweh (Eds.), *Differenzierung und Verselbständigung* [Differentiation and independence] (pp. 261–293). Campus.

Sun, T., Youn, S., Wu, G., & Kuntaraporn, M. (2006). Online word-of-mouth (or mouse): An exploration of its antecedents and consequences. *Journal of Computer-Mediated Communication, 11*, 1104–1127. https://doi.org/10.1111/j.1083-6101.2006.00310.x

Sunstein, C. R. (2006). *Infotopia.* Oxford University Press.

Surowiecki, J. (2005). *The wisdom of crowds.* Anchor Books.

Tapscott, D., & Williams, A. D. (2007). *Wikinomics.* Penguin.

Tilly, C. (2008). *Explaining social processes.* Paradigm Publishers.

van Dijk, J. (2012). *The network society* (3rd ed.). SAGE.

van Ginneken, J. (2003). *Collective behavior and public opinion.* Erlbaum.

Vasterman, P. (Ed.). (2018). *From media hype to Twitter storm: News explosions and their impact on issues, crises and public opinion.* Amsterdam University Press.

Waldherr, A. (2014). Emergence of news waves: A social simulation approach. *Journal of Communication, 64*, 852–873. https://doi.org/10.1111/jcom.12117

Waldherr, A. (2017). Öffentlichkeit als komplexes System. Theoretischer Entwurf und methodische Konsequenzen [The public sphere as a complex system. Theoretical outline and methodological consequences]. *Medien & Kommunikationswissenschaft, 62*, 534–549. https://doi.org/10.5771/1615-634X-2017-3-534

Waldherr, A., Geise, S., Mahrt, M., Katzenbach, C., & Nuernbergk, C. (2021). Toward a stronger theoretical grounding of computational communication science. *Computational Communication Research, 3*(2), 1-28. https://doi.org/10.17605/OSF.IO/PU9DQ

Walther J. B., & Valkenburg, P. M. (2017). Merging mass and interpersonal communication via interactive communication technology: A symposium. *Human Communication Research, 43*, 415–423. https://doi.org/10.1111/hcre.12120

Walther, J. B. (2017). The merger of mass and interpersonal communication via new media: Integrating metaconstructs. *Human Communication Research*, *43*, 559–572. https://doi.org/10.1111/hcre.12122

Walther, J. B., & Bunz, U. (2005). The rules of virtual groups: Trust, liking, and performance in computer-mediated communication. *Journal of Communication*, *55*, 828–846. https://doi.org/10.1111/j.1460-2466.2005.tb03025.x

Watts, D. J. (2004). The "new" science of networks. *Annual Review of Sociology*, *30*, 243–270. https://doi.org/10.1146/annurev.soc.30.020404.104342

Wehner, J., Passoth, J.-H., & Sutter, T. (2012). Gesellschaft im Spiegel der Zahlen – Die Rolle der Medien [Society in the mirror of numbers – The role of the media]. In F. Krotz & A. Hepp (Eds.), *Mediatisierte Welten* [Mediatized worlds] (pp. 59–86). Springer VS.

Weise, P. (1997). Konkurrenz und Kooperation [Competition and cooperation]. In M. Held (Ed.), *Normative Grundfragen der Ökonomik* [Normative basic questions of economics] (pp. 58–80). Campus.

Wellman, B. (1988). Structural analysis: From method and metaphor to theory and substance. In B. Wellman, Barry & S. D. Berkowitz (Eds.), *Social structures* (pp. 19–61). Cambridge University Press.

Werron, T. (2009). Der Weltsport und seine Medien [World sport and its media]. In F. Axster, J. Jäger, K. Sicks, & M. Stauff (Eds.), *Mediensport* [Media sport] (pp. 23–42). Fink.

Werron, T. (2010). Direkte Konflikte, indirekte Konkurrenzen. Unterscheidung und Vergleich zweier Formen des Kampfes [Direct conflicts, indirect competitions. Differentiation and comparison of two forms of struggle]. *Zeitschrift für Soziologie*, *39*, 302–318. https://doi.org/10.1515/zfsoz-2010-0403

Werron, T. (2014). On public forms of competition. *Cultural Studies – Critical Methodologies*, *14*, 62–76. https://doi.org/10.1177/1532708613507891

Wessler, H. (2004). Can there be a global public sphere? September 11 in the world's media. In F. Hardt (Ed.), *Mapping the world* (pp. 179–188). Francke.

Wessler, H. (2018). *Habermas and the media.* Polity.

Christoph Neuberger (Dr. phil., Catholic University of Eichstätt, Germany, 1995) is Full Professor at the Institute for Media and Communication Studies, Free University of Berlin, Germany, and Managing Director of the Weizenbaum Institute for the Networked Society, Berlin. His research focuses on the digital transformation of media, the public sphere, and journalism. He is a regular member of the Bavarian Academy of Sciences and Humanities (BAdW) and the German Academy of Science and Engineering (acatech). Wolfram Peiser was his colleague at the LMU Munich from 2011 to 2019.

How Does the Internet Change Group Processes?

Applying the Model of Collective Information Processing (MCIP) to Online Environments

Johanna Schindler

Abstract

The internet seems to be a breeding ground for both negative and positive social phenomena, e.g., not only radicalization and the spread of misinformation but also social connection and knowledge gain. Although these topics are inherently social, they are typically researched on the individual level. This contribution develops a theoretical framework to explore them on the group level, e.g., in e-communities, online social movements, or online discussions. Drawing on concepts like social identity and the model of collective information processing (MCIP), it adopts a collective information processing perspective on online group phenomena. Then it reviews how different collective processing modes (automatic vs. systematic and closed vs. open) can interact with the internet's core technical possibilities (participation, selectivity, interaction, interconnectedness, and automatization). Online spaces appear to work as a catalyst for any collective processing mode; however, closed and open modes may raise the greatest risks and opportunities for societies. This work may inspire new questions and approaches for future research on social phenomena online.

Digitalization has fundamentally changed the conditions of discourse. For society, these changes seem to be both a blessing and a curse. On one hand, they allow for an entirely new dimension of radicalization (e.g., Wojcieszak, 2010) and misinformation (e.g., Dan et al., 2021), amplifying hate (e.g., Brown, 2018) and polarization (e.g., Neudert & Marchal, 2019). On the other, they offer more possibilities for social connection (e.g., Ruesch, 2013) and knowledge gain (e.g., Engel et al., 2014), paving the way for new forms of empowerment (e.g., Brady et al., 2017) and deliberation (e.g., Min, 2007). What all these phenomena have in common is that they are inherently social. They usually refer to perceptions and behaviors of groups or individuals as group members. Therefore, they can unfold their full potential only through the collaboration of individuals. In a broader sense, they can be conceptualized as collective information processes and their outcomes (Hinsz et al., 1997; Schindler, in preparation). Yet, although human beings are specialized for group life, communication studies—and social sciences in general—have traditionally focused on the individual level (Brauner & Scholl, 2000; Poole et al., 2004). In the present contribution, I explore the flip side of the coin and focus on processes at the group level. From a group perspective, social habits that have evolved over thousands of years under offline conditions collide with entirely new technical possibilities online. A theoretical framework for the interaction between collective information processing and the infrastructure of online spaces might help us to understand what is unique about social phenomena online. Thereby, it may serve as an inspiration and foundation for future research. Although the present work focuses on the group level, several of its assumptions might also apply to individual information processing online.

Thus, this theoretical contribution seeks to conceptualize how online environments shape collective information processing. For this purpose, I extend the propositions of the model of collective information processing (MCIP, Schindler, in preparation; for a first draft see Schindler & Bartsch, 2019) from small, face-to-face groups to large groups online. In doing so, I link theoretical and empirical literature from multidisciplinary fields such as social psychology, small-group research, communication studies, and computer-supported cooperative work. My contribution begins with an overview of the foundations of collective information processing (i.e., the concepts of social identity, small groups as information processors, and their application to large groups online). On this basis, I introduce four basic modes of collective information processing based on the MCIP (i.e., automatic vs. systematic processing and closed vs. open processing). Next, I summarize core technical possibilities of online environments (i.e., participation, selectivity, interaction, interconnectedness, and automatization) based on Neuberger (2018). Drawing on these concepts, I then review how each mode of collective information processing might interact with the technical possibilities online. In the final sections, I discuss these insights and outline their implications for future research and for society.

The Foundations of Collective Information Processing

The following sections address the key concepts relevant to collective information processing. The first section introduces social identity (Tajfel

Johanna Schindler

& Turner, 1986) as a social psychological basis for group processes. The second section deals with the conceptualization of small groups as information processors as introduced by Hinsz et al. (1997) and adopted by the MCIP (Schindler, in preparation). In the third section, the idea of collective information processors is applied to large groups in online settings. This perspective provides the foundation for grasping collective processes on the internet.

Social Identity

For humankind, living in groups is existential. Belongingness is a basic human need (Fiske, 2000), and human cognition is "truly social" (Caporael, 1997, p. 277) in that individual processes are closely knit to their social environment. This background leads to the assumptions of social identity theory (SIT) (Tajfel & Turner, 1986): According to SIT, humans perceive not only others but also themselves through social categorization (Turner et al., 1987). They can, thus, not only take on a personal identity (I vs. you) but also a social identity as part of a social category or group (we vs. you). In this "we mode," individuals internalize their group membership as part of their self-concept and think as representatives of their ingroup. Through the lens of social identity, ingroups and outgroups are prototypical constructs accentuating differences between each other. Consequently, individuals perceive personal characteristics of themselves and others as less striking (depersonalization or stereotyping). Individuals can dynamically switch between various personal and social identities depending on which identity is salient in a specific situation. However, only one identity can be present at any given moment (Hogg et al., 2004; Tindale & Kameda, 2000).

There are two primary motivations behind social identity processes. The first is self-enhancement; humans strive for positive distinction, which they can achieve by joining a group and comparing it positively to other groups. The second motivation is uncertainty reduction. Social categorization helps reduce perceived uncertainty about the self and the social environment (Hogg et al., 2004).

Originally, SIT referred to intergroup processes between large social groups but was also applied to small groups later (Hogg et al., 2004). The social identity perspective helps explain how people can become part of a group and why they might adapt their perceptions and attitudes to align with this group.

Small Groups as Information Processors

The social orientation of human beings gives them special possibilities for cooperation. Concerning small groups, Hinsz et al. (1997) developed the concept of groups as information processors. Their comprehensive review of group research showed that collective and individual information processing involves highly similar elements. As on the individual level, information processing on the group level includes objectives, attention, encoding, storage, retrieval, processing, responses, and feedback. To process information collectively, however, groups need to fulfill two requirements. The first is that they need a basic amount of social sharedness, a concept referring to the extent to which states and processes are shared among group members. Social sharedness can, e.g., relate to information, attitudes, motives, norms, identities, cognitive processes (Tindale & Kameda, 2000), and plausibly also emotions (Smith, 1993; Smith et al., 2007; van Kleef & Fischer, 2016). It is, therefore, strongly linked to the concept of social identity (see above). The second requirement for collective information processing is a combination of contributions and relates to how groups (a) identify relevant contributions of group members and (b) combine these contributions on the group level. Such contributions can include resources, skills, and knowledge. Their combination works via an interactive process of aggregating, linking, or transforming (Hinsz et al., 1997).

Apart from structural commonalities, there are differences between individual and collective information processing. Only group processes are dependent on social sharedness and shaped by additional factors like group norms, majorities, and leaders. From a group-level perspective, these social influences are not confounders but part of the collective process. They allow the group to maintain its social identity and unity. Accordingly, they also benefit individual members as they depend on belonging to a group (see above; Hogg et al., 2004; Tindale & Kameda, 2000). As a result, groups tend to process information even more prototypically (i.e., accentuated and homogeneously) than individuals (Chalos & Pickard, 1985; Hinsz et al., 1997, p. 50).

The information processing perspective on groups has been adopted by the MCIP to describe, explain, and predict the collective processing of (media) information via different processing modes (Schindler, in preparation). Thus far, it has focused on small groups in face-to-face settings. However, it demonstrates that groups can be conceptualized as meaningful information processing units in general. In the following, this fundamental idea will be transferred to larger groups in online settings.

Johanna Schindler

Application to Large Groups Online

Collective information processing traditionally occurs face-to-face in small groups like families, friends, or co-workers. Such groups can, of course, use online channels as well to process information collectively; however, online spaces offer new possibilities for larger groups to engage in efficient collective information processing (see below for details). At the same time, not every group phenomenon on the internet meets the relevant criteria. Dolata and Schrape (2014) described online collective formations from an actor-based social theory perspective, differentiating between non-organized collectives (e.g., masses, crowds) and organized collectives (e.g., social movements, communities). Non-organized collectives may exhibit social sharedness to a minor degree but cannot perform combinations of contributions; their collective behavior can result only from an aggregate of individual actions. Organized collectives, in contrast, share a social identity, norms, or goals, which might generally enable them to act—or process information—collectively via some form of social sharedness and a combination of contributions (Dolata & Schrape, 2014). In the following, the term "groups" refers to collectives with at least some type of social sharedness performing at least some kind of combinations of contributions. Thus, it includes not only tight-knit online communities but also, e.g., groups of random users with the shared motivation to discuss an issue in a comments section.

Empirical evidence shows that larger groups in online spaces can, indeed, engage in collective processes similar to those of smaller face-to-face groups. This analogy is supported by findings from the field of computer-supported cooperative work (CSCW), an interdisciplinary research area focusing on how people collaborate with the aid of computer systems. Apart from organizations, the field investigates groups on social platforms as well, including social movements (e.g., #MeToo), peer production communities (e.g., Wikipedia), or gaming communities (e.g., World of Warcraft). In a systematic review of CSCW literature, Seering et al. (2018) provided evidence that the principles of social identity known from offline research also apply to groups in online spaces. For example, internet users seem to switch between different social identities and associated self-presentation and communication norms depending on specific contexts (e.g., Marwick & boyd, 2011). Moreover, it appears that online groups with the goal of advocating their identity have stronger social identities (e.g., De Choudhury et al., 2016). Members of online groups with strong social identities, in turn, seem to engage in more one-to-many reciprocity, i.e., collaboration with group members they don't know personally (e.g., Liu et al., 2016).

Social identity on the group level is directly linked to socially shared states and processes and the ability to combine contributions of individual members interactively (see above).

In summary, there is theoretical and empirical support that a basic collective information processing perspective can be helpful for conceptualizing group processes on the internet. Even though online groups might be large and lack direct contact between each of their members, they appear to be capable of social sharedness and combinations of contributions.

Modes of Collective Information Processing

I have demonstrated that online groups can act as information processing systems. Thus, general principles of human information processing known from individuals and small groups may also apply to them. In the following sections, I introduce two dimensions of information processing: (1) the automatic vs. systematic continuum and (2) the open vs. closed continuum. Both are well-known on the individual level and have already been transferred to small groups within the framework of the MCIP (Schindler, in preparation; Schindler & Bartsch, 2019). They could, thereby, also help to systematize different modes of information processing in online spaces.

Automatic vs. Systematic Processing

First, numerous dual-process models of individual information processing distinguish between an "automatic" and a "systematic" mode (but using different labels). These models include, e.g., the elaboration likelihood model of persuasion (ELM; Petty & Cacioppo, 1986), the heuristic-systematic model of information processing (HSM; Chaiken et al., 1989), the limited capacity model of motivated mediated message processing (LC4MP; Lang, 2006), and the affect infusion model (AIM; Forgas, 1995). Automatic information processing requires only minimal motivation and cognitive resources; it works superficially and often unconsciously. Systematic information processing, in contrast, is associated with high levels of motivation, mental effort, accuracy, and consciousness (Chaiken et al., 1989; Forgas, 1995; Lang, 2006; Petty & Cacioppo, 1986). Automatic processing is the default mode but can be supplemented by systematic processing, resulting in a continuum between both extremes (e.g., Petty & Wegener, 1999).

Johanna Schindler

Results of small-group research imply that the distinction between automatic and systematic information processing also applies to small groups in face-to-face settings (De Dreu et al., 2008; Hinsz et al., 1997). This assumption is supported by, first, qualitative (Schindler & Bartsch, 2019) and then quantitative (Schindler, in preparation) evidence. Thus, small groups can process information either automatically, relying on common knowledge and simple heuristic cues, or systematically, engaging deeply with the topic and related arguments. Later, the same distinction will be applied to interpreting research results on group processes online.

Closed vs. Open Processing

Second, some approaches differentiate between a "closed" and an "open" mode of individual information processing (applying different labels, again). These approaches include, e.g., the theory of lay epistemics (Kruglanski, 1989), the concept of motivated reasoning (Kunda, 1990), the HSM (Chaiken et al., 1989), and the AIM (Forgas, 1995). Closed information processing is directed toward reaching or maintaining a specific, predetermined result. Conversely, open information processing is associated with the willingness to accept different results. Again, both modes build a continuum rather than two completely distinct modes (Kruglanski, 1989). The automatic vs. systematic continuum and the closed vs. open continuum represent two orthogonal dimensions of information processing (Chaiken et al., 1989; Forgas, 1995; Kunda, 1990). Their respective modes can, therefore, be combined with each other, e.g., systematic and open processing.

Again, the distinction between closed and open information processing can be applied to small groups in face-to-face settings. A first qualitative (Schindler & Bartsch, 2019) and quantitative (Schindler, in preparation) study implies that small groups can process information either closed, reproducing and justifying established views, or open, engaging with new pieces of information and positions. Therefore, the same distinction will be applied later to review the literature on collective information processing in online spaces.

Technical Possibilities in Online Spaces

The last two sections have focused on grasping the concept of collective information processing, especially by groups in online spaces. It has been shown that, essentially, they engage in identity-driven processes similar to those of smaller face-to-face groups. However, the internet offers technical possibilities that are entirely new in human history. Based on Neuberger (2018, pp. 15–17), the next sections introduce five core technical possibilities of the internet relevant to a social dimension: (a) participation, (b) selectivity, (c) interaction, (d) interconnectedness, and (e) automatization (originally labeled "transparency"). The factor of selectivity has been added to Neuberger's (2018) original list as it seems critical for some group processes online. The following sections outline how these factors are connected to group processes in general, making collective information processing possible online. After that, they are linked to the different modes of collective information processing (see above) in order to better grasp what makes the internet such a special environment for groups.

Participation

The internet enables users to participate in public discourse and other social processes. Not only can online users passively follow these; they can actively contribute to them (Neuberger, 2018, p. 16). Hence, groups and individuals—particularly social or political minorities and their members—can become more involved and more visible online.

Selectivity

In many online contexts, it is common and easy for users to obscure specific individual characteristics and emphasize others. Thereby, they can choose any (social) identity, and accordingly, they can often decide how to act with no consequences for their offline lives. This freedom could be especially important for groups and their members who are less socially accepted. It also enables groups and individuals to easily violate societal norms.

Johanna Schindler

Interaction

While traditional media environments have offered few opportunities for follow-up communication, online spaces enable extensive and complex interactions. These can occur between various actors (Neuberger, 2018, p. 16). Interactions are a fundamental requirement for combinations of contributions (see above) and, therefore, for collective information processing within groups. Moreover, online environments enable interactions between groups and, therefore, pro-social and anti-social intergroup processes of all kinds.

Interconnectedness

The internet offers new possibilities for people to connect independent of time and space. In addition, content can be linked much more efficiently (Neuberger, 2018, p. 16). Consequently, individuals are able to build groups that wouldn't exist offline. The interconnectedness of groups' members and information (e.g., via hashtags) might generally contribute to effective collective information processing via social sharedness and a combination of contributions.

Automatization

Algorithms and artificial intelligence allow online information processing to become more effective—or biased—than it has ever been before. Furthermore, content can be precisely personalized to online users, as platform providers can collect fine-grained data on user characteristics (Neuberger, 2018, pp. 16–17). Thus, groups and their members have the ability to find exactly what they are looking for online. Platforms also actively offer information tailored to their needs.

Modes of Collective Information Processing in Online Spaces

Two factors are demonstrated in the previous two sections. First, groups seem to process information in different modes, i.e., on an (1) automatic vs. systematic continuum and on an (2) open vs. closed continuum. Second, online environments essentially offer five new possibilities in social terms, i.e., (a) participation, (b) selectivity, (c) interaction, (d) interconnectedness, and (e) automatization. These concepts build the foundation for exploring how online spaces might shape collective information processing. The following sections review each combination of processing mode and condition; they also address corresponding literature and empirical evidence.

For Automatic Processing

Online environments provide groups and their members with new and even more accessible opportunities for automatic information processing. The *participation* of many group members should lead to a broader foundation for majority cues. As in offline settings (Tindale & Kameda, 2000), group members in online settings tend to base decisions on majority cues within their group (Go et al., 2014).

Selectivity in terms of personal identity may lead to more apparent authority cues or expert cues in online spaces, as a small, selected set of user characteristics stands out more prominently. Leaders or experts have been shown to influence groups and their members offline (Hogg et al., 2004) and online (Kanthawala & Peng, 2021). Likewise, social identity cues can be more prominent online. They could, thus, reinforce any automatic mechanisms associated with ingroup or outgroup membership, e.g., the application of prejudice (Dotsch & Wigboldus, 2008; Dovidio et al., 2010).

Online *interaction* helps groups easily generate heuristic cues, e.g., identifying the majority position or asking trusted group members (see above). Similarly, the *interconnectedness* online facilitates access to existing heuristic cues, as they might be just one click away.

Finally, *automatization* provides an ultimate aid for automatic information processing in online spaces. Groups can find information with the least amount of effort or are even proactively recommended tailored content. Just as individuals do (Wirth et al., 2007), they might often process such pieces of information in an automatic mode.

For Systematic Processing

In contrast, the internet allows new and powerful possibilities for systematic information processing in groups. The *participation* of a large number of members enables an entirely new level of collective intelligence. Offline

Johanna Schindler

and online studies have demonstrated that groups can solve problems better than individuals (Laughlin et al., 2006; Schmidt et al., 2001). A meta-analysis on collective brainstorming has shown that larger groups outperform smaller groups—especially when they collaborate virtually (Dennis & Williams, 2007). One of the best-known examples is Wikipedia.

Selectivity online might also aid collective systematic information processing via a more salient social identity. As collective information processing depends on social sharedness (see above), a stronger social identity could facilitate group performance. This idea is supported by the results of an online experiment on creative performance in groups (Guegan et al., 2017).

Interaction is critical for collective information processing (see above) and especially for challenging tasks. Therefore, effective solutions for online group communication should promote systematic modes as well. It has been demonstrated for online and offline teams, for example, that more communication is associated with higher scores in a test of collective intelligence (Engel et al., 2014). Similar to measures of individuals' general intelligence, this test gives groups a variety of cognitive tasks to be performed together (A. W. Woolley et al., 2010).

Furthermore, the special tools for *interconnectedness* in online spaces could contribute particularly to collective systematic processing as they allow for a new level of combinations of contributions (see above). Various examples show how local communities have utilized such opportunities to perform highly effective crisis management online during violent attacks or natural disasters, e.g., to efficiently organize information and assistance (Büscher et al., 2014).

Ultimately, *automatization* can also aid systematic collective processes in a unique way. Algorithms allow for a broadly-based and in-depth information search not possible for human groups alone. Likewise, collaborations between humans and artificial agents may enable an entirely new level of intelligence, mutually compensating for the weaknesses of collective and artificial intelligence (Peeters et al., 2021).

For Closed Processing

Online spaces can support closed information processing in groups under entirely new conditions. As *participation* on the internet is hardly restricted, it is easier for any social and political groups to take part in public discourse. Through online social movements, they can recruit a large number of members to work collectively toward their goals (Jost et al., 2018).

How Does the Internet Change Group Processes?

Examples include the Fridays for Future, #BlackLivesMatter, or #MeToo but also right-wing extremist or Islamic extremist groups.

Selectivity online can also shift the focus to certain social identities instead of diverse personal identities (see above). Consequently, groups might develop stronger social sharedness of motivations and become prone to a closed processing mode. Meta-analyses show that anonymity, i.e., a lack of personal cues, in offline and online contexts leads individuals to act more in line with norms of their ingroup (Huang & Li, 2016; Postmes & Spears, 1998). If such norms are antisocial, this might, for example, foster hate toward outgroups and their members (Rösner & Krämer, 2016). Furthermore, selectivity in online environments makes it easier for individuals to participate in movements that are socially unacceptable in their offline community.

The special possibilities for *interaction* online can also support closed information processing. Groups strongly motivated to reach a goal tend to endorse leadership (Kruglanski et al., 2006), which can be particularly effective online. For example, hierarchy has been shown to enhance the abilities of teams playing the online game League of Legends (Kim et al., 2017). Moreover, the internet enables groups to interact more efficiently with others to achieve their goals. They can not only persuade potential ingroup members to join them (Bos et al., 2020) but also easily attack outgroups and their members with insults and threats (Brown, 2018).

Together with the potential for interaction, *interconnectedness* online may especially aid and reinforce a closed processing mode. Collective information processing depends on combinations of contributions (see above) that can work highly effectively online. Online social movements can continuously provide their members with practical information, ideological content, and support to accomplish their collective goals (Jost et al., 2018). However, strong online interconnectedness might also contribute ultimately to radicalization. A study conducted with members of neo-Nazi online forums, for instance, demonstrated that their extremism increased with participation (Wojcieszak, 2010).

Automatization on the internet may further boost a closed processing mode. Algorithms and artificial intelligence can potentially present groups with content accurately adjusted to their preexisting beliefs, including computational propaganda (S. C. Woolley & Howard, 2017). They could, thereby, support extreme forms of closed processing and lead to the spread of misinformation and polarization (Neudert & Marchal, 2019).

Johanna Schindler

For Open Processing

At the other end of the spectrum, the internet offers new possibilities for open collective information processing. Online spaces allow the *participation* of various people, including social and political minorities. As in offline contexts (Nemeth & Kwan, 1987), this may facilitate a creative, open collective processing mode. For example, gender and tenure diversity have been shown to enhance the productivity of programming teams (Vasilescu et al., 2015), and opinion diversity in online discussion forums has been shown to lead to a higher level of deliberation (Karlsson, 2012).

Selectivity may also aid open processing in groups when it hides members' attributes that might inhibit collaboration and shift the focus away from the idea itself (e.g., because of prejudices). Accordingly, a study on online brainstorming demonstrated that diverse groups who were also anonymous showed the highest level of group creativity (Garfield et al., 2007). Additionally, selectivity may help members of stigmatized groups to participate in open collective online processes. For example, anonymity has been shown to be critical in order for individuals to participate in the LGBTQ+ community and learn from each other (Fox & Ralston, 2016).

Furthermore, online tools for *interaction* can also contribute to openness in collective processes as they might help groups to generate new ideas effectively. As mentioned above, more communication in online teams correlates with higher collective intelligence—a construct including openness in brainstorming tasks, among others (Engel et al., 2014). An experiment also demonstrated that political deliberation as an open and rational communication process can be equally effective in face-to-face and online settings (Min, 2007). Regarding online interaction between groups, a study on the Israel–Palestine conflict on Facebook demonstrated that online spaces generally have the potential for open intergroup communication and prejudice reduction (Ruesch, 2013).

Interconnectedness has the potential to additionally amplify openness in collective information processing. Due to the unique possibilities for combinations of contributions (see above) on the internet, groups might be able to collaborate creatively and explore new connections. A study of individuals with diabetes, for example, showed that patient communities can generate information, advice, and empowerment for their members (Brady et al., 2017). Other examples of open-minded problem-solving are cases of online crisis management in local communities during violent attacks or natural disasters (see above; Büscher et al., 2014).

Finally, online *automatization* may foster collective open-mindedness in online spaces. Just as algorithms and artificial intelligence seem able to draw groups further toward a predetermined direction (see above; Neudert & Marchal, 2019), they could also nudge collective creativity, reflection, and the reevaluation of preexisting beliefs.

Discussion

The previous sections systematically elaborated on how different modes of collective information processing might interact with the technical infrastructure online. Based on the MCIP (Schindler, in preparation), they referred to the distinction between (1) automatic (i.e., simple) vs. systematic (i.e., thorough) and (2) closed (i.e., determined) vs. open (i.e., open-minded) information processing on the group level. The four different processing modes were then examined against the background of (a) participation, (b) selectivity, (c) interaction, (d) interconnectedness, and (e) automatization as core technical possibilities of the internet. A first literature review based on this framework suggests that each of these factors can facilitate each collective processing mode on an entirely new level. Certainly, whether this occurs depends on group characteristics, technical configurations, and situational factors. Under particular conditions, a given processing mode might also persist or diminish, as many of the aforementioned mechanisms may counterbalance or contradict each other. However, and most important, online spaces have the potential to reinforce any four collective processing modes—with all their consequences. In the following sections I discuss the implications of this potential separately for each dimension of information processing.

Automatic vs. Systematic Processing Online

On the continuum between automatic (i.e., simple) and systematic (i.e., thorough) information processing, online spaces may, on the one hand, promote an automatic mode. In online infrastructures, groups can easily access simple-to-grasp information like heuristic cues. Thus, they need to invest even less cognitive effort than in offline contexts. However, this should not necessarily be associated with lower-quality outcomes. In some cases, of course, online spaces may amplify biases due to automatic processing. Often, however, technical assistance might contribute to higher-quality results of automatic processing. Participation of many users might, for

Johanna Schindler

example, lead to better-founded majority cues and automatization to more carefully selected information.

On the other hand, online environments may accelerate systematic information processing in groups. Online spaces can assist groups to collaborate on a large scale and effectively combine their members' resources. At the same time, collective systematic information processing might require less effort online as it is partly supported by technology. Sometimes, it may fall into the trap of sophisticated misinformation, e.g., deepfakes (Dan et al., 2021). However, systematic information processing of groups might often produce even more elaborated outcomes when supported by an online infrastructure. For instance, the participation of many users might increase the number of available resources; interconnectedness may enable groups to better organize individual contributions; and automatization might help perform ideal systematical information searches.

Regarding the relationship between collective automatic and systematic information processing in online environments, both processing modes seem to be converging to some extent. Generally, automatic processing offers the benefit of low requirements but the drawback of lower-quality results, while the opposite is true for systematic processing. Online environments seem to compensate somewhat for both weaknesses simultaneously. Technical support can make the automatic parts of collective information processing more effective (i.e., lead to more accurate results) and the systematic parts more efficient (i.e., require less effort). Thus, we can assume that online environments may generally increase the elaborateness of collective information processing outcomes.

Closed vs. Open Processing Online

On the continuum between closed (i.e., determined) and open (i.e., open-minded) information processing, the internet might support a closed mode on the group level. Due to a larger sphere of influence and more and better-organized resources, groups can effectively work toward their common goals. Selectivity might, for example, increase the salience of internal group norms in relation to general societal norms; interaction may offer opportunities to recruit ingroup members or attack outgroup members; and automatization might reaffirm existing beliefs. Closed information processing is human and not harmful per se. To a certain extent, it can be functional for a pluralistic society by stimulating discourse between different camps or by allowing for reliable, shared principles (e.g., a constitution). However, depending on their design, online environments might also fuel an extreme form of closed information processing in groups, known as group centrism (Kruglanski et al., 2006), which refers to collective processes characterized by strong group norms and pressure to conform, ingroup favoritism, and support for autocratic leaders. When associated with a high level of elaborated, systematic processing (see above), extreme closedness should be the most challenging collective processing mode for society. Via an online infrastructure, skilled and extreme groups seem particularly capable of facilitating radicalization, misinformation, hate, and polarization.

At the same time, the internet allows for more-open collective information processing. Online spaces might inspire and support groups in exploring new perspectives and solutions together. Participation may, for instance, enhance diversity; interaction may boost creativity and allow for positive intergroup contact; and automatization could challenge preexisting beliefs. Again, the design of online environments is critical to realizing these opportunities. In conjunction with systematic processing (see above), an open collective processing mode could offer the most significant potential for society. It might contribute to new dimensions of social connection, knowledge gain, empowerment, and deliberation.

Unlike the automatic vs. systematic continuum, the ends of the closed vs. open continuum seem to be moving even farther apart in online spaces. Automatic and systematic processes are driven by a trade-off between effort and benefit as their opposition is caused simply by limited resources. Closed and open processing, however, are guided by specific motivations that are inherently and fundamentally opposed to each other. Their respective mindsets, beliefs, or ideologies might become even more accentuated when they encounter specific technical infrastructures. This dynamic suggests that online environments may essentially increase the gap between closed and open collective information processing—both in terms of how they operate and what their outcomes are.

Conclusion

In this contribution I have sought to develop a theoretical perspective on how online environments shape online group processes, e.g., in e-communities, online social movements, or online discussions. Applying the propositions of the model of collective information processing (MCIP, Schindler, in preparation), I have demonstrated that a collective information processing perspective might be a helpful lens for group phenomena online. An illustrative literature review indicates that the internet can function as a catalyst for any collective processing mode—depending on the interplay of a group, infrastructure, and situation. First, this applies to the continuum of automatic (i.e., simple) vs. systematic (i.e., thorough) processing on the group level. Due to technical support, however, both extremes seem to converge in becoming more efficient and effective at the same time. Second, online environments also seem to reinforce both ends of the continuum between closed (i.e., determined) vs. open (i.e., open-minded) processing in groups, and these appear to be drifting even farther apart on the internet. The continuum between closed and open processing, especially, appears to harbor for societies not only threats but also opportunities never before seen.

Of course, the present work has several limitations. It presents only a first draft of a theoretical framework for collective information processing in online spaces. More specifically, it can only begin to address the similarities and differences between collective processing in small, face-to-face groups and large groups online. Furthermore, the review of the connection between technical possibilities and collective processing modes is not exhaustive, and the interplay of both processing dimensions (automatic vs. systematic and closed vs. open) is only briefly discussed. Finally, the relationship between processes on the group level and on the individual level remains to be examined in greater detail. Future work should further develop and more comprehensively link this draft with existing literature, but most important, the presented framework needs to be tested empirically.

Nevertheless, the theoretical implications of the current contribution may inspire and benefit future research that focuses specifically on the group level. The most urgent issues of our time seem inseparably linked to group processes (e.g., the climate crisis, COVID-19 pandemic, or ideological polarization in general). A collective information processing perspective might, therefore, shed new light on seemingly well-researched areas. Future studies could explore questions such as the following: Under what circumstances do different collective processing modes occur in online spaces? How do groups utilize the same online infrastructure based on different processing modes? What role do algorithms and artificial intelligence play in this? How could extreme forms of closed collective information processing be attenuated? And how might online environments help collective intelligence and creativity reach their full potential? These kinds of questions are relevant not only for (social) scientists but also policymakers, platform developers, and citizens in general. Their answers could contribute to a deeper understanding of social phenomena online and, ultimately, their consequences for the offline world.

References

Bos, L., Schemer, C., Corbu, N., Hameleers, M., Andreadis, I., Schulz, A., Schmuck, D., Reinemann, C., & Fawzi, N. (2020). The effects of populism as a social identity frame on persuasion and mobilisation: Evidence from a 15-country experiment. *European Journal of Political Research*, *59*(1), 3–24. https://doi.org/10.1111/1475-6765.12334

Brady, E., Segar, J., & Sanders, C. (2017). Accessing support and empowerment online: The experiences of individuals with diabetes. *Health Expectations*, *20*(5), 1088–1095. https://doi.org/10.1111/hex.12552

Brauner, E., & Scholl, W. (2000). Editorial: The Information Processing Approach as a Perspective for Groups Research. *Group Processes & Intergroup Relations*, *3*(2), 115–122. https://doi.org/10.1177/1368430200003002001

Brown, A. (2018). What is so special about online (as compared to offline) hate speech? *Ethnicities*, *18*(3), 297–326. https://doi.org/10.1177/1468796817709846

Büscher, M., Liegl, M., & Thomas, V. (2014). Collective Intelligence in Crises. In D. Miorandi, V. Maltese, M. Rovatsos, A. Nijholt, & J. Stewart (Eds.), *Social Collective Intelligence* (pp. 243–265). Springer International Publishing. https://doi.org/10.1007/978-3-319-08681-1_12

Caporael, L. R. (1997). The Evolution of Truly Social Cognition: The Core Configurations Model. *Personality and Social Psychology Review*, *1*(4), 276–298. https://doi.org/10.1207/s15327957pspr0104_1

Chaiken, S., Liberman, A., & Eagly, A. H. (1989). Heuristic and systematic processing within and beyond the persuasion context. In J. S. Uleman & J. A. Bargh (Eds.), *Unintended Thought* (pp. 212–252). Guilford Press.

Chalos, P., & Pickard, S. (1985). Information choice and cue use: An experiment in group information processing. *Journal of Applied Psychology*, *70*(4), 634–641. https://doi.org/10.1037/0021-9010.70.4.634

Dan, V., Paris, B., Donovan, J., Hameleers, M., Roozenbeek, J., van der Linden, S., & von Sikorski, C. (2021). Visual Mis- and Disinformation, Social Media, and Democracy. *Journalism & Mass Communication Quarterly*, *98*(3), 641–664. https://doi.org/10.1177/10776990211035395

De Choudhury, M., Jhaver, S., Sugar, B., & Weber, I. (2016). *Social media participation in an activist movement for racial equality.* 92–101.

De Dreu, C. K. W., Nijstad, B. A., & van Knippenberg, D. (2008). Motivated Information Processing in Group Judgment and Decision Making. *Personality and Social Psychology Review*, *12*(1), 22–49. https://doi.org/10.1177/1088868307304092

Dennis, A. R., & Williams, M. L. (2007). A Meta-Analysis of Group Size Effects in Electronic Brainstorming: More Heads are Better than One. In N. Kock (Ed.), *Advances in E-Collaboration* (pp. 250–269). IGI Global. https://doi.org/10.4018/978-1-59904-393-7.ch013

Dolata, U., & Schrape, J.-F. (2014). Kollektives Handeln im Internet. Eine akteurtheoretische Fundierung. *Berliner Journal für Soziologie, 24*(1), 5–30. https://doi.org/10.1007/s11609-014-0242-y

Dotsch, R., & Wigboldus, D. H. J. (2008). Virtual prejudice. *Journal of Experimental Social Psychology, 44*(4), 1194–1198. https://doi.org/10.1016/j.jesp.2008.03.003

Dovidio, J. F., Hewstone, M., Glick, P., & Esses, V. M. (2010). Prejudice, Stereotyping and Discrimination: Theoretical and Empirical Overview. In J. F. Dovidio, M. Hewstone, & V. M. Esses (Eds.), *The SAGE Handbook of Prejudice, Stereotyping and Discrimination* (pp. 3–29). SAGE Publications Ltd.

Engel, D., Woolley, A. W., Jing, L. X., Chabris, C. F., & Malone, T. W. (2014). Reading the Mind in the Eyes or Reading between the Lines? Theory of Mind Predicts Collective Intelligence Equally Well Online and Face-To-Face. *PLoS ONE, 9*(12), 1–16. https://doi.org/10.1371/journal.pone.0115212

Fiske, S. T. (2000). Stereotyping, prejudice, and discrimination at the seam between the centuries: Evolution, culture, mind, and brain. *European Journal of Social Psychology, 30*(3), 299–322. https://doi.org/10.1002/(SICI)1099-0992(200005/06)30:3<299::AID-EJSP2>3.0.CO;2-F

Forgas, J. P. (1995). Mood and judgment: The affect infusion model (AIM). *Psychological Bulletin, 117*(1), 39–66. https://doi.org/10.1037/0033-2909.117.1.39

Fox, J., & Ralston, R. (2016). Queer identity online: Informal learning and teaching experiences of LGBTQ individuals on social media. *Computers in Human Behavior, 65*, 635–642. https://doi.org/10.1016/j.chb.2016.06.009

Garfield, M., Chidambaram, L., Carte, T., & Lim, Y.-K. (2007). Group diversity and creativity: Does anonymity matter? *ICIS 2007 Proceedings*, 1–22.

Go, E., Jung, E. H., & Wu, M. (2014). The effects of source cues on online news perception. *Computers in Human Behavior, 38*, 358–367. https://doi.org/10.1016/j.chb.2014.05.044

Guegan, J., Segonds, F., Barré, J., Maranzana, N., Mantelet, F., & Buisine, S. (2017). Social identity cues to improve creativity and identification in face-to-face and virtual groups. *Computers in Human Behavior, 77*, 140–147. https://doi.org/10.1016/j.chb.2017.08.043

Hinsz, V. B., Tindale, R. S., & Vollrath, D. A. (1997). The emerging conceptualization of groups as information processors. *Psychological Bulletin, 121*(1), 43–64. https://doi.org/10.1037/0033-2909.121.1.43

Hogg, M. A., Abrams, D., Otten, S., & Hinkle, S. (2004). The Social Identity Perspective: Intergroup Relations, Self-Conception, and Small Groups. *Small Group Research, 35*(3), 246–276. https://doi.org/10.1177/1046496404263424

Huang, G., & Li, K. (2016). The effect of anonymity on conformity to group norms in online contexts: A meta-analysis. *International Journal of Communication, 10*, 398–415.

Jost, J. T., Barberá, P., Bonneau, R., Langer, M., Metzger, M., Nagler, J., Sterling, J., & Tucker, J. A. (2018). How Social Media Facilitates Political Protest: Information, Motivation, and Social Networks: Social Media and Political Protest. *Political Psychology, 39*, 85–118. https://doi.org/10.1111/pops.12478

Kanthawala, S., & Peng, W. (2021). Credibility in Online Health Communities: Effects of Moderator Credentials and Endorsement Cues. *Journalism and Media*, 2(3), 379–396. https://doi.org/10.3390/journalmedia2030023

Karlsson, M. (2012). Understanding Divergent Patterns of Political Discussion in Online Forums—Evidence from the European Citizens' Consultations. *Journal of Information Technology & Politics*, 9(1), 64–81. https://doi.org/10.1080/1933168 1.2012.635965

Kim, Y. J., Engel, D., Woolley, A. W., Lin, J. Y.-T., McArthur, N., & Malone, T. W. (2017). What Makes a Strong Team? Using Collective Intelligence to Predict Team Performance in League of Legends. *Proceedings of the 2017 ACM Conference on Computer Supported Cooperative Work and Social Computing*, 27, 2316–2329. https://doi.org/10.1145/2998181.2998185

Kruglanski, A. W. (1989). *Lay Epistemics and Human Knowledge Cognitive and Motivational Bases*. Plenum. https://doi.org/10.1007/978-1-4899-0924-4

Kruglanski, A. W., Pierro, A., Mannetti, L., & De Grada, E. (2006). Groups as epistemic providers: Need for closure and the unfolding of group-centrism. *Psychological Review*, 113(1), 84–100. https://doi.org/10.1037/0033-295X.113.1.84

Kunda, Z. (1990). The case for motivated reasoning. *Psychological Bulletin*, 108(3), 480–498. https://doi.org/10.1037/0033-2909.108.3.480

Lang, A. (2006). Using the Limited Capacity Model of Motivated Mediated Message Processing to Design Effective Cancer Communication Messages. *Journal of Communication*, 56(1), 57–80. https://doi.org/10.1111/j.1460-2466.2006.00283.x

Laughlin, P. R., Hatch, E. C., Silver, J. S., & Boh, L. (2006). Groups Perform Better Than the Best Individuals on Letters-to-Numbers Problems: Effects of Group Size. *Journal of Personality and Social Psychology*, 90(4), 644–651. https://doi.org/1 0.1037/0022-3514.90.4.644

Liu, P., Ding, X., & Gu, N. (2016). "Helping Others Makes Me Happy": Social Interaction and Integration of People with Disabilities. *Proceedings of the 19th ACM Conference on Computer-Supported Cooperative Work & Social Computing*, 1596–1608. https://doi.org/10.1145/2818048.2819998

Marwick, A. E., & boyd, danah. (2011). I tweet honestly, I tweet passionately: Twitter users, context collapse, and the imagined audience. *New Media & Society*, 13(1), 114–133. https://doi.org/10.1177/1461444810365313

Min, S.-J. (2007). Online vs. Face-to-Face Deliberation: Effects on Civic Engagement. *Journal of Computer-Mediated Communication*, 12(4), 1369–1387. https://doi.org/10.1111/j.1083-6101.2007.00377.x

Nemeth, C. J., & Kwan, J. L. (1987). Minority Influence, Divergent Thinking and Detection of Correct Solutions. *Journal of Applied Social Psychology*, 17(9), 788–799. https://doi.org/10.1111/j.1559-1816.1987.tb00339.x

Neuberger, C. (2018). Journalismus in der Netzwerköffentlichkeit: Zum Verhältnis zwischen Profession, Partizipation und Technik. In C. Nuernbergk & C. Neuberger (Eds.), *Journalismus im Internet* (pp. 11–80). Springer Fachmedien Wiesbaden. https://doi.org/10.1007/978-3-531-93284-2_2

Neudert, L. M., & Marchal, N. (2019). *Polarisation and the use of technology in political campaigns and communication*. European Parliament.

Peeters, M. M. M., van Diggelen, J., van den Bosch, K., Bronkhorst, A., Neerincx, M. A., Schraagen, J. M., & Raaijmakers, S. (2021). Hybrid collective intelligence in a human–AI society. *AI & SOCIETY*, *36*(1), 217–238. https://doi.org/10.1007/s00146-020-01005-y

Petty, R. E., & Cacioppo, J. T. (1986). The Elaboration Likelihood Model of Persuasion. In L. Berkowitz (Ed.), *Advances in Experimental Social Psychology* (Vol. 19, pp. 123–205). Academic Press.

Petty, R. E., & Wegener, D. T. (1999). The elaboration likelihood model: Current status and controversies. In S. Chaiken & Y. Trope (Eds.), *Dual-process theories in social psychology* (pp. 41–72). Guilford Press.

Poole, M. S., Hollingshead, A. B., McGrath, J. E., Moreland, R. L., & Rohrbaugh, J. (2004). Interdisciplinary Perspectives on Small Groups. *Small Group Research*, *35*(1), 3–16. https://doi.org/10.1177/1046496403259753

Postmes, T., & Spears, R. (1998). Deindividuation and antinormative behavior: A meta-analysis. *Psychological Bulletin*, *123*(3), 238–259. https://doi.org/10.1037/0033-2909.123.3.238

Rösner, L., & Krämer, N. C. (2016). Verbal Venting in the Social Web: Effects of Anonymity and Group Norms on Aggressive Language Use in Online Comments. *Social Media + Society*, *2*(3), 1–13. https://doi.org/10.1177/2056305116664220

Ruesch, M. (2013). A peaceful net? Intergroup contact and communicative conflict resolution of the Israel-Palestine conflict on Facebook. In A. Ternes (Ed.), *Communication: Breakdowns and breakthroughs* (pp. 13–31). Brill.

Schindler, J. (in preparation). *The Model of Collective Information Processing (MCIP): Theory and Evidence on Predictors, Characteristics, and Outcomes of Information Processing in Groups.*

Schindler, J., & Bartsch, A. (2019). *Vorurteile – Medien – Gruppen: Wie Vorurteile durch Medienrezeption in Gruppen beeinflusst werden*. Springer VS. https://doi.org/10.1007/978-3-658-23218-4

Schmidt, J. B., Montoya-Weiss, M. M., & Massey, A. P. (2001). New Product Development Decision-Making Effectiveness: Comparing Individuals, Face-To-Face Teams, and Virtual Teams. *Decision Sciences*, *32*(4), 575–600. https://doi.org/10.1111/j.1540-5915.2001.tb00973.x

Seering, J., Ng, F., Yao, Z., & Kaufman, G. (2018). Applications of Social Identity Theory to Research and Design in Computer-Supported Cooperative Work. *Proceedings of the ACM on Human-Computer Interaction*, *2*, 1–34. https://doi.org/10.1145/3274771

Smith, E. R. (1993). Social Identity and Social Emotions: Toward New Conceptualizations of Prejudice. In D. M. Mackie & D. L. Hamilton (Eds.), *Affect, cognition and stereotyping: Interactive processes in group perception* (pp. 297–315). Elsevier.

Smith, E. R., Seger, C. R., & Mackie, D. M. (2007). Can emotions be truly group level? Evidence regarding four conceptual criteria. *Journal of Personality and Social Psychology*, *93*(3), 431–446. https://doi.org/10.1037/0022-3514.93.3.431

Tajfel, H., & Turner, J. C. (1986). The Social Identity Theory of Intergroup Behavior. In S. Worchel & W. G. Austin (Eds.), *Psychology of Intergroup Relations* (pp. 7–24). Nelson-Hall.

Tindale, R. S., & Kameda, T. (2000). 'Social Sharedness' as a Unifying Theme for Information Processing in Groups. *Group Processes & Intergroup Relations*, *3*(2), 123–140. https://doi.org/10.1177/1368430200003002002

Turner, J. C., Hogg, M. A., Oakes, P. J., Reicher, S. D., & Wetherell, M. S. (1987). *Rediscovering the social group: A self-categorization theory*. Basil Blackwell.

van Kleef, G. A., & Fischer, A. H. (2016). Emotional collectives: How groups shape emotions and emotions shape groups. *Cognition and Emotion*, *30*(1), 3–19. https://doi.org/10.1080/02699931.2015.1081349

Vasilescu, B., Posnett, D., Ray, B., van den Brand, M. G. J., Serebrenik, A., Devanbu, P., & Filkov, V. (2015). Gender and Tenure Diversity in GitHub Teams. *Proceedings of the 33rd Annual ACM Conference on Human Factors in Computing Systems*, 3789–3798. https://doi.org/10.1145/2702123.2702549

Wirth, W., Böcking, T., Karnowski, V., & von Pape, T. (2007). Heuristic and Systematic Use of Search Engines. *Journal of Computer-Mediated Communication*, *12*(3), 778–800. https://doi.org/10.1111/j.1083-6101.2007.00350.x

Wojcieszak, M. (2010). 'Don't talk to me': Effects of ideologically homogeneous online groups and politically dissimilar offline ties on extremism. *New Media & Society*, *12*(4), 637–655. https://doi.org/10.1177/1461444809342775

Woolley, A. W., Chabris, C. F., Pentland, A., Hashmi, N., & Malone, T. W. (2010). Evidence for a Collective Intelligence Factor in the Performance of Human Groups. *Science*, *330*, 686–688. https://doi.org/10.1126/science.1193147

Woolley, S. C., & Howard, P. (2017). *Computational Propaganda Worldwide: Executive Summary*. University of Oxford.

Johanna Schindler *(M.A., LMU Munich, 2017) is Research Associate at the Department of Media and Communication, LMU Munich, Germany. Her research interests lie in group phenomena with a special focus on digital communication, political communication, and media effects. She was a student of Wolfram Peiser from 2014 to 2016.*

Does Social Media Use Promote Political Mass Polarization?
A Structured Literature Review[1]

Katharina Ludwig & Philipp Müller

Abstract

In past years, a large amount of research was conducted to determine whether the use of social media causes political polarization. This research field, however, lacks clear terminological definitions and concepts such as fragmentation and selective exposure are often imprecisely equated with political polarization, which may explain the widespread assumption that social media cause political polarization. With this article, we aim to unravel conceptual confusion and offer distinct definitions of affective, ideological, and partisan polarization. We conducted a structured literature review of 88 studies addressing the potential effects of social media use on polarization. We find the operationalization of relevant concepts to differ significantly between research projects, making the comparability of results difficult and possibly contributing to inconsistent findings. No clear evidence is found to support the generalized perception of strong polarization effects through the use of social media. Implications for future research are proposed.

Since the internet's earliest days, theorists have voiced concerns about the risks of fragmentation and polarization effects (e.g., Dahlberg, 2007; Papacharissi, 2002; Sunstein, 2001). These concerns are amplified by the emergence and growth of social media platforms and algorithmic content-selection mechanisms and their growing importance in political information exposure (Bakshy, Messing, & Adamic, 2015). The so-called fragmentation thesis expresses the idea that discussions about politics are taking place in insulated groups, separated along party or ideological lines, with little or no contact between groups (Bright, 2018). This implies that people are captured in self-selected "echo chambers" (Sunstein, 2001) or algorith-

---

1 This research was supported by a grant from Baden-Württemberg Stiftung within the research program Responsible Artificial Intelligence.

mically induced "filter bubbles" (Pariser, 2011), communicating only with those who have similar ideological viewpoints and, thus, being exposed only to opinion-confirming information. As empirical studies have shown that, in social media, the fragmentation thesis is, at least partly, in place (e.g., Bright, 2018), theorists worry about the implications for democracy as the democratic formation of a collective will via deliberation requires citizens to be exposed to a range of diverse viewpoints (Gentzkow & Shapiro, 2010). If people, instead, are exposed only to like-minded content and, consequently, constantly reinforced in their beliefs, political polarization and societal disintegration might be the outcomes (e.g., Warner, 2010; Arceneaux & Johnson, 2010).

While the argument that growing segments of the electorate that use social media platforms to become informed might initiate such processes seems convincing at first (and is continuously popularized in public discourse), it remains largely unclear whether this notion is supported by empirical research. The main aim of this chapter is, therefore, to systematically review existing findings on polarization through social media usage and to disentangle different causal mechanisms of social-media-induced effects on polarization effects found in the literature. Before being able to do so, however, we must first clarify extant conceptual confusions that are caused by the frequent interchangeable use of terms such as "fragmentation," "group polarization," or "political polarization" in the literature. In the first part of this chapter, we propose a conceptual framework to disentangle these different types of polarization as well as each one's operationalization.

Moreover, our aim is not to determine whether political polarization *is represented* in social media environments but whether social media environments are *causing political polarization* and if so, to identify those exact mechanisms that play central roles in this process. In other words, if polarization can be documented within social media environments, does this mean that social media technologies can be held responsible for its occurrence? In particular, we are interested in clarifying whether algorithmic selection mechanisms or individual user decisions or predispositions affect political polarization processes. Furthermore, we perform an analysis to identify structural differences between different country contexts and researchers' methodological decisions. As the existing research on this topic lacks clear definitions and distinctions between concepts, operationalization, and methodologies, this is a necessary and important endeavor.

Ours is not the first attempt to provide a systematic overview of the questions discussed up to this point. As we were conducting this study, two literature reviews were published that follow a similar perspective;

they deal with (a.) group polarization in online discussions (Iandoli, Primario, & Zollo, 2021) and (b.) the role of (social) media use in political polarization (Kubin & von Sikorski, 2021). While we see a good amount of merit in these two studies, we believe that at least two arguments justify publishing a third literature review that follows a similar question. First, literature reviews can be seen as meta-empirical research that draws conclusions from a broad overview of the empirical observations of others. As such, the same argument that can be made for single empirical studies has to be made for literature reviews of empirical research; that is, empirical science is based on an accumulation of evidence and, therefore, one research team's observations and interpretations can never be sufficient to draw generalizable conclusions. That being said, reconsidering a question that has previously been investigated by others inevitably adds value to the state of knowledge, if it is only to provide reassurance that previous conclusions can be substantiated.

Second, we see specific limitations of the previous literature reviews that are addressed by our study. More specifically, Iandoli et al. (2021) offer a broad overview of all kinds of research revolving around the themes of social media and polarization. This breadth of focus necessarily restricts the review's ability to answer specific questions precisely. The review study looks at significantly different types of fragmentation and polarization processes without conceptually disentangling them. Furthermore, the review does not focus solely on social media *effects* on polarization but considers, in addition, manifestations of polarization on social media platforms as well as "other online conversational platforms" (p. 1). The second review, by Kubin and von Sikorski (2021), approximates our study in terms of its focus and procedure. Yet the two studies differ in nuance, and most importantly, their corpora vary for several reasons. For instance, we excluded several studies that, in our reading, used the term "polarization" but, instead, investigated what we would call "fragmentation" processes. Contrary to existing literature reviews, we categorize the type of polarization investigated in a study based on the operationalization used rather than on the labeling used by a study's authors. We argue that this process is necessary to achieve comparable results in light of the conceptual vagueness of the field and significantly large discrepancies between studies in terms of labeling and operationalization. At the same time, our literature search resulted in a larger number of studies indicating depolarizing effects of social media use than the review by Kubin and von Sikorski (2021). This leads us to question the conclusion that there is "agreement across studies that social media, in a variety of contexts, can exacerbate both ideological and affective political polarization" (Kubin & von Sikorski, 2021, p. 196).

In the following, the concept of political polarization and its different dimensions will be defined and subsequently distinguished from the concept of fragmentation. Then, we briefly discuss the origins and consequences of political mass polarization and the role that social media technologies might play in this context. Finally, we delve into a systematic review of empirical evidence about social media effects on polarization

Political Mass Polarization: Concept and Overview

Research on political sociology, particularly from the United States, has carved out political polarization as one of the major factors affecting societal and political processes in recent decades (e.g., Fiorina & Abrams, 2008; Baldassarri & Gelman, 2008). As pointed out by DiMaggio et al. (1996), there are two different ways in which time can be considered when defining polarization as a concept: "Polarization is both a state and a process. Polarization as a state refers to the extent to which opinions on an issue are opposed in relation to some theoretical maximum. Polarization as a process refers to the increase in such opposition over time" (p.693). More recent scholarly definitions align with the perspective of polarization as a process—because determining a definite threshold at which topics or groups are polarized seems unrealistic (Fiorina & Abrams, 2008). For this research endeavor, we therefore adopt the definition by McCoy, Rahman, and Somer (2018), who conceptualized polarization as "a process whereby the normal multiplicity of differences in a society increasingly align along a single dimension" (p.16).

Forms and Measurement of Political Mass Polarization

This phenomenon is exactly what we have been witnessing in past decades, not just in the context of the US with its political landscape becoming steadily more polarized (e.g., McCarty, Poole & Rosenthal, 2006; Iyengar, Sood & Lelkes, 2012) and, at the same time, with growing animosities between the parties' electorates (e.g., Abramowitz & Sounders, 2008). These observations are also the main forms of political polarization that are traditionally distinguished: *elite polarization*, respectively *party polarization*, and *mass polarization*. Party polarization describes the polarization between the ruling party and the opposition party at the political system level (Baldassarri & Gelman, 2008). Mass polarization depicts a division

Katharina Ludwig & Philipp Müller

along party lines of the public's attitudes toward political topics, policies, politicians, or opposing political camps within the electorate (e.g., Fiorina & Abrams, 2008; McCarty et al., 2006; Layman, Carsey & Horowitz, 2006). Some researchers assume party polarization to be the main reason for mass polarization, as partisans align with their party's ideals and engage in behaviors that are, seemingly, in line with their party's objectives (e.g., Layman, Carsey, & Horowitz, 2006). Other scholars theorize that the opposite holds true, with party polarization resulting from the publics' separation in opposing camps (see, e.g., Fiorina et al., 2005). While this study focuses on the second form of polarization, the polarization of the electorate, it is important to keep in mind that the strength and particular forms of mass polarization within a society appear to be causally related to party polarization at the system level. This is particularly important to acknowledge for a literature review that attempts to integrate empirical findings from a diverse set of national contexts. Another important theoretical differentiation can be made between the above-mentioned mass polarization, measured on the level of individuals, for example, through surveys or experiments, and group polarization, measured on a group level through, for instance, network or content analyses. While mass polarization studies can make statements about individual polarization effects through the use of social media, studies on group polarization can identify superordinate polarization patterns at the group level.

Recent research has pinpointed the fact that different dimensions of mass polarization have to be disentangled. Some scholars argue that it appears as if US citizens, in particular, are increasingly agreeing on many political issue positions while, at the same time, the strength of partisan identifications and animosities between different political camps have profoundly massively increased (e.g., Baldassarri & Gelman, 2008; Iyengar, Sood, & Lelkes, 2012). Others argue that polarization in both dimensions is still on the rise (e.g., Abramowitz & Sounders, 2008; Abramowitz, 2010). To distinguish these two concepts, researchers have coined the terms *ideological polarization* (DiMaggio, Evans & Bryson, 1996) and *affective polarization* (Iyengar et al., 2019).

Affective and ideological polarization are both characterized by a separation of individuals of different political camps, typically from the ideological left and right, over policy differences (Webster & Abramowitz, 2017). In the case of *affective polarization,* this manifests in a strong liking for one's partisan party and a close attachment to it, accompanied by the simultaneous and equally strong dislike of the opposing party and preference for distance from it or its members. Affective polarization, therefore, is usually measured by surveys and experiments through a "feeling thermometer" (Stroud, 2010) calculating the participants' warmth toward their preferred party or political camp minus their warmth toward an opposing camp to compare inter- or intra-individual polarity scores. Other modes of operationalization involve measures of trait ratings toward the different camps' partisans, asking respondents, for instance, to rate their intelligence, generosity, and character or asking respondents what aspects they like and dislike about political parties and their voters (e.g., Levendusky & Malhotra, 2016; Garrett et al., 2014). In addition, Iyengar and Westwood (2015) adapted the Implicit Association Test (IAT) to capture unconscious partisan bias. Similarly, studies dealing with group polarization, using for example network, content, and sentiment analysis and a combination of different content features, such as ingroup vs. outgroup references combined with sentiment or other features, e.g., expressions of anxiety, anger, and the use of profanity, can be used to measure affective polarization (Gruzd & Roy, 2014; Bliuc, Smith & Moynihan, 2020; Mentzer, Fallon, Prichard & Yates, 2020).

Such operationalization is easily used in dual-party systems but poses problems for multi-party systems, as coalitions in such political systems are formed temporarily (Sened, 1996) and are characterized by floating affinities and animosities between parties beyond ideology. Therefore, it is generally not possible to identify clear "counterparties" in such systems, which allow using the common affective polarization measures that are considered dyads of political camps. Nevertheless, it is possible to capture affective polarization in multi-party systems by calculating an index of like/dislike scores across different political parties (Wagner, 2020). However, to the best of our knowledge, no studies thus far have used this operationalization.

A simpler approach omits negative sentiment toward an opposing political camp and focuses instead on *partisan polarization*. Studies following this approach usually measure merely the degree of partisans' attachments to their political camps. That is, participants are typically asked about their party identity directly or asked to locate themselves on a left–right or liberal–conservative scale. Some studies have also used profile information to derive the political ideology of users, and network analyses additionally determine the partisanship of social media users through the co-following or co-retweet networks (Grover et al., 2019). This operationalization of political polarization, of course, reduces the concept's explanatory power as it considers only half of the affective polarization process. At the same time, it might be more appropriate to capture polarization dynamics in multi-party systems in which there is not always a clear bipolar relationship between opposing political camps. Another reason to include studies based on partisan polarization in the present research is that this concept is used by several social-media-oriented polarization studies and, thereby, cannot be omitted from a literature review.

Ideological polarization, also referred to as "issue polarization" (Dylko et al., 2017) or "positional polarization" (Yarchi, Baden & Kligler-Vilenchik, 2020), is measured similarly to affective polarization. However, measures are based on issue stances or attitudes toward political topics such as climate change, health care, gay marriage, abortion laws, gun policy, or immigration (e.g., Bail et al. 2018; Cho et al. 2018). Commonly in surveys and experiments, attitudes about polarized or non-polarized topics from both opposing political camps are operationalized as several items, and the aggregation of agreement or disagreement with these statements by the participants results in a polarity score that leans toward, for example, rather liberal or conservative attitudes. However, the measurement of ideological polarization is not limited to surveys. Content analyses can be used to investigate users' issue stances voiced in social media posts or expressions of sentiment toward a particular topic (e.g., Yardi & Boyd, 2010; Yarchi, Baden, & Kligler-Vilenchik, 2020). Another way to measure ideological polarization in social media networks is the so-called modularity approach (e.g., Del Vicario et al., 2017; Zollo, 2019). Here, for example, the balance of a user's likes on social media posts or pages confirming or opposing an issue position is calculated. It is then interpreted as an estimator for the respective user's ideological position on the specific issue (e.g., Vicario et al., 2017).

Beyond that, the literature on social-media-related polarization effects includes a large body of research that applies network analysis methods. Most of this research uses interaction networks, retweet networks, or post-sharing networks as indicators of polarized communities, which are bound by a shared attitude toward a topic. Notably, these analytical network approaches typically do not include negative feedback (such as dislikes), whereby only half of the operationalization of polarization is achieved. Therefore, many network analyses are complemented by additional data, for example from sentiment analyses or external opinion polls. Conceptually, this line of research cannot be clearly allocated to either affective or ideological polarization (even though this may be true for particular studies). This is because these studies usually do not measure individuals' attitudes or feelings toward political camps or issues but, rather, interaction patterns at the group level. These patterns may, of course, mirror the group members' levels of affective or ideological polarization, but they are, at best, coarse indicators for affective or ideological polarization. Consequently, network analyses dealing with social-media-related polarization apply a variety of labels such as "group polarization" (Yardi & boyd, 2010), "user polarization" (Bessi et al., 2016), "information polarization" (Usui, Yoshida, & Torium, 2013) or "online polarization" (Bliuc, Smith, & Moynihan, 2020). Conceptually, such approaches seem to draw from the idea of fragmentation as well as the above-defined understanding of political mass polarization.

Therefore, before turning to the role of social media technologies as potential drivers of polarization, we need to consider one of the major underlying facilitators of political polarization that is frequently confused with the latter: the phenomenon of political fragmentation.

Political Mass Polarization and Fragmentation

Broadly stated, a society or a network is fragmented if it is separated into or consisting of several parts. In other words, the more fragmented a society or network is, the more divisions between groups can be found (Bright, 2018). On a societal level, this dynamic has been observed in recent years especially in the US context (Arceneaux & Johnson, 2010). Parallel to polarization, elites, parties, media, and societies as a whole can be fragmented. As political fragmentation is accompanied by decreased contact between the fragmented groups, it can reduce group members' abilities to engage in perspective-taking with regard to outgroup individuals. This, in turn, may lead to distancing between social groups or may even promote group-related hostility and, thereby, result ultimately in political mass polarization (Arceneaux & Johnson, 2010).

Empirically, fragmentation is usually assessed at the group level where the degree of social homophily within groups (e.g., McPherson, Smith-Lovin, & Cook, 2001) and group seclusiveness (Bright, 2018) are typical indicators. From a communication perspective, this includes the degree of exposure to diverse political information sources. The technological developments of the past decades, such as the expansion in the numbers of radio and TV stations as well as of newspapers and magazines, have led to broad accessibility of news content (e.g., Arceneaux & Johnson, 2010). This development climaxed in the evolution of the internet as humanity's central communication tool. However, the wide diversification of potential news sources comes with the increased likelihood of decreasing the overlap between the various news repertoires of different members of a society, which in turn makes the fragmentation of information exposure more likely. However, it is important to note that fragmentation research aims at patterns of high social homophily within - and low interaction between

- groups, while mass polarization (as defined above) is typically studied by looking at how the separation of political camps within a society is reflected in individual persons' cognitions and emotions. Thus, the unit of analysis for fragmentation research is group composition and group-level behaviors, while for polarization research, it is individuals' group-oriented cognitions and emotions.

Similarly, political mass polarization can be seen as both a potential driver and outcome of fragmentation processes (Arceneaux & Johnson, 2010). As fragmented communities tend to narrow the scope of available information and reinforce existing beliefs, individual viewpoints might move farther away from more moderate attitudes and toward more extreme ones, and the differences and distance between ideological viewpoints may, in turn, grow (Arceneaux & Johnson, 2010). Of course, the opposite causal pathway almost certainly occurs at the same time, with mass polarization leading to a fragmented social landscape. As a result, mass polarization and fragmentation are mutually dependent. However, they do not refer to the same concept and, therefore, should not be equated in scientific research. Fragmentation and mass polarization are different processes and have different underlying mechanisms. Notably, fragmentation does not necessarily lead to political polarization, but it provides fertile ground for polarization.

Origins and Consequences of Political Mass Polarization

The societal consequences of increasing mass polarization are manifold. Partisan polarization, for instance, appears to strongly affect social relationships. This goes as far as leaning toward hiring staff with congruent partisanship (Iyengar & Westwood, 2015), preferences for romantic relationships, and the selection of friends who are co-partisans (e.g., Huber & Malhotra, 2017; Pew Research Center, 2017; Bakshy, Messing, & Adamic, 2015), and extends even to families becoming increasingly ideologically homogeneous. In 2018, 80% of married couples agreed on party identification; for parents and children, the agreement was 75% (Iyengar, Konitzer, & Tedin, 2018). Furthermore, people prefer living in areas comprised mostly of fellow partisans (Gimpel & Hui 2015). Studies have also identified economic transactions being affected by co-partisanship, with, for example, taxi drivers in Ghana demanding higher prices from counter-partisans (Michelitch, 2015) and US American citizens being willing to pay almost double for a gift card sold by a co-partisan in contrast to one sold by a counter-partisan (McConnell et al., 2018). Polarization also has consequences for political processes. Growing animosities between counter-partisans, for example, make it more difficult to reach consensus; they affect voting decisions (Bartels, 2000) and can lead to growing opinion radicalization (Baldassarri & Gelman, 2008) or even political violence (Jensen et al., 2012). Taking into consideration these various domains of societal life, which are in one way or another being affected by mass polarization, it does not seem overstated to argue that political mass polarization poses a serious threat to social cohesion at the structural level. Sociologically, this means that increasing mass polarization (as documented for a number of countries over the last several decades; see, for example, Boxell et al., 2020) has the potential to endanger the functioning of human coexistence within a society.

In light of these consequences, it is important to investigate the origins of increasing polarization. In the research landscape, three lines of argument are typically emphasized for this purpose: (1.) social-identity-based explanations, (2.) ideology-based explanations, and (3.) information-exposure-based explanations. Notably, while these three lines of reasoning can be distinguished, they are also intertwined in many respects and, therefore, have to be considered complementary rather than competing mechanisms.

The first line of argument, identity-based explanations, underscores how political parties or camps increasingly serve as donors of collective identity for partisans seeking positively charged social entities with which they can identify in order to gain a positive self-image. As a byproduct, this process is also deemed to facilitate outgroup prejudice (Brewer, 1999) and, thereby, increase affective polarization (Mason, 2016). Fundamental to this concept is partisan identity acquired at a young age and frequently expressed in recurring political campaigns. Consequently, partisans build a sense of group identity with their co-partisans that can become more or less central to their self-concept. While outgroup derogation is a potential consequence of all social-identity processes (Brewer, 1999), devaluing opposing partisan groups in a political context appears even more likely since different political camps are, by nature, in opposition to each other (Iyengar, Sood, & Lelkes, 2012).

The second line of argument, ideology-based explanations, asserts that political mass polarization occurs as a consequence of political parties' ideological disparities (Webster & Abramowitz, 2017). They assume that, if the ideological distance between the different parties of a political system grows, this will lead citizens to perceive candidates or parties as polarized. For partisans, this perception of ideological gap formation may induce an urge to reaffirm their own ideological beliefs and partisan identity and corroborate their rejection of diverging ideologies and identities (Rogowski & Sutherland, 2016). However, rather than regarding ideological conflict as a unilateral cause for partisan polarization, there seem to be mutual interrelations between both factors (Lelkes, 2018).

Finally, the third line of argument, information-exposure-based explanations, suggests that exposure to one-sided political content strengthens partisan identities and ideological beliefs, thereby facilitating political mass polarization (Garrett et al., 2014; Lau et al., 2017). While this research is set in the context of traditional mass-media channels, it has been argued that the internet's high-choice media environment (van Aelst et al., 2017) might have, once again, increased media impact on polarization processes.

Social Media Use: A Driver of Political Mass Polarization?

Within the debate about the internet's role in increasing political mass polarization, social media platforms are a crucial factor. When these technologies emerged, their services were predominantly understood as allowing "individuals to (1) construct a public or semi-public profile within a bounded system, (2) articulate a list of other users with whom they share a connection, and (3) view and traverse their list of connections and those made by others within the system" (boyd & Ellison, 2007). In the field of political communication research especially, the focus of attention has since shifted from users' abilities to self-present and connect via social media to the content to which they are exposed on these platforms. The infamous "news feed" and its algorithm-driven content selection now play a prominent role in the debate (see, e.g., Bode, 2016). From a business perspective, the central goal of social media's platform architectures is to maximize the time users spend on a platform because this maximizes ad revenues (Cohen, 2018). To achieve this goal, it is often argued that social media platforms' algorithms apply a "more-of-the-same" logic: They identify users' individual content preferences by tracking user behavior within the platform ecosystem (and beyond) and then attempt to serve individual users a content diet that aligns perfectly with their needs and interests. That being said, it is frequently assumed that, in terms of political content, this means users are going to encounter mainly messages that fit their political interests and convictions on social media platforms (which might reinforce their existing attitudes and partisan identities).

This potential mechanism has been popularized in Eli Pariser's (2011) "filter bubble" metaphor, which assumes that algorithmic content selection on social media platforms ultimately promotes political polarization. This is frequently referred to alongside the "echo chamber" metaphor offered by Cass Sunstein (2001). The latter argues that users' own content-selection choices in high-choice media environments (van Aelst et al., 2017) may lead to homogeneous information environments that could also contribute to mass polarization. However, empirical evidence on whether algorithmic content selection or users' own selection decisions produce such homogeneous information environments in online ecosystems is mixed at best (see, e.g., Bakshy et al., 2015; Bruns, 2019; Flaxman et al., 2016; Möller et al., 2018; Scharkow et al., 2020; Zuiderveen Borgesius et al., 2016), with the occurrence of "echo chambers" appearing somewhat more likely than the emergence of "filter bubbles" (Flaxman et al., 2016). Moreover, even if patterns of homogeneous information environments emerged on a larger scale within online ecosystems, whether or not these "echo chambers," "filter bubbles," or "rabbit holes" actually promoted political mass polarization would still be unclear. For instance, it might very well be that homogeneous information environments have calming instead of radicalizing effects on many individuals since they offer less irritation than exposure to cross-cutting messages (Bor & Petersen, 2021).

Moreover, the entire debate on social media environments potentially contributing to polarization seems somewhat limited to "filter bubble" and "echo chamber" perspectives. Yet various other features and modalities of social media use might also contribute to mass polarization, perhaps to an even greater extent; however, for the most part, these are left untouched in the debate. For instance, it could be argued that the overrepresentation of negative sentiment and hateful expressions of opinion on social media platforms might deepen cleavages between different political camps (Bor & Petersen, 2021; Harel et al., 2020). Or social media self-effects that occur if a person has (semi-)publicly made a political statement might contribute to a radicalization of that person's political convictions and identifications (Valkenburg, 2017). Therefore, the present literature review is not limited to the "filter bubble" or "echo chamber" perspectives but attempts instead to systematically disentangle what is known empirically about the different, potentially causal mechanisms between social media use and political mass polarization.

Procedure

Literature Selection

Articles for this literature review were selected from EBSCO's *Communication & Mass Media Complete* database as well as *Semantic Scholar*

Katharina Ludwig & Philipp Müller

and had to be published in the period between 2004 and May 2021. To include all relevant articles, we searched for different keyword combinations. We combined the terms "polarization"/"polarisation" with the keyword terms "filter bubble," "echo chamber" or "rabbit hole" and with "social media," in addition to the names of the most common social media platforms ("Twitter," "Facebook, "YouTube," "TikTok," "Instagram," "Reddit," "VKontakte," and "Weibo"). For *Semantic Scholar,* we restricted the search to the fields of sociology, psychology, political science, and computer science and the type of publication to journal articles and conference contributions. For *Communication & Mass Media Complete,* we confined the search to academic journals in the English language. This resulted in a list of roughly 300 articles each from the two databases.

Literature Categorization

After gathering the initial corpus of potentially relevant studies, several selection steps were performed to arrive at a final collection of studies of interest. First, as *Semantic Scholar* also includes preprints, we eliminated studies that were not yet published in peer-reviewed outlets (by the end of May 2021). In the next step, the more-specific eligibility for each publication was determined based on its title, abstract, and—in the case of uncertainty—a full-text read. We narrowed the corpus to a set of empirical articles that dealt explicitly with both social media platforms and political polarization; this meant that research looking at non-political polarization (such as gender or age polarization) was excluded. Likewise, the role of social media platforms had to be an operationalized variable as well. Therefore, either social-media-use variables had to be measured empirically; content had to be posted on social media platforms; relationships between social media users had to be analyzed, or the research had to be embedded in an experimental setting that included social media environments. Studies using social media or political polarization as mere interpretational concepts were eliminated. Furthermore, we excluded studies that relied fully on non-empirical data, such as simulations-based research. This selection step resulted in a total of $n = 88$ studies, for which the full texts were read and will be analyzed in the following.

To gain a better overview of the study results, we categorized them according to their operationalization of polarization: (a.) fragmentation studies, (b.) group polarization studies, and (c.) mass polarization studies.

Review of Studies

Fragmentation or Polarization?

Before going into detail concerning studies that have analyzed group polarization and mass polarization effects, we provide a brief insight into several studies we found through our literature research. We recognized that the operationalization of polarization in several studies was actually one of fragmentation. As previously described, fragmentation and its related concepts as homophily or information diversity are closely connected to polarization and may play a critical role in the polarization process. Nevertheless, a measurement of fragmentation aspects does not necessarily measure polarization (effects); however, almost half of the studies we gathered do not operationalize polarization per se but still frame their research endeavor in this way. This alone is an interesting observation that may help to disentangle the conceptual and operational confusion in this research area. Therefore, although they did not meet our previously defined criteria, we still decided to include a brief overview of these studies and their results. It is important to note, however, that our search does not include a full picture of fragmentation/homophily studies. We report only on studies that frame their research endeavor as a measure of polarization and, thus, were identified through our keyword search.

In this category, we found 41 studies. Their respective operationalization of polarization includes measures of network homophily (n = 19); the density of connections within a network (n = 6), for example, measured through modularity approaches; measures of content diversity (n = 5); and the application of community detection algorithms (n = 4), such as the random walk controversy (RWC). Additionally, we found studies (n = 9) that merely determined the number of partisan users on social media and compared that with poll or election results. These nine studies will not be discussed in greater detail as their results show simply that users on social media are as fragmented as the electorate and, therefore, constitute a reflection of the offline social world. All the aforementioned measures might yield results about polarization processes or effects when combined with other measurements, but used alone, these variants of operationalization cannot illustrate the full polarization process. This is because, as we have argued in the definitions section of this chapter, homophily, content diversity, or network structure alone are not sufficient indicators of political polarization.

It is noteworthy that of the 32 studies we consider as capturing fragmentation rather than polarization, 26 analyzed Twitter, whereas the actual

Katharina Ludwig & Philipp Müller

polarization studies consider a much more balanced variety of social media platforms. The majority of fragmentation studies found what is called "polarization" in their respective arguments (n = 16). Another 12 studies yielded mixed effects—for instance, that a retweet network is "polarized" whereas a mention network is not (Conover et al., 2011), that partisan users formed highly partisan networks, whereas moderate users did not (Kearney, 2019), or that partisanship was less dominant if users had many cross-stance relations (Lai et al., 2019). Additionally, one study found no effects (Garimella, Morales, Gionis, & Mathioudakis, 2017), and another identified a reduction in network homophily over time (Lee & Hahn, 2017). Furthermore, many studies in this category found that, before and during election periods, more fragmentation was present (e.g., Yang et al., 2017; Kearney, 2019; Lai et al., 2019).

The fact that many of these fragmentation studies claim to have documented "polarization" within social media environments might help to explain why the general perception that social media leads to political polarization is so widespread. This argument is further pronounced when comparing these findings with the more inconclusive results found in actual mass polarization studies (see the following sections). The studies discussed here help us observe processes of fragmentation and *potential* signs of political polarization on social media. However, they do not help us to clarify whether political mass polarization is actually enhanced by social media use. For this, we need to take a much closer, in-depth look at the evidence about group polarization and mass polarization effects caused by social media use.

Group Polarization

Analyses of group polarization allow the observation of group dynamics on a larger scale but not of the effects on single individuals. Group polarization occurs when, after participating or being exposed to a discussion or taking part in other group activities, group members are reinforced in their sense of belonging and, consequently, become more extreme in their ideological or affective positions in concordance with their group's collective position (Isenberg, 1986). The difference between this and mass polarization is that, in terms of group polarization, dynamics can be determined on a group level but not traced back to individual polarization processes and effects. These patterns can also be divided into ideological, affective, and partisan (de)polarization, but they should not be misinterpreted as describing *effects* of social media use.

In the category of group polarization, we found 18 studies published in 13 different journals plus five different conference proceedings (for a full overview, see Appendix 1). Of these 18 studies, 10 articles were published between 2019 and 2021 and the remaining eight between 2010 and 2018. In addition, 13 studies conducted network analyses, most in combination with other methods such as content or sentiment analyses; four studies performed qualitative or automated content analyses, and one study conducted an observation. In our sample, we found eight studies that analyzed Twitter, six that analyzed Facebook, one that researched YouTube, and three that compared two or more platforms. Six studies were conducted in the US American context; there were two studies each in Hong Kong and Israel, three in other country contexts (Italy, Canada, Australia), and two studies compared two or more countries. Four studies were conducted during election periods and four during heightened periods of political conflict (the Hong Kong protests and the Israeli–Palestinian conflict). The remaining studies were not conducted during election periods or at least did not specify so. Of these 18 studies, 10 looked at the development of group polarization over time, with time frames ranging from 24 hours to more than seven years. Eight studies were conducted in dual political systems, six in multi-party environments (but four of the six studies examined the dual contexts of Hong Kong and Israel–Palestine), and two studies compared several countries with different party systems. Nine studies in this category measured ideological polarization, five measured affective polarization, one study measured partisan polarization, another measured affective as well as ideological polarization, and two studies analyzed all three types of polarization.

Two studies that combined content analyses and opinion polls found that "cyberbalkanization" (fragmentation on the internet) and ideological polarization were related among young adults in Hong Kong (Chan & Fu, 2015, 2017). Another study that conducted an automated content analysis found that intergroup interactions characterized by direct dissent were drivers of affective polarization (Bliuc, Smith, & Moynihan, 2020). Furthermore, by comparing the two platforms Facebook and YouTube, one observation showed that the content, more than the algorithm, drove ideological polarization (Bessi et al., 2016). Concerning qualitative results from content analyses, one study found that right-wing users voiced a clear demarcation between (as well as the rejection and dehumanization of) the opposing political camp in Israel (Harel, Jameson, & Maoz, 2020). Another study found US Facebook and Twitter users to be polarized along party lines, whereas Dutch users demonstrated less party-related polarization. Instead, they drew a line between ordinary citizens and the elite

(Hameleers, 2020). The third qualitative study found tweets labeled as conservative to contain more negative perceptions toward the US healthcare reform, while tweets considered as liberal suggested the opposite and the majority of all tweets indicated some dislike of "the other" (Mendez, Cosby, & Mohanty, 2017).

Other studies that conducted content and network analyses found similarly differentiated results. For example, US American climate-change disbelievers on Twitter showed higher levels of hostility toward climate-change believers than vice versa (Tyagi, Uyheng, & Carley, 2020). In addition, conservatives in the US tweeted about ingroup candidates more positively and, simultaneously, more negatively about opposing candidates than did liberals (Mentzer, Fallon, Prichard, & Yates, 2020). Moreover, more Twitter users were found to be both positively and negatively polarized toward Hilary Clinton in comparison to Donald Trump (Grover et al., 2019), and men on Twitter appeared to voice less ingroup party support and less dislike of the out-group party than women did (Mentzer, Fallon, Prichard, & Yates, 2020). Furthermore, several studies identified homophily at work (Yardi & boyd, 2010; Gruzd & Roy, 2014), with interactions with like-minded individuals on Twitter strengthening group identity, whereas engagement with different-minded individuals reinforced ingroup and outgroup affiliations (Yardi & boyd, 2010). Moreover, higher engagement seems to have led to a higher number of polarized users (Grover et al., 2019), and users expressing negativity in their tweets were more ideologically polarized, while, surprisingly, negativity in the user's social environment had a depolarizing effect on ideological positions (Buder et al., 2021). Yarchi, Baden, and Kligler-Vilenchik (2020) analyzed Twitter, Facebook, and WhatsApp and found that only Twitter displays clear signs of political-group polarization. They found homophilic interaction patterns present, an increase in ideological polarization, and hostility between users of opposed camps—a sign of affective polarization. For WhatsApp, despite of the heterogeneous composition of the analyzed groups, a shared group identity and common purpose counteracted the polarization dynamics and even led to depolarization of its users. Facebook, in turn, was "found to be the least homophilic platform in terms of interactions, positions, and emotions expressed" (Yarchi, Baden and Kligler-Vilenchik, 2020, p. 1). Furthermore, we encountered four studies using modularity network approaches based on "likes" on Facebook. Contrary to the mixed and rather idiosyncratic results described above, the studies using a modularity approach all found ideological polarization present on Facebook. This might be due to the one-sidedness of the modularity approach: In all four cases, only the positive reactions (likes) were considered, whereas negative reactions and opinions are not captured. Therefore, only half of the operationalization of ideological polarization, as described above, is included, which might bias results.

To summarize, group polarization studies exhibit significantly differentiated results, often holding only for specific groups of people or certain circumstances. Thus, this line of research is unable to support the idea of strong, generalized group polarization on social media platforms.

Mass Polarization

Quantitative Review of Studies

In the final selection step, we considered only studies that *empirically tested ideological, affective,* or *partisan polarization effects at the individual level.* This means that a larger number of studies focusing on aspects such as network homophily within social media platforms or group polarization were omitted in this step since they do not offer points of comparison that would allow making causal inferences about individual social media effects on political polarization of the public. This selection process yielded 31 studies published between 2014 and 2021, with a large majority (n = 23) published between 2018 and 2021. Articles were published in 23 different journals and the proceedings of one conference; 16 studies conducted surveys, 13 conducted experiments, and two combined surveys with observations. Of these 31 studies, 23 were originally developed for this research purpose, and eight used secondary data provided, for example, by the National Annenberg Election Survey or the Eurobarometer. Sample sizes ranged from n = 21 to n = 37,494, and 14 studies use representative, quota, or stratified samples, five used student samples, and the remaining 12 studies used convenience samples or did not specify their sampling procedure.

The majority of the studies analyzed (the frequency of) social media use in general (n = 10) or news consumption habits in social media environments (n = 6) as predictors of polarization. But some also analyzed polarization effects on specific social media platforms, as follows: YouTube (n = 3), Twitter (n = 2), Facebook (n = 5), Facebook and Twitter (n = 3), Facebook and KakaoTalk (n = 1), and WhatsApp (n = 1). Of these studies, five focused additionally on the influence of algorithmic news recommendations and customization options. The vast majority of studies (n = 20) were conducted in the US; of the remaining studies, three were conducted in Hong Kong, four in South Korea, three in different European countries

Katharina Ludwig & Philipp Müller

(Norway, Denmark, Netherlands), one in multiple European countries simultaneously, and one in Kenya. Thereby, 20 studies were conducted in a dual-party system, and the remaining 11 were conducted in multi-party systems (including three studies from the dual context of Hong Kong and other countries with multi-party systems dominated by two major political parties, i.e., South Korea and Kenya). Seven studies in all were conducted during election periods and the remaining studies were not. Three other studies, nevertheless, were conducted during heightened political conflict in Hong Kong and one study prior to a referendum in the Netherlands.

Eight of the studies measured affective polarization; 12 analyzed ideological polarization; and five selected partisan polarization as their dependent variable of interest. In addition, three studies incorporated measures of both ideological and affective or partisan polarization, and three analyzed all three types of polarization.

Of the 31 studies, eight identified ideological polarization patterns through social media use; three studies found affective polarization effects and three found partisan polarization effects. Three studies found only depolarization effects (affective and ideological, which includes one study where depolarization could be observed after deactivating Facebook), and two studies identified depolarization effects and no polarization simultaneously (affective and ideological). Seven studies found no polarization effects at all (affective, ideological, or partisan). The remaining six studies found mixed results, such as both polarization effects and depolarization effects or no polarization.

Topics analyzed in terms of ideological polarization are, on one hand, commonly discussed issues such as immigration, the economy, education, crime, health care, taxes, same-sex marriage, and feelings and attitudes toward candidates. On the other hand, more specific topics, such as North Korea, relations between the US and China, or investigations regarding Russian interference in elections are discussed. Several studies included both polarized and less-polarized topics.

Qualitative Review of Studies

Across all types of political polarization (affective, ideological, and partisan), our analysis indicates that there are several groups of main factors that appear to influence individual political polarization and depolarization processes.

The first factor found to be politically polarizing is the *frequency of social media use* or reliance on social media for news and political information.

This factor was considered mostly in studies based on survey designs, including surveys using longitudinal data as well as those dependent on cross-sectional data. Although only longitudinal data can provide causal inferences, we found no structural differences in the results between these two designs; thus, all findings will be presented together. In such research, the reliance on social media for political information was shown to affectively polarize users (Johnson, Kaye, & Lee, 2017), and time spent on social media indirectly heightened ideological polarization, especially for those users who frequently encountered like-minded information (Lu et al., 2020). Similarly, when users deactivated Facebook, they encountered less opinion-confirming partisan information, which, in turn, led to a decrease in all three types of polarization (Allcott et al., 2020). Likewise, it was found that active social media users had a higher likelihood of becoming engaged in political processes, which led them, in turn, to become ideologically more polarized than non-users (Lee, Shin, & Hong, 2018). Furthermore, users of social media and partisans were shown to become ideologically more polarized, whereas people using traditional media did not (Ohme, 2021; Suk et al., 2020). In contrast, another study found that the use of partisan mass media, as well as demographic factors (e.g., gender, age), had a stronger influence on ideological polarization than the use of social media (Lee et al., 2018). In line with this, Nguyen and Vu (2019) showed that reliance on social media did not ideologically polarize users more than participants relying on traditional media for political information. In total, in this category, we find evidence focused almost exclusively on ideological polarization with significantly mixed results, which might stem from the very general operationalization of social media use as a frequency measure.

Second, the strength of *partisanship and party ties* was found to play a crucial role in the process of polarization (e.g., Min & Yun, 2018). Party ties seemed to be strengthened by the use of social media (Cho et al., 2018), with stronger ties enhancing selective exposure, which led, in turn, to ideological polarization (Johnson, Kaye, & Lee, 2017). Nevertheless, political orientation had a stronger effect on ideological polarization than the use of social media (Lee et al., 2018), and social media use was not related to partisan polarization for moderate partisans (Lee, Shin, & Hong, 2018). This evidence becomes most clear by comparing single identifiers with dual identifiers, which showed that people who identified with only one political camp become more polarized through the use of social media (for all three types of polarization), whereas depolarization was observed for people identifying with both political ideologies (Kobayashi, 2020). The influence of partisanship was found almost exclusively in dual political contexts. Therefore, it seems appropriate to conclude that people with strong party ties and a strong partisan identity in countries with clear opposing camps become more polarized through the use of social media, without generalizing these findings for all contexts and population groups.

Another group of factors that we discovered involves the *content* to which social media users are exposed or with which they engage. Here we differentiate between (a.) pro-attitudinal exposure, (b.) counter-attitudinal exposure, and (c.) pro- and counter-attitudinal expression.

Concerning pro-attitudinal exposure, research yielded highly mixed results. Twitter was found to heighten partisan polarization through the display of mostly opinion-confirming information (Hahn, Ryu, & Park, 2015). Facebook was also shown to reduce the likelihood of encountering counter-attitudinal news content, which increased affective polarization in comparison to counter-attitudinal news exposure (Levy, 2020), and Min and Yin (2018) found selective exposure toward political information to heighten affective polarization on KakaoTalk and, to a lesser extent, on Facebook. Similarly, the amount of time spent on social media indirectly heightened ideological polarization, especially for users who frequently encountered like-minded information (Lu et al., 2020). In contrast, Johnson et al. (2020) found that ideological polarization was not heightened through exposure to either pro- or counter-attitudinal information on Facebook. Likewise, Kim and Kim (2019) demonstrated that exposure to opinion-confirming comments did not affect ideological polarization.

Studies that looked at counter-attitudinal news exposure also found contradictory results. Beam, Hutchens, and Hmielowski (2018), for example, found counter-attitudinal news exposure on Facebook to increase over time, leading to a modest affective depolarization, whereas Levy (2020) found Facebook to decrease users' counter-attitudinal news exposure and, conversely, to increase pro-attitudinal news exposure, which heightened affective and ideological polarization. Furthermore, Bail et al. (2018) identified a backfire effect and an increase of ideological polarization through counter-attitudinal exposure for Republicans on Twitter. The latter study, however, forced users to expose themselves to counter-attitudinal news, which might have led to a negative predisposition and aversion toward the presented content beforehand.

Next to the causal dimensions of exposure to news content, behavioral components in the context of potentially polarizing content were also considered in past research. This includes pro- and counter-attitudinal expression, for example in the form of sharing news content as well as commenting on news or discussing it with other users. Turning to these studies investigating pro- and counter-attitudinal expression, Johnson et al. (2020) found that sharing pro-attitudinal news articles on Facebook led to ideological polarization, whereas sharing counter-attitudinal news articles reduced ideological polarization. Kibet and Ward (2018) found higher levels of political discussion on WhatsApp to increase ideological and affective polarization, whereas, somewhat contradictorily, for respondents commenting more frequently on news, a reduction of both kinds of polarization was observed. This is contrasted by Cho et al.'s (2018) study that found YouTube users who express opinions about election campaigns to be strengthened in their initial opinion and to be affectively polarized. These contradictions might be explained by Karlsen et al.'s (2017) finding showing that discussions with both opponents and supporters on Facebook or Twitter might reinforce the preexisting attitude, possibly because of the aforementioned backfire effect. They also found that these effects were stronger for individuals with strong attitudes compared to those with moderate attitudes. Additionally, Shmargad and Klar (2019) demonstrated that those who are aware of their social surroundings share more moderate news articles when confronted with an out-group environment, whereas those previously enclosed by echo chambers share their preexisting (and more extreme) views independently of their social environment in the context of social networks.

Connected to the latter is the factor of *network heterogeneity*. Here again, we find very mixed results. Network heterogeneity on social media in general was shown to decrease ideological polarization (Lee & Choi, 2020), whereas, in the case of WhatsApp in Kenya, higher levels of network heterogeneity increased ideological and affective polarization (Kibet & Ward, 2018). Representing greater differentiation, Lee et al. (2014) found higher levels of social network diversity to increase partisan polarization for individuals participating in more political discussions, whereas almost no effect was observed for those joining fewer political discussions.

The last group of factors comprises studies dealing with the role of **recommendation systems** or customization options implemented in social media. One study found that, in an experimental setup, customization on social media led to selective exposure, which heightened ideological polarization (Dylko et al., 2017). Similarly, affective polarization was heightened through YouTube's recommendation system in an experimental setup on the platform itself by providing opinion-confirming information (Hilbert et al., 2018). Other studies, by contrast, did not find affective polarization to be increased by users' customization preferences, and social preferences, i.e., the preferences of the users' social environment, were found in an experimental setup on YouTube as well as based on survey results to even reduce affective polarization (Cho et al., 2020; Feezell,

Katharina Ludwig & Philipp Müller

Wagner, & Conroy, 2021). Furthermore, sorting articles by popularity did not increase partisan polarization (Shmargad & Klar, 2020).

Nevertheless, probably the most-overlooked category in polarization research is that with null findings concerning polarization effects. Our analysis, however, demonstrates a considerable share of published empirical studies yielding null effects. For instance, ideological polarization was not affected in one study when users were exposed to uncivil commentary attacking the other side of an issue on YouTube (Hwang, Kim, & Huh, 2014). According to Munger et al. (2020), affective polarization was also not increased through partisan clickbait headlines on Facebook and Twitter. Lee and Choi (2020) demonstrated that individuals who fear others with opposing views and those who feel disadvantaged or excluded from dominant positions might adhere stick to their initial viewpoints; thus, ideological polarization was neither reduced nor heightened in this case either.

Overall, we find many mixed and often contradictory results. Therefore, in the following, we discuss structural differences between studies conducted in multi-party and dual-party contexts, studies that analyzed different social media platforms, and polarization and fragmentation studies—and the extent to which these differences might have affected the studies' results.

Evidence from Dual-Party Systems and Multi-Party Systems

Almost two-thirds of the studies analyzing mass polarization effects at the individual level were conducted in the US context; for studies analyzing group polarization, the US focus was slightly less dominant, yet still about half were conducted in this dual-party system. Another quarter of all studies concerning group and mass polarization effects were conducted in other countries with dual-party or multi-party systems dominated by two major political parties (e.g., the UK, South Korea, Kenya, Australia) or in countries with heightened political conflict between two groups (Hong Kong, Israel). This might be caused by polarization being a more severe problem in these contexts, but it may also be that measures are more easily operationalized if two clearly antagonistic groups contribute to this pattern. Both reasons may also help explain why, with very few exemptions, all studies considering affective polarization as an outcome of social media use were conducted in these dual contexts, whereas ideological and partisan polarization were analyzed almost exclusively in multi-party environments.

Specific Social Media Platforms and Method Choices

Most studies analyzing specific social media platforms focused on Facebook and Twitter, and a few each on YouTube, WhatsApp, and Kakao-Talk. Although researchers have complained about the dominance of Twitter studies (Kubin & von Sikorski, 2021), we found such research to be dominant only in the area of fragmentation studies and only using "polarization" as a label, whereas for actual group or mass polarization studies, we saw a more balanced focus on different social media platforms. The difference between studies researching group polarization and those analyzing mass polarization effects is interesting: While studies analyzing mass polarization effects on Facebook found an exceptionally high number of depolarization and null effects of social media use, studies analyzing group polarization on Facebook found polarization effects (with the exemption of Buder et al., 2021). Additionally, studies of group polarization on Twitter found numerous patterns of polarization, whereas studies of mass polarization effects on Twitter and YouTube returned mixed results. This suggests that differences in operationalization resulted in this disparity. While group polarization was analyzed using content and network analyses, mass polarization effects were detected through surveys and experiments. This means that content and network analyses appear to be more prone to identifying patterns of polarization mirrored on social media platforms at the group level, whereas surveys and experiments at the individual level show few actual polarization effects of using specific social media platforms.

That the operationalization of social media use plays a critical role is also suggested by examining studies that employ modularity approaches. All these found polarization effects due to their one-sided approach; as described above, only the positive reactions (likes) were considered, whereas negative reactions and opinions were not captured. This omits half of the theoretical concept of polarization. Another methodological decision stands out regarding the group of studies operationalizing the frequency of generalized social media use. These studies found comparatively few depolarization effects or null effects. This might be due to the broad operationalization of "frequency of" or "reliance on" social media use used in most of the surveys, through which it is not possible to fully capture the depth and facets of social media usage as participants' self-disclosure is vulnerable to forgetfulness, social desirability, and other distortions. Furthermore, only some surveys analyzed longitudinal data; hence, causality might not always be assumed. In total, 19 of 31 research projects conducted studies with designs that allowed causal inferences, such as analyzing longitudinal data or conducting experiments. As previously noted, no clear patterns within

Katharina Ludwig & Philipp Müller

this group of studies and no differences between them were found; these studies, in addition, found both polarization and depolarization effects as well as no polarization effects for all three forms of political polarization (affective, ideological, and partisan).

Fragmentation vs. Polarization Studies

Despite the general belief that before and during elections political polarization increases, we could not find any systematic evidence in this structured literature review that an election taking place during the study period heightened any kind of political polarization. Nevertheless, this was a recurring finding in the fragmentation studies found by our literature search since they used the label "polarization." This supports the assumption that inconsistencies in operationalization and concepts distort conclusions about polarization effects. Conclusively, it seems that fragmentation is heightened on social media platforms before and during electoral campaigns but not necessarily political mass polarization.

Another structural difference identified between the fragmentation and polarization studies in this review is the strong concentration of fragmentation studies on the homophily of users. This might stem from the methodological dominance of network analyses in this category, which inherently have a focus on the compilation of users in different clusters, whereas in studies conducting experiments and surveys, this aspect is more difficult to measure. While the homogeneity of users within clusters is seen as evidence of political polarization in the fragmentation studies, the studies on mass polarization present a more nuanced picture.

Furthermore, fragmentation studies find "polarization effects" almost exclusively, while studies analyzing group polarization and individual polarization effects also find many depolarization effects and more-differentiated results, with heightened polarization being identified only for a certain group of social media users, for example. Again, this supports the assumption that conceptual unclarities and different ways of operationalization in this research field resulted in an overstatement of the role social media plays in the political polarization process.

Takeaways and Research Desiderata

Overall, we found significantly heterogeneous findings, conceptually overlapping constructs, and an inconclusive empirical research landscape. As polarization research has gained increasingly more attention in the past decade, the term "polarization" seems to be used frequently as a catchword rather than being an actual essential concept in a research endeavor. Frequently, the concepts of fragmentation and polarization appear to be equated, and distinctions between group and individual polarization effects are often not clarified. Definitions of and differentiations between the different dimensions of political polarization may be lacking or not applied. Therefore, first and foremost, in future polarization research, we plead for conceptual clarity and the provision of definitions of relevant concepts. Our literature review has proposed a typology of patterns of fragmentation, group, and mass polarization that may help ensure greater precision in the research landscape.

Concerning the role social media plays in the political polarization process, it is difficult to make universal statements based on the empirical findings generated thus far. Nevertheless, one unambiguous statement we can make based on our systematic review of empirical literature is that people with strong party ties and a strong partisan identity in countries with clear opposing camps become more polarized through the use of social media. Therefore, partisanship seems to play a major role in the polarization process and should be an essential component of future research in this area.

The same applies to the content that users consume and interact with on social media platforms. A substantial amount of research already concentrates on this aspect, but findings are inconclusive. (De)polarization effects have been observed both for exposure to and interaction with attitude-confirming and attitude-opposing content. Future research should, therefore, focus on disentangling these effects by applying comparable definitions and operationalization.

Furthermore, research analyzing algorithms or including actual running algorithms remains scarce. Thus far, most studies have used proxies for the role played by algorithmic recommendation systems, such as experimental setups with mock recommendations or survey designs (sometimes combined with behavioral web-tracking data). This low external validity leads to disparities between real-world social media use and research results. Nevertheless, it seems that these few studies agree on the finding that attitude-congruent content exposure evoked by a recommendation system heightened polarization.

Finally, our review of extant research indicates many other influences on political polarization, such as the strength of partisanship, polarized contexts, use of traditional media, personal conversations, age, or gender. These variables are often included as controls in empirical studies focusing on the effects of social media use. However, in many studies these control variables proved to produce a much stronger impact on polarization than social media use did. This indicates that social media is not as polarizing as popular discourse assumes; rather, a combination of different factors has to come into play to create strong polarization effects. As social media use itself is co-varying with many of the aforementioned third variables, it is crucial for future research on social-media-induced polarization effects to include a multitude of control variables to avoid producing false positive results as a result of omitted variable bias (Clarke, 2009).

Turning toward the methodological decisions and their implementations, we found a strong bias for studies dealing with political polarization to be conducted in dual-party contexts, especially in the US. Regarding the mass polarization effects of social media use in particular, we did not observe systematic differences between dual-party and multi-party contexts. It appears that the same mechanisms play a central role both in multi- and dual-party contexts. However, methodologically, we see that, with very few exceptions, all studies interested in affective polarization were conducted in dual contexts, whereas in multi-party environments, ideological and partisan polarization were analyzed almost exclusively. Therefore, we plead for researchers to also analyze affective polarization in multi-party contexts, based for example on Wagner's (2020) like–dislike scoring, and to conduct more internationally comparative research. Furthermore, most studies have focused on single social media platforms. As different platforms are expected to have different effects on their users, more comparative research analyzing multiple platforms in direct comparison is also needed.

Other methodological implications stand out as well. It seems that studies analyzing group polarization on Facebook and Twitter have found many more polarization effects than studies analyzing mass polarization effects at the individual level on the same platforms. This suggests that differences in accessing polarization on social media, either through observing societal group dynamics, in the case of group polarization, or individual polarization effects, in the case of mass polarization, yielded a disparity of findings. In the latter group, it is further noticeable that many studies based their analyses on the self-disclosed "frequency of" or "reliance on" social media use. These studies find comparatively few depolarization effects or no polarization effects, which might be because these types of operationalization cannot possibly fully capture the depth and facets of social media usage and do not allow conclusions about the content to which participants were exposed or which they shared., Looking at the bigger picture, these findings show that the choice of how to access the concept of polarization and the choice of measurement play critical roles role in which polarization effects are found or if any can be found at all.

To put the present analysis into perspective, we may ask how our findings correspond to or differ from insights gleaned from other recent literature reviews. In line with Kubin and von Sikorski (2021), we found an increase in research over the past 10 years and a strong focus on the US context, but an increasing number of studies from other country contexts appearing in recent years. Likewise, our findings also correspond to the authors' insights that "political polarization is not consistently discussed, or measured, across the literature" (p. 197), that "ideological and affective polarization are not clearly defined, nor consistently measured" (p. 188), and that there is "a lack of research exploring ways (social) media can depolarize" (Kubin & von Sikorski, 2021, p. 188). However, contrary to the literature reviews conducted by Kubin and von Sikorski (2021) as well as Iandoli et al. (2021), we did not find a strong dominance of polarization studies that analyzed Twitter. What we have found is a hyperfocus on Twitter for those studies that have actually analyzed fragmentation. This difference in findings results again from the lack of conceptual differentiation between polarization and fragmentation studies discussed above. Moreover, contrary to Kubin and von Sikorski (2021), we did not find that pro-attitudinal media clearly exacerbates polarization (see, e.g., Johnson et al., 2020; Kim & Kim, 2019). Furthermore, also in contrast to Kubin and von Sikorski (2021), our literature review included several experiments that provided "insight into ways social media can decrease (or have no effect) on ideological [and affective] polarization" (e.g., Cho et al., 2020; Munger et al., 2020).

Overall, we can say that the landscape of political polarization research needs more conceptual clarity and more inclusion of and comparison across different political and national contexts—and that, in general, the causal role of social media in the process of political polarization seems overstated or can be, at least, strongly disputed.

References

Abramowitz, A. I. (2010). *The Disappearing Center. Engaged Citizens, Polarization, and American Democracy.* Yale University Press.

Abramowitz, A. I., & Saunders, K. L. (2008). Is polarization a myth? *The Journal of Politics*, 70(2), 542–555. https://doi.org/10.1017/S0022381608080493

Allcott, H., Braghieri, L., Eichmeyer, S., & Gentzkow, M. (2020). The welfare effects of social media. *American Economic Review*, 110(3), 629–676. https://doi.or g/10.1257/aer.20190658

Arceneaux, K. & Johnson, M. (2010). Does Media Fragmentation Produce Mass Polarization? Selective Exposure and a New Era of Minimal Effects. *APSA 2010 Annual Meeting Paper*. Retrieved from https://ssrn.com/abstract=1642723

Bail, C. A., Argyle, L. P., Brown, T. W., Bumpus, J. P., Chen, H., Hunzaker, M. B. F., Lee, J., Mann, M., Merhout, F., & Volfovsky, A. (2018). Exposure to opposing views on social media can increase political polarization. *Proceedings of the National Academy of Sciences*, 115(37), 9216–9221. https://doi.org/10.1073/pn as.1804840115

Bakshy, E., Messing, S., & Adamic, L. A. (2015). Exposure to ideologically diverse news and opinion on Facebook. *Science*, 348(6239), 1130–1132. https://doi.org/1 0.1126/science.aaa1160

Baldassarri, D., & Gelman, A. (2008). Partisans without constraint: Political polarization and trends in American public opinion. *American Journal of Sociology*, 114(2), 408–446. https://doi.org/10.1086/590649

Bartels, L. M. (2000). Partisanship and voting behavior, 1952-1996. *American Journal of Political Science*, 44(1), 35. https://doi.org/10.2307/2669291

Beam, M. A., Hutchens, M. J., & Hmielowski, J. D. (2018). Facebook news and (de)polarization: Reinforcing spirals in the 2016 US election. *Information, Communication & Society*, 21(7), 940–958. https://doi.org/10.1080/1369118X.2018.14 44783

Bessi, A., Zollo, F., Del Vicario, M., Puliga, M., Scala, A., Caldarelli, G., Uzzi, B., & Quattrociocchi, W. (2016). Users' polarization on Facebook and YouTube. *PLOS ONE*, 11(8), e0159641. https://doi.org/10.1371/journal.pone.0159641

Bliuc, A.-M., Smith, L. G. E., & Moynihan, T. (2020). "You wouldn't celebrate September 11": Testing online polarisation between opposing ideological camps on YouTube. *Group Processes & Intergroup Relations*, 23(6), 827–844. https://doi.o rg/10.1177/1368430220942567

Bode, L. (2016). Political news in the news feed: Learning politics from social media. *Mass Communication and Society*, 19(1), 24–48. https://doi.org/10.1080/15 205436.2015.1045149

Bor, A., & Petersen, M. B. (2021). The psychology of online political hostility: A comprehensive, cross-national test of the mismatch hypothesis. *American Political Science Review*, 1–18. https://doi.org/10.1017/S0003055421000885

Boxell, L., Gentzkow, M., & Shapiro, J. (2020). Cross-country trends in affective polarization (Nr. w26669; S. w26669). *National Bureau of Economic Research*. https://doi.org/10.3386/w26669

boyd, danah m., & Ellison, N. B. (2007). Social network sites: Definition, history, and scholarship. *Journal of Computer-Mediated Communication*, 13(1), 210–230. https://doi.org/10.1111/j.1083-6101.2007.00393.x

Brewer, M. B. (1999). The psychology of prejudice: Ingroup love and outgroup hate? *Journal of Social Issues*, *55*(3), 429–444. https://doi.org/10.1111/0022-4537.00126

Bright, J. (2018). Explaining the emergence of political fragmentation on social media: The role of ideology and extremism. *Journal of Computer-Mediated Communication*, *23*(1), 17–33. https://doi.org/10.1093/jcmc/zmx002

Bruns, A. (2019). *Are Filter Bubbles Real?* Polity Press.

Buder, J., Rabl, L., Feiks, M., Badermann, M., & Zurstiege, G. (2020). *Does negatively toned language use on social media lead to attitude polarization?* [Preprint]. PsyArXiv. https://doi.org/10.31234/osf.io/dx9ws

Cambridge Dictionary. (n.d.). Polarization. *dictionary.cambridge.org*. Retrieved December 4, 2021, from https://dictionary.cambridge.org/dictionary/english/polarization

Merriam-Webster. (n.d.). Polarization. *Merriam-Webster.com Dictionary*. Retrieved December 4, 2021, from https://www.merriam-webster.com/dictionary/polarization

Chan, C., & Fu, K. (2015). Predicting political polarization from cyberbalkanization: Time series analysis of facebook pages and opinion poll during the hong kong occupy movement. Proceedings of the ACM Web Science Conference, 1–2. https://doi.org/10.1145/2786451.2786509

Chan, C., & Fu, K. (2017). The relationship between cyberbalkanization and opinion polarization: Time-series analysis on Facebook pages and opinion polls during the Hong Kong occupy movement and the associated debate on political reform: cyberbalkanization and opinion polarization. *Journal of Computer-Mediated Communication*, *22*(5), 266–283. https://doi.org/10.1111/jcc4.12192

Cho, J., Ahmed, S., Keum, H., Choi, Y. J., & Lee, J. H. (2018). Influencing myself: Self-reinforcement through online political expression. *Communication Research*, *45*(1), 83–111. https://doi.org/10.1177/0093650216644020

Clarke, K. A. (2009). Return of the phantom menace: Omitted variable bias in political research. *Conflict Management and Peace Science*, *26*(1), 46–66. https://doi.org/10.1177/0738894208097666

Cohen, J. N. (2018). Exploring echo-systems: How algorithms shape immersive media environments. *Journal of Media Literacy Education*, *10*(2), 139–151. https://doi.org/10.23860/JMLE-2018-10-2-8

Conover, M., Ratkiewicz, J., Francisco, M., Goncalves, B., Menczer, F., & Flammini, A. (2021). Political polarization on Twitter. *Proceedings of the International AAAI Conference on Web and Social Media*, *5*(1), 89-96. Retrieved from https://ojs.aaai.org/index.php/ICWSM/article/view/14126

Dahlberg, L. (2007). Rethinking the fragmentation of the cyberpublic: From consensus to contestation. *New Media & Society*, *9*(5), 827–847. https://doi.org/10.1177/1461444807081228

Del Vicario, M., Zollo, F., Caldarelli, G., Scala, A., & Quattrociocchi, W. (2017). Mapping social dynamics on Facebook: The Brexit debate. *Social Networks*, *50*, 6–16. https://doi.org/10.1016/j.socnet.2017.02.002

DiMaggio, P., Evans, J., & Bryson, B. (1996). Have American's social attitudes become more polarized? *American Journal of Sociology*, 102(3), 690–755.

Dylko, I., Dolgov, I., Hoffman, W., Eckhart, N., Molina, M., & Aaziz, O. (2017). The dark side of technology: An experimental investigation of the influence of customizability technology on online political selective exposure. *Computers in Human Behavior*, *73*, 181–190. https://doi.org/10.1016/j.chb.2017.03.031

Feezell, J. T., Wagner, J. K., & Conroy, M. (2021). Exploring the effects of algorithm-driven news sources on political behavior and polarization. *Computers in Human Behavior*, *116*, 106626. https://doi.org/10.1016/j.chb.2020.106626

Fiorina, M. P., & Abrams, S. J. (2008). Political polarization in the American public. *Annual Review of Political Science*, *11*(1), 563–588. https://doi.org/10.1146/annurev.polisci.11.053106.153836

Fiorina, M. P., Abrams, S. J., & Pope, J. C. (2005). *Culture War? The Myth of a Polarized America*. Pearson Longman.

Flaxman, S., Goel, S., & Rao, J. M. (2016). Filter bubbles, echo chambers, and online news consumption. *Public Opinion Quarterly*, *80*(S1), 298–320. https://doi.org/10.1093/poq/nfw006

Garimella, K., De Francisci Morales, G., Gionis, A., & Mathioudakis, M. (2017). The effect of collective attention on controversial debates on social media. *Proceedings of the 2017 ACM on Web Science Conference*, 43–52. https://doi.org/10.1145/3091478.3091486

Garrett, R. K., Gvirsman, S. D., Johnson, B. K., Tsfati, Y., Neo, R., & Dal, A. (2014). Implications of pro- and counterattitudinal information exposure for affective polarization: Partisan media exposure and affective polarization. *Human Communication Research*, *40*(3), 309–332. https://doi.org/10.1111/hcre.12028

Gentzkow, M. & Shapiro, J.M. (2010). What drives media slant? Evidence from u. S. Daily newspapers. (2010). *Econometrica*, *78*(1), 35–71. https://doi.org/10.3982/ECTA7195

Gimpel, J. G., & Hui, I. S. (2015). Seeking politically compatible neighbors? The role of neighborhood partisan composition in residential sorting. *Political Geography*, *48*, 130–142. https://doi.org/10.1016/j.polgeo.2014.11.003

Grover, P., Kar, A. K., Dwivedi, Y. K., & Janssen, M. (2019). Polarization and acculturation in US Election 2016 outcomes – Can twitter analytics predict changes in voting preferences. *Technological Forecasting and Social Change*, *145*, 438–460. https://doi.org/10.1016/j.techfore.2018.09.009

Gruzd, A., & Roy, J. (2014). Investigating political polarization on twitter: A Canadian perspective: investigating political polarization on twitter. *Policy & Internet*, *6*(1), 28–45. https://doi.org/10.1002/1944-2866.POI354

Hahn, K. S., Ryu, S., & Park, S. (2015). Fragmentation in the twitter following of news outlets: The representation of South Korean users' ideological and generational cleavage. *Journalism & Mass Communication Quarterly*, *92*(1), 56–76. https://doi.org/10.1177/1077699014559499

Hameleers, M. (2020). Augmenting polarization via social media? A comparative analysis of Trump's and Wilders' online populist communication and the electorate's interpretations surrounding the elections. *Acta Politica, 55*(3), 331–350. https://doi.org/10.1057/s41269-018-0119-8

Harel, T. O., Jameson, J. K., & Maoz, I. (2020). The normalization of hatred: Identity, affective polarization, and dehumanization on Facebook in the context of intractable political conflict. *Social Media + Society, 6*(2), 205630512091398. https://doi.org/10.1177/2056305120913983

Hilbert, M., Ahmed, S., Cho, J., Liu, B., & Luu, J. (2018). Communicating with algorithms: A transfer entropy analysis of emotions-based escapes from online echo chambers. *Communication Methods and Measures, 12*(4), 260–275. https://do i.org/10.1080/19312458.2018.1479843

Huber, G. A., & Malhotra, N. (2017). Political homophily in social relationships: Evidence from online dating behavior. *The Journal of Politics, 79*(1), 269–283. https://doi.org/10.1086/687533

Hwang, H., Kim, Y., & Huh, C. U. (2014). Seeing is believing: Effects of uncivil online debate on political polarization and expectations of deliberation. *Journal of Broadcasting & Electronic Media, 58*(4), 621–633. https://doi.org/10.1080/08838 151.2014.966365

Iandoli, L., Primario, S., & Zollo, G. (2021). The impact of group polarization on the quality of online debate in social media: A systematic literature review. *Technological Forecasting and Social Change, 170*, 120924. https://doi.org/10.1016/j .techfore.2021.120924

Isenberg, D. J. (1986). Group polarization: A critical review and meta-analysis. *Journal of Personality and Social Psychology, 50*(6), 1141–1151. https://doi.org/10.1 037/0022-3514.50.6.1141

Iyengar, S., & Westwood, S. J. (2015). Fear and loathing across party lines: New evidence on group polarization: fear and loathing across party lines. *American Journal of Political Science, 59*(3), 690–707. https://doi.org/10.1111/ajps.12152

Iyengar, S., Konitzer, T., & Tedin, K. (2018). The home as a political fortress: Family agreement in an era of polarization. *The Journal of Politics, 80*(4), 1326–1338. https://doi.org/10.1086/698929

Iyengar, S., Lelkes, Y., Levendusky, M., Malhotra, N., & Westwood, S. J. (2019). The origins and consequences of affective polarization in the united states. *Annual Review of Political Science, 22*(1), 129–146. https://doi.org/10.1146/annure v-polisci-051117-073034

Iyengar, S., Sood, G., & Lelkes, Y. (2012). Affect, not ideology: A social identity perspective on polarization. *Public Opinion Quarterly, 76*(3), 405–431. https://doi. org/10.1093/poq/nfs038

Jackson, T. W., & Farzaneh, P. (2012). Theory-based model of factors affecting information overload. *International Journal of Information Management, 32*(6), 523–532. https://doi.org/10.1016/j.ijinfomgt.2012.04.006

Jensen, J., Kaplan, E., Naidu, S., & Wilse-Samson, L. (2012). Political polarization and the dynamics of political language: Evidence from 130 years of partisan speech. *Brookings Papers on Economic Activity*, (1), 1–81. https://doi.org/10.1353/e ca.2012.0017

Johnson, B. K., Neo, R. L., Heijnen, M. E. M., Smits, L., & van Veen, C. (2020). Issues, involvement, and influence: Effects of selective exposure and sharing on polarization and participation. *Computers in Human Behavior, 104*, 106155. https://doi.org/10.1016/j.chb.2019.09.031

Johnson, T. J., Kaye, B. K., & Lee, A. M. (2017). Blinded by the spite? Path model of political attitudes, selectivity, and social media. *Atlantic Journal of Communication, 25*(3), 181–196. https://doi.org/10.1080/15456870.2017.1324454

Karlsen, R., Steen-Johnsen, K., Wollebæk, D., & Enjolras, B. (2017). Echo chamber and trench warfare dynamics in online debates. *European Journal of Communication, 32*(3), 257–273. https://doi.org/10.1177/0267323117695734

Kearney, M. W. (2019). Analyzing change in network polarization. *New Media & Society, 21*(6), 1380–1402. https://doi.org/10.1177/1461444818822813

Kibet, A., & Ward, S. (2018). Socially networked heterogeneity: The influence of Whatsapp as a social networking site on polarisation in Kenya. *African Journalism Studies, 39*(4), 42–66. https://doi.org/10.1080/23743670.2018.1537979

Kim, Y., & Kim, Y. (2019). Incivility on Facebook and political polarization: The mediating role of seeking further comments and negative emotion. *Computers in Human Behavior, 99*, 219–227. https://doi.org/10.1016/j.chb.2019.05.022

Kobayashi, T. (2020). Depolarization through social media use: Evidence from dual identifiers in Hong Kong. *New Media & Society, 22*(8), 1339–1358. https://doi.or g/10.1177/1461444820910124

Lai, M., Tambuscio, M., Patti, V., Ruffo, G., & Rosso, P. (2019). Stance polarity in political debates: A diachronic perspective of network homophily and conversations on Twitter. *Data & Knowledge Engineering, 124*, 101738. https://doi.org/10. 1016/j.datak.2019.101738

Lau, R. R., Andersen, D. J., Ditonto, T. M., Kleinberg, M. S., & Redlawsk, D. P. (2017). Effect of media environment diversity and advertising tone on information search, selective exposure, and affective polarization. *Political Behavior, 39*(1), 231–255. https://doi.org/10.1007/s11109-016-9354-8

Layman, G. C., Carsey, T. M., & Horowitz, J. M. (2006). Party polarization in American politics: Characteristics, causes, and consequences. *Annual Review of Political Science, 9*(1), 83–110. https://doi.org/10.1146/annurev.polisci.9.070204.1 05138

Lee, J., & Choi, Y. (2020). Effects of network heterogeneity on social media on opinion polarization among South Koreans: Focusing on fear and political orientation. *International Communication Gazette, 82*(2), 119–139. https://doi.org /10.1177/1748048518820499

Lee, H., & Hahn, K. S. (2018). Partisan selective following on Twitter over time: Polarization or depolarization? *Asian Journal of Communication, 28*(3), 227–246. https://doi.org/10.1080/01292986.2017.1384845

Lee, F. L. F. (2016). Impact of social media on opinion polarization in varying times. *Communication and the Public, 1*(1), 56–71. https://doi.org/10.1177/205704 7315617763

Lee, P. S. N., So, C. Y. K., Lee, F., Leung, L., & Chan, M. (2018). Social media and political partisanship – A subaltern public sphere's role in democracy. *Telematics and Informatics, 35*(7), 1949–1957. https://doi.org/10.1016/j.tele.2018.06.007

Lee, C., Shin, J., & Hong, A. (2018). Does social media use really make people politically polarized? Direct and indirect effects of social media use on political polarization in South Korea. *Telematics and Informatics, 35*(1), 245–254. https://d oi.org/10.1016/j.tele.2017.11.005

Lelkes, Y. (2018). Affective polarization and ideological sorting: A reciprocal, albeit weak, relationship. *The Forum, 16*(1), 67–79. https://doi.org/10.1515/for-2018-00 05

Levendusky, M., & Malhotra, N. (2016). Does media coverage of partisan polarization affect political attitudes? *Political Communication, 33*(2), 283–301. https://do i.org/10.1080/10584609.2015.1038455

Levy, R. (2021). Social media, news consumption, and polarization: Evidence from a field experiment. *American Economic Review, 111*(3), 831–870. https://doi.org/1 0.1257/aer.20191777

Lu, Y., Ray, R., Ha, L., & Chen, P. (2020). Social media news consumption and opinion polarization on China's trade practices: Evidence from a U.S. national survey. *International Journal of Communication, 14*, 3478–3495.

Mason, L. (2016). A cross-cutting calm: How social sorting drives affective polarization. *Public Opinion Quarterly, 80*(S1), 351–377. https://doi.org/10.1093/poq/nfw 001

McCarty, N. M., Poole, K. T., & Rosenthal, H. (2006). *Polarized America: The Dance of Ideology and Unequal Riches*. MIT Press.

McConnell, C., Margalit, Y., Malhotra, N., & Levendusky, M. (2018). The economic consequences of partisanship in a polarized era. *American Journal of Political Science, 62*(1), 5–18. https://doi.org/10.1111/ajps.12330

McCoy, J., Rahman, T., & Somer, M. (2018). Polarization and the global crisis of democracy: Common patterns, dynamics, and pernicious consequences for democratic politics. *American Behavioral Scientist, 62*(1), 16–42. https://doi.org/1 0.1177/0002764218759576

McPherson, M., Smith-Lovin, L., & Cook, J. M. (2001). Birds of a feather: Homophily in social networks. *Annual Review of Sociology, 27*(1), 415–444. https://doi.o rg/10.1146/annurev.soc.27.1.415

Mendez, G.P.R, Cosby, A.G. & Mohanty, S.D. (2017). Obamacare and political polarization on Twitter: An application of machine learning and social network analysis. *Teorija in Praksa, 55*(2).

Mentzer, K., Fallon, K., Prichard, J. J. & Yates, D. (2020): Measuring and unpacking affective polarization on Twitter: The role of party and gender in the 2018 Senate races. *Proceedings of the 53rd Hawaii International Conference on System Sciences (HICSS)*. 1-10

Michelitch, K. (2015). Does electoral competition exacerbate interethnic or interpartisan economic discrimination? Evidence from a field experiment in market price bargaining. *American Political Science Review*, *109*(1), 43–61. https://doi.org/10.1017/S0003055414000628

Min, H., & Yun, S. (2018). Selective exposure and political polarization of public opinion on the presidential impeachment in south korea: Facebook vs. Kakaotalk. *Korea Observer - Institute of Korean Studies*, *49*(1), 137–159. https://doi.org/10.29152/KOIKS. 2018.49.1.137

Möller, J., Trilling, D., Helberger, N., & van Es, B. (2018). Do not blame it on the algorithm: An empirical assessment of multiple recommender systems and their impact on content diversity. *Information, Communication & Society*, *21*(7), 959–977. https://doi.org/10.1080/1369118X.2018.1444076

Munger, K., Egan, P. J., Nagler, J., Ronen, J., & Tucker, J. (2020). Political knowledge and misinformation in the era of social media: Evidence from the 2015 uk election. *British Journal of Political Science*, 1–21. https://doi.org/10.1017/S0007123420000198

Nguyen, A., & Vu, H. T. (2019). Testing popular news discourse on the "echo chamber" effect: Does political polarisation occur among those relying on social media as their primary politics news source? *First Monday*. https://doi.org/10.5210/fm.v24i6.9632

Ohme, J. (2021). Algorithmic social media use and its relationship to attitude reinforcement and issue-specific political participation – The case of the 2015 European immigration movements. *Journal of Information Technology & Politics*, *18*(1), 36–54. https://doi.org/10.1080/19331681.2020.1805085

Papacharissi, Z. (2002). The virtual sphere: The internet as a public sphere. *New Media & Society*, *4*(1), 9–27. https://doi.org/10.1177/14614440222226244

Pariser, E. (2011). *The Filter Bubble: What the Internet is Hiding from You*. Penguin Press.

Pew Research Center. (2017). The partisan divide on political values grows even wider. Retrieved April 10 2021, from https://www.people-press.org/2017/10/05/the-partisan-divide-on-political-values-grows-even-wider/.

Rogowski, J. C., & Sutherland, J. L. (2016). How ideology fuels affective polarization. *Political Behavior*, *38*(2), 485–508. https://doi.org/10.1007/s11109-015-9323-7

Scharkow, M., Mangold, F., Stier, S., & Breuer, J. (2020). How social network sites and other online intermediaries increase exposure to news. *Proceedings of the National Academy of Sciences*, *117*(6), 2761–2763. https://doi.org/10.1073/pnas.1918279117

Sened, I. (1996). A model of coalition formation: Theory and evidence. *The Journal of Politics*, *58*(2), 350–372. https://doi.org/10.2307/2960230

Shmargad, Y., & Klar, S. (2019). How Partisan Online Environments Shape Communication with Political Outgroups. *International Journal of Communication*, *13*, 27.

Shmargad, Y., & Klar, S. (2020). Sorting the news: How ranking by popularity polarizes our politics. *Political Communication, 37*(3), 423–446. https://doi.org/10.1080/10584609.2020.1713267

Stroud, N. J. (2010). Polarization and partisan selective exposure. *Journal of Communication, 60*(3), 556–576. https://doi.org/10.1111/j.1460-2466.2010.01497.x

Suk, J., Shah, D. V., Wells, C., Wagner, M. W., Friedland, L. A., Cramer, K. J., Hughes, C., & Franklin, C. (2020). Do improving conditions harden partisan preferences? Lived experiences, imagined communities, and polarized evaluations. *International Journal of Public Opinion Research, 32*(4), 750–768. https://doi.org/10.1093/ijpor/edz051

Sunstein, C. R. (2001). *Echo Chambers: Bush v. Gore, Impeachment, and Beyond.* Princeton University Press.

Tyagi, A., Uyheng, J., & Carley, K. M. (2020). Affective polarization in online climate change discourse on twitter. *arXiv:2008.13051* [cs]. http://arxiv.org/abs/2008.13051

Usui, S., Yoshida, M., & Toriumi, F. (2018). Analysis of information polarization during japan's 2017 election. *2018 IEEE International Conference on Big Data (Big Data)*, 4383–4386. https://doi.org/10.1109/BigData.2018.8622143

Valkenburg, P. M. (2017). Understanding self-effects in social media. *Human Communication Research, 43*(4), 477–490. https://doi.org/10.1111/hcre.12113

van Aelst, P., Strömbäck, J., Aalberg, T., Esser, F., de Vreese, C., Matthes, J., Hopmann, D., Salgado, S., Hubé, N., Stępińska, A., Papathanassopoulos, S., Berganza, R., Legnante, G., Reinemann, C., Sheafer, T., & Stanyer, J. (2017). Political communication in a high-choice media environment: A challenge for democracy? *Annals of the International Communication Association, 41*(1), 3–27. https://doi.org/10.1080/23808985.2017.1288551

Wagner, M. (2021). Affective polarization in multiparty systems. *Electoral Studies, 69*, 102199. https://doi.org/10.1016/j.electstud.2020.102199

Warner, B. R. (2010). Segmenting the electorate: The effects of exposure to political extremism online. *Communication Studies, 61*(4), 430–444. https://doi.org/10.1080/10510974.2010.497069

Webster, S. W., & Abramowitz, A. I. (2017). The ideological foundations of affective polarization in the U. S. electorate. *American Politics Research, 45*(4), 621–647. https://doi.org/10.1177/1532673X17703132

Yang, M., Wen, X., Lin, Y.-R., & Deng, L. (2017). Quantifying content polarization on Twitter. *2017 IEEE 3rd International Conference on Collaboration and Internet Computing (CIC)*, 299–308. https://doi.org/10.1109/CIC.2017.00047

Yarchi, M., Baden, C., & Kligler-Vilenchik, N. (2021). Political polarization on the digital sphere: A cross-platform, over-time analysis of interactional, positional, and affective polarization on social media. *Political Communication, 38*(1–2), 98–139. https://doi.org/10.1080/10584609.2020.1785067

Yardi, S., & boyd, D. (2010). Dynamic debates: An analysis of group polarization over time on Twitter. *Bulletin of Science, Technology & Society, 30*(5), 316–327. https://doi.org/10.1177/0270467610380011

Zollo, F. (2019). Dealing with digital misinformation: A polarised context of narratives and tribes. *Proceedings of the Third EFSA Scientific Conference: Science, Food and Society*. https://doi.org/10.2903/j.efsa.2019.e170720

Zuiderveen Borgesius, F. J., Trilling, D., Möller, J., Bodó, B., de Vreese, C. H., & Helberger, N. (2016). Should we worry about filter bubbles? *Internet Policy Review*, 5(1). https://doi.org/10.14763/2016.1.401

Katharina Ludwig *(M.A., U of Mannhheim, 2020) is Research Associate in the Mannheim Centre for European Social Research (MZES) and the Institute for Media and Communication Studies, University of Mannheim, Germany. Her research interests concern the perception, usage and effects of political communication in news media and social networks with special emphasis on (1) polarization, fragmentation and extremism, (2) migration, flight, and racism/discrimination, (3) quantification and effects of (self-transcendent) emotions.*

Philipp Müller *(Dr. phil., LMU Munich, 2015) is Senior Lecturer in the Institute for Media and Communication Studies, University of Mannheim, Germany, and Project Director in the Mannheim Centre for European Social Research (MZES). His research deals with questions of political communication and media change, with a special focus on digital news consumption and its effects on democracy and societal cohesion. Wolfram Peiser was his PhD advisor in Munich. Philipp worked as research and teaching associate with his chair from 2010 to 2014.*

Does Social Media Use Promote Political Mass Polarization?

Appendices

Appendix 1: Overview of Group Polarization Studies

Title	Country	Method	S.M. Platform	Type of Polarization	Results on Polarization
Bessi, A., Zollo, F., Vicario, M. D., Puliga, M., Scala, A., Caldarelli, G., Uzzi, B., & Quattrociocchi, W. (2016): Users' polarization on Facebook and Youtube. doi: 10.1371/journal.pone.0159641	USA	Observation	Facebook & Youtube	ideological	The content more than the algorithm drove polarization
Bliuc, A., Smith, L. G.E., & Moynihan, T. (2020): "You wouldn't celebrate September 11": Testing online polarisation between opposing ideological camps on YouTube doi: 10.1177/1368430220942567	Australia	Automated Content Analysis	Youtube	affective	Mostly intergroup interaction, when direct dissent is expressed, drives polarisation.
Brugnoli, E., Cinelli, M., Quattrociocchi, W. & Scala, A. (2019): Recursive patterns in online echo chambers doi: 10.1038/s41598-019-56191-7	Italy	Network Analysis - Modularity Approach	Facebook	ideological	Polarized communities: polarized users tend to remain confined within groups of very few pages and reinforce their preexisting beliefs by leveraging the activity of their like-minded neighbors
Buder, J., Rabl, L., Feiks, M., Badermann, M., & Zurstiege, G. (2021): Does negatively toned language use on social media lead to attitude polarization? doi: 10.1016/j.chb.2020.106663	/	Network Analysis & Sentiment Analysis	Twitter	ideological	Negativity in tweets is linked to a polarized attitude. Negativity in a user's social environment had a slightly depolarizing effect on attitude extremity.
Chan, C. & Fu, K. (2015): Predicting political polarization from cyberbalkanization: Time series analysis of Facebook pages and opinion polls during the Hong Kong Occupy Movement doi: 10.1145/2786451.2786509	Hong-Kong	Network Analysis & Opinion Polls	Twitter	ideological	Cyberbalkanization and opinion polarization are connected for young adults.

Title	Country	Method	S.M. Platform	Type of Polarization	Results on Polarization
Chan, C. & Fu, K. (2017): The Relationship between cyberbalkanization and opinion polarization: Time-series analysis on Facebook pages and opinion polls during the Hong Kong occupy movement and the associated debate on political reform. doi: 10.1111/jcc4.12192	Hong-Kong	Network Analysis & Opinion Polls	Facebook	ideological	Cyberbalkanization and opinion polarization are connected for young adults.
Del Vicario, M., Zollo, F., Caldarelli, G.,Scala, A. & Quattrociocchi, W. (2017): Mapping social dynamics on Facebook: The Brexit debate. doi: 10.1016/j.socnet.2017.02.002	UK	Network Analysis - Modularity Approach	Facebook	ideological (towards news pages)	Polarized communities: users are divided into two main distinct groups and confine their attention on specific pages.
Grover, P., Kar, A. K., Dwivedi, Y. K., & Janssen, M. (2019): Polarization and acculturation in US Election 2016 outcomes – Can twitter analytics predict changes in voting preferences. doi: 10.1016/j.techfore.2018.09.009	USA	Content, Network & Sentiment Analysis	Twitter	partisan	Higher engagement leads to a higher number of polarized users.
Gruzd, A., & Roy, J. (2014): Investigating political polarization on Twitter: A Canadian perspective. doi: 10.1002/1944-2866.POI354	Canada	Network Analysis & Content Analysis	Twitter	affective	Clustering effect around shared political views; Evidence of cross-ideological connections and exchanges characterized by hostility.
Hameleers, M.(2020): Augmenting polarization via social media? A comparative analysis of Trump's and Wilders' online populist communication and the electorate's interpretations surrounding the elections. doi: 10.1057/s41269-018-0119-8	USA, Netherlands	Qualitative Content Analysis	Facebook & Twitter	affective	U.S. citizens find themselves fragmented along partisan lines. In the Netherlands, the divide between the ordinary people and the others (elite) is more central.
Harel, T., Jameson, J., & Maoz, I., (2020): The Normalization of Hatred:Identity, Affective polarization, and dehumanization on	Israel	Qualitative Content Analysis	Facebook	affective	Individuals on the right-wing FB-page seem polarized.

Does Social Media Use Promote Political Mass Polarization?

Title	Country	Method	S.M. Platform	Type of Polarization	Results on Polarization
Facebook in the context of intractable political conflict. doi: 10.1177/2056305120913983					
Mendez, G., Cosby, A.G.,, & Mohanty, S.D. (2017): Obamacare and political polarization on Twitter: An application of machine learning and social network analysis.	USA	Qualitative Content Analysis & Sentiment Analysis	Twitter	partisan & ideological & affective	Users are polarized along party lines; Influencers have a growing capacity to polarise the public's views and opinions; Ideologically opposing tweets express opposing perceptions about health care; Majority of the tweets indicate they are against 'the other'.
Mentzer, K., Fallon,K., Prichard, J. J. & Yates, D. (2020): Measuring and Unpacking affective polarization on Twitter: The role of party and gender in the 2018 Senate races. doi: 10.24251/hicss.2020.301	USA	Network Analysis & Sentiment Analysis	Twitter	affective	greater level of polarization, and larger fluctuations in polarization, among Conservatives over Liberals; women and Conservatives expressed stronger in-group party support and greater dislike of out-group party than men or Liberals
Schmidt, A.L., Zollo, F., Scala, A., C. Betsch, C. & Quattrociocchi, W. (2018): Polarization of the vaccination debate on Facebook. doi: 10.1016/j.vaccine.2018.05.040	/	Network Analysis - Modularity Approach	Facebook	ideological	polarized communities
Tyagi, A., Uyheng, J., & Carley, K. M. (2020): Affective polarization in online climate change discourse on Twitter. arXiv:2008.13051v1	USA	Network Analysis & Sentiment Analysis	Twitter	affective	Climate change Disbelievers tended to exhibit high levels of hostility toward climate change Believers; Disbelievers had similarly valenced interactions toward in-group and out-group members
Williams, H.T.P., McMurray, J.R., Kurz, T. & Lambert, F. H. (2015: Network analysis reveals open forums and echo chambers in soci-	/	Network Analysis	Twitter	ideological	High ideological polarisation; social media discussion of climate change is characterised by strong attitude-

Title	Country	Method	S.M. Platform	Type of Polarization	Results on Polarization
al media discussions of climate change. doi: 10.1016/j.gloenvcha.2015.03.006					based homophily and widespread segregation into like-minded communities. Users exposed to diverse views in mixed attitude communities were less likely to hold a polarised view; polarized members were more likely to express negative sentiment towards others with differing views.
Yarchi, M., Baden, C., & Kligler-Vilenchik, N. (2020): Political polarization on the digital sphere: A cross-platform, over-time analysis of interactional, positional, and affective polarization on Ssocial media. doi: 10.1080/10584609.2020.1785067	Israel	Content Analysis & Network Analysis	Facebook, Twitter, WhatsApp	affective, ideological	Dependent on platform: Twitter is polarized; WhatsApp less, Facebook not.
Yardi, S., & Boyd, D. (2010): Dynamic debates: An analysis of group polarization over time on Twitter. doi: 10.1177/0270467610380011	USA	Content Analysis & Network Analysis	Twitter	ideological	Users were more likely to interact within their like-minded group, which strengthend group identity, but also actively engaged with ideologically competing groups, which reinforced in-group and out-group affiliation

Title	Country	Method	S.M. Platform	Type of Polarization	Results on Polarization
Zollo, F. (2019): Dealing with digital misinformation: Apolarised context of narratives and tribes. doi: 10.2903/j.efsa.2019.e170720	Italy, USA, UK	Network, Content - Modularity Approach & Sentiment Analysis	Facebook	ideological	polarized communities: reinforcement of world view by opinion-confirming content and interaction with like-minded people who; sentiment of polarised users tend to be more negative than general ones

Appendix 2: Overview of Mass Polarization Studies

Title	Country	Method	S.M. Platform	Type of Polarization	Results on Polarization
Allcott, H., Braghieri, L., Eichmeyer, S., & Gentzkow, M. (2020). The welfare effects of social media. doi: 10.1257/aer.20190658	USA	Experiment	Facebook	affective, ideological, partisan	Deactivation of Facebook reduced political polarization.
Bail, C. A., Argyle, L. P., Brown, T. W., Bumpus, J. P., Chen, H., Hunzaker, M. B. F., Lee, J., Mann, M., Merhout, F., & Volfovsky, A. (2018). Exposure to opposing views on social media can increase political polarization. doi: 10.1073/pnas.1804840115	USA	Experiment	Twitter	ideological	No evidence that exposing Twitter users to opposing views reduces polarization. Evidence for backfire effects and increase of polarization through counter-attitudinal views.
Beam, M. A., Hutchens, M. J., & Hmielowski, J. D. (2018). Facebook news and (De)polarization: Reinforcing spirals in the 2016 US election. doi: 10.1080/1369118X.2018.1444783	USA	Survey	Facebook	affective	Facebook news use was related to a modest over-time spiral of depolarization. Counter-attitudinal news exposure increased over time, which resulted in depolarization. We found no evidence of a parallel model, where pro-attitudinal exposure stemming from Facebook news use resulted in greater affective polarization.
Cho, J., Ahmed, S., Hilbert, M., Liu, B. & Luu, J. (2020). Do search algorithms endanger democracy? An experimental investigation of algorithm effects on political polarization. doi: 10.1080/08838151.2020.1757365	USA	Experiment	Youtube	affective	Affective polarization is not heightened by videos YouTube recommends – based on either users' self-preferences or preferences of users' social networks – as affective polarization in both conditions is no greater than that in the control condition. However, there is a tendency for videos recommended based on "social" preferences to reduce affective polarization.

Title	Country	Method	S.M. Platform	Type of Polarization	Results on Polarization
Cho, J., Ahmed, S., Keum, H., Choi, Y. J., & Lee, J. H. (2018). Influencing myself: Self-reinforcement through online political expression. doi: 10.1177/0093650216644020	USA	Survey	Social Media	ideological, partisan	Results show that expressing opinions about election campaigns strengthened the expresser's initially held opinions.
Dylko, I., Dolgov, I., Hoffman, W., Eckhart, N., Molina, M., & Aaziz, O. (2017). The dark side of technology: An experimental investigation of the influence of customizability technology on online political selective exposure. doi: 10.1016/j.chb.2017.03.031	USA	Experiment	Social Media	ideological	Customizability increased political polarization indirectly, via its effect on political selective exposure.
Feezell, J. T., Wagner, J. K., & Conroy, M. (2021). Exploring the effects of algorithm-driven news sources on political behavior and polarization. doi: 10.1016/j.chb.2020.106626	USA	Survey	Facebook & Twitter	affective	Neither non-algorithmic media nor user-driven or socially-driven algorithms influenced political polarization
Hahn, K. S., Ryu, S., & Park, S. (2015). Fragmentation in the twitter following of news outlets: The representation of south korean users' ideological and generational cleavage. doi: 10.1177/1077699014559499	South Korea	Survey & Webbrousing	Twitter	partisan	Partisan and generational selectivity sharply polarizes news following on Twitter; Results imply that the network of Twitter following mirrors the landscape of offline political polarization.
Hilbert, M., Ahmed, S., Cho, J., Liu, B., & Luu, J. (2018). Communicating with algorithms: A transfer entropy analysis of emotions-based escapes from online echo chambers. doi: 10.1080/19312458.2018.1479843	USA	Experiment	Youtube	affective	Besides user selectivity and homogeneous networking, algorithm-based recommender systems seem to function as a structural factor promoting polarization by providing confirmatory information and thus reinforcing prior predispositions.
Hwang, H., Kim, Y., & Huh, C. U. (2014). Seeing is believing: Effects of uncivil online debate on political polarization and expectations of deliberation. doi: 10.1080/08838151.2014.966365	USA	Experiment	Youtube	ideological	Exposure to uncivil online discussion in which commenters uncivilly attacked the other side of the issue did not affect participants' attitude polarization.

Title	Country	Method	S.M. Platform	Type of Polarization	Results on Polarization
Johnson, B. K., Neo, R. L., Heijnen, M. E. M., Smits, L., & van Veen, C. (2020). Issues, involvement, and influence: Effects of selective exposure and sharing on polarization and participation. 10.1016/j.chb.2019.09.031	Netherlands	Experiment	Facebook	ideological	Pro- and counter-attitudinal information exposure did not have any main effects on opinion polarization and political participation. Sharing of pro-attitudinal news articles about refugees and equal pay had positive effects on opinion polarization. Also, the sharing of counter-attitudinal news articles about refugees and equal pay were negatively associated with opinion polarization.
Johnson, T. J., Kaye, B. K., & Lee, A. M. (2017). Blinded by the spite? Path model of political attitudes, selectivity, and social media. doi: 10.1080/15456870.2017.1324454	USA	Survey	Social Media	affective	Social media influence selective exposure and selective avoidance and political polarization.The only exception is that reliance on blogs does not lead to political polarization. The indirect effects model shows that strength of party ties and reliance influence confidence in the president and Congress indirectly through polarization and selective exposure through social media use.
Karlsen, R., Steen-Johnsen, K., Wollebæk, D., & Enjolras, B. (2017). Echo chamber and trench warfare dynamics in online debates. doi: 10.1177/0267323117695734	Norway	Experiment	Facebook, Twitter	ideological	Both discussing with opponents and supporters might lead to a reinforcement of the original opinion. Effects are stronger for individuals with strong attitudes than individuals with moderate attitudes.
Kibet, A., & Ward, S. (2018). Socially networked heterogeneity: The influence of whatsapp as a social networking site on polarisation in kenya. doi: 10.1080/23743670.2018.1537979	Kenya	Survey	Whats App	ideological, affective	Respondent's age and commenting on news reduces all forms of polarization, whereas, Ethnic identity, Political discussion, Class ideology, and Social network heterogeneity increase the three types of polarization.

Title	Country	Method	S.M. Platform	Type of Polarization	Results on Polarization
Kim, Y., & Kim, Y. (2019). Incivility on Facebook and political polarization: The mediating role of seeking further comments and negative emotion. doi: 10.1016/j.chb.2019.05.022	USA	Experiment	Facebook	ideological	Whether supporting evidence is provided or not in comments did not have any significant effect on respondents' ideological polarization.
Kobayashi, T. (2020). Depolarization through social media use: Evidence from dual identifiers in Hong Kong. doi: 10.1177/1461444820910124	Hong Kong	Survey & behavioral data	Social Media	affective, ideological, partisan	The political use of social media polarizes the attitudes and affects of single identifiers, whereas it has depolarizing effects on dual identifiers.
Lee, C., Shin, J., & Hong, A. (2018). Does social media use really make people politically polarized? Direct and indirect effects of social media use on political polarization in South Korea. doi: 10.1016/j.tele.2017.11.005	South Korea	Survey	Social Media	partisan	Social media did not directly push users into political extremes, whether they were neutrals or moderate partisans but indirectly affected polarization through increased political engagement. Social media use was negatively associated with a shift of neutrals toward a conservative view and positively associated with a shift toward a liberal view. Social media was not related to polarization in any direction for moderate partisans.
Lee, F. L. F. (2016). Impact of social media on opinion polarization in varying times. doi: 10.1177/2057047315617763	Hong-Kong	Survey (3)	Social Media	ideological	Political communication via social media can contribute to political polarization when the context itself is polarizing.
Lee, J., & Choi, Y. (2020). Effects of network heterogeneity on social media on opinion polarization among South Koreans: Focusing on fear and political orientation. doi: 10.1177/1748048518820499	South Korea	Survey	Social Media	ideological	Exposure to diverse opinions on social media hat potential to mitigate polarization. Individuals who feel disadvantaged or excluded from dominant position and those who are afraid of others with opposing views may stick to their initial viewpoints.

Title	Country	Method	S.M. Platform	Type of Polarization	Results on Polarization
Lee, J.K., Choi, J., Kim, C. & Kim, Y. (2014). Social media, network heterogeneity, and opinion polarization. doi: 10.1111/jcom.12077	USA	Survey	Social Media	affective, ideological, partisan	The higher level of SNS diversity led to more partisanship polarization for individuals participating in more political discussions whereas it had almost no effects on partisanship polarization for those joining fewer political discussions. It showed a similar pattern for ideological polarization.
Lee, P. S. N., So, C. Y. K., Lee, F., Leung, L., & Chan, M. (2018). Social media and political partisanship – A subaltern public sphere's role in democracy. doi: 10.1016/j.tele.2018.06.007	Hong-Kong	Survey	Social Media	ideological	The frequent use of social media contributed to a positive assessment of "the importance of democratic development in Hong Kong" but a negative view of "the importance of national interest," "trust in the central government," "social situation of Hong Kong two decades after returning to China," and "the future of Hong Kong". Political orientation, demographic factors and mass media had stronger relationships with the stance toward political values and social issues than social media use.
Levy, R. (2021). Social media, news consumption, and polarization: Evidence from a field experiment. doi: 10.1257/aer.20191777	USA	Experiment	Facebook	ideological, affective	Exposure to counter-attitudinal news decreases negative attitudes toward the opposing political party. No evidence that the political leanings of news outlets affect political opinions: Exposure to pro-attitudinal news increases affective polarization compared to counter-attitudinal news.
Lu, Y., Ray, R., Ha, L., & Chen, P. (2020). Social media news consumption and opinion	USA	Survey	Social Media	ideological	Time spent on social media is indirectly associated with opinion polarization on China's trade practice. Social media had

Title	Country	Method	S.M. Platform	Type of Polarization	Results on Polarization
polarization on China's trade practices: Evidence from a U.S. national survey.					a mediationg effect among those who frequently encounter like-minded information.
Min, H., & Yun, S. (2018). Selective exposure and political polarization of public opinion on the presidential impeachment in south korea: Facebook vs. Kakaotalk. doi: 10.29152/KOIKS. 2018.49.1.137	South Korea	Survey	Facbook, Kakao Talk	affective	It shows that politically motivated selective exposure predicted a significant increase in political polarization. In addition, education, political interest, and political ideology strength were also positively related to political polarization. The online activity on KakaoTalk has more of an impact on the increase of political polarization than online activity on Facebook.
Munger, K., Egan, P. J., Nagler, J., Ronen, J., & Tucker, J. (2020). Political knowledge and misinformation in the era of social media: Evidence from the 2015 uk election. doi: 10.1017/S0007123420000198	USA	Experiments	Facebook, Twitter	affective	No polarization through partisan cklickbait headlines.
Nguyen, A., & Vu, H. T. (2019). Testing popular news discourse on the "echo chamber" effect: Does political polarisation occur among those relying on social media as their primary politics news source? doi: 10.5210/fm.v24i6.9632	EU	Survey	Social Media	ideological	There is little (no) evidence for an increase in polarisation of EU related attitudes through social media compared to traditional media.
Ohme, J. (2021). Algorithmic social media use and its relationship to attitude reinforcement and issue-specific political participation – The case of the 2015 European immigration movements. doi: 10.1080/19331681.2020.1805085	Denmark	Survey	Social Media	ideological	The likelihood to report attitude reinforcement was twice as high for citizens who strongly rely on social media than for those who strongly rely on nonalgorithmic or offline media. Algorithmic news selection in combination with the homophily of social media can affect po-

Title	Country	Method	S.M. Platform	Type of Polarization	Results on Polarization
					litical attitudes of citizens in a reinforcing way.
Semaan B. C. Robertson, S., Douglas, S. & Maruyama, M. (2014). Social media supporting political deliberation across multiple public spheres: towards depolarization. doi: 10.1145/2531602.2531605	USA	Survey – qualitative	Social Media	/	We found that people's broader online interactions were depolarized in nature.
Shmargad, Y., & Klar, S. (2019). How partisan online environments shape communication with political outgroups.	USA	Experiment	News in social online contexts	partisan	Those who are attentive to their social surroundings learn over time how to moderate in the face of diversity. When they are subsequently exposed to our outgroup treatment, they choose to share more moderate news articles. Those who are surrounded by echo chambers respond to political outgroups by clinging to their preexisting views and sharing these views with a disagreeing audience.
Shmargad, Y., & Klar, S. (2020). Sorting the news: How ranking by popularity polarizes our politics. doi: 10.1080/10584609.2020.1713267	USA	Experiment (2)	News in social online contexts	partisan	No evidence that sorting news articles by popularity increases affective polarization.
Suk, J., Shah, D. V., Wells, C., Wagner, M. W., Friedland, L. A., Cramer, K. J., Hughes, C., & Franklin, C. (2020). Do improving conditions harden partisan preferences? Lived experiences, imagined communities, and polarized evaluations. doi: 10.1093/ijpor/edz051	USA	Survey	Social Media	partisan	Partisans' use of digital media strengthened their polarizing attitudes toward Obama evaluations.

Journalism or Public Relations?
Proposal for Conceptualizing a User-Oriented Research Program on the Confounding of the Two Genres Online

Romy Fröhlich

Abstract

The Internet makes it easier for strategic communicators to address their PR audiences directly in a way that has never been seen before. This is even more true as media users increasingly turn to the Internet as an alternative source of information, especially in times of crisis and controversy. As a result, new forms of 'particular-interest oriented persuasive simulations of journalism' (PIoPS) are spreading over the Internet. This chapter provides a first theoretical review and foundation of the troubled situation and briefly explains why and from which perspective we are actually dealing with a 'problem.' On this basis, it conceptualizes a user-oriented research program that enables us to measure whether and, if so, how PR's simulations of journalism can be distinguished from actual journalistic products/content. The contribution discusses theoretical implications for a text-oriented approach that could be suitable for describing and operationalizing criteria of distinctiveness. It also yields theoretical implications for a reception-oriented perspective which helps to describe users' concrete differentiation behaviors and procedures in the reception of PR and journalism and operationalize these for respective reception studies. In conclusion, specific challenges that will inevitably arise for the outlined research program are outlined.

The Internet has fundamentally changed the conditions under which the public sphere and public communication[1] are created. This particularly affects the two societal sub-systems of public communication: 'journalism'[2]

---

1 For definitions of 'public communication,' see e.g., Godulla (2017), Kohring (2006), and Pfetsch and Bossert (2013).
2 In this contribution understood as "institutionalized journalism" as defined by Wolf (2014, p. 72).

167

and 'public relations' (PR) (cf. for example Pietzcker, 2017), also and especially in their interplay in the production of public communication and the public sphere (cf. Ward-Johnson & Guiniven, 2008, among others). Distinguishing these two fields becomes problematic when formal and content-related measures are used to make PR on the web look like journalistic reporting without labeling the respective content as PR. While the integration of PR or marketing content into editorial content is regulated by separation principles in professional self-obligations and in laws[3] to safeguard editorial independence and protect media users[4] from being misled, there are no labeling obligations for original PR communication published beyond original journalistic media. However, as the Internet now offers the possibility for organizations whose primary field of activity is not publishing to expand their communication channels, their role as communicators changes and a new problematic situation arises. Lloyd and Toogood (2015) describe this situation as follows: "Every organization is a media organization' has developed from being a slogan into becoming a growing reality" (p. vii). Years ago, Henry (2007) had already warned that "PR firms have become increasingly effective at churning out advertising that looks and sounds just like mainstream journalism" (p. 180).

There has always been a certain 'closeness' between journalism and PR on the content and formal levels. This arises primarily from the fact that PR in the area of media relations must prepare its services for journalists such that they fit the professional journalistic criteria for form and content. To be perceived and ultimately processed by the media system/journalism, PR messages intended as source and research material for journalists (media relations, press releases) must meet journalistic standards. These demands include the expectation that the respective PR material fulfills the criterion of truthfulness while also meeting the general technical rules of journalistic texting/writing as well as the special requirements derived from theories of news selection and newsworthiness (news factors/values). With regards to its journalistic target group, PR has therefore always been guided by journalistic skills. If it is done well, PR in

---

3 The 'principle of separation' is regulated in Germany in the *Pressekodex* (the 'Press Code' is a voluntary commitment; Presserat, 2019) in section 7 on the separation of advertising and editorial work. Moreover, it is legally stipulated in section 8 of the State Media Treaty (MStV) (for the latest version of April 2020, see here https://www.rlp.de/fileadmin/rlp-stk/pdf-Dateien/Medienpolitik/MedienEventstaatsvertrag.pdf).

4 The terms user(s), recipient(s), and audience are used synonymously in this contribution.

Journalism or Public Relations?

the field of media relations has thus typically 'simulated'[5] journalism (cf. for example Fröhlich, 2015, p. 115). This is done because the closer PR products are in form and content to what is relevant for journalists in their work, the greater the chance that journalists will perceive and process PR products in their work and the greater the chance that PR can establish itself as a source of information for journalists. Or – to put it differently following Hoffjann and Arlt (2015) – public relations imitates journalism in its press and media work to "[...] become the subject of journalism with its self-representations" (p. 94).[6] However, as far as PR's target groups beyond journalism are concerned, PR now has the opportunity to bypass journalism altogether from the outset. Using new digital communication channels, PR can reach the relevant stakeholders online, thereby overcoming the spatial and temporal barriers that previously existed (cf. Wendelin, 2014, p. 80). The Internet thus makes it easier to address PR audiences directly in a way that has never been seen before. This is even more true as media users increasingly turn to the Internet as an alternative source of information, especially in times of crisis and controversy. As a result, online PR now increasingly simulates journalism in direct communication with its non-journalistic audiences. This is quite reasonable because journalistic procedures and programs represent "(...) professional instructions for the production of public communication offers, i.e., typified action patterns and rules. Those who wish to address the public be it as a group or individual can greatly maximize the success of these efforts by using the professional and organizational programs of journalism" (Altmeppen & Quandt, 2002, p. 58). As a consequence, authoritative self-representations (i.e., PR), as Hoffjann and Arlt (2015) have described it, can increasingly be found on the Internet disguised as authoritative external representations (journalism). This appears to be facilitated by a view dominant in large parts of the German population that PR is a form of journalism (77%, Bentele & Seidenglanz, 2005, p. 211).

(1) The described problematic situation on 'particular-interest oriented persuasive simulation of journalism' (PIoPS), as I call it, has not been well studied so far. This is especially true for newer forms of persuasive journalism simulations spreading over the Internet. This article provides a first theoretical analysis of this situation. In this context, I

---

5 All quotations from non-English language sources were translated into English by the author.
6 The phenomenon of "churnalism" has reinforced this reasoning in recent years (Hummel,2009, p. 59; cf. also Hummel, 2016).

Romy Fröhlich

understand PIoPS of journalism as PR texts that can unequivocally be identified as products of strategic-persuasive communicators/sources,
(2) closely follow journalistic rules and conventions in terms of form and content-related quality criteria,
(3) seemingly imitate journalism by strongly leaning towards the visual and textual appearance and formal style of journalistic texts, and
(4) primarily pursue the goal of having a persuasive effect on a target audience, i.e., persuading people of a claim, product, opinion, attitude, etc.[7]

Two examples of PIoPS in the Internet are shown in the following:

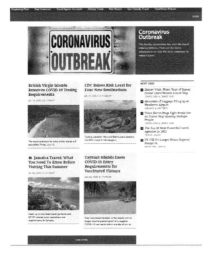 

https://www.travelpulse.com   https://alles-rund-ums-auto.de

This contribution elaborates on the possibilities for a theoretical foundation that enables us to measure whether and if so, how, PR's simulations of journalism can be distinguished from actual journalistic products/content. On the one hand, this question relates to theoretical implications for (1) a text-oriented approach that could be suitable for describing criteria of distinctiveness as textual features and operationalizing them for the con-

---

7 Journalistic texts of specific genres, such as commentary, must be distinguished from this, as they may also pursue a certain kind of persuasive intention.

Journalism or Public Relations?

tent-analytical testing of corresponding texts. On the other hand, it yields theoretical implications for (2) a reception-oriented perspective, which helps to describe users' concrete differentiation behaviors and procedures in the reception of PR and journalism and operationalizing them for respective reception studies.

At an early stage, Bucher (2000) pointed out the need for empirical studies on recipients' perceptions of the quality of *online* journalism to be conducted with a reference to the specific online products in question. More precisely, he speaks of the necessity of a "product-oriented" approach that "relates reception findings and product/content attributes to each other" (p. 155). Ideally, the reception-related question should be combined with the text-related question, and the relevant stimulus material from the reception study should then be the basis for the content analysis or vice versa.

The following section will describe the outlined problem and its causes in more detail. It will also briefly explain why and from which perspective this is actually a 'problem.' In a second step, existing theoretical components are presented that appear to be helpful for a scientific treatment of the specific, two-part object of interest. Based on this, in a third step, initial considerations for the empirical operationalization of concrete research questions are made. Finally, particular challenges for operationalization are discussed that arise when empirically implementing the outlined approach, especially if it is product-oriented in Bucher's sense.

Causes, Relevance, and Consequences of the Problem

The constant proliferation of media products and services is nothing new; in fact, it is even typical for the emergence and development of "mediated public spheres" (Wendelin, 2011). In this context, the technology driven development of "owned media" mentioned above is one among a number of processes that increase the sheer amount of media offerings as part of the (further) development of mediated public spheres. And of course, the communicative offers of strategic-persuasive communication from a wide variety of organizations not primarily active in the field of journalistic publishing (e.g., companies, NGOs, political parties, etc.) have long provided alternatives to the media offers of journalistic editorial departments and media organizations. PR has thus always been involved in the production of the public (sphere) (Röttger, Preusse & Schmitt, 2014, p. 5). From the perspective of democracy and norms theory, however, journalism, PR, and their products should be distinguishable, both explicitly and above all for the recipients (cf. among others Gonser & Rußmann, 2017, pp. 3-4). After all, PR is a form of self-referential persuasive communication that acts in an interest- and client-driven manner (= self-referential) and whose "controlled communication activities (...) are intended to contribute (...) to the realization of overarching organizational goals (...)" (Zerfaß & Pleil, 2015, p. 47). In contrast, journalism's hetero-referential communication is committed to the common good. From this fact, some essential protection rights are derived for journalism and media companies (e.g., the right to refuse to testify/to give evidence; 'Tendenzschutz,' a protective regulation for media enterprises serving ideological purposes/tendencies). Such specific protective rights do not exist for PR.

While journalism, from a normative point of view, is still committed to hetero-referentiality, i.e., to the "public description(s) of society, namely of the society that is currently happening" (Hoffjann & Arlt, 2015, p. 40), PR can act both self- and hetero-referentially in the sense of a flexible situational adaptation to specific communication topics and intended communication goals. Depending on the situation, PR can, therefore, either generate "self-representation for image cultivation" or construct "desirable realities" via external representations (Merten & Westerbarkey, 1994, p. 208) – e.g., via issues management. On the Internet, PR is increasingly also found in the form of hetero-referential communication. The probability of this is high because PR must also be understood as a "performance system of publicity" (Hoffjann & Arlt, 2015, p. 39). From a theoretical point of view, one can conclude against this background that journalistic and PR publications should/must be distinguishable from each other (in a way that is easily recognizable to the audience) – today more than ever. This is the ideal-typical way of looking at things. It is also reflected in different attributions of responsibility in rules laid down by professional policy and in the establishment of special professional control bodies (in Germany: German Press Council, DPR, and German Council for Public Relations, DRPR) to monitor compliance with these rules.

However, the prerequisites for PR's involvement in the creation and production of the public sphere are quite different today than they were in pre-digital times. These prerequisites concern, for example, the functional characteristics of strategic-persuasive communication: Due to the dwindling credibility attributed by recipients to traditional advertising, which is subject to labeling requirements, label-free PR is increasingly taking over functions previously attributed to brand marketing (cf. Ries & Ries, 2004). It is hoped that this will lead to higher credibility attributions for the persuasive messages among the respective target groups – always assuming that the PR communication in question in such cases does not then come along again in a form that is easily identifiable as 'advertising.'

One way of avoiding the impression of advertising in PR is to give the PR texts in question a journalistic appearance, that is, to 'simulate' journalism. This also leads to a 'proliferation of media offerings,' whereby the Internet decisively facilitates the dissemination of journalistic-looking PR directly to the intended PR target groups. In this context, Gonser and Rußmann (2017) even speak of a "planned deception of users" in the online sphere by PR communicators "overstepping the boundaries of ethically correct behavior" (p. 7). In contrast, Pleil (2015a) takes a more neutral stance on the matter when he describes this development as a process by which companies, for example, succeed better today than in pre-digital times in offering their reference groups "new mechanisms of orientation alongside journalistic orientation" (p. 22). Regardless of the perspective with which one views this development, it promotes a blurring of the boundaries between journalism and PR.

Another trend contributes to the problem: Media companies are adapting to the advances of the Internet and the migration of users to the Internet by expanding their online presence (see Beck, Reineck & Schubert, 2010; Godulla, 2015; Neuberger & Kapern, 2013, pp. 196-213). Accordingly, the number of users who also search for and use media coverage on the Internet beyond paid online or offline newspaper or magazine subscriptions has been multiplying steadily for years (cf. Beisch & Schäfer, 2020; cf. also Keen, 2007). The probability that they will encounter content that looks like journalism but is not journalism (such as "PR, service, archive and reference functions, and lay communication;" Weischenberg et al., 2006, p. 348) is high. This is not a problem as long as users are able to recognize it. However, in the course of the developments described above, the distinction between journalism and simulations of journalism is seeming to become increasingly difficult for recipients (Bucher, 2000; Neuberger, 2011); they usually appear to lack the media competence required for this (Gonser & Rußmann, 2017, p. 7; see also Pietzcker, 2017, p. 73; Henry, 2007, p. 23).

Meanwhile, fears are growing that, through its digital transformation, the public sphere is increasingly losing its normatively desirable effective selectivity between journalism and PR, and that the shortage of editorial capacity is further exacerbating this problem (as a result of cost-cutting measures by media organizations; cf. for example Neuberger, 2018). Ruß-Mohl (2017, p. 17) even speaks of a "digitization-induced power shift" between journalism and PR. Against this background, Neuberger et al. (2019) diagnose "that professional journalism has forfeited its extensive

Romy Fröhlich

monopoly as a scrutinizing control authority on the current public sphere: audiences and speakers [in the sense of 'senders'; R. F.] can bypass journalism and dispense with its services, they can more easily criticize it publicly or take on scrutinizing tasks themselves, which are thus no longer the exclusive preserve of professional journalism, which is moreover weakened by an economic crisis. As a result, the previous order is weakening." (p. 175)

This 'softening' is even inherent in some theoretical models of journalism. Haller (2003), for example, writes that journalism must pursue the goal of "successful social communication." This "(...) succeeds when journalism creates a media reality that is used by the communication partners (actors and recipients) as an orientation on current event contexts, or is at least understood as such" (p. 181).[8] Here, the 'success' of specific journalistic goals and functions depends on the perception of the communication partners of journalism and thus also on the recipients' perceptions and assessments of journalism and its products. This means, firstly, that journalism does not achieve its 'goal' if recipients do not use or understand the media reality as an orientation on current event contexts. This happens completely independently of whether or not recipients are correct in their respective perception and assessment (as reflected in the pejorative keyword 'lying/mendacious press' when recipients in Germany believe the media report is not the truth but propaganda). Secondly, considering the theoretical foundations of the distinction between journalism and PR scenarios are also conceivable in which recipients may prefer to understand current event contexts by using 'media' which originates from strategic-persuasive communicators (from organizations and institutions beyond the publishing industry, e.g., companies, NGOs, political parties, etc.). This may occur because these PR texts (1) are sometimes less complex and less diverse and thus appear more comprehensible, because (2) they better hit the core of the recipients' particular interests, because (3) they have an entertaining character, or other reasons. This would mean that a situation would exist in which strategic persuasive communication (and not journalism) would achieve 'successful social communication' – even if

---

8 See also Arnold (2008) on the journalistic criterion of "applicability." According to this criterion, journalistic offerings "should be attractive [to recipients; R. F.] and applicable in the users' living environment" (p. 499). PR communication can also fulfill this criterion as well as the criterion of being "entertaining." Under certain circumstances, PR can even meet these criteria better than journalism. Unlike journalism, it does not have to consider other criteria that might run counter to these goals here, such as 'diversity' or 'balance.'

Journalism or Public Relations?

only in certain thematic areas and/or only among some of the recipients (keywords 'fake news,' 'post-truth,' or 'disinformation'). That this scenario is not at all improbable is indicated by findings from an unpublished, initial study of recipients (Kiefl et al., 2020) that I will come back to later.

It is, therefore, "not a matter of course that the audience is almost automatically interested" in the "professional and independent communication of relevant information" by journalism (Godulla & Wolf, 2017, p. 233; cf. similarly Schweiger, 2007, p. 264). The audience may even become less and less interested in this kind of independent communication in the future. Non-journalistic sources and communicators may fulfill the individual and specific information needs of recipients better than journalism. This can result in a reception-functional overlap between journalism and PR, which in turn presents journalism with new challenges of an attention-economic nature, especially on the web. The consequence of this could be that journalistic products change significantly.

There are also further reception-functional overlaps between journalism and PR. For example, Bentele and Seidenglanz (2005, p. 216) found in a representative population survey that the German population expects truthful communication, objectivity, honesty, and social responsibility from PR, as well – criteria and expectations that are also (and actually primarily) attributed to journalism. Bentele (2013, p. 46) assumes that the boom in corporate media (corporate publishing) is mainly responsible for this. Journalism has long been simulated in this PR field as well, both online and offline. In recent years, large publishing houses have increasingly invested in corporate publishing and maintained independent units to produce corporate publications. The commissioning companies benefit from the journalistic expertise and appeal and the associated high credibility of their publications among recipients (Ruß-Mohl, 2017). Increasingly, however, 'corporate publishing' products (available online and offline free of charge) represent serious competition to classic journalistic products, which "(...) can potentially offer a more critical view (...) less influenced by the need for positive self-promotion" but "have to sell at the newsstand" (Ruß-Mohl, 2017, p. 19).

The general public, at any rate, has surprisingly similar value expectations and quality perceptions of the two (normatively and functionally quite different) publishing performance systems (Bentele & Seidenglanz, 2005). It can be assumed that this attitude of the audience additionally aggravates the problem of the increasingly difficult differentiation between digital forms of journalistic and PR texts. However, there is still a dearth of research on the problematic situation described regarding PR that simulates journalism (as defined above). This applies to research on the form and

Romy Fröhlich

content of such simulations as well as to research on the question of the reception and impact of such simulations. A short overview of the state of research on this subject area is given in the following.

State of Research

Previous research on 'journalism and PR' has focused primarily on the working relationship between the two professions. In particular, studies have investigated the extent to which both sides are oriented towards or adapt to each other in the production of public communication. This research is primarily interested in the extent to which journalistic products are influenced and determined by PR interventions (e.g., PR's influence on the timing and the topics of media coverage, c.f. Baerns, 1991). In Anglo-American research, studies on this topic are usually referred to as "information subsidy" (Gandy, 1982; cf. also Kiousis et al., 2007; Manning, 2001). In contrast, research on the 'intereffication model' assumes a mutual orientation, adaptation, and enabling of journalism and PR (Bentele et al., 1997; cf. also Bentele & Fechner, 2015). Corresponding research also addresses the question of the extent to which PR imitates formal selection criteria of journalism in order to influence the reporting process in a way that is favorable to the respective strategic communicator (Hoffjann & Arlt, 2015, p. 92). However, this research does not get to the core of the problem described here regarding the distinguishability between journalistic and PR products.

Godulla et al. (2017) are closer to this issue with their study on differences in digital long-form journalism and corporate publishing (CP). Some of their content-analytic findings have the potential to be transferred to the comparative analysis of journalistic texts and PIoPS of journalism. Among other things, the audio elements and graphics, as well as photos, were found significantly more frequently in journalistic online articles than in the online CP offers examined. Moreover, the online CP texts were also considerably shorter in comparison. Conversely, the occurrence of hyperlinks in CP items was more than three times higher than in the journalistic items. There were also apparent differences in terms of the design of the reception structure: While the linear reception structure (from top to bottom or, less frequently, from left to the right) dominated in corporate publishing (83%), less than half (44%) of the journalistic contributions had this "rigid" structure, as the authors describe it. The "elastic, parallel or ramified narrative structure and storytelling in strands" practiced in 38% of journalistic posts occurs in only 10% of CP posts, and only 7% of

CP posts have a "concentric narrative structure" or "narrate in chapters" compared to 19% of journalistic posts (pp. 216-217).

Against this background, it is hardly surprising that the journalistic articles were more complex in structure than the CP articles, which had a significantly more straightforward and more homogeneous appearance. Godulla et al. (2017) interpret this as an indication that the two compared text types pursue principally different narrative approaches. They write:

> "Aspects such as objectivity, completeness, and comprehensibility are traditionally emphasized as qualities in journalism (...). A narrative consisting of many sense units can meet these postulates. Thus, the consideration of many aspects theoretically leads to a more versatile (and thus also more complete) picture, which becomes more comprehensible through supplementary information. In corporate publishing, on the other hand, the focus seems to be on formulating an accentuated message, even in digital long-forms, which would lose conciseness if there were too many segments since users could set their own priorities" (p. 215).

Overall, the study offers some interesting starting points for examining differences between journalistic and PR texts. However, it must be remembered that the analyzed criteria apply specifically to textual long forms, and their generalizability is therefore limited.

Another study by Theis-Berglmair and Kellermann (2017) is the only one to date that explicitly addresses the distinction between journalistic and PR texts. In a pilot study, they investigate whether and, if so, how original journalistic texts can be distinguished from original PR texts. In describing this extant research gap, the authors argue that "[t]he problem of classifying and evaluating texts (...) can neither be solved satisfactorily with regard to the (professional) status of the actors nor concerning the traditional quality debate in journalism" (p. 107). They assume that due to the increasingly blurred boundaries between journalism and PR and the changing work roles and new communicative offers on both sides, the previous actor- and organization-related approaches are becoming increasingly useless. Therefore, they propose a descriptive differentiation approach on the text level. The approach aims to develop a survey system that can be used for content analyses and that overcomes the time-consuming operationalization of other (primarily normative) differentiation criteria.

Theis-Berglmair and Kellermann (2017) assume unique and typical linguistic characteristics that can be distinguished for both types of texts. For this purpose, they develop and test a text-analytical procedure based on theoretically founded text-immanent and textual meta-elements, by means of which (unambiguous) assignments of texts to journalism or PR can be made. Such text-immanent elements include, for example, certainty-reducing clauses, which are regarded in journalism as a quality feature in situations of uncertainty. A first qualitative pilot study of the two researchers with small text samples indeed provides evidence that their assumption is correct. However, an empirical test on a large scale is still pending. The approach sounds promising for the research interest explicated here regarding the distinguishability of journalism and PR texts. Therefore, it will be presented in more detail later in this article in a section on the contingency-oriented linguistic dimension at the text level to provide a theoretical foundation for the stated research interest.

The question of whether the democracy-theory and norm-based differences between journalistic texts and PIoPS of journalism are actually reflected in the respective text products of PR and journalism is only one side of the coin. Without a doubt, whether recipients can distinguish the two types of texts is also essential – including the questions of whether recipients even expect that the two text types can be distinguished, whether they want to distinguish them at all, and whether they can then actually do so. However, there has been no research on this complex of questions. What is available so far are studies that deal with the recipient perspective on journalistic quality and studies specifically on the quality of online journalism from the recipient perspective (e.g., Neuberger, 2012). From such studies, one could conclude that if recipients can judge journalistic quality, they should also be able to identify communication that does not meet these quality criteria as something other than 'journalism.' They would thus be able to differentiate. However, the findings of relevant audience studies are ambiguous (cf., e.g., Rössler, 2004 vs. Dahinden et al., 2004). Moreover, most studies equate 'quality of journalistic products from a users' perspective' with 'users' expectations of journalistic products' (e.g., Wolling, 2002; as an exception, see Jungnickel, 2011). In most cases, no distinction is made between content producers' professional quality criteria and content users' quality criteria (which may greatly differ; for exceptions, see Rössler, 2004; Wicke, 2022). The question of whether and how the online media audience can judge professional 'journalistic quality' on the Internet at all, and if so, how they go about it, has not been solidly researched so far. The qualitative survey by Wladarsch (2020) does provide the first current assumptions that complement and substantiate older findings by Neubeger et al. (2012), however.

The findings of an as yet unpublished empirical study of recipients (Kiefl et al., 2020) raise initial doubts about the ability of the media audience to distinguish between journalistic texts and PIoPS of journalism on

Journalism or Public Relations?

the web. The pilot study in question was product-oriented in the sense of Bucher (2000, p. 155). Therefore, it was supplemented by a parallel content analysis of the relevant stimulus material of the recipient study. Most of the respondents expressed an interest in distinguishing between journalism and PR on the Internet and slightly more than 50% were able to classify respective texts correctly. Nevertheless, 38% of the respondents in the experimental study were still unable to accurately identify the presented texts[9] as journalism or PR. Here, actual journalistic texts were identified as PR, and actual PR texts as journalistic texts. Adding the "don't know" residual response category, the number of those who found the task too difficult is quite large. Therefore, there is some evidence that assumptions about a lack of recipients' media competence (see above), which have not been particularly well supported empirically, are probably correct. On the other hand: This result does not have to be due to the audience's deficient media competence. It can also emerge because the respective PR texts simply do a good job in simulating journalism.

The pilot study also revealed initial interesting insights into which formal and content-related criteria the respondents use to identify and distinguish journalism and PR on the Internet (method: thinking aloud). Except for the criteria 'neutrality' and 'diversity,' it is not the classic quality criteria, e.g., according to Arnold (2009) or others (see above), that are used here, but completely different measures, through which individual ideas of journalism and PR come into play. Furthermore, it has been shown that the test persons found the actual PR texts, which they mistook for journalism, more appealing than the actual journalistic texts, which they took for PR. In addition, quite a few test subjects rated the PR texts they had correctly identified as more interesting and relevant than the journalistic texts they had correctly identified. In addition, it made no difference to the perceived credibility of the text stimuli presented whether the subjects had previously identified a text as journalism or as PR. The majority of respondents based their attribution of credibility on their individual perception of the truthfulness of the information provided and not on the more formal question of whether the text was written by journalists or PR authors and what the author's intentions were. In addition, it was shown that for demographic characteristics of the test persons, only age showed slight effects in the response behavior. The same applies at a low level to the frequency of reception of online content (Internet experience).

---

9 Real journalistic texts existing on the web (i.e., not 'built' for the study) and real journalism simulations of PR sources on the topic of 'Diesel-Gate.'

Romy Fröhlich

The state of the research summarized above means the current scientific knowledge on our topic is sparse. Above all, there is a lack of an initial and coherent theoretical foundation for the research interests introduced above. In the following, possibilities for a theoretical foundation of the two-part subject of research will be explored. For this purpose, existing theoretical components will be brought into play that can be helpful for our problem.

Theoretical Implications for the Distinction Between Journalistic Texts/Products and 'Particular-Interest Oriented Persuasive Simulations' of Journalism (PIoPS)

As already explained, two intertwined sets of questions arise for the overarching research interest of communication studies in the problem context described above:

1. the questions of which theoretical approaches could be suitable for identifying criteria of indistinguishability between journalistic and PR texts and how these criteria can be described in such a way that they allow for a content analytical operationalization to assess text products. The corresponding question here would be whether said differences could be recognizable for users/recipients at all because the two text types are (or are not) designed differently (formally and/or in terms of content);
2. the question of which theoretical approaches could be suitable in audience research that intends to investigate whether recipients (want to) identify differences between the text products in question, how well or poorly they ultimately succeed in doing so, and what criteria they use in trying to distinguish the two.

At this point, it should be recalled once again that one should ideally address both sets of questions in a combined, one-to-one approach within the framework of a "product-oriented" research agenda (cf. Bucher, 2000, p. 155).

Additionally, a third set of questions is conceivable: How do professional communicators from journalism and PR/strategic-persuasive communication actually think about the problem complex described? Do they perceive the overlapping boundaries between journalism and PR and the challenges of difficult distinguishability that may go hand in hand with them as a problem at all? And if so, how do they describe this problem, with what consequences for whom or what, etc.? However, the theoretical foundation for this vital complex of questions is fed by other theoretical

Journalism or Public Relations?

approaches (e.g., professionalization research, role research, organizational research), depending on the specific knowledge interest, and therefore cannot be dealt with here. It deserves a separate consideration, which would, however, far exceed the framework set here.

Differentiation Dimensions from the Content Perspective

At the center of the product-oriented research interest is the question of which differentiation *dimensions* appear suitable for distinguishing between PIoPS of journalism and actual journalistic texts/content. As described, this question focuses on border shifts/transgressions between PR and journalism, which are especially intensified by the digitalization of public communication. Consequently, the following explanations address the essential content-related and format/design-related peculiarities of journalism and PR as well as selected peculiarities of online texts/content of journalism and PR. A whole range of different dimensions can be used to derive measurement criteria for operationalizing this research interest. Referring back to my explanations in the previous chapters, these measurement criteria can be systematized as follows. However, there is no claim of completeness here: 1. the dimension *'journalistic quality,'* 2. the dimension *'advertency (control),'* 3. the c*ontingency-oriented linguistic dimension* at the text level and 4. the dimension *'persuasion and ethics in PR.'*

The 'Journalistic Quality' Dimension

This dimension focuses on what professional and scientific discourse largely consensually define as good and sincere journalistic online products. To simplify, one can assume thereby: The more online PR texts/content correspond in form and content to these (relevant) journalistic quality criteria, the greater the similarities between PR content and journalistic content on the web.

The public interest orientation of journalism described above, which in most liberal democracies also legitimizes important protective rights of institutionalized journalism, gives rise to two assumptions: First, that a whole series of quality features characterize products of institutionalized journalism in an ideal-typical manner, and second, that products of institutionalized journalism are therefore recognizable by such quality criteria. These assumptions hold true at least for quality journalism.

For PR, there are no such distinguishable quality criteria (Hoffmann, 2007, p. 558). This does not automatically mean, however, that PR products in general or PIoPS of journalism generally do not exhibit such journalistic criteria. However, from the point of view of professional practice and technique, it can certainly be assumed that journalism simulations – understood as the product of commissioned persuasive communication – fulfill these criteria less often or clearly than journalistic products committed to the common good. This would open up a first theoretical horizon for the measurability of differences between journalistic and PR products: approaches and models for 'journalistic quality.'

In 2008, Arnold presented a first systematization proposal for the wide-ranging discourse on the quality of journalism in communication studies. For this purpose, he developed a three-level model (cf. also Arnold, 2009): (1) For the connection between function and quality of journalistic products, the functional-system-oriented level of the social function of journalism (key phrase "public good orientation"), (2) for the connection between values and quality of journalistic products, the normative democracy-oriented level of fundamental social values, and (3) for the connection between audience benefit and quality of journalistic products, the audience-based action-oriented level of marketing driven expectations. Arnold assigns corresponding quality criteria to each level which could be operationalized both for a content-analytical approach to our research interest and in the context of user studies:

– Functional-system-oriented criteria such as diversity (of topics, arguments, sources, and actors), topicality/novelty value (in the sense of an "observation of society connected to the present" (Arnold, 2008, p. 494)), relevance (in the sense of the journalistic selection program based on news value theory), credibility (not in the sense of assessment by recipients but in the sense of a plausible linking of facts and opinions), independence (in the sense of the norm that journalism does not submit to the logic of other systems), research (in the sense of self-observation "that goes beyond the interests of the performing actors of individual subsystems" (p. 495)), criticism (in the sense of criticizing communication and actions from other social subsystems), accessibility (in the sense of presenting information as comprehensibly, clearly, and vividly as possible), background reporting, regional/local reference;
– Normative democracy-oriented criteria such as balance/neutrality/separation of news and opinion (including legal regulations on impartiality), protection/respect for personal privacy or protection from libel or slander (regulated in media laws and press codices);

Journalism or Public Relations?

– Audience-oriented criteria such as applicability (journalistic products should be attractive to recipients and applicable in their life setting), entertainment value (in the sense of an entertaining format of information), transparency (in the sense of a minimum requirement for naming sources of information), design.

Other authors arrive at other systematizations, specify and expand this catalog of criteria, or assign specific quality criteria to other levels than Arnold. For example, Pöttker (2000) simply distinguishes between quality criteria that are aimed at the subject of reporting (accuracy, completeness (relevance), truthfulness, distinctiveness) and quality criteria that are important with regard to the audience and its expectations of journalism (independence, topicality, comprehensibility, entertaining nature). On the other hand, other authors point out which criteria are considered irrelevant, less relevant to quality, or even hostile to quality in journalistic products and for what reasons they are placed in these categories. Concerning hostility to quality, Neuberger (2012, p. 44) mentions, e.g., individual or participatory aspects such as views from a personal perspective. Differentiation dimensions can also be operationalized from such 'negative nominations.' Finally, PR products have greater freedom to thematize individual, participatory, or particularistic aspects. The occurrence of such aspects in relevant text products could therefore indicate that a respective text is a PR text.

Arnold's systematization of criteria represents "core qualities" of journalism (Arnold, 2016, p. 558). Depending on the object of investigation and journalistic genre (e.g., opinionated forms such as reportage) or media type (e.g., online journalism or broadcasting), they must be adapted or differentiated. Arnold (2016) emphasizes that this necessity does not make the core qualities obsolete or that "completely different quality grids have to be developed in each case; rather, the quality criteria can be concretized, modified, and weighted accordingly" (p. 557).

For the operationalization of the criterion 'journalistic quality' in the context of our epistomological interest, it must also be taken into account that the classic journalistic quality criteria have so far been developed predominantly for offline journalism. For the online context relevant here, they must be supplemented by quality criteria specifically for online journalism (cf. for example Mehlis, 2014). These include, above all (but not limited to), hypertextuality (cf. Ryfe et al., 2015), interactivity, and multimediality. These web-typical criteria for the quality of online journalism possibly reinforce the similarity between PR and journalism on the Internet because these criteria are also characteristics of professional online

PR (cf. Pleil, 2015a; Radl et al., 2015, and others). Nevertheless, they are also seen as quality criteria of online journalism in the relevant quality research. Hypertextuality, for example, allows for more transparency of research sources and enables the presentation of further contexts (cf., Neuberger, 2011, p. 108). Interactivity offers recipients better and faster opportunities for feedback to and contact with editorial teams and even enables them to communicate in dialog (cf. Bucher, 2000, pp. 155-156). Multimedia possibly improves the quality of communicating complex issues. For the concrete operationalization of these criteria, however, it is essential to bear in mind that the quality of online journalism is not guaranteed per se by such criteria, but that it depends in turn on the concrete quality of the specific design of these features, functions, and offerings. A difference between journalistic text products and those of online PR could become apparent in the particular design of these criteria. First indications of this can already be found in Godulla et al. (2017) – at least as far as long-text forms of journalism and PR on the Internet are concerned. The only remaining question is whether these findings can be transferred beyond long-text forms and sustainably to other textual formats, which would then make these typical online quality criteria universally distinguishable.

As an overview in McQuail (1992) shows, by the early 1990s, there was already a whole series of studies that examined either individual journalistic quality criteria or larger groups of these criteria. As with McQuail, more recent synopses by Beck et al. (2010, pp. 28-37) or Arnold (2016) show that content analyses dominate quality research. Concrete proposals for the operationalization of journalistic quality criteria, including ideas for improving, adapting, and further developing existing measures, are thus available in large numbers; no fundamental pioneering work needs to be done here.

The 'Attention' Dimension

Less relevant than the criterion 'journalistic quality' is the criterion 'attention' (attention control). The importance of this criterion for the stated research interest arises primarily from the fact that PR and journalism operate in the same online distribution space and are thus, unlike in the offline world, direct communication competitors (cf. Ruß-Mohl, 2017; Altmeppen et al., 2002). Here, their content products are only a single click away from each other. Audience studies have shown that recipients are strongly guided by the formal design of web content when selecting information (Seibold, 2002, p. 37). Thus, in comparison to the offline scenario,

Journalism or Public Relations?

strategic considerations for attracting (and/or controlling) attention gain enormous importance in the somewhat "chaotic" Internet (Pleil, 2015b, p. 1017), both in PR and in journalism (cf. Franck, 2014).[10]

News factors represent a comparatively classic instrument of attention control. They not only control the journalistic selection process in news production. As research has shown, they also influence the selective use and information processing of news by recipients (e.g., Eilders, 1997, 2006; Eilders et al., 1999; Fretwurst, 2008; Temmerman et al., 2021), especially when they increase the newsworthiness of an article simply by appearing in headlines (see also Seibold, 2002). Therefore, news factors can also be regarded as an instrument for controlling the attention of recipients and are given a corresponding relevance for the dimension 'attention.' In addition to these content-related aspects of news value logic, it is primarily aspects of the design layout and narrative structure that can control the recipients' attention. These include the ranking and positioning of an article, graphic design of headlines and the rest of the text, specifics of the layout, type of imagery, narrative structure (elastic, parallel, ramified, concentric, etc.; Godulla et al., 2017), and, on the Internet in particular, features such as brevity and conciseness, but also size and conspicuity of the typography (especially of the headline) (Seibold, 2002).

However, in journalism there are normative expectations of adherence to certain reliable design rules. These give journalistic products a specific value of recognition and therefore appear to be suitable as a criterion for distinguishing between journalistic and non-journalistic text products in general. In online journalism, design aspects extend far beyond simple rules such as 'headline, title, lead.' They also depend on the type of presentation (e.g., interview, report), whether the format is more opinion-driven or information-driven, whether it is 'hard' or 'soft' journalism, and much more. Also, the web offers more possibilities for creative attention control of textual products than the offline area (unique technical features, multimedia, etc.). In this context, PR has more leeway for the use of different attention-grabbing strategies (e.g., more conspicuous typographical features; tabloid characteristics) than offline and online journalism. They both are subject to expectations and professional requirements based on normative standards (e.g., seriousness and credibility through creative presentation). However, one can assume that in PR texts that aim to have a journalistic appearance, this leeway will not be exploited, and instead, the products

---

10 It should be remembered here that the simulation of journalism by PR is already per se a strategy for attracting attention (cf. also Hoffjann et al., 2015).

Romy Fröhlich

will be oriented in terms of content and form towards the stricter and narrower rules of journalistic attention-creation. Or vice versa: A journalism-like text that aims to gain/increase attention by employing online strategies that are rather unusual or even undesirable for journalism is probably the journalism simulation of a strategic-persuasive communicator.

The Contingency-Oriented Linguistic Dimension at the Text Level

The pilot study by Theis-Berglmair and Kellermann (2017) offers an interesting approach to distinguishing journalism from PR at the text level. The aim is to overcome the limitations and research pragmatic hurdles of classical actor, role and organizational dimensions, including journalistic quality criteria. The authors propose a contingency-oriented approach. The orientation on the construct 'contingency' is crucial: The approach assumes that journalistic contributions can be distinguished from PR content similar to journalism by looking at contingency. In this case, contingency simply means "that something can be one way or another" (Theis-Berglmair et al., 2017, p. 108). The measurement of distinctiveness between journalistic and PR texts is derived from the specific contingency character of each of the texts under investigation. This is because, according to Theis-Berglmair et al., the space and potential possibilities for the 'this way or another' are more extensive and more diverse in journalism (second-order observation) than in PR (self-referential observation). This is reflected in journalistic texts by, for example, a larger number of different sources, a greater variety of perspectives and reference horizons, and/or more independent reference observers such as experts/scientists or other organizations (p. 109). Conversely, Theis-Berglmair et al. expect significantly higher degrees of certainty in PR texts than in journalistic texts. Thus, a journalistic text would be characterized by an open contingency (a great deal of internal plurality) and a PR text by a closed contingency (little internal plurality). As clauses 13.1 and 14 of the Press Code of the German Press Council (2019) show, this assumption is also plausible from a norm-theoretical perspective; there is nothing comparable for PR products.

Theis-Berglmair et al. propose to investigate precisely this difference by means of text-linguistic procedures, e.g., a content-analytical survey of the occurrence of certainty-reducing modal verbs and modal adverbs in texts. Linguistically, certainty reduction is expressed via modal adverbs of conditional validity such as 'probably,' 'possibly,' 'perhaps,' 'presumably,' etc., as well as via modal verbs such as 'can,' 'may,' 'should,' etc. (Theis-Berglmair

& Kellermann, 2017, p. 110; see also Simmerling & Janich, 2016; Janich & Simmerling, 2015). In a first pilot study, the authors showed that PR texts contain far fewer, if any, certainty-reducing clauses than journalistic texts (p. 111).

The approach presented by Theis-Berglmair et al. is not entirely new, but its application to the measurement of differences between journalism and PR products is. There are already studies on the handling of linguistic forms of certainty reduction and the expression of uncertainty in journalism, especially content analyses on science journalism (e.g. Collins, 1987). From this research on journalists' grammatical, stylistic, and rhetorical choices for the linguistic depiction of 'uncertainty,' theoretical implications in the sense of Theis-Berglmair et al. can also be derived and survey indicators identified that are relevant for the operationalization of our specific research interest. These include, for example, the occurrence of so-called "qualifying indications" (e.g., 'obviously,' 'unambiguously,' 'presumably,' 'apparently') (Kepplinger, 2011, p. 101), "restrictive formulations" (e.g., 'presumably,' 'possibly') but also "formulations in the subjunctive" (Maurer, 2011, p. 62; see also Collins, 1987) or the investigation of tense, expressions of negation, and certain patterns of word formation like the use of particular affixes, etc. (Simmerling & Janich, 2016, p. 964-965; see also Janich & Simmerling, 2015; Stocking & Holstein, 2009). Given such a linguistic orientation of operationalization, the goal set by Theis-Berglmair et al. to overcome the limitations and research pragmatic hurdles of classical actor, role, and organizational dimensions could probably be realized in the context of automated computational linguistic content analyses.

The Dimension 'Persuasion and Ethics in PR'

The working definition for PR's journalism simulation presented above assumes that the textual messages in question are persuasive in nature. As a reminder: The definition suggests that journalism simulations by strategic communicators (PR) primarily pursue the goal of having a persuasive effect on a target audience, i.e., persuading them of a fact, a product, an opinion/attitude, etc. Conversely, this means that original journalistic texts of high quality (quality journalism) do not pursue persuasive goals in this sense – at least from a normative and ideal-typical point of view.[11] The question is whether the persuasive character can be identified in journalism-simulating PR and would be recognizable for users of such simulations. To clarify this question, the occurrence of 'persuasion' or the persuasive character of a text product has to be operationalized. For this purpose, I propose the following indicators, which do not all have to occur simultaneously. This means that 'persuasion' can also occur on a sliding scale:

– a less pronounced separation of news and opinion (in contrast to journalism, PIoPS of journalism does not have to separate information/facts and opinion or explicitly identify the author's individual position as his/her 'opinion');
– less pronounced labeling of promotional content (e.g., product PR)
– less background reporting;
– fewer different and independent opinions and consequently less diversity, balance, and neutrality;
– less criticism/polarization (prioritizing positive coverage/sentiment).

The extent to which these criteria of persuasive impression are used at all in successful PIoPS of journalism has not yet been investigated. Their use is rather unlikely because they interfere with the intended (non-persuasive) journalistic impression and are thus somewhat counterproductive for journalism simulations. However, for the question of the more or less well recognizable persuasive character of PIoPS of journalism (and thus for the operationalization of distinctiveness), they are indispensable as dimensions of investigation as a start.

While the quality debate in journalism research has developed numerous indicators for 'good' journalism on the basis of demands and expectations grounded in democracy theories and its normative implications, no "separable indicators" have yet been developed for PR (Hoffmann, 2007, p. 558). One exception to this is the quality requirements for PR in media relations which are specifically geared to the target group of journalism. For professional reasons, the requirements here are very closely aligned with what is known from the quality discourse in journalism research; it can therefore come as no surprise that the parallels to the quality of journalism are obvious here. Beyond media relations, quality

---

11 Extreme tabloid journalism can be seen as a typical exception to this rule. And I have already mentioned the special forms of opinionated journalism such as commentary or feature reporting. They, too, can or even should have a persuasive character.

Journalism or Public Relations?

standards for PR are described and discussed under the heading of 'ethics in PR,' some of which are very close to those of journalism or have even been adopted one-to-one from journalism (cf. Pleil, 2015a). These include requirements such as credibility/reliability (e.g., Bentele & Seidenglanz, 2015) and transparency/full disclosure (about sources of content and sender transparency), timeliness, or completeness. Other quality criteria of PR that are rather atypical for journalism concern authenticity, symmetrical dialog orientation (Grunig et al., 1984), consensus-oriented communication (Burkart, 1993; 2004), respect for differing viewpoints, veracity or honesty (cf., Parsons, 2016, Ikonen et al., 2017; Deutscher Rat..., 2012, among others).

As we have seen, there are several possible text-oriented operationalization dimensions for the comparative analysis of the two online text types in question. As mentioned, this overview does not claim to be complete. For example, one could also consider what role the occurrence of typical Internet advertising plays for our question. This includes the content of advertising, its design and placement or the way it is embedded, its number, etc. – from pop-up ads to banner ads to links that lead to external advertising websites.

Differentiation Dimensions from an Audience Perspective: Recipient Characteristics and Reception Behavior

The question of whether recipients would even have the chance to detect differences between the two types of texts on the Internet is covered by content-analytical procedures. Content analysis can be used to clarify whether corresponding texts exhibit distinguishing features at all and whether this chance, therefore, at least potentially exists. It is, however, unable to answer whether recipients are able to recognize such features, whether they use these features as criteria in their attempt to distinguish between text types, whether they possibly apply wholly different or even their own distinguishing criteria, whether these finally lead to the goal of a 'correct' distinction, or how important it is to recipients that the types of texts are distinguishable and that the recipients themselves are able to distinguish between the types. For this, an audience-oriented approach is needed which enables us to describe the concrete differentiation behaviors and procedures of recipients and offers possibilities of operationalization for reception studies. This dimension includes the usual socio-demographic characteristics of recipients, which can be assumed to determine their ability to discriminate and the concrete procedures they use to do so. Following existing assumptions about the quality of media literacy in general and online media literacy in particular (cf., for example, Bucher, 2000; Gonser et al., 2017; Henry, 2007; Neuberger, 2011; Pietzcker, 2017), it is quite plausible to assume that, in addition to sociodemographic characteristics, characteristics of recipients' media literacy also influence their individual discrimination behavior and procedures. However, media competence is difficult to operationalize. A helpful approach would be to survey the respondents' general media use (quantity and/or quality of media use, depending on the specifics of the research question) on an individual level and, with a view to our specific research interest, also ask about the characteristics of their Internet use in particular. This is based on the assumption that respondents with more Internet experience may practice different discrimination behaviors and procedures than respondents with less Internet experience. The individual level of media literacy could also impact the question of how important it is to recipients in general that journalism and PR are distinguishable from one another and/or whether they want to distinguish between the two at all.

Operationalization Concept: Design of a Structural Model

The operationalization concept proposed in the following is to be understood as a first attempt to empirically implement a research goal that has not yet been investigated in a theoretically well-founded way. For this purpose, we recall the specific research interest from the beginning of this contribution: Can persuasive journalism simulations of PR on the Internet be distinguished from actual journalistic products/content on the Internet and, if so, how? The research interest is twofold:

(1) Do theoretically derived features that are assumed to be typical occur in both types of texts on the Internet, and if so, to what extent and in what form? That is, are the texts actually characterized by different features? This is aimed at the question of whether it is even possible for recipients to recognize differences?

(2) Do recipients have the skills to distinguish between the two types of texts on the Internet and what criteria, means, and procedures do they use for this? How important or unimportant is it for recipients to be able to distinguish between the two types?

Following Bucher (2000), the approach will be product-oriented. As discussed above, this means that reception findings (user studies) are related to text/content characteristics (content analysis) in the same project, i.e.,

Journalism or Public Relations?

a recipient study is combined with a content analysis of the relevant stimulus material from the recipient study. Table 1 summarizes the derived theoretical dimensions according to the chosen system (cf. the sections on differentiation dimensions) and names the respective objectives. It serves as a basis for developing an operationalization concept.

Table 1: Theoretically Derived Differentiation Dimensions, Research Areas/Methods and Knowledge Objectives

Differentiation Dimensions	Research Area & Method	Knowledge Objective
Text feature 'journalistic quality' Text feature 'attention' (including narrative structure) e'Contingency-oriented linguistic features at the text level' Text feature 'persuasion and ethics in PR'	Media content research: – Quantitative methods of content analysis, including computer-assisted automated methods – Qualitative methods of content analysis – Combinations of quantitative and qualitative methods	Identification of assumed distinguishing features, the weighting of their (gradual) relevance as well as the degree of their discriminatory power between text types → Derivations for recipient study
Recipient characteristics and reception behavior	Reception research: – Quantitative & qualitative methods of inquiry – Thinking aloud – Participatory observation – Eye-tracking as well as mixed methods or method triangulation	Identification & description of: – Characteristics of recipients' individual *intention* to discriminate – Characteristics of the relevance of the basic discrimination *possibility* for recipients – Characteristics of the *individual discrimination behavior/procedure* ... based on the function and relevance of content-analytically identified differentiating features (differentiation dimensions 4.1.1. to 4.1.4) ... beyond the content-analytically identified differentiating features. – Analysis of the importance of individual user-specific recipient characteristics (e.g., socio-demographics & media competence)

From this scheme, a large catalog of research-guiding questions can be derived. Table 2 outlines these questions for the text-oriented part of the declared knowledge interest. In this context, I also refer to the relevant basic literature for each aspect (cf. the section on the state of research).

Romy Fröhlich

Table 2: *Possible Research-Guiding Questions for the Text-Oriented Part of the Stated Research Interest (Media Content Research) According to Knowledge Objectives*

Knowledge Objective (Each of which has specific implications/derivations for audience-focused research)	Research-Guiding Questions
– Identification of various distinguishing features of the dimension '*journalistic quality*,' the weighting of their (gradual) relevance as distinguishing features as well as their general discriminatory potential	• *Do the two types of texts on the Internet differ with regard to the norm-theoretically founded and ideal-typically attributed classical criteria for 'quality'?* [Occurrence, type, and frequency] (e.g., Arnold, 2016; Beck et al., 2010; Deutscher Rat..., 2012; Ikonen et al., 2017; McQuail, 1992; Mehlis, 2014; Neuberger 2012, 2011; Parsons, 2016; Pleil, 2015a; Pöttker, 2000). • *Do the two types of text on the Internet differ concerning Internet-specific criteria for 'quality' such as, in particular, multimedia, interactivity, and hypertextuality?* [Occurrence, type, and frequency of multimedia, interactive and hypertextual tools] (e.g., Bucher, 2000; Godulla et al., 2017; Mehlis, 2014; Neuberger; 2011; Pleil, 2015a; Radl et al., 2015)
– Identification of various distinguishing features of the dimension '*attention*' (*including narrative structures*), the weighting of their relevance as suitable distinguishing features, as well as determination of their general discriminatory potential	• *Do the two types of text on the Internet differ in their content and/or formal design to attract/enhance attention?* [Occurrence, type, and frequency of means to attract/enhance attention, including news factors/values] (e.g., Altmeppen et al., 2002; Eilders, 1997, 2006; Eilders et al., 1999; Franck, 2014; Fretwurst, 2008; Godulla et al., 2017; Pleil, 2015b; Ruß-Mohl, 2017; Seibold, 2002).
– Identification of *contingency-oriented linguistic distinguishing features at the text level*, the weighting of their relevance as suitable distinguishing features, and their general discriminatory potential	• *Do the two text types on the Internet differ concerning contingency-oriented linguistic features at the text level?* [Occurrence, type, and frequency of linguistic forms of certainty reduction and expression of uncertainty] (e.g., Collins, 1987; Deutscher Presserat, 2019; Janich et al., 2015; Kepplinger, 2011; Maurer, 2011; Simmerling et al., 2016; Stocking et al., 2009; Theis-Berglmair et al., 2017
– Identification of various distinguishing features of the dimension '*persuasion and ethics in PR*,' the weighting of their relevance as suitable distinguishing features, and their general discriminatory potential	• *In PIoPS of journalism on the Internet, how does the persuasive nature of PR manifest itself (if at all), and (how) does the implementation of ethical standards of PR become apparent?* [Occurrence, type, and frequency of persuasive characteristics and ethical standards of PR] (e.g., Bentele & Seidenglanz, 2015; Burkart, 1993, 2004; Deutscher Rat..., 2012; Grunig at al., 1984; Ikonen et al., 2017; Parsons, 2016; Pleil, 2015a)

The operationalization concept outlined here for the content-analytical distinction between journalistic products and journalism simulation on the Internet is certainly not complete. For example, it could also be relevant to investigate whether and, if so, in what way advertising plays a role, as it is embedded in or surrounds the respective text products. It could also be investigated whether and, if so, how much advertising the two types of text have, how much advertising surrounds the texts in each case or is

Journalism or Public Relations?

embedded in the texts – from pop-up advertising to advertising banners to links that lead to external advertising websites. PR texts are likely to have greater leeway here than journalistic products, which could result in a differentiating criterion.

From the content-analytical examination of the presented differentiation dimensions, two contrasting result scenarios in the sense of a continuum are conceivable, between which further gradually graded scenarios could be distinguished. Result scenario 1: The two types of text can be distinguished (more or less beyond doubt) on the basis of the dimensions and criteria analyzed. This means that recipients have at least the potential to distinguish between original journalism and simulated journalism on the basis of product-immanent characteristics. Result scenario 2: The two types of text cannot be (easily) distinguished on the basis of the analyzed dimensions and criteria. The similarities between journalism simulation (PIoPS) and actual/original journalism are too considerable. The recipients have no/few possibilities to distinguish between original journalism and simulated journalism on the basis of product-immanent characteristics. From these two result scenarios (if necessary, gradually staged) derivations can and must then be made for a corresponding recipient study. Depending on the resulting scenario, a large catalog of research-guiding questions can also be derived for recipient-oriented research based on the systematization presented in Table 1. Table 3 outlines corresponding questions for the user-oriented part of the research.

Beyond these research-guiding questions derived from the preceding theoretical considerations regarding the stated research interest, one can, of course, deduce quite different research questions from other theoretical contexts. For example, in an evaluation-theoretical PR context, it seems interesting to ask whether the assignment of a text on the Internet to journalism or PR by the recipients influences its perceived credibility, seriousness, transparency, etc.—and in which way. Interestingly, such patterns were not found in the pilot study by Kiefl et al. (2021). The study's results indicate that the perception of a text as credible, serious, transparent, or balanced is independent of whether respondents had previously classified this text (correctly or incorrectly) as PR or as journalism. The uses-and-gratifications approach represents an entirely different, alternative theoretical anchoring of the described problem context. From this perspective, it could be interesting to ask which motivational and reward conditions users on the Internet prefer for one or the other type of text. Here, too, Kiefl's et al. pilot study produced some interesting initial findings, according to which the test subjects made highly individual

Romy Fröhlich

Table 3: Possible Research-Guiding Questions for the Reception-Oriented Part of the Stated Research Interest by Knowledge Objective (Reception Research)

Knowledge Objectives	Research-Guiding Questions
– Identification & relevance of the user-specific **discrimination intention** [also wholly independent of the result scenario content analysis].	‣ *Do users even want to (be able to) distinguish between the two types of text on the Internet? How important is this to them? How do they justify their respective attitude?* [Characteristics of intention/willingness to distinguish and reasons for this]
– Identification & relevance of recipients' **basic discrimination ability**.	‣ *Are users able to distinguish (correctly) between both types of text on the Internet? If not, how great is the recipients' uncertainty in this regard, and what exactly do these uncertainties consist of?* [Duration of the decision-making process; quality of the decisions made; reasons/causes for a particular decision, etc.]
– Identification & relevance of recipients' **individual discrimination behavior/procedure** ... ... according to the function and relevance of content-analytically identified differentiation dimensions as well as ... beyond the content-analytically identified differentiation characteristics (user-specific differentiation criteria).	‣ *Which (classical vs. own content-related and/or formal) criteria/procedures do recipients use to distinguish between both text types on the Internet?* [Particular characteristics of the differentiation behavior of recipients, including procedures beyond the content-analytically identified differentiation dimensions such as consultation of the imprint, etc.]
– Identification of the influence of recipients' **socio-demographic characteristics** and characteristics of their **media competence**.	‣ *Do specific recipient characteristics influence the response behavior of the respondents?* [e.g., socio-demographics, quantity & quality of general media/Internet use; media literacy]

benefit assessments, again irrespective of whether they considered a text to be journalism or PR.

Challenges for Operationalization

For the operationalization of the research interest outlined here, a series of challenges arise. From a methodological point of view, the realization of the product-oriented approach demanded by Bucher (2000) that was presented above, i.e., the combination of content analysis and reception study, is only a minor difficulty. However, the product-oriented approach entails several particular features for the selection of the investigation and stimulus material. These are due to the fact that this material must be identical in the reception study and the content analysis and must therefore meet the requirements of the research question for a content analysis as well as for a user study. The specific conditions that have to be taken into account in selecting a study design and stimulus material and the kind of care that has to be taken in the content analysis will be briefly outlined in the following two sections.

Selection of Study Design and Stimulus Material for Audience Research

Since there is no established procedure for identifying PR texts on the Internet, it is not possible to systematically select the text samples for PIoPS of journalism. On the other hand, when selecting stimulus material for a study according to the outlined approach, it has to be taken into account that the respective media brands strongly determine recipients' quality expectations, perceptions, and evaluations (cf., for example, Slater et al., 1996; Urban et al., 2014; Voigt, 2016; Wladarsch, 2020). This speaks against selecting prominent, widely known media brands for recipient-oriented research on the issues under consideration here. The journalistic product could then be identified by the subjects from the outset quite simply via the media brand. The search for journalistic stimulus material suitable for the research interest outlined here thus represents a challenge that should not be underestimated. Artificially constructing a corresponding text as investigation and stimulus material, as experimental media effects research does in many cases, is not a solution. The specific research question requires authentic text material which can actually be found on the Internet.

This also applies to the selection of a suitable content topic for both types of text. It must be a topic that is very likely to arouse widespread interest to minimize the influence of the topic on the response behavior of the recipients (interest in the topic, being personally affected by the topic, etc.). The recommended topic for journalistic and PR stimulus material should be a socially relevant problem. To ensure that different perspectives are presented (e.g., internal plurality/diversity as a quality feature of journalistic reporting), it should also be sufficiently controversial or crisis-related. After all, strategic communicators from different social subsystems should (want/be able/have to) express themselves. The probability of this increases in the case of crisis-related topics. Kiefl et al. (2020), for example, solved these challenges as follows: The research team decided to use the diesel scandal ('Diesel-Gate') of the German car industry as a topic for the study. This topic was quite current at the time of the survey. In addition to journalism, many companies also commented on it – especially car companies as part of their crisis PR. The aim was to restore confidence and minimize the damage done to their image. To this end, a number of

German car companies affected deliberately relied on stakeholder communication in the form of journalistic simulation.

This topic also made it possible for Kiefl et al. (2020) to find corresponding journalistic reporting on the Internet beyond the comparatively prominent media brands that are easily recognizable. In the case of Kiefl et al., specialist media sites proved to be well-suited for this purpose. The researchers therefore chose journalistic online contributions from *managermagazin.de* and *gute-fahrt.de* for the pilot study in question and PIoPS of journalism from the PR-products *fleetdriver.de* and *meinautomagazin.de*. The vast majority of participants in the study were not familiar with either media brand.

The stimulus material of the PR text type 'journalistic simulation' must come from stakeholder media. According to Hoffmann (2007), these cannot "intuitively be attributed to either PR or journalism, [since they] often have a professional journalistic makeup" (p. 555). One can easily find such texts, for example, on industry-specific, subject-specific online sites.[12] Nevertheless, great care must be taken when checking whether the corresponding material actually originates from strategic-persuasive communicators (e.g., through detailed checks of the information in the imprint of a website). This is all the more relevant because journalistic simulations are, by definition, similar to actual journalistic reporting. At first glance, therefore, it must not be recognizable whether a text is journalism or PR.

The second challenge consists of checking whether this PR material also represents a sufficiently clear journalistic simulation – sufficiently clear in the sense of the declared research interest. For this purpose, a precise and easily applicable definition of 'journalistic simulation' (content-related and formal criteria) that can be easily applied to the selection process must be established in advance.

Quite a few of the research questions listed above as examples for reception studies and content analyses also require the sender/author of the stimulus material to be clearly identifiable in the imprint of the website in question. This is not always the case, especially not with hybrid models such as blogs. There is a surprisingly large number of texts on such websites that cannot be unequivocally identified as either journalism or PR. Here, too, broad exploratory work may have to be done first.

---

12 For the sake of completeness, it should be mentioned here that Kiefl et al. (2020) selected their PR stimulus texts (journalism simulations) on the topic of 'Diesel-Gate' from the PR platforms *fleetdriver.de* and *meinautomagazin.de*.

Journalism or Public Relations?

Content Analyses

Apart from selecting suitable stimulus material for content analysis and reception study, there are further challenges, especially for the content analysis part. It is already known from the many existing studies on journalistic quality that an enormously sophisticated system of categories is needed for a correspondingly comprehensive survey, and this system must be broken down into many different dimensions and characteristics (cf., also Theis-Berglmair et al., 2017). Because of the need for intersubjectively verifiable coding, great care must be taken in defining categories. Given the complexity of sub-dimensions of the construct 'journalistic quality' (e.g., credibility, transparency, diversity), the same applies to developing corresponding coding instructions. Because of the long tradition of (also internationally comparative) content-analytical research on journalistic quality, one does not have to reinvent the wheel here. However, it must be clarified, for example, whether and how individual quality dimensions should potentially be weighted or how one deals data-analytically with the problem that quality criteria are not entirely independent of one another.

Concluding Remarks

The digitization of communication and the emergence of the Internet have not only sustainably changed the conditions of interaction between journalism and PR in the production of public communication and the public (sphere). The reception of their respective products by the intended target groups has also changed. While the first aspect – change in the *interaction* of journalism and PR in the production of public communication and the public – is comparatively well researched, the latter – change in the *reception and expectations* of journalism and PR – still remains a blind spot in communication science. This is surprising because it is a field in change. Fields in change are always well-suited for research. In addition, they are well-suited to improving and advancing dialogue and mutual stimulation between science and the respective professional practice. In the present case, journalism and PR are involved likewise – also explicitly with a view to each other.

This theoretical contribution is intended to show in which direction(s) the outlined research interest could be developed. In doing so, two questions were deliberately omitted: First, could relevant studies on the comparison of journalistic texts and persuasive journalism simulations also offer an answer as to whether journalistic products actually provide higher quality

Romy Fröhlich

(from whose perspective?) than persuasive journalism simulations produced and disseminated by strategic communicators (PR)? As already mentioned, initial research results (Kiefl et al., 2020) indicate that this question may be answered differently from the recipients' viewpoint than from a normative perspective taken by experts and professional representatives. However, further research on this interesting and important issue, which is highly relevant for the future of journalism in liberal democracies, requires different theoretical foundations than those outlined here.

Second, to what extent do the audience's perceptions go hand in hand with what journalists and strategic PR communicators see as their own professional tasks and experts see as the quality of journalism and PR texts. Concerning journalism, communication scholars are now working on this question (see, e.g., Loosen et al., 2020); concerning PR, interest in the issue is still minimal. In any case, the research interest outlined in this chapter can contribute initial answers to these two questions. However, concrete theoretical foundations for the study of these two questions would have to differ in various aspects as compared to the ones presented here, which particularly considered the distinguishability and differentiation between journalism and persuasive journalism simulations.

References

Altmeppen, K. D., & Quandt, T. (2002). Wer informiert uns, wer unterhält uns? Die Organisation öffentlicher Kommunikation und die Folgen für Kommunikations- und Medienberufe [Who informs us, who entertains us? The organization of public communication and the consequences for communication and media professions]. *M & K, Medien & Kommunikationswissenschaft, 50*(1), 45-62.

Arnold, K. (2008). Qualität im Journalismus – ein integratives Konzept [Quality in journalism – an integrative concept]. *Publizistik, 53*, 488-508.

Arnold, K. (2009). *Qualitätsjournalismus. Die Zeitung und ihr Publikum* [Quality journalism. The newspaper and its audience]. Konstanz: UVK.

Arnold, K. (2016). Qualität des Journalismus. In M. Löffelholz & L. Rothenberger (Eds.), *Handbuch Journalismustheorien* (pp. 551-562). Wiesbaden: Springer

Baerns, B. (1991). *Öffentlichkeitsarbeit oder Journalismus? Zum Einfluss im Mediensystem* [Public relations or journalism? On influence in the media system]. Köln: Verlag Wissenschaft u. Politik.

Beck, K., Reineck, D., & Schubert, C. (2010). *Journalistische Qualität in der Wirtschaftskrise. Eine Studie im Auftrag des deutschen Fachjournalisten-Verbandes (DFJV)* [Journalistic quality in the economic crisis. A study commissioned by the German Association of Professional Journalists (DFJV)]. Berlin: Freie Universität Berlin. Retrieved 24.3.2022 from Studie_Journalistische_Qualitaet_03_2010.pdf

Journalism or Public Relations?

Beisch, N., & Schäfer, C. (2020). Ergebnisse der ARD/ZDF-Onlinestudie 2020. Internetnutzung mit großer Dynamik: Medien, Kommunikation, Social Media [Results of the ARD/ZDF online study 2020. Internet use with great dynamics: Media, communication, social media]. *Media Perspektiven, no vol.*(9), 462-481.

Bentele, G. (2013). Corporate Publishing. In G. Bentele, H.-B. Brosius, & O. Jarren (Eds.), *Lexikon Kommunikations- und Medienwissenschaft* [Encyclopedia communication and media Studies] (2nd ed., p. 46). Wiesbaden: Springer VS.

Bentele, G. & Fechner (2015). Intereffikationsmodell [Intereffication Model]. In R. Fröhlich, P. Szyszka, & G. Bentele (Eds.), *Handbuch der Public Relations. Wissenschaftliche Grundlagen und berufliches Handeln* [Handbook of Public Relations. Scientific foundations and professional action] (pp. 319-340). Wiesbaden: Springer.

Bentele, G., Liebert, T. & Seeling, S. (1997). Von der Determination zur Intereffikation. Ein integriertes Modell zum Verhältnis von Public Relations und Journalismus [From determination to intereffication. An integrated model of the relationship between public relations and journalism]. In G. Bentele, & M. Haller (Eds.), *Aktuelle Entstehung von Öffentlichkeit. Akteure, Strukturen, Veränderungen* [Current emergence of the public sphere. Actors, structures, changes] (pp. 225-250). Konstanz: UVK.

Bentele, G., & Seidenglanz, R. (2005). Das Image der Image-(Re-)Konstrukteure: Ergebnisse einer repräsentativen Studie zum Image der Public Relations in der deutschen Bevölkerung und einer Journalistenbefragung [The image of the image-makers. A representative study concerning the population's image of the professional field and a survey of journalists]. In E. Wienand, J. Westerbarkey & A. Scholl (Eds.), *Kommunikation über Kommunikation. Theorien, Methoden und Praxis* [Communication about communication. Theories, methods and practice] (pp. 200-222). Wiesbaden: VS.

Bentele, G., & Seidenglanz, R. (2015). Vertrauen und Glaubwürdigkeit. Begriffe, Ansätze, Forschungsübersicht und praktische Relevanz [Trust and credibility. Concepts, approaches, research overview and practical relevance]. In R. Fröhlich, P. Szyszka, & Bentele, G. (Eds.), *Handbuch der Public Relations. Wissenschaftliche Grundlagen und berufliches Handeln. Mit Lexikon* [Handbook of Public Relations. Scientific foundations and professional action] (pp. 411-429). Wiesbaden: Springer VS.

Bucher, H.-J. (2000). Publizistische Qualität im Internet. Rezeptionsforschung für die Praxis [Journalistic quality on the internet. Reception research for practice]. In K.-D Altmeppen, H.-J. Bucher, & M. Löffelholz (Eds.), *Online-Journalismus. Perspektiven für Wissenschaft und Praxis* [Online Journalism. Perspectives for science and practice] (pp. 153-172). Wiesbaden: Westdeutscher Verlag.

Burkart, R. (1993). *Public Relations als Konfliktmanagement. Ein Konzept für verständigungsorientierte Öffentlichkeitsarbeit. Untersucht am Beispiel der Planung von Sonderabfalldeponien in Niederösterreich* [Public relations as conflict management. A Concept for understanding-oriented public relations. Examined using the example of hazardous waste landfill planning in Lower Austria.]. Wien: Braumüller.

Burkart, R. (2004). Consensus-oriented public relations (COPR) – A conception for planning and evaluation of public relations. In B. van Ruler, & Dejan Vercic, (Eds.). *Public relations in Europe. A nation-by-nation introduction to public relations theory and practice* (pp. 446-452.). Berlin, New York: Mouton De Gruyter.

Collins, H. M. (1987). Certainty and the Public Understanding of Science: Science on Television. *Social Studies of Science, 17*(4), 689-713.

Dahinden, U., Kaminski, P., & Niederreuther, R. (2004). Qualitätsbeurteilung aus Angebots- und Rezipientenperspektive [Quality assessment from supply and recipient perspectives.]. In K. Beck, W. Schweiger, & W. Wirth (Eds.), *Gute Seiten – schlechte Seiten. Qualität in der Onlinekommunikation* [Good pages – bad pages. Quality in online communication] (pp. 103-126). München: Reinhard Fischer.

Davies, N. (2009). *Flat earth news*. London: Vintage.

Deutscher Rat für Public Relations (Ed., 2012). Deutscher Kommunikationskodex. Retrieved 24.3.2022 from http://www.kommunikationskodex.de/wp-content/upl oads/Deutscher_Kommunikationskodex.pdf

Eilders, C. (1997). *Nachrichtenfaktoren und Rezeption. Eine empirische Analyse zur Auswahl und Verarbeitung politischer Information [News factors and reception. An Empirical Analysis of the Selection and Processing of Political Information]*. Opladen: Westdeutscher Verlag.

Eilders, C. (2006). News factors and news decisions. Theoretical and methodological advances in Germany. *Communications, 31*(1), 5-24.

Eilders, C., & Wirth, W. (1999). Die Nachrichtenwertforschung auf dem Weg zum Publikum: Eine experimentelle Überprüfung des Einflusses von Nachrichtenfaktoren bei der Rezeption [Newsworthiness research on the way to the audience: an experimental review of the influence of news factors in reception]. *Publizistik, 44*(1), 35-57.

Franck, G. (2014). Jenseits von Geld und Information: Zur Ökonomie der Aufmerksamkeit [Beyond money and information: On the economy of attention]. In A. Zerfaß, & M. Piwinger (Eds.), *Handbuch Unternehmenskommunikation. Strategie – Management – Wertschöpfung* [Corporate communications handbook. Strategy – management – value creation] (2nd ed., pp. 193-202). Wiesbaden: Springer Gabler.

Fretwurst, B. (2008). *Nachrichten im Interesse der Zuschauer. Eine konzeptionelle und empirische Neubestimmung der Nachrichtenwerttheorie* [News in the interest of the audience. A conceptual and empirical redefinition of news value theory]. Konstanz: UVK.

Fröhlich, R. (2015). Zur Problematik der PR-Definition(en) [On the problem of PR definition(s)]. In R. Fröhlich, P. Szyszka, & G. Bentele (Hrsg.), *Handbuch der Public Relations* [Handbook of public relations] (pp. 1003-120). Wiesbaden: Springer.

Gandy, O. H. (1982). Beyond agenda setting: Information subsidies and public policy. Norwood, NJ: Ablex.

Journalism or Public Relations?

Godulla, A. (2015). Mehr als lousy pennies? Etablierte vs. alternative Geschäftsmodelle im Online-Journalismus [More than lousy pennies? Established vs. alternative business models in online journalism]. In O. Hahn, R. Hohlfeld, & T. Knieper (Eds.), *Digitale Öffentlichkeit(en)* [Digital public(s)] (pp. 135-148). Konstanz: UVK.

Godulla, A. (2017). *Öffentliche Kommunikation im digitalen Zeitalter: Grundlagen und Perspektiven einer integrativen Modellbildung* [Public Communication in the digital age: Foundations and perspectives of integrative modeling]. Wiesbaden: Springer VS.

Godulla, A., & Wolf, C. (2017). *Digitale Langformen im Journalismus und Corporate Publishing. Storytelling – Webdokumentationen – Multimediastorys* [Digital longforms in journalism and corporate publishing. Storytelling – web documentaries – multimedia stories]. Wiesbaden: Springer VS.

Gonser, N., & Rußmann, U. (2017). Verschwimmende Grenzen Abgrenzung zwischen Journalismus, PR, Werbung und Marketing [Blurring boundaries demarcation between journalism, PR, advertising and marketing]. In N. Gonser & U. Rußmann (Eds.), *Verschwimmende Grenzen zwischen Journalismus, PR Werbung und Marketing. Aktuelle Befunde aus Theorie und Praxis* [Blurring boundaries between journalism, PR advertising and marketing. Current findings from theory and practice] (pp. 1-12). Wiesbaden: Springer.

Grunig, J. E., &. Hunt, T. (1984). *Managing Public Relations.* New York: Rinehart and Winston.

Haller, M. (2003). Qualität und Benchmarking im Printjournalismus [Quality and benchmarking in print journalism]. In H.-J. Bucher, & Altmeppen, K.-D. (Eds.), Qualität im Journalismus. Grundlagen – Dimensionen – Praxismodelle [Quality in journalism. Fundamentals – dimensions – practice models] (pp. 181–201). Wiesbaden.

Harcup, T, & O'Neill, D. (2017). What is News? *Journalism Studies, 18*(12), 1470-1488.

Henry, N. (2007). *American carnival: Journalism under siege in an age of new media.* Berkeley, CA: University of California Press.

Hoffjann, O., & Arlt, H.-J. (2015). *Die nächste Öffentlichkeit. Theorieentwurf und Szenarien* [The Next Public. Draft of theory and scenarios]. Wiesbaden: Springer VS.

Hoffmann, J. (2007). Mitgliederpresse: Journalismus für die Organisation, PR für die Gesellschaft [Member press: Journalism for the organization, PR for society]. *M & K, Medien und Kommunikaitonswissenschaft, 55*(4), 555-574.

Hummel, R. (2016). *Churnalism.* In Deutscher FachjournalistenVerband (Ed.), *Journalistische Genres* [Journalistic genres] (pp. 133-138). Köln: Herbert von Halem Verlag.

Ikonen, P., Luoma-aho, V. & Bowen, S. A. (2017) Transparency for sponsored content: Analysing codes of ethics in public relations, marketing, advertising and journalism. *International Journal of Strategic Communication, 11*(2), 165-178.

Janich, N., & Simmerling, A. (2015). Linguistics and ignorance. In M. Gross, & L. McGoey (Eds.), *Routledge international handbook of ignorance studies* (pp. 125-137). London, New York, NY: Routledge.

Jungnickel, K. (2011). Nachrichtenqualität aus Nutzersicht. Ein Vergleich zwischen Leserurteilen und wissenschaftlich-normativen Qualitätsansprüchen [News quality from the user's perspective. A comparison between reader judgments and scientific-normative quality claims]. *M & K – Medien- und Kommunikationswissenschaft, 59*, 360-378.

Keen, A. (2007). *The cult of the amateur: How today's internet is killing our culture.* New York: Doubleday.

Kepplinger, H.-M. (2011). *Realitätskonstruktionen* [Constructions of reality]. Wiesbaden: VS Verlag.

Kohring, M. (2006). Öffentlichkeit als Funktionssystem der modernen Gesellschaft [Public sphere as a functional system of modern society]. In A. Ziemann (Ed.), *Medien der Gesellschaft – Gesellschaft der Medien* [Media of the society - society of the media] (pp. 161-181). Konstanz: UVK.

Kiefl, F., Sauter, S., Pohl, E., & Fröhlich, R. (2020). *Journalistische Simulationen persuasiver Kommunikation im WWW. Eine Untersuchung zur Konvergenz von Journalismus und PR aus Nutzersicht* [Journalistic simulations of persuasive communication on the WWW. An investigation into the convergence of journalism and PR from the user's perspective]. Paper presentd at the conference of the DGPuK Division „OC/PR", 30.10.2020, Mainz, Germany

Kiousis, S., Popescu, C., Mitrook, M. (2007). Understanding influence on corporate reputation: An examination of public relations efforts, media coverage, public opinion, and financial performance from an agenda-building and agenda-setting perspective. *Journal of Public Relations Research, 19*, 147-165.

Lloyd, J, & Toogood, L. (2015). *Journalism and PR. News media and public relations in the digital age.* London, New York, Oxford: Tauris and Reuters Institute for the Study of Journalism at University of Oxford.

Loosen, W., Reimer, J., & Hölig, S. (2020). What journalists want and what they ought to do (in)congruences between journalists' role conceptions and audiences' expectations. *Journalism Studies, 21*(12), 1744-1774.

Manning, P. (2001). *News and news sources. A critical introduction.* London, Southand Oaks, New Delhi: Sage.

Maurer, M. (2011). Wie Journalisten mit Unsicherheit umgehen. Eine Untersuchung am Beispiel der Berichterstattung über die Folgen des Klimawandels. [How journalists deal with uncertainty. An investigation using the example of reporting on the consequences of climate change]. *Medien- und Kommunikationswissenschaft, 59*, 60-74.

McQuail, D. (1992). *Media performance. Mass communication and the public interest.* London, Newbury Park, New Delhi: Sage.

Mehlis, K. (2014). Entwicklung einer mehrdimensionalen Skala zur Messung der Qualität von Online-Nachrichtenangeboten aus Publikumssicht [Development of a multidimensional scale to measure the quality of online news offerings from the audience's point of view]. In W. Loosen & M. Dohle (Eds.), *Journalismus und (sein) Publikum* [Journalism and (its) audience] (pp. 253-271). Wiesbaden: Springer.

Merten, K., & Westerbarkey, J. (1994). Public Opinion und Public Relations [Public Opinion and Public Relations]. In K. Merten, S. Schmidt, & S. Weischenberg (Eds.). *Die Wirklichkeit der Medien. Eine Einführung in die Kommunikationswissenschaft* [The reality of media. An introduction to communication science] (pp. 188-211). Opladen: Westdeutscher Verlag.

Neuberger, C. (2011). Im Netz nichts Neues: Presse und Rundfunk bleiben konkurrenzlos wichtig [Nothing new on the Net: Press and Broadcasting Remain Unrivaled in Importance]. *Fachjournalist*, Issue 3, 12-17. Retrieved 24.3.2022 from http://www.fachjournalist.de/PDF-Dateien/2012/05/FJ_3_2011-Presse-und-Rundfunk-bleiben-konkurrenzlos-wichtig.pdf

Neuberger, C. (2012). Journalismus im Internet aus Nutzersicht: Ergebnisse einer Onlinebefragung [Journalism on the internet from the user's perspective: Results of an online survey]. *Media Perspektiven*, (1), 40-55.

Neuberger, C. (2018). Journalismus in der Netzwerköffentlichkeit. Zum Verhältnis zwischen Profession, Partizipation und Technik [Journalism in the network public sphere. On the relationship between profession, participation and technology]. In C. Nuernbergk & C. Neuberger (Eds.), *Journalismus im Internet: Profession – Partizipation – Technisierung* [Journalism on the internet: profession – participation – technization] (2nd ed., pp. 10-80). Wiesbaden: Springer VS.

Neuberger, C., & Kapern, P. (2013). *Grundlagen des Journalismus* [Basics of journalism].Wiesbaden: Springer VS.

Neuberger, C., Bartsch, A., Reinemann, C., Fröhlich, R., Hanitzsch, T., & Schindler, J. (2019). Der digitale Wandel der Wissensordnung. Theorierahmen für die Analyse von Wahrheit, Wissen und Rationalität in der öffentlichen Kommunikation [The digital transformation of the knowledge order. Theoretical framework for the analysis of truth, knowledge and rationality in public communication]. *M & K Medien & Kommunikationswissenschaft*, 67(2), 167-186.

Parsons, P. J. (2016). *Ethics in public Relations: A guide to best practice* (3rd ed.). London: Kogan.

Pfetsch, B., & Bossert, R. (2013). Öffentliche Kommunikation [Public communication]. In G. Bentele, H.-B. Brosius, & O. Jarren (Eds.), *Lexikon Kommunikationsund Medienwissenschaft* [Encyclopedia communication and media studies] (2nd ed., pp. 248-249). Wiesbaden: Springer VS.

Pietzcker, D. (2017). Anything Goes 2.0: Zur Selbstdefinition der Medienberufe im digitalen Informationszeitalter [Anything goes 2.0: On the self-definition of media professions in the digital information age]. In N. Gonser, & U. Rußmann (Eds.), *Verschwimmende Grenzen zwischen Journalismus, Public Relations, Werbung und Marketing. Aktuelle Befunde aus Theorie und Praxis Praxis* [Blurring boundaries between journalism, PR advertising and marketing. Current findings from theory and practice] (pp. 65-77). Wiesbaden: VS.

Pleil, T. (2015a). Kommunikation in der digitalen Welt [Communication in the digital world]. In A. Zerfaß, & T. Pleil (Eds.), *Handbuch Online-PR: Strategische Kommunikation in Internet und Social Web* [Handbook online PR: Strategic communication on the internet and social web] (pp. 17-38). München: UVK.

Pleil, T. (2015b). Online-PR. Vom kommunikativen Dienstleister zum Katalysator für ein neues Kommunikationsmanagement [Online PR. From communicative service provider to catalyst for a new communication management]. In R. Fröhlich, P. Szyszka, & G. Bentele (Eds.), *Handbuch der Public Relations* [Handbook of Public Relations] (pp. 1017-1038). Wiesbaden: Springer Fachmedien Verlag.

Radl, B. A., & Wittenbrink, H. (2015). Content-Strategie [Content strategy]. In A. Zerfaß, & T. Pleil (Eds.), *Handbuch Online-PR: strategische Kommunikation in Internet und Social Web* [Handbook Online-PR: Strategic communication on the internet and social web] (pp. 127-140). München: UVK Verlagsgesellschaft mbH.

Pöttker, H. (2000). Kompensation von Komplexität. Journalismustheorie als Begründung journalistischer Qualitätsmaßstäbe [Compensating complexity. Journalism Theory as the Justification of Journalistic Quality Standards]. In M. Löffelholz (Ed.), *Theorien des Journalismus. Ein diskursives Handbuch* [Theories of Journalism. A discursive handbook] (pp. 375-390). Wiesbaden: Westdeutscher Verlag

Presserat (2019). *Publizistische Grundsätze (Pressekodex). Richtlinien für die publizistische Arbeit nach den Empfehlungen des Deutschen Presserats* [Journalistic principles (Press Code). Guidelines for journalistic work in accordance with the recommendations of the German Press Council]. Berlin: Deutscher Presserat. Retrieved 24.3.2022 from https://www.presserat.de/pressekodex.html

Ries, A., & Ries, L. (2004). *The fall of advertising and the rise of PR*. New York: Harper Collins.

Rössler, P. (2004). Qualität aus transaktionaler Perspektive. Zur gemeinsamen Modellierung von ›User Quality‹ und ›Sender Quality‹: Kriterien für Online-Zeitungen [Quality from a Transactional Perspective. On the joint modeling of 'user quality' and 'sender quality': criteria for online newspapers.]. In K. Beck, W. Schweiger, & W. Wirth (Eds.), *Gute Seiten – schlechte Seiten. Qualität in der Onlinekommunikation* [Good pages - bad pages. Quality in online communication] (pp. 127-145). München: Reinhard Fischer.

Röttger, U., Preusse, J., & Schmitt, J. (2014). *Grundlagen der Public Relations. Eine kommunikationswissenschaftliche Einführung* [Fundamentals of Public Relations. An introduction to communication science] (2nd ed.). Wiesbaden: Springer VS.

Journalism or Public Relations?

Ruß-Mohl, S. (1992). „Am eigenen Schopfe …". Qualitätssicherung im Journalismus – Grundfragen, Ansätze, Näherungsversuche ["By their own …". Quality assurance in journalism – Basic questions, approaches]. *Publizistik, 37*, 83-96.

Ruß-Mohl, S. (2017). Wie sich die Machtbalance zwischen Journalismus und PR verschiebt. Die „antagonistische Partnerschaft" in der digitalen Aufmerksamkeitsökonomie – eine verhaltensökonomische Analyse [How the balance of power between journalism and PR is shifting. The "antagonistic partnership" in the digital attention economy – a behavioral economic analysis]. In N. Gonser & U. Roßmann (Eds.), *Verschwimmende Grenzen zwischen Journalismus, Public Relations, Werbung und Marketing. Aktuelle Befunde aus Theorie und Praxis* [Blurring boundaries between journalism, PR advertising and marketing. Current findings from theory and practice] (pp. 13-30). Wiesbaden: Springer VS.

Ryfe, D., Mensing, D., & Kelley, R. (2015). What's the meaning of a news link? *Digital Journalism, 41*, 41-54.

Sallot, L. M., Steinfatt, T. M., & Salwen, M. B. (1998). Journalists' and public relations practitioners' news values: Perceptions and cross-perceptions. *Journalism & Mass Communication Quarterly, 75*(2), 366-377.

Schweiger, W. (2007). *Theorien der Mediennutzung. Eine Einführung* [Theories of media use. An introduction]. Wiesbaden: VS.

Seibold, B. (2002). *Klick-Magnete: Welche Faktoren bei Online-Nachrichten Aufmerksamkeit erzeugen* [Click magnets: which factors generate attention in online news]. München: Fischer.

Simmerling, A., & Janich, N. (2016). Rhetorical functions of a 'language of uncertainty' in the mass media. *Public Understanding of Science, 25*(8), 961-975.

Slater, M., & Rouner, D. (1996). How message evaluation and source attributes may influence credibility assessment and belief change. *Journalism & Mass Communication Quarterly, 73*(4), pp. 974-991.

Stocking, H. S., & Holstein, L. W. (2009). Manufacturing doubt: Journalists' roles and the construction of ignorance in a scientific controversy. *Public Understanding of Science, 18*(1), 23-42.

Temmerman, M., & Mast, J. (Eds., 2021). *News values from an audience perspective.* Cham: Palgrave Macmillan.

Theis-Berglmair, A., & Kellermann, H. (2017). Kontingenz oder Qualität? Die Entwicklung eines textanalytischen Verfahrens zur Differenzierung zwischen journalistischen und PR Angeboten – Ein Werkstattbericht. [Contingency or quality? The development of a text-analytical method for differentiating between journalistic and PR products – A workshop report]. In N. Gonser & U. Rußmann (Eds.), *Verschwimmende Grenzen zwischen Journalismus, PR Werbung und Marketing. Aktuelle Befunde aus Theorie und Praxis* [Blurring boundaries between journalism, PR advertising and marketing. Current findings from theory and practice] (pp.103-114). Wiesbaden: Springer VS.

Urban, J., & Schweiger, W. (2014). News quality from the recipients' perspective. *Journalism Studies, 15*(6), pp. 821-840.

Voigt, J. (2016). *Nachrichtenqualität aus Sicht der Mediennutzer. Wie Rezipienten die Leistung des Journalismus beurteilen können* [News quality from the perspective of media users. How recipients can judge the performance of journalism]. Wiesbaden: Springer VS.

Ward-Johnson, F., & Guiniven, J. E. (2008). The social media release and its implications for PR-journalist relations. *Journal of New Communications Research, II*(2), 63-72.

Weischenberg, S., Malik, M., & Scholl, A. (2006). Journalismus in Deutschland 2005 [Journalism in Germany 2005]. *Media Perspektiven,* (7). 346-361.

Wendelin, M. (2011). *Medialisierung der Öffentlichkeit. Kontinuität und Wandel einer normativen Kategorie der Moderne* [Medialization of the public. Continuity and change of a normative category of modernity]. Köln: Herbert von Halem Verlag.

Wendelin, M. (2014). Transparenz von Rezeptions- und Kommunikationsverhalten im Internet. Theoretische Überlegungen zur Veränderung der Öffentlichkeitsdynamiken zwischen Journalismus und Publikum [Transparency of reception and communication behavior on the Internet. Theoretical considerations on the change in dynamics of the public sphere between journalism and the audience]. In W. Loosen, & M. Dohle (Eds.), *Journalismus und (sein) Publikum. Schnittstellen zwischen Journalismusforschung und Rezeptions- und Wirkungsforschung* [Journalism and (its) audience. Interfaces between journalism research and reception and effects research] (pp. 73-90). Wiesbaden: Springer VS.

Wicke, N. (2022). Eine Frage der Erwartungen? [A question of expectations?] *Publizistik, 67*(1), 51-84.

Wladarsch, J. (2020). *Metakommunikation und die Qualität des Journalismus. Einfluss von Metakommunikation auf Qualitätserwartungen und -bewertungen bei Nachrichtennutzern im Internet* [Metacommunication and the quality of journalism. influence of metacommunication on quality expectations and evaluations among news users on the internet]. Baden-Baden: Nomos.

Wolf, C. (2014). *Mobiler Journalismus: Angebote, Produktionsroutinen und redaktionelle Strategien deutscher Print- und Rundfunkredaktionen* [Mobile journalism: Products, production routines, and editorial strategies of German print and broadcast editorial offices.]. Baden-Baden: Nomos.

Wolling, J. (2002). Aufmerksamkeit durch Qualität? Empirische Befunde zum Verhältnis von Nachrichtenqualität und Nachrichtennutzung [Attention through quality? Empirical findings on the relationship between news quality and news usage]. In A. Baum, & S. J. Schmidt (Eds.), *Fakten und Fiktionen: Über den Umgang mit Medienwirklichkeiten* [Facts and fictions: On dealing with media realities] (pp. 202-216). Konstanz: UVK.

Zerfaß, A., & Pleil, T. (Eds.). (2015). *Handbuch Online-PR. Strategische Kommunikation in Internet und Social Web* [Handbook online PR. Strategic communication on the Internet and social web (2nd updated and expanded edition)]. Konstanz: UVK.

Journalism or Public Relations?

Romy Fröhlich *is a Professor of Communication Science and Media Research in the Department of Media and Communication at Ludwig-Maximilians University Munich, Germany. She is former President of the German Association for Communication Research and former head of the German Public Relations Association's Commission for Education in Public Relations. She served as the coordinator and principal investigator of the international collaborative FP7-EU-Projekt INFOCORE about media and persuasive communication in violent conflicts. Her emphases in research are persuasive communication/PR, war and media, and gender-sensitive communication research. She knew Wolfram Peiser since 1990 when both were doctoral students with Klaus Schönbach at the Hanover University of Music and Drama (Germany), where they shared an office (and countless highly inspiring scholarly discussions).*

Political Advertising – Good or Bad?
The Heterogeneity of U.S. Research Findings and Their Limited Validity for Europe

Christina Holtz-Bacha

Abstract

Political advertising has always been a contentious issue. In general, this can be explained by the uneasy feeling that advertising, which comes, after all, from the world of commerce, has no place in serious politics. Derived from this, the concern focuses on the presumed effects of advertising on recipients and, in particular, those that go beyond the actual purpose of the advertising (which primarily seeks to affect voter turnout, sympathy for one or the other party or candidate, and the voting decision) and more generally influence attitudes toward politics. Controversies regarding political advertising arise in almost every election campaign because its content is perceived as unfair to opponents, because it "hits below the belt," or because it violates human dignity. Therefore, concerns about undesirable effects relate primarily to negative campaigning because, unlike the case in commercial advertising, negative advertising in politics is commonplace. Against this background, this chapter summarizes the research on political advertising to determine whether there is a reasonable basis, on the one hand, for the expectations of its sponsors and, on the other hand, for the concerns about its negative effects on target audiences.

Political advertising worldwide is a contentious issue. In general, the question whether politics and advertising, which comes, after all, from the world of commerce, are compatible at all arises. Deriving from this, the concern focuses on the presumed effects of advertising on recipients and, in particular, those that exceed the actual purpose of the advertising (effects on voter turnout, sympathy for one party or candidate or the other, and the voter's decision) and more generally influence attitudes toward politics.

Controversies regarding political advertising come up in almost every election campaign because its content is perceived as unfair to opponents,

Political Advertising – Good or Bad?

because it "hits below the belt," or because it violates human dignity. This already demonstrates that concerns about its undesirable effects relate primarily to negative campaigning because, unlike commercial advertising, which usually presents an idyllic world, negative advertising in politics is common. However, the public's critical reactions toward the design and content of political advertising do not deter political actors from entering the electoral fray with attacks on their opponents.

Against this background, this chapter summarizes the research on political advertising to determine whether there is a reasonable basis, on the one hand, for the expectations of its sponsors and, on the other hand, for the concerns about its negative effects on target audiences. First, this chapter establishes a definition of political advertising to narrow the subject of this review. It then looks at the framework conditions for political advertising, which reflect international differences in attitudes toward these kinds of political messages, before assessing the state of research on its effects. Ultimately, it answers the twofold question of whether the high hopes that campaigners seem to place in election advertising are justified and the extent to which the advertising can be dysfunctional.

Defining Political Advertising

Since most of the research on political advertising originated in the United States and due to the importance of televised spots during U.S. election campaigns, political advertising is often associated with television ads. In her 2004 review of research on political advertising, Lynda Kaid demonstrated how early concepts were oriented toward commercial advertising and, accordingly, assumed that the airtime would be purchased. Especially under the impression of international comparative research, which began around the 1990s, the purchase aspect recedes as a defining feature to consider the fact that, in many countries, the allocation of broadcasting time is controlled and conducted free of charge. In U.S. research, however, the term "advertising" is still used most often. This is explained, on the one hand, by the conditions in the United States where political advertising must be paid for; on the other hand, it emphasizes the purpose of the messages, namely, to promote the sponsor or client.

Eventually, the perspective expands beyond election campaigns and considers advertising media other than television. Thus, Kaid (2004, p. 156) finally developed a broad definition that understands political advertising "as any message primarily under the control of a source used to promote political candidates, parties, policy issues, and/or ideas through

209

mass channels." The extension beyond election-related advertising is intended to include promotional activities in any type of political campaign. This definition also incorporates third-party advertising intended to support individual candidates or parties. By specifying "mass channels" as the relevant means of distribution, the definition associates the transmission of advertising through traditional mass media or the internet, which was just emerging as a medium for political advertising at that time, and finally, social networks. Yet the definition is only able to grasp the mass distribution of election posters on the streets to a limited extent.

Due to the extensive body of research on political advertising's effects, to which European research has contributed significantly in the last two or three decades, this chapter is limited to audiovisual political advertising in the run-up to congressional and presidential elections in the United States. In addition, this focus is interesting against the background that election advertising on television—and especially negative advertising—has also stimulated the debate about the Americanization of European election campaigns that peaked around the turn of the millennium. With the ubiquitousness of the internet and social networks, new channels have emerged for audiovisual election advertising, opening up a new perspective for the question raised here.

Framework Conditions

Any examination of the benefits or undesirable effects of audiovisual election advertising must bear in mind that political—just as commercial advertising—depends on the cultural context in which it is embedded. That applies to the visuals and to the verbal elements of the advertising. Election advertising must, therefore, be understood against the background of the respective political and electoral systems, and that holds true for the outcome of the relevant research as well.

This has consequences particularly for research on audiovisual election advertising, which comes from the United States, or the comparison of U.S.-based results with research from European countries as the US is an outlier not only because of its electoral system but also regarding the regulation of political advertising. Unlike European countries, there are virtually no restrictions on political advertising in the US, which in this respect is treated the same as commercial advertising. Election advertising on television is not subject to any time restrictions; political actors can buy advertising slots at any time, not only before elections, and as much as their budget allows. The only requirement is that candidate ads show

Political Advertising – Good or Bad?

a picture of the contender; candidates must also reaffirm in the ad that they approve the message (cf. Just & Crigler, 2017, p. 283). In addition, U.S. regulations allow third parties to support candidates through the purchase of advertising time. In every election campaign, political action committees (PACs) appear promoting one candidate or the other and are characterized, above all, by the use of aggressive advertising. Although the names of the sponsors are displayed, those who are really behind the PACs and what they stand for often remains in the dark. This low level of regulation can be explained by the U.S. interpretation of the basic right to freedom of expression, which is placed first and foremost here, without concern about the potential effects of the advertising on its audience. In contrast, European countries have comparatively strong restrictions on political advertising, which is usually allowed only as election advertising in the last several weeks before election day (cf. Holtz-Bacha, 2017). This, along with the fact that there are countries that do not even allow electoral advertising, rather points to an approach of social responsibility that does not want to leave ideological advertising to the free play of market forces. On top of that, the regulations as well as occasional discussions about abolishing or introducing election advertising reflect uncertainties about the effects on the electorate.

In addition to the peculiarities of the respective electoral system, in particular whether votes are given to candidates or parties, the differences in regulation have consequences for the period, amount, and scope of election advertising, and these, in turn, affect its content and design. Some countries even go so far as to impose specifications on the style and visual design of advertising. If there are such restrictions, they are typically aimed at preventing manifestations of negative advertising. For the visual packaging, there may be bans on the use of national symbols to keep them out of the electoral battle. The country-specific regulations thus determine whether the political actors have access to television at all for their advertising and to what extent advertising time is available to them. Any regulatory specifications for the design of advertising restrict them in their strategies, which are manifested in the text and visuals. The interpretation of the results of international comparative studies on the amount and the verbal and visual content of election broadcasts should, therefore, consider the legal framework and not simply attribute differences to nation-specific strategies.

Christina Holtz-Bacha

What Do We Know About the Effects of Political Advertising?

The figures for audiovisual election advertising in the 2020 US presidential campaign reflect the importance attached to the ads, and in comparison with European countries, for example, they demonstrate the exceptional role the use of ads has for US elections. For the 2019/2020 election cycle, Ridout, Fowler, and Franz (2021, p. 467) recorded 2.35 million airings of political advertising on television. The period between early September, when party conventions nominated the presidential candidates, and Election Day in early November accounted for 804,000 airings in 2020. Compared with the previous presidential election, these figures represent a doubling. And the election revealed one more factor: While candidates have significantly increased their online advertising, it has not been at the expense of traditional television advertising (Fowler et al., 2020, p. 57; Franz, 2020). Although 2020 can be expected to have been an exceptional year in terms of audiovisual advertising due to the pandemic and candidates' reducing personal appearances, thereby relying all the more on ads, these figures clearly highlight the discrepancy with the situation in Europe. In Germany, for example, parties receive a maximum of eight slots each for their spots on the two public service channels, and parties not represented in the Bundestag receive only two. Moreover, the commercial channels, where advertising time must be paid for, are booked only by the larger parties that can afford the costs. Therefore, unrestricted access has given election advertising on U.S. television a starring role in political campaigns. In addition, the election campaigners benefit from an element of surprise due to the interstitial placement of ads. With the significant number of broadcasts, they can count on a repetition effect. The high level of investment in audiovisual election advertising also indicates campaigners' belief that this type of voter appeal has an impact. Indeed, there are numerous studies that have fed this hope. By and large, there is a consensus that ads matter, but determining how they matter is not as easy.

Since electoral advertising has been a feature in the US since the 1950s and because of the large numbers of ads, which have increased steadily from election to election, there is an extensive body of research on U.S. political advertising. The majority of this research is devoted to content analyses; the findings, however, are relevant to the question posed here only if they are related to effects. The investigation of effects is naturally of particular interest to those who commission the advertising. First and foremost, their concern is whether the financial outlay is worthwhile and whether the ads work in the campaigners' interests, i.e., whether they win them votes. This question is expanded since indirect effects can be

Political Advertising – Good or Bad?

assumed, i.e., the ads have an effect on variables that influence the voting decision. The interests of academic research, however, are broader than those of campaigners because they also investigate the effects of advertising that go beyond the immediate electoral context and may also affect those not yet eligible to vote.

Similar to media-effects research in general, overviews of studies on the effects of audiovisual electoral advertising have demonstrated that any effects, if they appear at all, are dependent on a multitude of variables, making generalizations difficult if not impossible (e.g., Fowler et al., 2022, ch. 7, 8; Kaid, 2004). Such influencing variables include the electoral level in U.S. presidential elections or down-ballot elections. Furthermore, regarding the ads, the following variables can play a role: characteristics of the sponsor of the advertisement, the channel (in the case of audiovisual advertising on television, the internet, or social media), and characteristics of the formal design and content of an ad. On the part of viewers variables such as personal characteristics and, for example, their political interests or party identification may also have an influence on the effects of the advertising.

Effects can arise in the aggregate and in the individual voter. However, several studies indicated that ads have little impact on voter turnout. Sides et al. (2021, p. 15) suggested that the main effect of ads lies less in mobilization than in persuasion. Similarly, from their research, Spenkuch and Toniatti (2018) concluded that campaign advertising has virtually no effect on the overall voter turnout but does have an influence on vote shares. This is supported in a study by Law (2021, p. 544), who calculated estimates based on data from the 2008 election that 60% to 70% of advertising effects can be attributed to persuasion and only 30% to 40% to mobilization. Donald Trump's 2016 election campaign has shown that political advertising is also used to demobilize voters and present them with reasons why they should not vote for the opponent (Magleby, 2020, p. 369).

In an electoral system in which candidates are determined not by the parties but in primaries and finance their campaigns largely out of their own pockets, election advertising also plays a significant role in fundraising. In fact, a major portion of any candidate's electoral war chest comes from donations of individuals (Magleby, 2020, p. 362) who are targeted by all kinds of advertising and personal contacts. In addition, findings on whether larger expenditures on election advertising and the intensity of airings lead to greater success at the polls are not definitive (Coppock et al., 2020, p. 6). Liberini et al. (2020) noted that the 2016 Trump campaign invested more in Facebook ads than Hillary Clinton did and managed to get his supporters to turn out to vote, and that this advertising had a negative effect on Clinton's liberal supporters. Konitzer et al. (2019, p. 12), however, found evidence that there could be a boomerang effect in vote intention through additional spending late in the campaign, which the authors interpret as a consequence of oversaturation.

A meta-analysis of 40 field experiments supplemented by nine original experiments provided evidence that campaign contacts, including different types of advertising, have minimally persuasive effects (Kalla & Broockman, 2018). These findings are further corroborated by 59 real-time experiments that varied sender, message, receiver condition, and context (Coppock et al., 2020). Other research has suggested that the effects of ads in U.S. presidential elections are rather small but can make a difference in down-ballot elections (Sides et al, 2021, p. 2). A plausible explanation is that voters in lower-level elections have less information about candidates and issues than in presidential elections. In fact, voters are more likely to be persuaded by a candidate they don't know much about, and this includes considerable changes in beliefs and vote choice (Broockman & Kalla, 2021). Ads broadcast after Labor Day, i.e., in the last two months of the election campaign, prove to be effective, while those broadcast earlier in a campaign do not significantly influence the outcome of the election.

According to the persuasion decay concept (e.g., Gerber et al., 2011), persuasive effects of electoral ads subside over time, and a large part of them decays quickly. Whereas the immediate effects in subnational elections are more substantial than those at the national level, they also deteriorate more quickly (Hill et al., 2013). However, this process does not seem to apply to all groups of voters predisposed in the same way (Bartels, 2014, p. 538). The fact that candidates, nevertheless, buy airtime for their ads on a large scale even in the early phase of election campaigns may mean that their objective is to become known and to position themselves at an early stage before attacks by opponents attempt to tarnish their image (Magleby, 2020, p. 372).

How uncertain the potential impact of ads is can also be illustrated by the example of negative advertising—considered a hallmark of US election advertising. Negative advertising in the US is a must for election campaigns, and that can be attributed, on the one hand, to the political and electoral system centering on candidates and, on the other hand, to the virtual absence of any restrictions on election advertising.

Moreover, negative advertising in the US is usually equated with attacks on one's political opponent or with a format that contrasts the opponents' characteristics and political positions. Generally, although negative advertising is supposed to be unpopular with the electorate, it appears to succeed.

Voters learn about the character and political positions of the targeted candidate through the ads, and possibly about those of the attacking candidate as well, and they remember negative ads better than positive ads (cf. Basil, Schooler, & Reeves 1991; Lau, Sigelman, & Rovner, 2007). Campaigners, however, fear negative advertising's potential backlash effect. This occurs when a negative ad has an unfavorable effect on its sponsor, instead of, as intended, on the attacked, which can happen when viewers perceive the attack as unfair (e.g., Fridkin & Kenney, 2004; Garramone, 1988; Pinkleton, 1997). To avoid this risk, candidates often prefer to hold back negative ads and leave the attacks on their opponents to the party or the Political Action Committees. Female candidates may even be subject to a double bind regarding the use of negative ads and, thereby, face an additional risk (e.g., Bauer & Santia, 2021; Gordon, Shafie, & Crigler, 2003): Whereas aggressive advertising is a common campaign tool in the US and women must prove themselves to be tough enough for politics and for the position they seek, attacking people does not align with the female role stereotype. Therefore, they run the risk of being rejected by the electorate for using aggressive ads.

Regarding the effects of negative advertising on turnout, research has yielded contradictory results. There are good reasons to assume that aggressive advertising alienates citizens from politics and diminishes their willingness to vote. With a view to the effects on general attitudes toward politics, political institutions, and actors, the potential effects of negative advertising point beyond the electoral context. Conversely, the image that negative ads provide of politics and political actors could also mobilize people to participate in elections. With their studies on the detrimental effects of exposure to negative advertising, Ansolabehere et al. (1994, 1999) have fueled the discussion. Their findings pointed to demobilizing effects, a weakening of political efficacy, and further polarization of the electorate. Therefore, Ansolabehere and Iyengar claimed that "[n]egative campaigning transforms elections into an entertaining spectator sport" (1995, p. 145). Other research, however, has been unable to confirm these findings. Based on their meta-analyses of studies on negative campaigning, Lau and collaborators concluded that, although negative ads are unsuitable for attracting votes, they have no detrimental effects on turnout and attitudes toward politics (Lau & Rovner, 2009; Lau, Sigelman, & Rovner, 2007). Other authors have suggested that negative campaign messages can even stimulate participation in the political process. For instance, research by Brooks and Geer (2007), who distinguished between negative and uncivil message content, did not find evidence of adverse effects on political engagement and attitudes toward politics. Rather, they found evidence that the least-liked candidate messages, namely negative, uncivil, and trait-based messages, increase political interest and the likelihood of participating in an election (p. 12). Similarly, Crigler et al. (2006) compared responses to different types of negative campaign communication and argued that their effect is mediated by the emotions they arouse among voters. Their results confirm the harmful effect of attack ads on the attacking candidate and offer some support for their demobilizing effect, whereas issue-based, fear-arousing communication can encourage democratic participation (pp. 153–154). The complexity of the process, with a variety of intertwined variables, leads the authors to conclude, "The jury is still out on the impact of attack advertising" (Crigler et al., 2006, p. 155).

An additional incentive for campaigners to employ negative advertising is that negativity and conflict have high news value, and aggressive commercials, therefore, often become the subject of reporting and, thereby, generate broader public attention. Television repeats the ads, and newspapers describe them in discussions about their form and content, giving the sponsor free advertising time. The classic example of an ad that was broadcast only once but that everyone knows to this day due to the public response is the so-called Daisy Girl spot, produced for Lyndon B. Johnson's campaign for the 1964 presidential election. The powerful, contrasting images of a little girl counting the petals of a daisy and an exploding atomic bomb represent a prime example of a negative spot that received lasting attention. This kind of free media exposure is suited to generate indirect persuasive effects (Konitzer et al., 2019).

With the widespread use of the internet and social media, election campaigners opened up new channels for audiovisual election advertising. These are also less expensive than purchasing television airtime, and they allow the micro-targeting of specific market segments and individual voters. Along with the employment of social media for electoral advertising came new phenomena such as big data and its marriage to neuromarketing (Hegazy, 2019), dark ads (e.g., Madrigal, 2017), and all kinds of deceptions such as deepfakes (Kietzmann et al., 2020) that have further provided new research challenges. While television advertising is public and, thereby, subject to public discussion and possibly fact-checking, social media ads target a narrowly defined audience and, therefore, easily escape public scrutiny.

Since channel, content, and reception situations differ, it is to be expected that digital ads also have different effects than those broadcast on television. It appears that, regardless of content, the channel alone makes a difference (Kaid, 2003). However, comparative content analyses demonstrated that electoral ads on social media are different from those on television (e.g., Crigler et al., 2011; Fowler et al., 2021). This suggests that digital ads serve different campaign goals than classic TV ads do; in fact, Motta and Fowler (2016) ascertained that using TV commercials is preferable for persuasion, while online ads are especially effective for mobilizing partisans. This was also the assumption of Fowler et al. (2021, p. 147) based on their content analysis of the online and TV ads used in the 2018 election campaigns that showed reduced negativity, lower issue content, and increased partisanship for Facebook ads. Accordingly, the mobilizing function, aimed at supporters and followers, is seen as an amplifier for political polarization.

While Broockman and Green (2014, p. 281) expressed doubt that online ads have substantial impact, Liberini et al. (2020), whose study yielded significant effects on voter behavior, concluded that micro-targeted ads on Facebook matter. These effects were particularly pronounced among users who were targeted based on ethnicity, gender, location, and political orientation (p. 29). The authors also found that highly targeted users are less inclined to change their minds and more likely to adhere to their voting choices than less-targeted users, and they interpreted these findings as evidence that advertising on Facebook intensifies political polarization (p. 30).

Micro-targeting, however, is not always as well-received as campaigns hope it will be due to the personalized approach. A study by Hersh and Schaffner (2013) showed that voters apparently prefer broad-based appeals of non-targeted advertising to the particularistic promises of micro-targeting. Moreover, mistargeting has negative consequences when mistargeted voters penalize the ad sponsor because they get the impression that the candidate has different priorities and does not represent the voter's interests.

Since online ads also encourage users to share the content (Kaid, 2006), ads are further spread via social networks, reaching a larger audience and possibly gaining credibility. By clicking, sharing, and commenting on the ads, recipients deliver immediate feedback to the campaigns on the ads' effectiveness (Brodnax & Sapiezynski, 2020).

Conclusion

All in all, this small excerpt from the extensive research on the effects of election advertising in the US shows that the findings are mixed. Studies have looked at all kinds of effects—cognitive, attitudinal, affective, and behavioral—and findings range from "no impact" to "significant impact."

Christina Holtz-Bacha

Effects, if they exist, are mediated by a variety of variables that lie with the ad's sponsor, its design, and its content (formal properties, visual design, text, theme, tone, etc.) as well as with the characteristics of the individual viewer. In addition, the findings of these numerous studies cannot be easily summarized or compared because they chose different methodological approaches and often referred to small samples and regionally specific situations.

As election campaigners hope, persuasion, according to Coppock, Hill, and Vavreck (2020, p. 1) "is presumed to be conditional on who says what to whom and when, and getting this recipe right is thought to be critical for changing minds." This assessment confirms the difficulty of identifying implications or success for election campaigners from the many studies conducted on election advertising in the US. It also reflects that research is continually in search of influencing variables and also seems strongly attached to the traditional S-O-R model.

Since the US is, in addition, an exceptional case with regard to election advertising, the findings of U.S. research can hardly be transferred to European countries. Election advertising is too closely linked to the political system, the media system, and the way election campaigns are conducted in the United States. It is not only the legal regulations that affect the employment of audiovisual election advertising in Europe but also the differences in (political) culture that are expressed in advertising. Just like commercial advertising, election advertising is shaped by the (political) culture of a country, which is expressed, not least, in the visuals: "In order to generate attention, advertisers must try to couple the advertising messages with such ideas, beliefs, values and cultural patterns [...] or with such socio-cultural developments [...] that they assume will be accepted or even desired by their clients and the target audience and in any case connotated with positive emotions" (Schmidt, 2002, pp. 103–104, translated by the author). Advertising is, therefore, always culturally bound, and this results in differences that make it difficult to generalize findings from US research to European countries, for example. To be able to assess the effects of election advertising in Europe, considerably more research would be needed.

Is political advertising good or bad? Research does not allow an answer to this question because of the heterogeneity of the findings and methodological uncertainties. The fact that campaigns invest heavily in advertising suggests that they expect to benefit from it in the political competition. But which scientific results they rely on when they spend millions and millions of dollars on election advertising remains their secret. There are numerous concerns and fears about the effects of election advertising on voters and on those not yet eligible to vote; whether they are justified cannot be answered unequivocally. We know a lot—but still not enough.

References

Ansolabehere, S., & Iyengar, S. (1995). *Going negative. How political advertisements shrink and polarize the electorate*. New York: The Free Press.

Ansolabehere, S., Iyengar, S., & Simon, A. (1999). Replicating experiments using aggregate and survey data: The case of negative advertising and turnout. *The American Political Science Review*, *93*, 901–909.

Ansolabehere, S., Iyengar, S., Simon, A., & Valentino, N. (1994). Does attack advertising demobilize the electorate? *The American Political Science Review*, *88*, 829–838.

Bartels, L. M. (2014). Remembering to forget: A note on the duration of campaign advertising effects. *Political Communication*, *31*, 532–544.

Basil, M., Schooler, C., & Reeves, B. (1991). Positive and negative political advertising: Effectiveness of ads and perceptions of candidates. In F. Biocca (Ed.), *Television and political advertising, Vol. 1. Psychological processes* (pp. 245–262). Hillsdale, NJ: Lawrence Erlbaum.

Bauer, N. M., & Santia, M. (2921). Going feminine: Identifying how and when female candidates emphasize feminine and masculine traits on the campaign trail. *Political Research Quarterly*, 1–15, DOI: 10.1177/10659129211020257.

Brodnax, N., & Sapiezynski, P. (2020). Evolution of digital advertising strategies during the 2020 US presidential primary, https://arxiv.org/pdf/2012.05859.

Brooks, D. J., & Geer, J. G. (2007). Beyond negativity: The effects of incivility on the electorate. *American Journal of Political Science*, *51*, 1–16.

Broockman, D. E., & Kalla, J. L. (2021). When and why are campaigns' persuasive effects small? Evidence from the 2020 US presidential election, *OSF Preprints*, 10.31219/osf.io/m7326.

Coppock, A., Hill, S. J., & Vavreck, L. (2020). The small effects of political advertising are small regardless of context, message, sender, or receiver: Evidence from 59 real-time randomized experiments. *Science Advances*, *6*(36), 1–6, DOI: 10.1126/sciadv.abc4046.

Crigler, A., Just, M., Hume, L., Mills, J., & Hevron, P. (2011). YouTube and TV advertising campaigns. Obama versus McCain in 2008. In R. L. Fox & J. M. Ramos (Eds.), *iPolitics. Citizens, elections, and governing in the new media era* (pp. 103-124). Cambridge: Cambridge University Press.

Crigler, A., Just, M., & Belt, T. (2006). The three faces of negative campaigning. The democratic implications of attack ads, cynical news, and fear-arousing messages. In D. P. Redlawsk (Ed.), *Feeling politics. Emotion in political information processing* (pp. 135–163). Houndmills: Palgrave Macmillan.

Fowler, E. F., Franz, M. M., & Ridout, T. N. (2020). The blue wave: Assessing political advertising trends and democratic advantages in 2018. *PS. Political Science & Politics*, *53*, 57–63.

Fowler, E. F., Franz, M. M., Martin, G. J., Peskowitz, Z., & Ridout, T. N. (2021). Political advertising online and offline. *American Political Science Review*, *115*, 130–149.

Fowler, E. F., Franz, M. M., & Ridout, T. N. (2022). *Political advertising in the United States* (second edition). New York: Routledge.

Franz, M. (2020). The utility and content of traditional ads. In E. Suhay, B. Grofman & A. H. Trechsel (Eds.), *The Oxford handbook of persuasion* (pp. 203–223). New York: Oxford University Press.

Fridkin, K. L., & Kenney, P. J. (2004). Do negative messages work? The impact of negativity on citizens' evaluations of candidates. *American Politics Research*, *32*, 570–605.

Garramone, G. (1984). Voter responses to negative political ads. *Journalism Quarterly*, *61*, 250–259.

Gerber, A. S., Gimpel, J. G., Green, D. P., & Shaw, D. R. (2011). How large and long-lasting are the persuasive effects of televised campaign ads? Results from a randomized field experiment. *The American Political Science Review*, *105*, 135–150.

Gordon, A., Shafie, D. M., & Crigler, A. N. (2003). Is negative advertising effective for female candidates? An experiment in voters' uses of gender stereotypes. *Press/Politics*, *8*(3), 35–53.

Hegazy, I. M. (2021). The effect of political neuromarketing 2.0 on election outcomes. The case of Trump's presidential campaign 2016. *Review of Economics and Political Science*, *6*, 235–251.

Hersh, E. D., & Schaffner, B. F. (2013). Targeted campaign appeals and the value of ambiguity. *The Journal of Politics*, *75*, 520–534.

Hill, S. J., Lo, J., Vavreck, L., & Zaller, J. (2013). How quickly we forget: The duration of persuasion effects from mass communication. *Political Communication*, *30*, 521–547.

Holtz-Bacha, C. (2017). Regulation of political advertising in Europe. In C. Holtz-Bacha, E. Novelli & K. Rafter (Eds.), *Political advertising in the 2014 European Parliament elections* (pp. 27–37). London: Palgrave Macmillan.

Just, M. R., & Crigler, A. (2017). The wild, wild West. Political advertising in the United States. In C. Holtz-Bacha & M. R. Just (Eds.), *Routledge handbook of political advertising* (pp. 279–291). New York: Routledge.

Kaid, L. L. (2003). Comparing Internet and traditional media: Effects on voters. *American Behavioral Scientist*, *46*, 677–691.

Kaid, L. L. (2004). Political advertising. In L. L. Kaid (Ed.), *Handbook of political communication research* (pp. 155–202). Mahwah, NJ: Lawrence Erlbaum.

Kaid, L. L. (2006). Political web wars: The use of the Internet for political advertising. In A. P. Williams & J. C. Tedesco (Eds.), *The Internet election: Perspectives on the web in campaign 2004* (pp. 67–82). Lanham, MD: Rowman & Littlefield.

Kalla, J. L., & Broockman, D. E. (2018). The minimal persuasive effects of campaign contact in general elections: Evidence from 49 field experiments. *American Political Science Review*, *112*, 148–166.

Kietzmann, J., Lee, L. W., McCarthy, I. P., & Kietzmann, T. C. (2020). Deepfakes: Trick or treat? *Business Horizons*, *63*, 135–146.

Konitzer, D. R., Hill, S., & Wilbur, K. C. (2019). Using big data and algorithms to determine the effect of geographically targeted advertising on vote intention: Evidence from the 2012 U.S. presidential election. *Political Communication*, *36*, 1–16.

Lau, R. R., & Rovner, I. B. (2007). Negative campaigning. *Annual Review of Political Science*, *12*, 285–306.

Lau, R. R., Sigelman, L., & Rovner, I. B. (2007). The effects of negative political campaigns: A meta-analytic reassessment. *The Journal of Politics*, *69*, 1176–1209.

Law, W. (2021). Decomposing political advertising effects on vote choices. *Public Choice*, *188*, 525–547.

Liberini, F., Redoano, M., Russo, A., Cuevas, A., & Cuevas, R. (2020). Politics in the Facebook era. Evidence from the 2016 US presidential elections (CESifo Working Paper No. 8235). Munich: Center for Economic Studies and ifo Institute, http://hdl.handle.net/10419/216631.

Madrigal, A. C. (2017, October 12). What Facebook did to American democracy. And why it was so hard to see it coming. *The Atlantic*, https://www.theatlantic.com/technology/archive/2017/10/what-facebook-did/542502/.

Magleby, D. B. (2020). How electoral spending relates to political persuasion. In E. Suhay, B. Grofman & A. H. Trechsel (Eds.), *The Oxford handbook of persuasion* (pp. 358–379). New York: Oxford University Press.

Motta, M. P., & Fowler, E. F. (2016). The content and effect of political advertising in U.S. campaigns. In Oxford Research Encyclopedias. *Oxford research encyclopedia of politics*, DOI: 10.1093/acrefore/9780190228637.013.217.

Pinkleton, B. (1997). The effects of negative comparative political advertising on candidate evaluations and advertising evaluations: An exploration. *Journal of Advertising 26*(1), 19–29.

Ridout, T. N., Fowler, E. F., & Franz, M. M. (2021). Spending fast and furious: Political advertising in 2020. *The Forum*, *18*, 465–492.

Schmidt, S. J. 2002. Werbung oder die ersehnte Verführung. In H. Willems (Ed.), *Die Gesellschaft der Werbung. Kontexte und Texte. Produktionen und Rezeptionen. Entwicklungen und Perspektiven*, (pp. 101–119). Wiesbaden: Westdeutscher Verlag.

Sides, J., Vavreck, L., & Warshaw, C. (2021). The effect of television advertising in United States elections. *The American Political Science Review*. DOI: 10.1017/S000305542100112X.

Spenkuch, J. L., & Toniatti, D. (2018). Political advertising and election results. *Quarterly Journal of Economics*, *133*, 1981–2036.

Christina Holtz-Bacha

Christina Holtz-Bacha *(Dr. phil.) is Professor Emerita at Friedrich-Alexander-Universität Erlangen-Nürnberg. Her research interests lie in the field of political communication, media policy, and gender and media. As an assistant professor, Wolfram Peiser worked with her from 1995 until 2004 at the University of Mainz, where he also completed his habilitation under her supervision.*

Does the Media System Explain Individual Media Use and Media Effects?

Findings From a Systematizing Literature Review

Cornelia Wallner

Abstract

Based on a comprehensive literature review, this article explores evidence about connections between the media system as explanatory macro-level for media use and media effects on an individual, micro-level. Addressing this context from a comparative, media system-related perspective, N=42 papers were reviewed and systematized by thematic area. Core results show that systematic connections exist between structural differences of media systems and patterns of individual media use and media effects. More findings are available for newspapers and television than for the internet and social media. Empirical evidence is given for media system-related differences in political knowledge, and the degree of political parallelism in media systems matters for political participation. Overall, the studies show that the media system as a context matters for explaining individual media use and effects. Perspectives for future research are derived from the current state of research.

Media use and media effects depend on multiple factors, and the micro-level plays a key role in explaining them. Beyond that, however, the question of whether micro-level findings are universally valid between different media environments arises. Concurrently, the question of whether there are explanatory factors at the macro-level, specifically the media system, that can explain communication phenomena at the micro-level is raised. These issues constitute the starting point for the following remarks. Based on a comprehensive literature review, this paper elaborates on the relationship between media systems, media use, and media effects and systematizes insights by thematic area.

In comparative media system research, we seek to explain why media for a certain area, usually a country, are the way they are, why they differ from media in other countries, what connections exist between media and other characteristics of the respective society, and how these relations differ between countries. Siebert, Peterson, and Schramm defined this research interest in 1956, and it continues to guide researchers engaged in media system research today. Thus, comparative media system research is also about the explanatory relevance of the macro-level, the "contextual environment for communication outcomes" (Esser & Pfetsch, 2020, preprint, p. 5) and how this macro-level shapes communication phenomena differently. The comparative research "is based on the assumption that different parameters of political and media systems differentially promote or constrain communication roles and behaviors of organizations and actors within those systems" (Esser & Pfetsch, 2020, preprint p. 5) The analysis of media systems involves the actual status as well as developments and interdependencies over time. It is about the answers to questions *within individual* media systems, as well as *comparing between* media systems. The latter is the focus of this paper.

Thus, comparative research examines the context of media and communication, and this context is relevant in two ways: "Not only are individual-level processes better understood through the consideration of contextual factors, but the significance of macro-level characteristics only becomes visible when different national political communication arrangements are compared with each other" (Esser, 2019, p. 680). Against the background of rapid media change and globalization, Livingstone pointed out that "it is no longer plausible to study one phenomenon in one country without asking, at a minimum, whether it is common across the globe or distinctive to that country or part of the world" (Livingstone, 2012, p. 417). Consequently, the comparative perspective can also be profitable for understanding media use: "Considering media use as embedded in higher-level structures will thus enable a more comprehensive, encompassing, and arguably theoretically enhanced understanding of the role of media in contemporary societies" (Boomgaarden & Song, 2019, p. 547). As such, we are interested in how different types of media systems are aligned with different patterns of media use and effects.

Different Models of Media Systems

The most prominent and widely employed study to date by Hallin and Mancini (2004) presented the "three models of media and politics." The authors examined 18 Western countries in Europe and North America in regard to their media and political systems and applied political science concepts to communication studies issues. They referred to historical press

Does the Media System Explain Individual Media Use and Media Effects?

and media development, political parallelism between media and politics, the professionalization of journalism, and the role of the state in the media system. The authors drew on the criteria elaborated by Blumler and Gurevitch (1995) to capture the relationship between media and politics. Based on an elaborated theoretical discussion, Hallin and Mancini (2004) derived their typology of three models of media and politics: the Mediterranean model (polarized pluralistic), the Northern European model (democratic corporatistic), and the North Atlantic model (liberal). Hallin and Mancini saw the models in the sense of ideal types according to Max Weber: "(...) and the media systems of individual countries fit them only roughly" (Hallin & Mancini, 2004, p. 11). Their typology has been used as the common ground for many comparative studies; thereby, Hallin and Mancini laid an essential foundation for the further development of comparative media systems research. However, this typology is "far from the last word" (Benson, 2010, p. 615). Empirical "tests" do not completely reproduce the typology (e.g., Brüggemann et al., 2014; Humprecht et al., 2022). Although Hallin and Mancini (2017) did not consider this to be a refutation of their model, they considered different approaches behind it, namely a theoretical and a data-centric one.[1]

In any case, there are clear differences between media systems in European and North American countries, with strong similarities between some countries. At the same time, clear differences between other countries can be identified. Hallin and Mancini's 2004 typology is important to mention here because it is often used to select countries for comparative empirical studies, as shown by the studies reviewed below.

Media Systems and Media Content

Shortly after the publication of Hallin and Mancini's typology, comparative media system studies increased significantly (Wallner, 2016). Initially, these studies focused particularly on whether and how media content differs between media systems, and it was consistently found that the differences in media content were related to the specific structures of the media

---

1 There is still a focus on Western countries in comparative media systems research that is definitely worthy of criticism (e.g., Sparks, 2018). In recent years, few works have been published that broaden the geographic scope. For an overview of media system typologies based on Hallin and Mancini (2004) and expanding their model in terms of indicators and geographic scope, see the overview in Hallin (2016, updated 2021).

systems. Studies of Western media systems have shown a relationship between the structures of a media system and the political information environments, i.e., "the supply and demand of political news and political information within a certain society" (Van Aelst et al., 2017, p. 4). In the case of television, the information environment varies depending on the degree of commercialization of a media system (Aalberg, van Aelst, & Curran, 2010), and media systems with public service broadcasting provide increasingly more frequent opportunities to consume political news content (Curran et al., 2009; Iyengar et al., 2010). In countries with *strong* public service broadcasting, the news supply is greater, especially during prime time (Esser et al., 2012). Thus, political information environments differ between media systems, which, in turn, offer different information opportunities, i.e., "access points in the political information environment that provide incentives for people to enter the news discourse" (Esser et al., 2012, p. 249).

Moving on, the question of whether the media system structures are accompanied by certain patterns of media use or even media effects arises. One of the first studies on structural influences of media use (Prior, 2007) in the US found "that news consumption, learning about politics, and electoral volatility have changed not so much because people are different today, but rather because the media environment is different. People have not necessarily changed; they have merely changed the channel" (Prior, 2007, p. 19). Althaus et al. (2009) demonstrated that, for the US, the demographic characteristics of a region together with the supply-side characteristics, market size, and complexity explain *more of* the self-reported news exposure than the demand characteristics for news at the individual level.

Based on an extensive literature review, I discuss the state of research regarding the relationship between media systems, their structures, and media use and effects.

Systematizing Literature Review

First, a note on the unit of analysis: macro-perspective studies, such as the one in focus here, continue to use a nation-state as the unit of analysis. Although the state is becoming increasingly inadequate as a unit of analysis due to global-communication networks, this continues to be necessary for empirical studies at the same time, in particular due to the data situation (Esser, 2013). Herein, studies are considered that explicitly address the

Does the Media System Explain Individual Media Use and Media Effects?

media system as a contextual level of individual media use/effects and/or societal media effects.

The literature search strategy was limited to articles published in peer-reviewed journals collected from the database Communication & Mass Media Complete. Journal articles were chosen for their relevance in determining the status of a subject (Brosius & Haas, 2009; Weaver & Wilhoit, 1988). No contributions from edited volumes or monographs were included (for the procedure, c.f. Hanusch & Vos, 2020; Matthes et al., 2019; Wallner, 2016). The database was searched through April 2022, with defined search terms (media system OR cross-cultural AND media use OR media exposure OR media effect OR screen time). For the selection of studies in the sense of comparative research, the criterion of multilevel comparison was applied, i.e., studies with at least three elements of comparison (i.e., media systems) related to an object of investigation relevant to communication studies (Esser & Hanitzsch, 2012) were selected, in this case, media use or media effects and media systems. These are multilevel comparative approaches in the sense of cross-national research (Boomgaarden & Song, 2019). Intra-state analyses were excluded, as well as research unrelated to the key interest of the review. The initial result yielded 330 articles, which were reviewed based on title, keywords, and abstract, and after removing duplicates, the literature search comprised 24 papers. This result was supplemented by other thematically related, peer-reviewed journal articles known from my own work on the topic and others not published in journals listed in CMMC (e.g., in sociological journals). Finally, 42 articles were included in the literature review.

Results

The aim is to provide a comprehensive overview of the current state of research that is as complete as possible. An interpretation of the (increasing) number of articles (c.f. Table 1) in the field of comparative media system research is not possible due to the steadily growing number of journal publications (e.g., Engels, Ossenblok, & Spruyt, 2012).

Table 1: Year of Publication

2007	2008	2009	2010	2011	2012	2013	2014	2015	2016	2017	2018	2019	2020	2021	Q1 2022
1	1	2	3	3	2	4	6	2	2	3	3	1	4	3	2

Cornelia Wallner

Table 2 provides an overview of the publication journals.

Table 2: Journals

Political Communication	6
The International Journal of Press/Politics	5
European Journal of Communication	3
International Journal of Communication	3
Journal of Communication	3
Communication Research	2
Communication Today (under evaluation)	2
Digital Journalims	2
Information, Communication & Society	2
International Communication Gazette	2
Acta Politica	1
Central European Journal of Communication	1
International Journal of Comparative Sociology	1
International Journal of Public Opinion Research	1
Journal of Broadcasting & Electronic Media	1
Journal of Elections, Public Opinions and Parties	1
Journalism	1
Journalism Practice	1
Journalism Studies	1
New Media & Society	1
Political Science and Research Methods	1
Social Media + Society	1
Total N =	*42*

In all, 24 studies examined more than 10 countries (multi-state comparisons), and 17 examined between three and 10 countries. For one study, which was a meta-study (Matthes et al., 2019), the number of countries could not be coded. About half of the data sources used are existing sources such as the European Social Survey, the European Election Survey, or the Reuters Institute Digital News Report. A number of studies additionally or exclusively use self-collected data, and some use combinations of surveys and content analyses as well as experimental designs (Steppat et al., 2022) and web-tracking data (Stier et al., 2020). The studies examine the relationship between media system structures and media use as well as media effects at different levels and include the following categories:

1. Studies that look at media use and/or media effects in a comparative perspective, examining in general differences between certain countries;
2. Studies that make comparisons between countries in terms of specific characteristics and classify country similarities and differences; and
3. Studies that include the media system in their statistical explanatory models for selected phenomena (i.e., country as a variable) and show explicitly the explained variance contributed by the media system.

Political communication is the focus in all studies, in particular, news usage, political knowledge, political interest, political participation, diversity of topics and opinions, fragmentation of audiences, selective exposure, media freedom, and the development of democracy. The following overview of key findings is structured along the thematic focus.

Media Use

In Western countries, television is the most important medium for political news (Nielsen & Schröder, 2014), with online media and traditional daily newspapers coming in second. In television-centric countries, the internet is used more for political news than the press (Papathanassopoulos et al., 2013). At the individual level, the studies examine the well-known relationships between media use of political media content and education, age, socioeconomic status, political interest, and political knowledge, each of which also has explanatory power. Across many countries, there is a positive correlation between social status and television use for information purposes, as well as an "upper-class bias" in daily newspaper use (Shehata, 2010).

Research shows cross-country variations in the use of social media for news and, in particular, the use of online news videos (Kalogeropoulos, 2018). Internet use in general is explained by individual factors but also by the media system at the macro-level, with people in Northern and Central European and North Atlantic countries using the internet more than people in Southern European countries (Meilan & Wu, 2017). However, interestingly, the explanatory relevance of individual characteristics for social media news use is obviously lower than for traditional media. Höhlig, Hasebrink, and Behrig (2021, p. 1816) pointed out that "sociodemographic patterns of news use are structurally similar *within* a range of otherwise distinctive countries but also sociodemographic characteristics only predict differences of news use *between* countries to a limited extent," which indicates the relevance of macro-level explanations rather than individual ones for social media news use.

For traditional media, the explanatory power of the macro-level for individual media consumption has previously been examined in several studies. Using data on media use from the European Social Survey for European countries, Elvestad and Blekesaune (2008) showed, by means of multilevel analysis, that 6.5% of individual newspaper use can be explained by variables at the country level. However, there is no uniform picture according to the country classification of Hallin and Mancini (2004): Not all countries that are assigned to a type show uniform patterns regarding newspaper consumption. Aalberg, Blekesaune, and Elvestad (2013) found a similar result for television: 5% of individual television-viewing time, in general, and 5.1% of individual television-news viewing can be explained by systematic differences across countries. Shehata and Strömbäck (2011) also revealed a connection between media system characteristics and individual media use: There is a positive relationship between newspaper centrism and the use of daily newspapers and television for political information that goes beyond individual explanatory factors. Political interest has a stronger influence on television-news use in television-centric countries than in newspaper-centric countries: "A one-unit increase in political interest increases television news consumption by 0.370 units in the least newspaper-centric country, a one-unit increase in political interest amounts to roughly 11 more min of viewing in the least newspaper-centric country, compared to 6 min in the most newspaper-centric country. That is, political interest has a positive influence in all countries but is substantially weaker in media environments that are newspaper-centric" (Shehata & Strömbäck, 2011, p. 126). Regarding individual characteristics, their study suggests that "the influence of education and political interest on television news consumption does depend on media environment characteristics" (Shehata & Strömbäck, 2011, p. 127).

Similarly, Perusko, Vozab, and Cuvalo (2015) highlighted the relevance of structural macro characteristics for explaining individual media use. By adding structural macro characteristics to individual characteristics, the explanatory power of models of individual media use improves, from 53% to 64% for television, from 36% to 40% for daily newspapers, and from 17% to 27% for mobile television use.

Political Knowledge

A central question in several studies is the role of the media for political knowledge and participation. Differences in people's knowledge about current affairs can be partially explained by the available media outlets in their respective countries (Curran et al., 2009; Elenbaas et al., 2014) and thus by different media system structures. For example, 25% of knowledge about international news topics can be explained by the amount of international news coverage (Aalberg et al., 2013), and this amount differs across media systems. Here, the use of public broadcasting has a significant positive effect on knowledge about political issues (Park & de Zuniga, 2021), while the use of commercial TV shows a negative effect (Fraile & Iyengar, 2014; Curran et al., 2014). Thus, it can also be stated that "the virtuous circle of democratic reinforcement operates primarily in relation to public service television" (Curran et al., 2014, p. 823).

A similar finding was made regarding the use of print media. The use of quality newspapers, which typically contain more hard news, has a positive effect on political knowledge, while the use of tabloids, which contain more soft news, has a negative effect (Fraile & Iyengar, 2014). This, again, refers to different types of media systems with different degrees of importance regarding quality press.

Nir (2012) found that cross-national differences explain 10% of the variability in political knowledge and 6% of the variability in political interest, where the characteristic "shared news" (operationalized as the share of regular newspaper readership of the largest newspaper and the share of regular viewership of the most-watched prime-time news program per country) is found to be an important covariate for the relevance of the country variable (Nir, 2012).

Obviously, the information environment matters. Accordingly, we distinguish information-rich media environments (strong public broadcasting, strong quality newspapers) and information-poor media environments (weak public broadcasting or only commercial TV and tabloids) as characteristics of media systems as well as differentiations between them. In information-rich environments, the explanatory power of individual characteristics such as interest or socioeconomic status on political knowledge is lower than in information-poor environments (Iyengar et al., 2010; Fraile, 2013). Very few cross-country comparative results are available on the role of social media for political knowledge; thus far, it is known that social media use has minimal effects on political knowledge (Park &

de Zuniga, 2021).[2] However, for non-institutional political participation (e.g., boycotts, legal and illegal demonstrations, occupations), Mosca and Quaranta (2016) showed that there is no influence from media system characteristics such as the degree of commercialization or from political characteristics such as a majoritarian or consensual system on patterns of non-institutional participation.

The Relevance of Political Parallelism

Another feature of media systems is political parallelism, "...a pattern or relationship where the structure of the political parties is somewhat reflected by the media organizations" (de Albuquerque, 2018), which Hallin and Mancini (2004) considered a crucial distinguishing criterion of media systems and which proves to be explanatory for distinguishing media systems in empirical comparative media system studies (Brüggemann et al., 2014). In countries with strong parallelism, citizens are more likely to go to the polls (Van Kempen, 2007); at the same time, the responsiveness of political authorities is perceived to be lower; the (biased) portrayal of political reality in the media influences perceptions of politics (Bene, 2020); and satisfaction with democracy is lower (Lelkes, 2016, with parallelism on television playing a somewhat greater role than parallelism in daily newspapers).

In an exhaustive analysis with data from the World Values Survey, Tsfati and Ariely (2014) showed that trust in media, in addition to individual-level predictors, was positively associated on the macro-level with post-materialism. However, and of special interest from the perspective of media system researchers, government ownership has no significant influence on trust in media when controlling for democracy and economic development. In contrast, Macháčková and Tkaczyk (2020) found higher levels of trust for democratic corporatist countries, and they concluded that higher newspaper circulation and lower control on Public Service Broadcasters (PBS) are positively related to trust in media. These findings, as well as possible moderation effects, are certainly important factors for future media system research.

---

2 For a case study in Sweden, Dimitrova et al. (2011) showed a low effect of social media use on political knowledge but more-significant effects on political participation.

Does the Media System Explain Individual Media Use and Media Effects?

Cross-Cutting Exposure

The greater the parallelism in a media system, the less cross-cutting exposure recipients have, referring to confrontation with opinions that do not correspond to their own (Goldman & Mutz, 2011). Thus, if a country has many media with a higher degree of parallelism to political parties, it may be easier for individuals to avoid cross-opinion or cross-party political discourse. The preference for news with a shared point of view is partially explained by the country as a variable, and together with interest for politics, they explain news preference better than individual sociodemographic characteristics can (Rodriguez-Virgili et al., 2022).

At the country level and considering national media-use patterns, it appears that television provides more opportunities for cross-cutting exposure than daily newspapers do (Goldman & Mutz, 2011). In countries with strong public broadcasting, the degree of individual political interest plays a smaller role for cross-cutting exposure (Castro-Herrero et al., 2018), and individuals from a country with strong public broadcasting are more willing to consume news from sources that disagree with their views, reducing the risk for echo chambers (Castro-Herrero et al., 2018). At the same time, differences by political system emerge: "The news media made a greater contribution to citizens' cross-cutting exposure in consensus systems that represent people and political interests more inclusively than in more power-concentrating systems or settings with a hegemonic tradition" (Castro & Nir, 2020).

Matthes et al. (2019) conducted a statistical meta-study on cross-cutting exposure and found that its effects regarding political participation were not larger for online vs. offline exposure (Matthes et al., p. 533). As an individual characteristic of the respondent, the region of origin (Europe, Asia, Africa, North America, Central and South America) was examined as a moderator. Yet the effect of cross-cutting exposure on political participation does not depend on respondents' regions. However, it is important to note that the "region" level in this case does not consider the differences between media systems within a region—which are evident, for example, between European media systems.

Audience Fragmentation

Another question is whether the development of high-choice media environments leads to a fragmentation of media users. Here, little overall fragmentation of recipients is shown for offline and online media, and therefore, it is not possible to speak of audience fragmentation (or echo chambers) (Fletcher & Nielsen, 2017; Steppat et al., 2022). However, there are, again, differences between media systems. Fletcher and Nielsen (2017) found the UK to have a more fragmented audience than Denmark, Germany, France, Spain, and the US, and Denmark to have a more fragmented audience than Spain and the US. In countries with a higher degree of fragmentation, a higher selective exposure is found (Steppat et al., 2022).

Regarding the media use of individuals with populist attitudes, web-tracking data showed that these people use more hyper-partisan news but still get their news primarily from established sources. A strong correlation was found between individual news diets and national media supply, although no consistent patterns have yet been identified across countries (Stier et al., 2020).

Online Political Participation

In regard to social media, participation aspects are compared between countries. Online participation in political discourse is more widespread in Italy, Spain, and the United States than in Denmark, Germany, and the United Kingdom (Kalogeropoulos, Negredo, Picone, & Nielsen, 2017; Nielsen & Schröder, 2014). In this regard, Nielsen and Schröder (2014, p. 472) noted that these country differences in participation do not correspond to differences in internet use, leading them to conclude that "more than mere availability shapes the role of social media as part of people's news habits."

When it comes to the spread of fake news via social media, the intensity of the use of social media, the use of alternative media, and the following of populist parties are explanatory factors across all the countries studied. People with higher social media use and activity are less likely to refrain from spreading disinformation, with some differences between countries. Thus, country-specific differences and, therefore, the respective information environments are significant deciding factors in whether fake news is further disseminated. Interestingly, the use of public service broadcasting does not strengthen resilience against disinformation except in France (Humprecht et al., 2021). This is particularly noteworthy because in several studies, as explained earlier, the country characteristic of strong PBS or the use of it seems to be consistently explanatory.

Political expression on social networks is positively related to the heterogeneity of the social network on which users share discussions, with this relationship being stronger in countries with lower freedom of expression

Does the Media System Explain Individual Media Use and Media Effects?

(Barnidge et al., 2018). Freedom of the media and freedom of expression are, in turn, positively related to political knowledge (Schoonvelde, 2013; Park & de Zuniga, 2021), and lower media freedom, i.e., a strong state role, is associated with higher information-seeking media behavior (Loveless, 2015).

Media and Social Change

Finally, the question of what role media change plays in social change arises. To answer it, Groshek (2011, 2010, 2009) examined the relationship between media distribution and the development of democracy over time. The correlation analyses are based on the assumptions of the media system dependency theory formulated by Ball-Rockeach and De Fleur (1976), which discusses the connections between media, recipients, their environment, social structure, and the economy. Groshek (2011) investigated whether media have a positive effect on the development of institutionalized democracy in those countries where media are widely distributed and, therefore, fulfill key social functions, including the information function, as well as in those countries with greater sociopolitical instability. Both assumptions were partially confirmed. The results revealed that, in countries where a certain level of media penetration already exists, a positive influence of TV and radio—but not newspapers—on the development of democracy could be seen. Media distribution also promotes the development of institutionalized democracy in countries with sociopolitical instability. In regard to the internet, for the period 1994–2003 Groshek (2009) showed that increasing internet penetration is associated with increasing democratic development in the context of developed countries or countries where democratic approaches are at least partially in place. A correlation also emerges in countries with high political instability. However, Groshek (2010) demonstrated that internet penetration has no *causal* effects on the development of democracy. Thus, mere media dissemination cannot be seen as a guarantor but rather as a component of democracy development. In addition, a certain minimum level of democratic politics must be in place for the internet to lead to an increase in democratic politics because if national politics restrict communication freedoms on the internet, then even relatively high internet penetration will *not* lead to a democratization effect. A study of Asian and African countries concluded that internet *penetration* is not a predictor, but internet *use* is a predictor of "demand for democracy," and internet penetration strengthens this relationship (Nisbet, Stoycheff, & Pearce, 2012). Similar to Groshek (2009),

Cornelia Wallner

these authors found that, in countries with higher democratization, the relationship between individual internet use and demand for democracy is higher.

Synopsis

This systematizing literature review aimed to provide a comprehensive picture of the current state of research regarding the relationships between media systems and media use as well as media effects. Several overarching findings can be derived from the studies discussed, and these may add to the question of whether certain parameters of media systems shape communication differently or, in other words, how context matters. Important for research on media systems as well as research on media use and effects, the critical finding is that media use differs depending on media system characteristics and that the media system can proportionately explain individual media use.

Furthermore, empirical evidence is provided for media system-related differences in political knowledge, with information-rich environments having a positive influence on political knowledge. The role of the state and political parties in the media sector appears to be an important characteristic for differentiating media systems. The "political parallelism" of a media system proportionately explains political participation in terms of voter turnout, perceptions of politics and democracy, and cross-cutting exposure. In summary, low political parallelism and strong public broadcasting seem to lead to higher news usage and more political knowledge, while more-commercialized media markets offer less political information and fewer information opportunities. Thus, based on studies of media use and effects, information-rich media environments with various opportunity structures are desirable characteristics of media systems from the perspective of democratic theory.

Comparative studies of media systems revealed that fragmentation of online and offline audiences is consistently low, but apparently, there are differences between media systems. More in-depth research on this issue is desirable. For online media in general, the country-specific information environment is an explanatory factor for media use and participation. Media change at the macro-level shows the role of the internet for social change, i.e., democratization processes.

In summary, the results of this systematizing literature review illustrate that we have well-documented empirical findings on certain relationships between structures and use, especially for newspapers and television. Regarding the internet and social media in particular, evidence for associations between structures and use and effects is scarce, and based on the current state of research, concluding statements can be made only with caution.

Concluding Remarks

Encouragingly, we already know quite a lot about the connections between the macro- and micro-levels of communication. However, many questions remain on a wide variety of topics that have not (yet) been addressed in empirical research. To name a few, these include questions regarding gradual expressions of media freedom at the macro-level and individual communication phenomena; historical developments of media systems and individual communication, especially regarding the merging of old and new media logics in hybrid media systems (Chadwick 2013); and the role of individual media effects for the development of the media system.

From a methodological point of view, in addition to the now well-established multilevel analyses, more moderator and mediator analyses should be encouraged in order to explain the multiple interrelationships within the macro-level as well as at the micro-level. Furthermore, Esser (2019) pointed out the necessity of qualitative research for a deeper understanding of the context. In the field of political communication, Matthes et al. (2019) suggested that states with varying degrees of democracy need to be studied in order to better examine structural influences on political participation aspects.

This leads me to a critical yet decisive remark. Inherent in almost all studies is a normative view of public communication in that more political information is considered beneficial; political knowledge as well as participation in the political process is considered important; and ultimately, a functioning democracy is implicitly or explicitly assumed as the target variable of public communication in the sense of a public sphere as well as in the sense of the political organization of a country. And here the reflection also ties in with what Wolfram Peiser (2009) expressed regarding the question of what ideas about media effects are held by communication scholars themselves. Reflecting on these implicit assumptions at the theoretical level for media systems research would be an important contribution, especially in the sense of international comparative media systems research that goes beyond Western countries. If one applies the normative criteria of the Western public sphere to non-Western and non-democratic states, one will always find a deficit in public communication. If one wants to examine public negotiation processes, which may well include political negotiation—also in less-free media environments—and analyze the relevance of media (structures), then a different heuristic concept must be used as a basis, one that enables a search not for deficits but for realization options of political communication.

Finally, the results discussed could also be considered on a meta-level, with an interesting task for scientific research. If we assume, based on the findings presented here, that media system structures matter, at least to some extent, for media effects and, at the same time, assume based on Wolfram Peiser's remarks (2009) on "general ideas about media effects" that the perspective taken when researching media effects also depends on the individual media socialization of the researcher, we can ask what the socialization of communication scientists into a certain media system means for the research of media effects.

Altogether, the review of the literature shows that the media system context and, thus, comparative media system research can provide important contributions to explaining communication at the individual level.

References

Aalberg, T., Blekesaune, A., & Elvestad, E. (2013). Media choice and informed democracy: Toward increasing news consumption gaps in Europe? *International Journal of Press/Politics, 18*(3), 281-303. https://doi.org/10.1177/1940161213485990

Aalberg, T., Papathanassopoulos, S., Soroka, S., Curran, J., Hayashi, K., Iyengar, S., Jones, P. K., Mazzoleni, G., Rojas, H., Rowe, D., & Tiffen, R. (2013). International TV news, foreign interest and public knowledge. *Journalism Studies, 14*(3), 387-406. https://doi.org/10.1080/1461670X.2013.765636

Aalberg, T., van Aelst, P., & Curran, J. (2010). Media Systems and the political information environment: A cross-national comparison. *The International Journal of Press/Politics, 15*(3), 255-271. https://doi.org/10.1177/1940161210367422

Althaus, S. L., Cizmar, A. M. & Gimpel, J. G. (2009). Media supply, audience demand, and the geography of news consumption in the United States. *Political Communication, 26*(3), 249-277, https://doi.org/10.1080/10584600903053361

Ball-Rokeach, S. J., & DeFleur, M. L. (1976). A dependency model of mass-media effects. *Communication Research, 3*(1), 3–21. https://doi.org/10.1177/009365027600300101

Barnidge, M., Huber, B., de Zúñiga, H. G., & Liu, J. H. (2018). Social media as a sphere for "risky" political expression: A twenty-country multilevel comparative analysis. *The International Journal of Press/Politics, 23*(2), 161–182. https://doi.org/10.1177/1940161218773838

Bene, M. (2020). Does context matter? A cross- country investigation of the effects of the media context on external and internal political efficacy. *International Journal of Comparative Sociology*, *61*(4), 264-286. https://doi.org/10.1177/0020715 220930065

Benson, R. (2010). What makes for a critical press? A case study of French and U.S. immigration news coverage. *The International Journal of Press/Politics*, *15*(1), 3-24.

Blumler J., & Gurevitch, M. (1995). *The crisis of public communication*. Routledge.

Boomgarden, H. G. & Song, H. (2019). Media use and its effects in a cross-national perspective. *Kölner Zeitschrift für Soziologie und Sozialpsychologie*, *71*(1), 545-571. https://doi.org/10.1007/s11577-019-00596-9

Brosius, H. B., & Haas, A. (2009). Auf dem Weg zur Normalwissenschaft. *Publizistik*, *54*(2), 168-190.

Brüggemann, M., Engesser, S., Büchel, F., Humprecht, E., & Castro, L. (2014). Hallin and Mancini revisited: Four empirical types of western media systems. *Journal of Communication*, *64*(6), 1037-1065. https://doi.org/10.1111/jcom.12127

Castro-Herrero, L., Nir, L., & Skovsgaard, M. (2018). Bridging gaps in cross-cutting media exposure: The role of public service broadcasting. *Political Communication*, *35*(4), 542–565. https://doi.org/10.1080/10584609.2018.1476424

Castro, L., & Nir, L. (2020). Political power sharing and crosscutting media exposure: How institutional features affect exposure to different views. *International Journal of Communication*, *14*, 2707-2727.

Chadwick, A. (2013). *The hybrid media system: Politics and power*. Oxford Studies in Digital Politics.

Curran, J., Coen, S., Soroka, S., Aalberg, T., Hayashi, K., Hichy, Z., Iyengar, S., Jones, P., Mazzoleni, G., Papathanassopoulos, S., Rhee, J. W., Rojas, H., Rowe, D., & Tiffen, R. (2014). Reconsidering 'virtuous circle' and 'media malaise' theories of the media: An 11-nation study. *Journalism*, *15*(7), 815–833. https://doi.org/10. 1177/1464884913520198

Curran, J., Iyengar, S., Lund, A. B., & Salovaara-Moring, I. (2009). Media system, public knowledge and democracy: A comparative study. *European Journal of Communication*, *24* (1), 5-26.

De Albuquerque, A. (2018). *Political Parallelism*. Oxford Research Encyclopedias. https://doi.org/10.1093/acrefore/9780190228613.013.860

Dimitrova, D. V., Shehata, A., Strömbäck, J., & Nord, L. W. (2014). The effects of digital media on political knowledge and participation in election campaigns: Evidence from panel data. *Communication Research*, *41*(1), 95–118. https://doi.or g/10.1177/0093650211426004

Elenbaas, M., de Vreese, C., Schuck, A., & Boomgaarden, H. (2014). Reconciling passive and motivated learning: The saturation-conditional impact of media coverage and motivation on political information. *Communication Research*, *41*(4), 481–504. https://doi.org/10.1177/0093650212467032

Elvestad, E., & Blekesaune, A. (2008). Newspaper readers in Europe: A multilevel study of individual and national differences. *European Journal of Communication*, *23*(4), 425-447. https://doi.org/10.1177/0267323108096993

Engels, T. C. E., Ossenblok, T. L. B. & Spruyt, E. H. J. (2012). Changing publication patterns in the social sciences and humanities, 2000–2009. (2012). *Scientometrics, 93*(2), 373–390. https://doi.org/10.1007/s11192-012-0680-2

Esser, F. (2013). The emerging paradigm of comparative communication inquiry: Advancing cross- national research in times of globalization. *International Journal of Communication*, 7, 113-128. https://doi.org/10.5167/uzh-91247

Esser, F. (2019). Advances in comparative political communication research through contextualization and cumulation of evidence. *Political Communication*, *36*(4), 680-686, https://doi.org/10.1080/10584609.2019.1670904

Esser, F., & Pfetsch, B. (2020). Political Communication. In D. Caramani (Ed.), *Comparative Politics* (5th ed., pp. 336-358). Oxford University Press. Note: the preprint version has been quoted.

Esser, F., de Vreese, C. H., Strömbäck, J., van Aelst, P., Aalberg, T., Stanyer, J., Lengauer, G., Berganza, R., Legnante, G., Papathanassopoulos, S., Salgado, S., Sheafer, T., & Reinemann, C. (2012). Political information opportunities in Europe: A longitudinal and comparative study of thirteen television systems. *The International Journal of Press/Politics*, *17*(3), 247–274. https://doi.org/10.1177/1940161212442956

Esser, F., & Hanitzsch, T. (2012). On the why and how of comparative inquiry in communication studies. In F. Esser, & T. Hanitzsch (Eds.). *The handbook of comparative communication research* (pp. 3-22). Routledge.

Fletcher, R., & Nielsen, R. K. (2017). Are news audiences increasingly fragmented? A cross-national comparative analysis of cross-platform news audience fragmentation and duplication. *Journal of Communication*, *67*(4), 476-498. https://doi.org/10.1111/jcom.12315

Fraile, M., & Iyengar, S. (2014). Not all news sources are equally informative: A cross-national analysis of political knowledge in Europe. *The International Journal of Press/Politics*, *19*(3), 275–294. https://doi.org/10.1177/1940161214528993

Fraile, M. (2013). Do information rich contexts reduce knowledge inequalities? The contextual determinants of political knowledge in Europe. *Acta Politica, 48*(2), 119–43. https://doi.org/10.1057/ap.2012.34

Goldman, S. K., & Mutz, D. C. (2011). The friendly media phenomenon: A cross-national analysis of cross-cutting exposure. *Political Communication*, *28*(1), 42-66. https://doi.org/10.1080/10584609.2010.544280

Groshek, J. (2009). The democratic effects of the internet, 1994-2003: A cross-national inquiry of 152 countries. *International Communication Gazette*, *71*(3), 115-136. https://doi.org/10.1177/1748048508100909

Groshek, J. (2010). A time-series, multinational analysis of democratic forecasts and internet diffusion. *International Journal of Communication*, 4, 142-174.

Groshek, J. (2011). Media, instability, and democracy: Examining the granger-causal relationships of 122 countries from 1946 to 2003. *Journal of Communication*, *61*(6), 1161-1182. https://doi.org/10.1111/j.1460-2466.2011.01594.x

Does the Media System Explain Individual Media Use and Media Effects?

Hallin, D. C. (2016). Typology of media systems. Oxford Research Encyclopedia of Politics. Last update 2021. E-pub retrieved from DOI https://doi.org/10.1093/acr efore/9780190228637.013.205 (last retrieval June 21, 2022).

Hallin, D. C., & Mancini, P. (2004). *Comparing media systems. Three models of media and politics.* Cambridge University Press.

Hallin, D. C., & Mancini, P. (2017). Ten years after comparing media systems: What have we learned? *Political Communication, 34*(2), 155-171.

Hanusch, F., & Vos, T. P. (2020). Charting the development of a field: A systematic review of comparative studies of journalism. *International Communication Gazette, 82*(4), 319–341. https://doi.org/10.1177/1748048518822606

Hölig, S., Hasebrink, U., & Behre, J. (2021). Keeping on top of the world: Online news usage in China, the United States and five European countries. *New Media & Society, 23*(7), 1798-1823. https://doi.org/10.1177/14614448211015982

Humprecht, E., Castro Herrero, L., Blassnig, S., Brüggemann, M., & Engesser, S. (2022). Media systems in the digital age: An empirical comparison of 30 countries. *Journal of Communication, 72*(2), 145–164. https://doi.org/10.1093/joc/jqab054

Humprecht, E., Esser, F., van Aelst, P., Staender, A., & Morosoli, S. (2021). The sharing of disinformation in cross-national comparison: Analyzing patterns of resilience. *Information, Communication & Society,* 1-21. https://doi.org/10.1080/13 69118X.2021.2006744

Humprecht, E., Herrero, L.C., Blassnig, S., Brüggemann, M., & Engesser, S. (2022). Media systems in the digital age: An empirical comparison of 30 Countries. *Journal of Communication, 72*(2), 145–164, https://doi.org/10.1093/joc/jqab054

Iyengar, S., Curran, J., Lun, A. B., Salovaara-Moring, I., Hahn, K. S., & Coen, S. (2010). Cross-national versus individual-level differences in political information: A media systems perspective. *Journal of Elections, Public Opinion and Parties, 20*(3), 291–309.

Kalogeropoulos, A. (2018). Online news video consumption: A comparison of six countries. *Digital Journalism, 6*(5), 651-665. https://doi.org/10.1080/21670811.201 7.1320197

Kalogeropoulos, A., Negredo, S., Picone, I., & Nielsen, R. K. (2017). Who shares and comments on news? A cross-national comparative analysis of online and social media participation. *Social Media + Society, 3*(4). https://doi.org/10.1177/20 56305117735754

Lelkes, Y. (2016). Winners, losers, and the press: The relationship between political parallelism and the legitimacy gap. *Political Communication, 33*(4), 523-543. https://doi.org/10.1080/10584609.2015.1117031

Livingstone, S. (2012). Challenges to comparative research in a globalizing media landscape. In F. Esser & T. Hanitzsch (Eds.), *Handbook of comparative communication research* (pp. 415-429). Routledge.

Loveless, M. (2015). Contextualizing media behavior: Media environments and individuals' media use in the European Union. *Central European Journal of Communication, 8*(14), 112–131.

Macháčková, H., & Tkaczyk, M. (2020). The effect of media and political beliefs and attitudes on trust in political institutions. A multilevel analysis on data from 21 European countries. *Communication Today, 11*(2), 64-83.

Matthes, J., Knoll, J., Valenzuela, S., Hopmann, D. N., & Von Sikorski, C. (2019). A meta-analysis of the effects of cross-cutting exposure on political participation. *Political Communication, 36*(4), 523-542. https://doi.org/10.1080/10584609.2019.1619638

Meilán, X., & Wu, H. D. (2017). Factoring media use into media system theory—An examination of 14 European nations (2002–2010). *International Communication Gazette, 79*(5), 533-551. https://doi.org/10.1177/1748048516688132

Mosca, L., & Quaranta, M. (2016). News diets, social media use and non-institutional participation in three communication ecologies: Comparing Germany, Italy and the UK. *Information, Communication & Society, 19*(3), 325-345. https://doi.org/10.1080/1369118X.2015.1105276

Nielsen, R. K., & Schrøder, K. C. (2014). The relative importance of social media for accessing, finding, and engaging with news. *Digital Journalism, 2*(4), 472-489. https://doi.org/10.1080/21670811.2013.872420

Nir, L. (2012). Public space: How shared news landscapes close gaps in political engagement. *Journal of Broadcasting & Electronic Media, 56*(4), 578-596, https://doi.org/10.1080/08838151.2012.732145

Nisbet, E.C., Stoycheff, E., & Pearce, K. E. (2012). Internet use and democratic demands: A multinational, multilevel model of internet use and citizen attitudes about democracy. *Journal of Communication, 62*(2), 249–265. https://doi.org/10.1111/j.1460-2466.2012.01627.x

Papathanassopoulos, S., Coen, S., Curran, J., Aalberg, T., Rowe, D., Jones, P., Rojas, H., & Tiffen, R. (2013). Online threat, but television is still dominant: A comparative study of 11 nations' news consumption. *Journalism Practice, 7*(6), 690–704. https://doi.org/10.1080/17512786.2012.761324

Park, C. S., & Gil de Zúñiga, H. (2021). Learning about politics from mass media and social media: Moderating roles of press freedom and public service broadcasting in 11 Countries. *International Journal of Public Opinion Research, 33*(2), 315-335. https://doi.org/10.1093/ijpor/edaa021

Peiser, W. (2009). Allgemeine Vorstellungen über Medienwirkungen. In C. Holtz-Bacha, G. Reus, L. B. Becker (Eds.), *Wissenschaft mit Wirkung* (pp.143-159). VS Verlag für Sozialwissenschaften. https://doi.org/10.1007/978-3-531-91756-6_11

Perusko, Z., Vozab, D., & Čuvalo, A. (2015). Digital mediascapes, institutional frameworks, and audience practices across Europe. *International Journal of Communication, 9*, 342-364.

Prior, M. (2007). *Post-broadcast democracy: How media choice increases inequality in political involvement and polarizes elections.* Cambridge University Press.

Rodríguez-Virgili, J., Sierra, A., & Serrano-Puche, J. (2022). Motivations from news exposure in different media systems. A comparative study of Germany, Spain and the United Kingdom. *Communication Today, 13*(1), 59-72.

Schoonvelde, M. (2014). Media freedom and the institutional underpinnings of political knowledge. *Political Science Research & Methods*, 2(2), 163–178. https://doi.org/10.1017/psrm.2014.13

Shehata, A. (2010). Pathways to politics: How media system characteristics can influence socioeconomic gaps in political participation. *The International Journal of Press/Politics*, 15(3), 295-318. https://doi.org/10.1177/1940161209360930

Shehata, A., & Strömbäck, J. (2011). A matter of context: A comparative study of media environments and news consumption gaps in Europe. *Political Communication*, 28(1), 110–134. https://doi.org/10.1080/10584609.2010.543006

Siebert, F., Peterson T.B., & Schramm W. (1956). Four theories of the press: The authoritarian, libertarian, social responsibility, and soviet communist concepts of what the press should be and do. University of Illinois press.

Sparks, C. (2018). Changing concepts for a changing world. *Journal of Communication*, 68(2), 390-398. https://doi.org/10.1093/joc/jqx026

Steppat, D., Herrero, L. C., & Esser, F. (2022). Selective exposure in different political information environments – How media fragmentation and polarization shape congruent news use. *European Journal of Communication*, 37(1), 82–102. https://doi.org/10.1177/02673231211012141

Stier, S., Kirkizh, N., Froio, C., & Schroeder, R. (2020). Populist attitudes and selective exposure to online news: A cross-country analysis combining web tracking and surveys. *The International Journal of Press/Politics*, 25(3), 426-446. https://doi.org/10.1177/1940161220907018

Tsfati, Y., & Ariely, G. (2014). Individual and contextual correlates of trust in media across 44 countries. *Communication Research*, 41(6), 760–782. https://doi.org/10.1177/0093650213485972

Van Aelst, P., Strömbäck, J., Aalberg, T., Esser, F., de Vreese, C., Matthes, J., Hopmann, D., Salgado, S., Hubé, N., Stępińska, A., Papathanassopoulos, S., Berganza, R., Legnante, G., Reinemann, C., Sheafer, T. & Stanyer, J. (2017). Political communication in a high-choice media environment: A challenge for democracy? *Annals of the International Communication Association*, 41(1), 3-27, https://doi.org/10.1080/23808985.2017.1288551

Van Kempen, H. (2007). Media-party parallelism and its effects: A cross-national comparative study. *Political Communication*, 24(3), 303-320. https://doi.org/10.1080/10584600701471674

Wallner, C. (2016). Theorien und Methoden in der komparativen Mediensystemforschung: Forschungsstand und Herausforderungen. In B. M. von Rimscha, S. Studer, M. Puppis (Eds.), *Methodische Zugänge zur Erforschung von Medienstrukturen, Medienorganisationen und Medienstrategien* (pp. 17-33). Nomos.

Weaver, D. & Wilhoit, G. C. (1988). A profile of JMC educators. Traits, attitudes and values. *Journalism & Mass Communication Educator*, 43(2), 4-41.

Cornelia Wallner

Cornelia Wallner *(Dr. phil., University of Vienna) is Post-Doc and Habilitandin at the Department of Media and Communication, Ludwig-Maximilians-Universität, Germany. Her research is focused on the comparative analysis of media systems, media policy and the public sphere, as well as on media dynamics and social change. Wolfram Peiser was member of her habilitation mentorate in Munich. Cornelia worked as a Post-Doc with his chair from 2010 to 2021.*

Do People Really Not Agree on What Can be Said?
Individual Differences in the Perception of Microaggressive, Derogatory and Hate Speech Against Women

Carsten Reinemann & Anna-Luisa Sacher

Abstract

In recent years, Western democracies have seen an increase in controversies about what can be said publicly. These controversies often lead to more general discussions about freedom of speech, "political correctness," "cancel culture," or the consequences of hateful and discriminatory speech spread on the Internet. However, till date, not much is known about the fundamental question of whether citizens perceive potentially harmful statements in similar ways and what might explain their varying perceptions. Against this backdrop, the current study investigates how microaggressive, derogatory, and hate speech against women are perceived depending on sociodemographics, experiences of discrimination, political attitudes, and trust in media. We develop a set of hypotheses and test these based on a standardized survey with a quota sample resembling the German population between 18 and 65 (N = 943). The survey included a split-ballot in which half of the respondents were asked to judge whether they regarded eight statements directed at women as acceptable and hurtful. The findings showed a great deal of consensus in the perception of those statements. While gender does not prove to be a key factor for explaining individual differences, age, experiences of discrimination, and media trust turn out to be significant predictors.

How free should speech be? How should free speech be? With these questions, Timothy Garton Ash (2016) outlines the tension between freedom of speech and discourse culture, which has become an issue of public debate in Western democracies in recent years. In the context of discussions about "political correctness" and "cancel culture," discriminatory and non-discriminatory speech, or the increase of hate speech on the Internet (e.g., Reimer, 2019), we have seen heated and controversial debates about whether certain statements fall within the space of what can be said and what is socially or legally acceptable. However, the kind of statements being discussed, what exactly is criticized, and the standards used to judge varies throughout and is by no means completely obvious in every case: sometimes, it may be a matter of legal categories, i.e., the question of whether a statement constitutes a justiciable insult, incitement of the people, or even approval of a war of aggression; other discussions revolve around whether statements are discriminatory, misogynistic, anti-Semitic, Islamophobic, or disparaging in some other way; it may be a matter of whether statements represent disinformation or "fake news"; or the questions are discussed of whether statements should be disseminated (unchallenged) in the media or whether controversial content or accounts should be deleted from social networks.

On a more abstract level, these kinds of debates often turn into more general discussions about whether freedom of expression is increasingly in danger or whether, on the contrary, freedom of speech tends to be abused to a more frequent extent, especially in the online environment. From a jurisprudential perspective, these discussions are often referred to as the "democratic dilemma," which describes the tension between freedom of expression and freedom from discrimination and is considered one of the greatest challenges for modern democracy (e.g., Marker, 2013; Struth, 2019).

At any rate, the German population currently seems rather skeptical about the state of freedom of speech in their country: According to a survey conducted by the Allensbach Institute for Public Opinion Research in 2021, the number of citizens who believe that it is better to be cautious when voicing political opinions in Germany has reached an all-time high with 45% of the population agreeing (Petersen, 2021). Although research is only starting to examine the reasons for these perceptions, the results seem to indicate that, first, almost half of the citizens have experienced or at least heard of instances in which voicing certain political opinions had negative consequences. Second, these findings might also indicate an insecurity or lack of consensus about what can be said freely and the kind of statements that might trigger a backlash of critical remarks, counter-speech, or even hate—justifiably or not. However, this does not seem to be the case for all kinds of statements. Recent findings show that while the evaluation of some statements that have been the subject of public debate diverges significantly among the population, there is quite a large consensus on others (Petersen, 2021). Thus, it seems that perceptions vary based on the statement.

Such differences can not only be seen in the general population but also in the judiciary, where they are even more consequential because they

Do People Really Not Agree on What Can be Said?

result in divergent legal assessments of potentially justiciable statements by different judicial bodies. Prominent examples in Germany include differing verdicts on insulting statements against well-known German politicians (e.g., Berlin District Court, 2020; Hong, 2020) and diverging evaluations of political campaign posters of a right-wing extremist party (e.g., Kister, 2021). However, while these examples show the complexity of the topic even in court, the discussions about the judgement of statements usually begin well before a possible legal dispute and often do not occupy the courts. In most cases, the question is not whether statements violate legal norms but whether they violate social norms by, for example, making discriminatory claims. Therefore, given recent heated debates, it is important to investigate where the boundaries lie between the "sayable" and "unspeakable" for citizens, how much of a consensus there is about these classifications, and what individual-level factors might explain differing assessments of statements. The answers to these questions are addressed in the present article.

Moreover, the issues we investigate here are socially relevant, especially because the lack of a minimum consensus on the social acceptability of speech can be seen as a danger to social integration (e.g., Quiring et al., 2020). If one segment of society is under the constant impression that its freedom of speech is restricted while another feels that it is constantly belittled or insulted, then feelings of deprivation and social distrust, affective polarization, or even social intergroup conflicts are potential consequences.

In this study, we start with two assumptions. First, we assume that the perception of what can be considered a socially acceptable statement varies between individuals (e.g., Mummendey et al., 2009) and that individual predispositions play a central role in explaining those differences (e.g., Valkenburg & Peter, 2013). For example, in the context of motivated reasoning, numerous studies on information processing show that attitudes, identities, and values have a considerable influence on how information is perceived and interpreted (e.g., Kahan, 2013; Taber & Lodge, 2006). Further, findings from research into polarization suggest that statements about a certain group are perceived differently by group members and non-members and that outgroup derogation can increase attitude polarization (Wojcieszak et al., 2021).

Second, we assume that individual differences are not the same across statements. As shown in previous research, there are statements, terms, and expressions that are likely to be either rejected or accepted relatively uniformly, while there probably is less consensus in terms of others (Petersen, 2021). This could apply, for example, to more subtle forms of discrimination, which have also been discussed for some time as "microaggressions" (e.g., Lilienfeld 2017; Sue, 2010; Torino et al., 2018). Dissent over the evaluation of such statements could indicate that these evaluations are changing because, for example, social power relations are shifting. Furthermore, it could also be due to interest groups (from less powerful or marginalized groups) articulating and problematizing their critical views on statements and forms of speech that were previously considered "unproblematic" by a majority or the actors dominating public discourse. It is these kinds of developments that point to the necessity for democratic societies to find a minimal common ground at least about what can be regarded as discriminatory speech in order to strengthen respectful and inclusive public discourse.

Against this background, we want to explore the actual degree of social consensus in the assessment of potentially controversial and harmful statements and what individual characteristics might help explain possible individual-level differences. To this end, we conducted a quantitative survey, in which we presented respondents with a set of statements and asked whether they considered these statements as acceptable or unacceptable and as hurtful or not. Given that gender plays a central role in victimization through hate speech and in the debates about non-discriminatory speech, we decided to use statements about women as examples, among which there were those that could be regarded as discriminatory, hateful, and therefore (potentially) harmful.

Freedom of Speech and (Potentially) Harmful Speech

One of the starting points for this paper is the idea that public controversies about the social acceptability of certain statements might be a reason for the widespread impression that freedom of speech is increasingly restricted. This does not mean, of course, that a pluralistic democratic society should aim for a situation in which no such controversies exist. This is neither desirable nor realistic. Some scholars also argue that perceptions of "taboos" and perceived social restrictions to speech are entirely normal and even necessary because even a free and democratic society has to rely upon at least some consensus on speech norms (e.g., Quiring et al., 2020). Nevertheless, we argue that it is important to understand how and why citizens differ in their perceptions of speech norms, as these might turn into more fundamental doubts about the ability to voice one's opinions and maybe even about the functioning of democracy per se. At the same time, if freedom of speech is indeed restricted by state authorities, Internet companies, or a toxic culture of hateful discourse, this might also pose a threat to democracy (e.g., Quiring et al., 2020).

Although not much research has been published on this issue, referring to the case of Germany, public interest in perceptions of freedom of speech and of specific statements has been on the rise in recent years. In fact, public debate about "political correctness" and "cancel culture" in the country has also been driven by polls published by the Institut für Demoskopie at Allensbach (IfD). Although the institute has long been interested in "taboo issues", "political correctness," what is "sayable," as well as related subjects for decades—in the footsteps of its founder Elisabeth Noelle-Neumann—public interest has been especially intense since seemingly alarming results were published in 2019 and again in 2021 (Köcher, 2019; Petersen, 2021). For example, the most recent study found that just as many people felt that one should "rather be careful" in expressing political opinions (44%) as those that held the view that one can "express one's opinion freely" (45%) (Petersen, 2021, p. 22).

Besides data for general perceptions of freedom of speech in Germany, the IfD has also been exploring contested and sensitive issues (Noelle-Neumann, 1996; Petersen, 2013; Köcher, 2019). Results show that topics such as "foreigners," "asylum seekers" and "refugees," "Muslims/Islam," "Judaism/Israel," or Germany's National Socialist past are among the issues that have been perceived as sensitive for decades (Köcher, 2019, p. 15). In addition, the IfD has been asking respondents for their perceptions of more concrete political statements (e.g., "Refugees are criminal"), examples of non-discriminatory speech that were sometimes labelled as being a part of a trend toward "political correctness" (e.g., Köcher, 2019, pp. 15–17; Petersen, 2021), and statements that could be viewed as "especially sensitive." Respondents were asked, for example, to decide whether such statements should be forbidden or whether they could get into hot water for the same (e.g., Petersen, 2013). However, although these data are interesting, the published findings are confined to descriptive aggregate-level analysis for the most part. Nevertheless, more in-depth systematic analyses of the reasons for these perceptions are missing. This includes the characteristics of the statements and issues that should be judged or the individual-level characteristics of citizens that drive these perceptions. So, the questions of who perceives certain potentially controversial statements in a particular way and why this is the case have remained largely unanswered.

Till date, the only German study to date that has provided a more in-depth analysis of the aforementioned kind is a recent investigation into perceived "speech bans" (Quiring et al., 2020). Taking four contested issues as examples, they investigated whether restrictions on free speech were perceived in relation to them, how this perception was connected to personal opinions on those issues, and who was most likely to perceive speech restrictions on those issues (Quiring et al., 2020, p. 61). In line with assumptions derived from Noelle-Neumann's work, they found that restrictions on freedom are more likely to be perceived in terms of morally loaded issues and those on which the public opinion is split (in this case, religion, migration, and criminality). In addition, they found the dissonance between an individual's opinion and that of the (perceived) majority makes the perception of restrictions more likely (Quiring et al., 2020, pp. 67–68). Furthermore, women and respondents who are less satisfied with democracy, have a lack of trust in traditional media, and are less socially integrated tended to perceive more restrictions on speech about these contested issues.

While Quiring et al. (2020) investigated the perceptions of speech bans for specific political issues, we set a slightly different focus here by investigating the perception of everyday utterances that people might encounter more generally among personal contacts, on social media, and in online comments sections. In addition, we do not ask about "speech bans" but whether people perceive certain statements as acceptable and potentially hurtful. This might change the perspective of respondents to a certain degree by putting a greater focus on those who may be negatively affected by a speech act and by not implying that there may be actors, institutions, or powers that would be able to "order" a speech ban. However, the fundamental question remains the same: Is there consensus or disagreement in the perception of statements and what drives potential differences?

Freedom of Speech in the Context of Misogynistic Statements

While free speech is discussed in relation to various topics, we examine the issue using the example of misogynistic speech. This topic was chosen for two reasons. The first is because of the continued relevance of the research topic: despite increasing awareness of gender equality, the sexist treatment of women in the form of stereotypically derogatory expectations and expressions is still present as shown by recent studies (e.g., Lui & Quezada, 2019; Foster, 2009). In the context of microaggressions, Sue (2010) even referred to gender as probably the most restrictive force in everyday life (p. 160ff). In addition, women run a higher risk of being victims of online hate speech (e.g., Chen et al., 2020).

The second reason is that it has been shown that there might be a gender difference in the perception of freedom of speech. A study at

American universities, for example, asked students about their assessment of the relevance of an unrestricted right to freedom of speech. When seeing gender as a binary concept, the results showed apparent differences between men and women. Nearly 60% of women thought an inclusive, open society was more important than freedom of speech as compared to only 28% of men (Knight Foundation, 2019, p. 6). Nearly half of female students also said Americans need to be more careful in their own choice of words, while only 26% of men agreed. In contrast, 74% of men were of the opposite opinion, saying people too often overreact to statements (p. 8f). In addition, 53% of women thought that hate speech should not be protected by the First Amendment, while 74% of men disagreed (p. 10). Even though these findings are restricted to the American context, gender may also impact the aforementioned perceptions in other countries such as Germany.

Types of (Potentially) Harmful Speech

Before investigating individual characteristics that may lead to different perceptions of controversial, (potentially) harmful statements, it is crucial to first define the characteristics of these statements. Previous research usually did not distinguish between different types of speech (e.g., Petersen, 2021; Wegner et al., 2020) or only focused on the perception of one specific type of discriminatory language, such as hate speech or microaggressive speech (e.g., Sue, 2010), without connecting it to the larger picture of freedom of speech. Even if the discussions surrounding certain controversial statements do not exclusively revolve around the juxtaposition of freedom of expression and freedom from discrimination, the discourse can mostly be traced to the controversy between these two fundamental freedoms (e.g., Struth, 2019). In order to get closer to understanding the perception of this conflict in the general population, in this study, we try to distinguish different degrees of discriminatory statements against women based on their extremity and the blatancy of the insult they represent. In doing so, we refer to the definition of discrimination by Dovidio et al. (2010), who defined it as behavior that "creates, maintains, or reinforces advantage for some groups and their members over other groups and their members" (p. 10).

One type of potentially discriminatory language that has been increasingly discussed in recent years, especially in the context of political correctness, is that of *microaggressions*. It refers to an implicit and subtle devaluation of discriminated social groups that can be verbally or behaviorally elicited (Sue et al., 2007). The concept of microaggressions describes insults that are less obviously recognizable as disparagement than other forms of discrimination. However, at the same time, they are in no way considered to be less derogatorily motivated (Lilienfeld, 2017, p. 139). With this type of potentially harmful language in particular, subjectivity plays a significant role. In order to label microaggressions as such, the individual assessment of the person affected is required: "First, the person must determine whether a microaggression has occurred" (Sue et al., 2007, p. 279). Moreover, the affected person does not necessarily have to assume that the communicator intended to offend. Instead, the pejorative may have also been uttered unconsciously (Sue et al., 2007, p. 278). This highlights that microaggressions, in particular, are in the eye of the beholder according to current research, and it depends on the individual whether a statement can be considered problematic at all. This means that not even all members of the respective social group may perceive microaggressive speech as discriminatory or hurtful (e.g., Sue, 2010; Lilienfeld, 2017)

In contrast to subtle microaggressive speech, is blatant discrimination in the form of hate speech. It can be understood as speech "that involves the advocacy of hatred and discrimination against groups on basis of their race, colour, ethnicity, religious beliefs, sexual orientation, or other status" (Boyle, 2001, p. 489). In the present research context, the victims of sexist hate comments are women. Moreover, the difference between hate and microaggressive speech becomes clear in terms of the perceived communicator's intentionality. Here, the intention to offend others is not questioned by the person affected by the hate speech (Marker, 2013), especially since the explicit use of offensive language also shapes it. In terms of perception, studies have found that hate speech is recognized as such by the majority of people and that it is perceived as disturbing, although this also depends on various subjective factors such as gender (e.g., Costello et al., 2019).

As microaggressive and hate speech represent extreme points of (potentially) hurtful speech in terms of the blatancy of discrimination, we will also include an intermediate type of speech in the present study. This will help us examine grey areas within the spectrum of speech as well. We will call this form of discriminatory, that are potentially harmful and controversial statements, "derogatory speech." It describes a more overt expression of discrimination than microaggressive speech and differs from hate speech in so far as the choice of words is less offensive and violent.

Thus, in the following, we distinguish three types of speech: microaggressive, derogatory and hate speech. With regard to the perception of this spectrum, research has so far been devoted, for example, to the psychological consequences after reception (for example, mental illnesses as a result of hate messages; for e.g., Leets, 2002). Moreover, comparing the different forms, some literature suggests that these psychological consequences are even worse for more subtle statements, such as verbal microaggressions (e.g., Williams & Mohammed, 2013; Sue, 2010). However, we know relatively little about a concrete comparison of perceptions of different forms of discriminatory speech (Lui & Quezada, 2019), especially in the context of freedom of speech debates. This research gap will therefore be addressed in the present study.

Predictors of the Perception of (Potentially) Harmful Speech

As argued above, we assume that individual characteristics impact the way potentially controversial, microaggressive, derogatory, or hateful speech against women is perceived. In this analysis, we will test four sets of potential predictors.

The first set of predictors are sociodemographic factors that can also be regarded as being indicative of different social identities. This is, of course, especially true for gender. It almost seems self-evident to assume that women will perceive derogatory and other problematic or controversial statements about women as less acceptable than men. In fact, research shows that gender does affect perceptions and attitudes on a gender-related issue like gender-neutral speech or gendered job announcements (e.g., Budziszewska et al., 2014; Gustafsson Sendén et al., 2015). Moreover, as noted earlier, it was found that women more often prioritize inclusive, cautious language over free speech (Knight Foundation, 2019) and more frequently perceive hateful language as disturbing than men (e.g., Costello et al., 2019). We, therefore, put forward our first hypothesis below.

H1: Women will perceive microaggressive, derogatory, and hateful statements against women as less acceptable than men.

In addition, it can be assumed that the way women are addressed and talked about has been the subject of social change over the last decades that have seen processes of emancipation and growing societal awareness of questions of gender equality (e.g., Inglehart & Norris, 2003; Scarborough et al., 2019). Consequently, we can assume that younger generations have grown up and socialized in an environment that has become much more positive with respect to gender equality. Therefore, we assume that younger people should also be more critical of discriminatory speech against women. We, therefore, put forward our second hypothesis below.

H2: Members of younger generations will perceive microaggressive, derogatory, and hateful statements against women as less acceptable than members of older generations.

The final sociodemographic factor we investigate is education. Generally, it can be shown that more educated people hold less traditional and more progressive values. Further, they have also been shown to be less sexist, although it has to be stressed that sexist attitudes are, of course, not restricted to the less formally educated (e.g., Pew Research Center, 2019). In addition, formal education has been shown to correlate with a stronger awareness and preference for gender equality (Pew Research Center, 2019). As we have not included direct measures of traditional and progressive values, sexism, and attitudes towards gender equality, we therefore view formal education as a proxy for these in the context of this study. In addition, it can also be argued that less formal education may also have a more direct effect on perceptions of speech because it may correlate with a more frequent usage of harsh language, although this is a topic of debate in linguistics (e.g., Love, 2021). We therefore assume the following.

H3: More formally educated people will perceive microaggressive, derogatory, and hateful statements against women as less acceptable than people with less formal education.

The second set of factors we consider here are experiences of discrimination based on, for example, migration background, sexual orientation, gender, etc. Discrimination, in general, may not only result in anger, anxiety, stress, or even mental health problems, but people experiencing verbal or non-verbal discrimination may also perceive future social interactions differently due to their experiences (e.g., Mummendey, 2009). One potential effect may be that people become increasingly aware of and sensitive to discrimination in general and discriminatory speech in particular and thus regard even more subtle forms of microaggressive speech as less acceptable. In contrast, extreme forms of non-verbal discrimination in particular may also raise the bar for verbal discrimination to be perceived as "real" discrimination ("I've experienced worse.") and thus lead to a de-sensitizing effect. However, as the literature mostly suggests that it is more likely that experiences of discrimination tend to raise awareness and make people more sensitive towards it, we assume the following.

H4: The more that people have experienced discrimination, the less acceptable they will find microaggressive, derogatory, and hateful statements against women.

In addition, this effect of discrimination should be especially pronounced in the case of statements against women for people who have been discriminated against based on their gender. We therefore assume:

Do People Really Not Agree on What Can be Said?

H5: The more that people have experienced discrimination based on their gender, the less acceptable they will find microaggressive, derogatory, and hateful statements against women.

The third set of factors we include are political predispositions. Generally, we can assume that politically more conservative and right-wing individuals will have more traditional values and preconceptions about gender roles and be more critical of gender equality in general and non-discriminatory speech in particular (e. g., Christley, 2021). In addition, they may be more inclined to be critical about issues around "political correctness" and what they perceive as dangers to freedom of speech, as recent research indicates (e.g., Petersen, 2021). Moreover, concerning hate speech, some studies have already shown that the perception of certain statements varies depending on how left or right people locate themselves on the political spectrum (e.g., Costello et al., 2019). This may be especially true for voters of the right-wing populist Alternative for Germany (AfD), which has—like other right-wing populist parties—positioned itself as a strong critic of progressive gender-equality policies (e.g., Abi-Hassan, 2017; Petersen, 2021). In contrast, people who are politically more progressive and those on the left of the political spectrum can be regarded as more sensitive toward gender-equality issues. We therefore assume the following.

H6: The more left-wing political attitudes people have the less they will perceive microaggressive, derogatory, and hateful statements against women as acceptable.

H7: Voters of right-wing populist AfD will perceive microaggressive, derogatory, and hateful statements against women as more acceptable than voters of other parties.

Finally, we also include trust in traditional media and trust in online user-generated content as potential drivers of differences in the perception of discriminatory speech. We opted for these indicators because trust in media can be a better predictor of certain media effects than media usage itself (e.g., Fawzi et al., 2021). This is because the processing and interpretation of information are strongly affected by the trust people have in a source and because not all people using a certain source actually regard it as trustworthy (Strömbäck et al., 2020). In addition, we argue that trust in different types of media sources may be connected to differing perceptions of controversial statements about women because it also reflects a certain degree of agreement with the basic values apparent in the content of these media. Against this backdrop, we first assume that most German traditional journalistic sources tend to position themselves against discrimination and more in favor of gender equality—although there are definitely exceptions and differences. Second, we assume that

Carsten Reinemann & Anna-Luisa Sacher

user-generated content online tends to contain more discriminatory, hateful, and misogynistic speech than the content of traditional journalistic news sources. Therefore, people trusting user-generated content might also be more likely to regard such speech as more acceptable because they are more often confronted with this kind of speech, might get used to it, and thus regard it as more appropriate ("normalization"). We, therefore, put forward our last hypothesis as follows.

H8: The higher their trust in traditional media, the less will people perceive microaggressive, derogatory, and hateful statements against women as acceptable.

H9: The higher their trust in online user comments and posts, the more will people perceive microaggressive, derogatory, and hateful statements against women as acceptable.

Methods

To test our hypotheses, we conducted a quantitative online survey. It was part of a research seminar at the Department of Media and Communication at LMU Munich. With the help of an access panel from a market researcher (*Dynata*), a quota sample was drawn within the age range of 18 to 65 years of the German voting population. Quotas were applied for gender, age brackets, and education. After intense pretesting, the survey was conducted in January 2020. Straightliners and respondents with an interview duration of less than six minutes were excluded from the sample. In addition, due to the very small group size, respondents who classified themselves as non-binary when stating their gender were excluded from the analysis (N = 2). Overall, 20% of original respondents were excluded for quality assurance purposes resulting in N = 943.

However, the questionnaire contained a split-ballot section on the perception of discriminatory statements. One half of the sample was presented with statements against people with a migration background and the other with statements against women. Since the latter constitutes the core of the present paper, the following section will assume that there were only half of the subjects. This results in a sample size of N = 447 respondents for the descriptive analyses and N = 401 for the explanatory analyses.

Dependent Variables

The core of this study is the evaluation of statements against women. To this end, the respondents were presented with a series of comments against women, which corresponded to the spectrum of forms of expression previously described: two statements each that can be assigned to the levels of microaggressive, derogatory statements, and hate speech; two neutral statements that we regarded as non-discriminatory for comparison purposes.

The conceptualization of these statements was based on previous research on discriminatory language against women (Sue, 2010). Here, such statements were defined based on their sexualization and objectification of women or viewing them as less competent and intelligent. Based on these preliminary considerations, actual comments from Internet forums were used for the operationalization and subsequently adapted to the respective levels. The statements not only differed in their extremity but also in the choice of words, which explicitly distinguishes the two levels of derogatory and hate speech.

Respondents also saw two neutrally phrased control items. This resulted in a total of eight items, which were randomized and presented to the respondents twice for evaluation. First, respondents were asked to evaluate the respective statements more rationally by asking whether they considered the items acceptable or thought they went too far. This was measured in each case on a seven-point scale (1 = "is acceptable", 7 = "goes too far"; the "don't know" option was also available). The second question was aimed at assessing the potential of the statement to elicit a negative emotional response by a potential receiver. Here, respondents were asked whether they thought that the statements could be hurtful ("Would you classify these statements as hurtful or would you say they are not hurtful?"; 1 = "not hurtful," 7 = "hurtful"; the "don't know" option was also available). Both questions were immediately asked one after the other (Table 1)[1].

---

1 The conceptualization and operationalization of the statements were undertaken by Danilo Harles, Lilli Fischer, Velina Chekelova, and Anna-Luisa Sacher.

Carsten Reinemann & Anna-Luisa Sacher

Table 1: Set of (Potentially) Harmful Statements Against Women

Perception of acceptability		Perception of potential to hurt
"Now it is about very specific statements: Imagine the following comments are made to a woman. Do you find these statements acceptable, or do you think they go too far?"		"Below, you find the comments from the previous question again. Regardless of whether you find them acceptable in principle, would you classify these statements as hurtful, or would you say they are not hurtful?"
Neutral speech	"Are you free for a short meeting tomorrow?"	
	"Have you seen, it is really nice weather today."	
Micro-aggression	"You must be on your period, right?"	
	"I think that is brave, though, that you have a career on top of having kids."	
Derogatory Speech	"Well, of course, you earn less, this should be the case for you women."	
	"You women just do not belong in the office, you should be taking care of the household."	
Hate Speech	"Stupid and ugly, it takes a woman's quota for you to get a job."	
	"If you dress like that, don't be surprised if you get raped."	

Independent Variables

Sociodemographics

Next to gender (47.5% female; 52.1% male), another sociodemographic factor of interest is age (M = 48.21, SD = 12.26), which is also measured using generations ("Baby Boomers": 1945–1964; "Generation X": 1965–1981; "Generation Y": 1982–1994; "Generation Z": 1995–2010). Since our sample is limited to the age range of 18 to 65, the generations under study are also limited to 1954 to 2001. In addition, respondents' education was obtained, and the variable was dichotomized to indicate whether they had received a high school diploma or not (1 = no diploma, 42.8%; 2 = diploma, 57.2%).

Experiences of Discrimination

Concerning previous experiences of discrimination, respondents were presented with nine items on a five-point scale to indicate how often they had already been disadvantaged or discriminated against for a variety of reasons (1 = never, 5 = very often). Potential reasons mentioned were, for example, migration background, appearance, sexual orientation, and gender. For the following analyses, this variable is relevant in two ways. First, the influence of "experiences of discrimination based on one's gender" is considered individually (M = 1.63; SD = 1.037). Second, a mean index was formed from all items (M = 1.48; SD = 0.66; α = .876) in order to make a statement about the effect of "the variety of previous experiences of discrimination." Respondents with more frequent and diverse experiences will score higher on this index.

Political Predispositions

In order to also examine the influence of political attitude on the perception of statements, two factors were considered. First, we examined "general political positioning" using an 11-point left-right scale (1 = left, 11 = right; M = 5.87, SD = 2.04). Second, we measured "party preference" using the so-called Sunday question, in which respondents indicated which party they would vote for if an election were held next Sunday (CDU/CSU: 16.1%; Green Party: 18.7%; AfD: 11.5%; SPD: 9.2%; FDP: 6.7%; The Left: 9.8%; others: 5.2%).

Media Trust

Finally, subjects' "media trust" was measured by four items in one question. Due to very high correlations between two indicators ("User generated commentary and posts online" and "Social media") and more than 200 "don't know" responses for another item ("Alternative media"), we only included two of the items in the analysis. Here, respondents were asked to rate their trust using a five-point scale (1 = no trust, 5 = very high trust) regarding traditional media (e.g., newspapers, news magazines, radio, television; M = 3.65, SD = 1.14) and posts or comments by Internet users (e.g., in forums, blogs, or comment sections; M = 2.17, SD = 1.05).

Results

Descriptive Analyses of Perceptions of (Potentially) Harmful Statements

The first result of our analysis is, rather surprisingly, that respondents perceived the statements very similarly no matter whether they were asked to evaluate their acceptability or hurtfulness. We only found a slight deviation in the perceptions of the statements. The distinction between the more rational assessment of whether the statements are acceptable and the more emotional assessment of whether they are hurtful does not seem relevant to respondents. This may be caused by the fact that the two assessment dimensions are interwoven and thus cover the same construct: if one classifies a statement as acceptable, this may also mean that one would interpret the degree of violation as low and vice versa. However, this could also be due to a response bias in the form of consistency effects since respondents were presented with the two item batteries immediately, one after the other. Thus, they possibly rated the statements consistently on the five-point scale despite different types of randomization. Since the evaluations of the more rational and emotional assessment dimensions were so similar, the results will be considered together as an index for each level in the following analyses. Reliability coefficients and index means are documented in Table 2.

Second, neutral control statements were indeed overwhelmingly perceived as acceptable and not hurtful (M = 1.88; SD = 1.26). However, it is interesting to note that the statement "Are you free for a short meeting tomorrow?" was rated as somewhat more hurtful and unacceptable (M = 2.14; SD = 1.51) than the statement about the weather (M = 1.62; SD = 1.29)—and as expected from a neutral item. Here, respondents possibly interpreted this statement in the context of the discriminatory comments as a courtship towards women and thus did not understand it as completely neutral. The difference is nevertheless small.

In terms of microaggressive speech, there was a striking difference between the two items as shown below. The statement "I think it's brave that you have a career while raising children" was rated below the midpoint of the scale for both dimensions (M = 3.34; SD = 1.95). However, respondents considered the item "You certainly have your period, don't you?" to be less acceptable, with the mean being way above the midpoint (M = 5.69; SD = 1.58). A comment regarding a woman's role image that it is courageous to be employed while raising children seems to be socially viewed as more "sayable" than a statement referring to her period, which is likely perceived as a violation of a woman's sphere of intimacy.

Concerning the results of the two extreme discriminatory levels, derogatory language and hate speech, it was found that all four statements were rated similarly. Accordingly, it did not seem to make a difference whether the statements were provided with extreme wording, as with hate speech (e.g., "Stupid and ugly … it takes a woman's quota for you to get a job"). The apparent disparagement provided a perceived boundary-crossing for all items at both levels. Overall, the theoretical differentiation proved to

Do People Really Not Agree on What Can be Said?

not be completely in line with the respondents' perception. This is especially true for the derogatory and hate speech statements, with the former being perceived as even more unacceptable than one of the statements we had classified as hate speech (Table 2).

Table 2: Perceptions of (Potentially) Hurtful Statements (M, SD, Indices)

Neutral speech	"Are you free for a short meeting tomorrow?"	M = 2.14 SD = 1.51	M = 1.88 SD = 1.26 r = .564***
	"Have you noticed the really nice weather today?"	M = 1.62 SD = 1.29	
Micro-aggression	"You must be on your period, right?"	M = 5.69 SD = 1.58	M = 4.51 SD = 1.44 r = .264***
	"I think that it is brave, though, that you have a career on top of having kids."	M = 3.34 SD = 1.95	
Derogatory speech	"Well, of course, you earn less ... this should be the case for you women."	M = 6.38 SD = 1.11	M = 6.32 SD = 1.09 r = .685***
	"You women just do not belong in the office ... you should be taking care of the household."	M = 6.26 SD = 1.22	
Hate speech	"Stupid and ugly ... it takes a woman's quota for you to get a job."	M = 6.49 SD = 1.12	M = 6.29 SD = 1.11 r = .425***
	"If you dress like that, don't be surprised if you get raped."	M = 6.09 SD = 1.43	

Note. Based on N = 401 respondents. Spearman-Brown r, *** p < .001

One of the questions we started with was whether there is a consensus about assessing potentially harmful statements about women among German citizens. Figure 1, which contains descriptive results for the acceptability assessment, suggests that this is mostly the case at least for the statements we classified as hate and derogatory speech. Moreover, only between 2% and 7% of respondents consider these statements to be more or less acceptable, which itself is rather surprising. Meanwhile, the consensus is almost as high for the statement regarding a women's period, although the share of respondents choosing the extreme point of complete acceptability is, in fact, lower. Then, the most diverse responses were regarding the statement that addresses the conflict between having kids and a career. While just more than half of the respondents find the statement rather acceptable, this is not the case for almost another 30%. Obviously, this statement could be a trigger for controversy, probably be hurtful for a least some women, or touches a hot topic that is still a social taboo (Figure 1).

Figure 1: Distribution of Answers – Perceptions of (Potentially) Harmful Statements

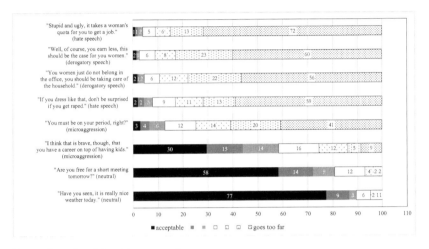

Note. Based on N = 401 respondents.

While the grouping of the statements examined was based on theoretical assumptions, the results indicate other clustering and thus the items were subsequently examined using an exploratory factor analysis (Varimax). First, the Kaiser-Meyer-Olkin criterion was fulfilled (KMO=.76), and Bartlett's test was found significant (χ^2 (28) = 1174.96, p< .001). Here, two factors can be extracted, each of which has an Eigenvalue greater than 1. They support the assumptions described above: One factor covers the neutral statements and the microaggression regarding a woman's career choice. The second factor, in contrast, includes the second microaggression regarding the female menstrual cycle, which was considered to be less acceptable, as well as the statements representing the more extreme types of speech. Accordingly, the statements we regarded as microaggressions were not perceived similarly by our respondents. While one resembles a neutral item more closely, the second was perceived almost in the same way as derogatory and hate speech. Together, the two factors can explain 60.58% of the variance.

Explanatory Analyses of Predictors of the Perceptions of (Potentially) Harmful Statements

We ran four regression models to explain individual perceptions of the different types of statements. However, the variance explained by the models was rather small and did not differ much, with a range between 10% and 13%. Of course, this is not that surprising given that the overall variance of perceptions is somewhat limited, especially in the case of neutral, derogatory, and hateful statements. In addition, the number of cases in the analysis was reduced to N = 403 due to missing values in the questions on media trust (Table 3).

The first remarkable finding is that only in one case did gender make a difference in perceptions when controlling for the other included factors. Further, only in the case of hate speech did women perceive the statements as slightly less acceptable and harmful than men. H1 is therefore rejected for most types of statements. As for age, a more consistent picture across types of statements is apparent, but it is rather surprising: most notably, members of generation X perceive all types of statements as more acceptable than the reference group of Boomers. For the neutral statements, this is also true for generation Y. In contrast, there mostly are no differences between the younger generations Y and Z and the Boomers. Therefore, H2 has to be rejected as only generation X seems perceive the statements as more acceptable. As for education, we only see a small effect in the case of the neutral statements, with higher education even contributing to a less critical view of these statements. H3 is therefore rejected. More generally, the explanatory power of sociodemographics is rather limited in our analysis, with age showing the most consistent impact.

The picture is slightly different for our indicators of experiences of discrimination that show a rather complex pattern of influences. For neutral statements, we found a significant effect of our cumulative measure of various types of discrimination with various experiences contributing to a more critical perception of the neutral statements. Meanwhile, microaggressive speech had different results. Respondents who have experienced various types of discrimination perceived these kinds of statements as "more" acceptable, whereas those who have experienced discrimination with respect to their gender regard these as "*less*" acceptable. However, this result has to be interpreted cautiously because, as we have seen, the two statements combined in the index were evaluated rather differently. For the derogatory statements, none of the indicators produced significant effects, but the cumulative indicator pointed in the same direction as that for microaggressions. Finally, the same indicator showed a significant effect on the perception of hate speech with more diverse experiences of discrimination again contributing to a less critical stance towards hate speech. Overall, these results suggest a sensitizing effect of gender-specific discrimination concerning microaggressions and a de-sensitization or habituation effect for more varied experiences of discrimination in terms of microaggressive and hate speech, with the coefficient for derogatory speech at least pointing in the same direction. Accordingly, H4 has to be completely rejected, and H5 has to be mostly rejected because it can only be confirmed for microaggressive speech.

Moreover, only a small number of significant effects can be identified concerning political attitude factors. The more conservative the respondents ranked themselves on the left-right scale, the less negative they perceived the microaggression, while there was no effect for the other types of speech. That means that we can only partially confirm H6. With regard to party preferences, we can also confirm our assumptions only partially: respondents with voting intentions for the AfD considered derogatory statements to be more acceptable. This means that we can also only partially confirm H7. Meanwhile, other effects were only found in one other case, with a preference for the FDP resulting in neutral statements being rated as less acceptable.

Finally, there were several significant effects in terms of the two trust indicators. As it turns out, neutral, microaggressive, and derogatory statements were perceived as less acceptable by respondents who tend to have a higher trust in traditional media. Therefore, this is in line with H8, which can be mostly confirmed. The picture is less clear for trust in posts and comments from Internet users. While neutral statements were regarded as less acceptable for those who have a higher trust in user posts and comments, derogatory speech was perceived as more acceptable by those with a higher trust in user posts. In addition, no effects could be found for microaggressive and hate speech. Therefore, H9 has to mostly be rejected (Table 3).

Do People Really Not Agree on What Can be Said?

Table 3: Predictors of the Perception of (Potentially) Harmful Speech

Predictors	Neutral statements Beta	Micro-aggression Beta	Derogatory Speech Beta	Hate Speech Beta
	Sociodemographics			
Gender (0 = male. 1 = female)	-,030	-,024	,067	,101[+]
Gen. Z (18-25 years)	-,064	-,056	-,020	-,016
Gen. Y (26-39 years)	-,130*	,011	,072	,008
Gen. X (40-54 years)	-,122*	-,105*	-,107[+]	-,109*
High School Diploma (0 = no. 1 = yes)	-,112*	-,004	-,081	,028
R^2	*.029*	*.022*	*.027*	*.032*
	Experiences of discrimination			
Discrimination based on gender	-,007	,235**	-,065	,035
Discrimination in general	,179*	-,177*	-,106	-,244***
R^2	*.063*	*.049*	*.065*	*.089*
	Political predispositions			
Political attitude (left-right scale)	-.006	-,156*	-.019	.006
Party preference (0 = no. 1 = yes)				
CDU/CSU	,082	,062	-,018	,006
Green party	,049	,002	-,042	,104
AfD	,036	-,012	-,150*	-,104
SPD	,049	,012	-,060	-,036
FDP	,122*	,019	-,030	-,052
The Left	,051	-,079	,043	,082
R^2	*.085*	*.087*	*.106*	*.128*
	Media trust			
Traditional media	,110*	,138*	,159**	,046
Posts/comments by Internet users	,165**	,061	-,102*	,011
R^2	*.118*	*.104*	*.135*	*.130*

Note. Table entries are beta coefficients from linear regression analyses. Based on N = 401. * $p < .05$; ** $p < .01$; *** $p < .001$

Conclusion

The starting point of this paper was the notion that it is important to understand where people draw the line between acceptable and unacceptable speech and what drives these perceptions. This is because differences in the perception of (potentially) discriminatory speech are at the heart of the frequently recurring disputes about controversial statements. Further, these controversies are important because, at least in Germany, they are potentially one factor contributing to the widespread perception that freedom of speech has become increasingly restricted. Against this background, we asked two rather basic questions: (a) whether and to what extent people differ in their perception of (potentially) harmful speech against women; and (b) which individual-level characteristics might explain such differences. The results of our analyses that are based on a survey conducted in early 2020 can be summarized as follows:

(1) Our respondents' answers did not vary much when they were asked to evaluate the acceptability and harmfulness of statements. Whether this is a methodological artefact because of consistency effects or whether this indicates that the acceptability of statements is to a large extent driven by the evaluation of their harmfulness cannot, however, be decided on the basis of our data.

(2) Most of the statements that we came up with based on real Internet comments and that we asked our respondents to evaluate were perceived rather similarly. This means that there was a large consensus about their evaluation. This is especially true for the statements against women that we had previously classified as derogatory and hate speech. Here, no more than about 10% of respondents regarded them as more or less acceptable. Our theoretical distinction between the two groups based on particularly offensive language was not supported by the results; the factor analysis subsumed them into one factor. Accordingly, our results confirm findings from previous studies that offensively discriminatory statements are also recognized as such by a majority and are thus strongly rejected (e.g., Costello et al., 2019). Although this might sound like good news, it should be noted that even a small number of people can make a difference in (online) discourses. In this context, given the extremity of the statements, there is still worry about the number of people viewing them as acceptable.

(3) The statements we had classified in advance as microaggressions were evaluated very differently. This was already evident based on the descriptive statistics but became apparent in the subsequent exploratory factor analysis, which did not support our grouping based on theoretical assumptions. Instead, two factors were distinguished that separated the two microaggressions based on the results. One statement was almost rated as unacceptable as the derogatory and hate speech statements, while the other was perceived in more diverse ways, but closer to the rating of the neutral statements. The obvious discrepancy between the a-priori classification and the respondents' perception is interesting in itself and highlights the difficulty of determining in advance how some statements may go down with an audience. In addition, the fact that there was no consensus on one of the statements reflects the more subtle and unclear nature of microaggressions that might result in controversy and misunderstanding because of entirely different perceptions and interpretations. Therefore, the central role of the subjective views on microaggression, which has been discussed in previous studies (e.g., Sue et al., 2007; Sue, 2010), is also

reflected in our results. Moreover, they also point to potential conceptual challenges with the construct of microaggression that remain to be resolved in future research (e.g., Lilienfeld, 2017).

(4) The individual characteristics we included did not explain much of the (mostly) rather small perceptual differences we encountered. This is particularly interesting in terms of the individual affectedness based on respondents' own gender being discussed. In contrast to our expectation that women's direct involvement might result in different perceptions, there were few to no differences. Thus, in terms of perceptions of discrimination against women, group membership did not play a central role in our study, so we could not replicate previous findings (e.g., Knight Foundation, 2019; Costello et al., 2019). However, this could also be due to methodological reasons, which we will discuss later. In this context, since there are certainly structural differences between discriminated groups, replications with other target groups would be of interest.

(5) Considering the other predictors analyzed, the most consistent effects across different types of statements appeared to come from age and trust in traditional media. In general, members of Generation X found the statements somewhat more acceptable than all other generations, younger and older. The reasons for this unexpected finding are unclear and will have to be identified in further analyses. The consideration that younger people have been socialized more sensitively due to increasing awareness of gender equality (e.g., Inglehart & Norris, 2003; Scarborough et al., 2019) can therefore not be confirmed on the basis of our data. In addition, people who trust traditional media more found three out of four types of statements "less" acceptable. This suggests a normative impact of traditional media on what is considered acceptable speech, which is an aspect that should also be investigated further.

(6) The results are less straightforward for experiences of discrimination and political attitudes. First, for the former, it seems that more frequent and diverse experiences instead led to a small de-sensitizing effect in terms of microaggression and hate speech. In contrast, experiences with gender-specific experiences contribute to a sensitizing effect for microaggressions. On a general level, this is consistent with previous findings that prior experiences with hurtful statements influence perceptions of future ones (e.g., Mummendey, 2019). In specific terms, however, the differentiated results also raise new questions concerning the further research that would be fruitful. Nevertheless, at this point, at least the importance of further research on microaggressions again becomes clear.

(7) Political attitudes were not as important as assumed. Two effects, however, point in the assumed direction. Political self-positioning proved

influential for microaggressions, with people on the right perceiving these statements as more acceptable, and the AfD preference has the same effect in terms of derogatory statements. These results are also consistent with previous studies on perceptions of freedom of expression (e.g., Costello et al., 2019; Petersen, 2021). However, while it has often been assumed that political factors, in particular, could be a key factor in these debates, we could not find such definite results within the framework of our method.

(8) Finally, we found surprising effects concerning the neutral control items, for which there could be methodological as well as substantial reasons: either the other overtly discriminating statements affected the evaluation of the neutral statements by producing a halo effect, or predispositions actually led to a differing assessment of even everyday statements. Further, the respective (imagined) context—i.e., the conversation partners and the situation—can also decisively influence the perception of the statements. As we cannot judge, either way, further research is needed here as well.

Although our results provide important indications of whether and how perceptions of statements vary across society, they are limited by some apparent factors. For example, the topic of statements about women is, of course, only one of many relevant to the question of social consensus. However, even within the topic itself, the number of statements examined was very limited with only two items per level. While they provided an initial basis for our exploratory approach, they did not, of course, cover the full range of discriminatory statements. Accordingly, the results cannot immediately be generalized to other topics or groups and thus require replications for other forms of discrimination and a wider range of statements. In addition, it should be mentioned that the number of respondents was relatively small due to the application of a split ballot design. Accordingly, besides the thematic limitation, the results are also limited with regard to sample size.

Overall, it can be summarized that the study provides initial insights into whether a social consensus exists in terms of which statements are currently socially accepted and which are considered unspeakable as well as what predispositions might impact these perceptions. Based on an initial exploratory framework that examined different types of discrimination, this study broadens the view from a specific phenomenon to a general perspective of freedom of expression. Accordingly, this conceptual view could also serve as a starting point for future research regarding the tension between freedom of expression and freedom from discrimination. While free speech is a fundamental basis of democracy, it can be simultaneously argued that democratic societies will do well to find common ground about what they regard as discriminatory speech in order to strengthen respectful public discourse. As far as this study is concerned, the controversial area of conflict does not seem to evolve around offensive discrimination but rather more subtle expressions. This study thus provides initial insights on the kinds of potentially controversial statements on which there is a general consensus and those that we as a society still need to discuss. Future research should follow up on these conclusions.

References

Abi-Hassan, S. (2017). Populism and gender. In C. R. Kaltwasser, P. A. Taggart, P. O. Espejo, & P. Ostiguy (Eds.), *The Oxford handbook of populism* (pp. 426–444). Oxford University Press.

Berlin District Court. (2020). *Beschluss vom 21.01.2020, 27 AR 17/19: Anspruch auf Auskunft zu einem beleidigenden Nutzer eines sozialen Netzwerks* [Decision of 21.01.2020, 27 AR 17/19: Right to disclosure of information about an offending user of a social network]. https://gesetze.berlin.de/bsbe/document/KORE534882020

Boyle, K. (2001). Hate speech— The United States versus the rest of the world? *Main Law Review*, *53*, 487–502. https://digitalcommons.mainelaw.maine.edu/mlr/vol53/iss2/7

Budziszewska, M., Hansen, K., & Bilewicz, M. (2014). Backlash over gender-fair language: The impact of feminine job titles on men's and women's perception of women *Journal of Language and Social Psychology*, *33*(6), 681–691. https://doi.org/10.1177/0261927x14544371

Chen, G. M., Pain, P., Chen, V. Y., Mekelburg, M., Springer, N., & Troger, F. (2020). 'You really have to have a thick skin.' A cross-cultural perspective on how online harassment influences female journalists. *Journalism*, *21*(7), 877–895. https://doi.org/10.1177/1464884918768500

Christley, O. (2021). Traditional gender attitudes, nativism, and support for the radical right. *Politics & Gender*, 1–27. https://doi.org/10.1017/S1743923X21000374

Costello, M., Hawdon, J., Bernatzky, C., & Mendes, K. (2019). Social group identity and perceptions of online hate. *Sociological Inquiry*, *89*(3), 427–452. https://doi.org/10.1111/soin.12274

Dovidio, J. F., Hewstone, M., Glick, P., & Esses, V. M. (2010). Prejudice, stereotyping and discrimination: Theoretical and empirical overview. In J. F. Dovidio (Ed.), *The SAGE handbook of prejudice, stereotyping and discrimination* (pp. 3–28). SAGE. https://doi.org/10.4135/9781446200919.n1

Fawzi, N., Steindl, N., Obermaier, M., Prochazka, F., Arlt, D., Blöbaum, B., Dohle, M., Engelke, K. M., Hanitzsch, T., Jackob, N., Jakobs, I., Klawier, T., Post, S., Reinemann, C., Schweiger, W., & Ziegele, M. (2021). Concepts, causes and consequences of trust in news media – A literature review and framework. *Annals of the International Communication Association*, *45*, 154–174. https://doi.or g/10.1080/23808985.2021.1960181

Foster, M. (2009). The dynamic nature of coping with gender discrimination: Appraisals, strategies and well-being over time. *Sex Roles*, *60*(9), 694–707. https://doi.org/10.1007/s11199-008-9568-2

Garton Ash, T. (2016). *Free speech: Ten principles for a connected world*. Yale University Press.

Gustafsson Sendén, M., Bäck, E. A., & Lindqvist, A. (2015). Introducing a gender-neutral pronoun in a natural gender language: The influence of time on attitudes and behavior. *Frontiers in Psychology*, *6*, 893. https://doi.org/10.3389/fps yg.2015.00893

Hong, M. (2020). Meinungsfreiheit und ihre Grenzen [Freedom of speech and its limits]. *Politik und Zeitgeschichte*. https://www.bpb.de/apuz/306444/meinungsfrei heit-und-ihre-grenzen

Inglehart, R., & Norris, P. (2003). *Rising tide: Gender equality and cultural change around the world*. Cambridge University Press.

Kahan, D. M. (2013). Ideology, motivated reasoning, and cognitive reflection: An experimental study. *Judgment and Decision Making*, *8*(4), 407–424. http://dx.doi.o rg/10.2139/ssrn.2182588

Kister, K. (2021, September 15). Zwickau: Die absurde Entscheidung des Verwaltungsgerichts Chemnitz [Zwickau: The absurd decision of the Administrative Court of Chemnitz]. *Süddeutsche Zeitung*. https://www.sueddeutsche.de/meinun g/verwaltungsgericht-chemnitz-neonazis-zwickau-1.5410637

Knight Foundation. (2019). *Freedom of speech at college campuses*. https://knightfoun dation.org/reports/free-expression-college-campuses/

Köcher, R. (2019). *Grenzen der freiheit* [Limits to freedom]. Allensbach Institute for Public Opinion Research. https://www.ifd-allensbach.de/fileadmin/user_upload/ FAZ_Mai2019_Meinungsfreiheit.pdf

Leets, L. (2002). Experiencing hate speech. Perceptions and responses to anti-Semitism and antigay speech. *Journal of Social Issues*, *58*, 341–361. http://dx.doi.org/10 .1111/1540-4560.00264

Lilienfeld, S. O. (2017). Microaggressions: Strong claims, inadequate evidence. *Perspectives on Psychological Science*, *12*(1), 138–169. https://doi.org/10.1177%2F17 45691616659391

Love, R. (2021). Swearing in informal spoken English: 1990s–2010s. *Text & Talk*, *41*(5-6), 739–762. https://doi.org/10.1515/text-2020-0051

Lui, P. P., & Quezada, L. (2019). Associations between microaggression and adjustment outcomes: A meta-analytic and narrative review. *Psychological Bulletin*, *145*(1), 45–78. https://doi.org/10.1037/bul0000172

Marker, K. (2013). Know your enemy. Zur Funktionalität der Hassrede für wehrhafte Demokratien [On the functionality of hate speech for defensible democracies]. In J. Meibauer (Ed.), *Hassrede. Interdisziplinäre Beiträge zu einer aktuellen Diskussion* [Hate speech. Interdisciplinary contributions to a current discussion] (pp. 59–94). Gießener Elektronische Bibliothek. http://geb.uni-giessen.de/geb/vo lltexte/2013/9251/pdf/HassredeMeibauer_2013.pdf

Mummendey, A., Kessler, T., & Otten, S. (2009). Sozialpsychologische Determinanten-- Gruppenzugehörigkeit und soziale Kategorisierung [Social psychological determinants-- Group membership and social categorization.]. In A. Beelmann, K. J. Jonas, A. Beelmann, & K. J. Jonas (Eds.), *Diskriminierung und Toleranz. Psychologische Grundlagen und Anwendungsperspektiven* [Discrimination and Tolerance. Psychological foundations and application perspectives] (pp. 43–60). Wiesbaden.

Noelle-Neumann, E. (1996). *Öffentliche Meinung: Die Entdeckung der Schweigespirale* [Public opinion: The discovery of the spiral of silence]. Ullstein.

Petersen, T. (2013). *Tatsächliche und gefühlte Intoleranz* [Actual and perceived intolerance]. Allensbach Institute for Public Opinion Research. https://www.ifd-alle nsbach.de/fileadmin/kurzberichte_dokumentationen/Maerz13_Intoleranz.pdf

Petersen, T. (2021). *Die Mehrheit fühlt sich gegängelt* [The majority feels it's being restrained]. Allensbach Institute for Public Opinion Research. https://www.ifd-a llensbach.de/fileadmin/kurzberichte_dokumentationen/FAZ_Juni2021_Meinun gsfreiheit.pdf

Pew Research Center. (2019). *A changing world: Global views on diversity, gender equality, family life and the importance of religion.* https://www.pewresearch.org/gl obal/2019/04/22/how-people-around-the-world-view-gender-equality-in-their-cou ntries/

Quiring, O., Jackob, N., Schemer, C., Jakobs, I., & Ziegele, M. (2020). „Das wird man doch noch sagen dürfen…" – Wahrgenommene Sprechverbote und ihre Korrelate ["One is still allowed to say that…" – Perceived speech prohibitions and their correlates]. In N. Jackob, O. Quiring, & M. Maurer (Eds.), *Traditionen und transformationen des öffentlichen: Soziale wahrnehmung und soziale kontrolle in zeiten gesellschaftlichen Wandels* [Traditions and transformations of the public sphere: Social perception and social control in times of social Change] (pp. 49–71). Springer VS. https://doi.org/10.1007/978-3-658-29321-5_3

Reimer, F. (2019). Freiheit der Meinungsäußerung: eine rechtsvergleichende perspektive – Deutschland [Freedom of expression: A comparative law perspective - Germany]. *EPRS / Wissenschaftlicher Dienst des Europäischen Parlaments.* https://w ww.europarl.europa.eu/RegData/etudes/STUD/2019/642269/EPRS_STU(2019)6 42269_DE.pdf

Scarborough, W. J., Sin, R., & Risman, B. (2019). Attitudes and the stalled gender revolution: Egalitarianism, traditionalism, and ambivalence from 1977 through 2016. *Gender & Society, 33*(2), 173–200. https://doi.org/10.1177/08912432188096 04

Strömbäck, J., Tsfati, Y., Boomgaarden, H. G., Damstra, A., Lindgren, E., Vliegenthart, R., & Lindholm, T. (2020). News media trust and its impact on media use: Toward a framework for future research. *Annals of the International Communication Association, 44*, 139–156. https://doi.org/10.1080/23808985.2020.1755338

Struth, A. K. (2019). *Hassrede und freiheit der meinungsäußerung* [Hate speech and freedom of speech]. Springer.

Sue, D. W. (2010). *Microaggressions in everyday life: Race, gender, and sexual orientation*. John Wiley & Sons.

Sue, D. W., Capodilupo, C. M., Torino, G. C., Bucceri, J. M., Holder, A., Nadal, K. L., & Esquilin, M. (2007). Racial microaggressions in everyday life: Implications for clinical practice. *The American Psychologist, 62*(4), 271-286. https://doi.org/10.1037/0003-066X.62.4.271

Taber, C. S., & Lodge, M. (2006). Motivated skepticism in the evaluation of political beliefs. *American Journal of Political Science, 50*(3), 755–769. https://doi.org/10.1111/j.1540-5907.2006.00214.x

Torino, G. C., Rivera, D. P., Capodilupo, C. M., Nadal, K. L., & Sue, D. W. (Eds.). (2018). *Microaggression theory: Influence and implications*. John Wiley & Sons.

Valkenburg, P. M., & Peter, J. (2013). The differential susceptibility to media effects model. *Journal of Communication, 63*(2), 221–243. https://doi.org/10.1111/jcom.12024

Wegner, J., Prommer, E., & Collado Seidel, C. (2020). Free speech under pressure: The effect of online harassment on literary writers. *Media and Communication, 8*(4), 145–157. https://www.ssoar.info/ssoar/bitstream/document/70232/2/ssoar-mediacomm-2020-4-wegner_et_al-Free_Speech_Under_Pressure_The.pdf

Williams, D. R., & Mohammed, S. A. (2013). Racism and health I: Pathways and scientific evidence. *The American Behavioral Scientist, 57*(8). https://doi.org/10.1177/0002764213487340

Wojcieszak, M., Sobkowicz, P., Yu, X., & Bulat, B. (2021). What information drives political polarization? Comparing the effects of in-group praise, out-group derogation, and evidence-based communications on polarization. *The International Journal of Press/Politics*. https://doi.org/10.1177%2F19401612211004418

Do People Really Not Agree on What Can be Said?

Carsten Reinemann *(Dr. phil., U of Mainz, 2003) is a Professor at the Department of Media and Communication, LMU Munich, Germany. His research currently deals with populism, extremism, changing opinion power in hybrid media systems and issues of freedom of speech. Wolfram Peiser was a PostDoc at the U of Mainz when Carsten Reinemann graduated there in 1997 (M.A.). They became colleagues when Carsten Reinemann started his PhD in Mainz in late 1997 until Wolfram Peiser went to LMU Munich in 2006 to become a Professor. In 2008, their ways crossed again when Carsten Reinemann also joined the Munich department as a Professor.*

Anna-Luisa Sacher *is a Research Associate and PhD student at the Department of Media and Communication (IfKW) at Ludwig-Maximilians-Universität Munich, Germany. Her research interests focus on the perception, use and impact of political communication, where she is particularly concerned with aspects of the tension between freedom of speech and freedom from discrimination.*

How Does One's Season of Birth Influence Television- and Music-Genre Preferences? And Why?

An Exploratory Analysis

Klaus Schönbach

Abstract

This study investigates the influence of season of birth on preferences for music- and television genres later in life. As early as in 1994, Wolfram Peiser and I had published survey data showing that people with fewer summer months during their first half year after birth in Germany tend to be less cheerful. In the meantime, an impressive body of research has accumulated similar evidence also for other countries in the north of the northern hemisphere. In a recently published study, I had applied mood-management theory to show that media content may be used to alleviate less cheerfulness due to one's birth climate in the Middle East and in North Africa as well. This article further explores such a benefit of media use with a secondary analysis of a large and representative survey in Germany. The study reveals that people with more winter months soon after birth tend to prefer "mainstream" entertainment offerings a little more —even after age, education and gender are controlled for. In addition, age shows significant moderating effects.

Does our month of birth have an impact on us later in life? Believers in horoscopes are convinced of it. But we do not need astrology to make this point: An impressive body of scientific evidence from Europe, East Asia and the U.S. has revealed all kinds of effects of when in the course of a year one was born. A recent analysis of large surveys from the MENA region (Middle East and North Africa) showed that one's season of birth even influences the *media genres* one prefers (Schoenbach, 2018). The following article further explores this effect—with a secondary analysis of a large and representative survey in Germany.

So far, our knowledge about the impact of one's season of birth has originated almost exclusively from biology, medicine, psychiatry and neuroscience (overviews, e.g., in Zhang et al., 2019; Schoenbach, 2018; Martinez-Bakker et al., 2014, and Axt & Axt-Gadermann, 2004)–sometimes based on huge datasets (e.g., Lewis et al., 2021). As examples, just a few more recent results: People born in spring or early summer of the north of the northern hemisphere—compared to those born in the fall and early winter—have a significantly higher chance to die of a cardiovascular disease (Uji et al., 2021; Zhang et al., 2019). They suffer slightly more often of macular degeneration (Longo et al., 2017), autoimmune Adisson's disease (Pazderska et al., 2016) and coeliac disease (Namatovu et al., 2016).

But also certain *personality traits* are related to one's season of birth. Again, some examples: There is ample evidence that early-spring-born babies have a greater tendency to develop schizophrenia (Hori et al., 2012). But in a fascinating U.S. study, Marzullo (1996) claims that to be born in February or March—as opposed to in August or September—is also more often related to creativity and artistry. A similar pattern was found in Germany (Axt & Axt-Gadermann, 2004, p. 82 f.). Or—more trivial: People born in spring or summer of the northern hemisphere more often are "night owls," i.e., evening persons (Natale & Milia, 2011).

Almost 30 years ago, Wolfram Peiser and I had found that also a desirable *temperament* was more widespread among people born in spring or early summer in Germany: They tended to be more cheerful, to experience more joy of life (Peiser & Schoenbach, 1994). In the meantime, the amount of evidence has increased impressively confirming that spring- and summer-borns in the north of the northern hemisphere do not only enjoy at least a little more cheerfulness, but also more liveliness, less shyness (overviews in Schoenbach, 2018, but already also in Cortmaker et al., 1997) and better self-control (Lee, Lee & Lee, 2021). No surprise, then, that they more often regard themselves as "a lucky person" (Chotai & Wiseman, 2005) and seem to be less aggressive (Asano et al., 2016).

Season-of-birth research has suggested a number of reasons for differences between those born in spring or early summer and other people (see overviews in Zhang et al., 2019; Schoenbach, 2018; Antonsen et al., 2013)—for instance: The seasonally different amount of light influences *chemical* reactions in our brains—e.g., the melatonin-dopamine ratio (Cortmaker et al., 1997) and the vitamin-D level (Day et al., 2015). Also, seasonal fluctuations in nutrition availability have been discussed as a cause (see, e.g., Chodick et al., 2009). The impact of one's month of birth on school-starting age—in the U.S. the difference between being born before September and later—has been investigated, too, as a cause of specific developments in personality (Dhuey et al., 2017). Finally, the warmer and sunnier environment during summers in the north certainly offers more stimuli and a richer social life for a newborn—and, in addition, also

Klaus Schönbach

about one year later, when toddlers usually begin to walk (e.g., Peiser & Schoenbach, 1994). At any rate, our first year after birth seems to be a particularly decisive year for physical and mental well-being later in life (e.g., Roseboom, 2018).

The basic premise of the analysis conducted for the MENA region (Schoenbach, 2018) and the following one is: If one's season of birth influences how cheerful and lively one is later in life, *media use* could help compensate lower levels of these personality traits. Such a function of the media is deducted from a broader reading of Dolf Zillmann's "mood management" theory (1988). Zillmann had applied it to situational "affective states" only (p. 328). He assumed that a bad mood makes us turn to exciting and absorbing media content (p. 331)—"cheerful programs, such as comedies," for instance (p. 335; see also Carpentier et al., 2008). Knobloch (2003) added "energetic-joyful" music for the same purpose.

So, the media genres entertaining enough to alleviate a bad mood obviously are defined by a *hedonic* approach to well-being (Whitaker, Velez & Knobloch-Westerwick, 2012). Hedonism equates well-being with pleasure, enjoyment and the avoidance of pain—as opposed to the *eudaimonic* perspective, originally described by Aristotle (about 340 BC/2000; see also, e.g., Kahneman et al., 1999, and Waterman, 1993). To achieve well-being, the eudaimonic approach suggests "seeking for meaningfulness," for the "gratification of greater insights," more than seeking for pleasure (Oliver & Raney, 2011, p. 987). An eudaimonic orientation therefore aims at "the cultivation of personal strengths and contribution to the greater good…, the realization of one's true potential" (McMahan & Estes, 2011, p. 93 f.).

In the MENA study, it was suggested that hedonic media offerings should not only be a choice for people who feel sad temporarily but also for those who feel less lucky and are less cheerful than others as their *permanent* emotional traits (Schoenbach, 2018)—thereby following Swedish researchers Karl-Erik Rosengren and Sven Windahl. They had proposed—as early as in 1972—that media consumption often serves as a "functional alternative" to experiences generally missing in everyday life.

The 2018 MENA study indeed revealed slightly different preferences for hedonic media genres, depending on one's season of birth (Schoenbach, 2018). That analysis was based on large and representative surveys in six countries of the MENA region—from Tunisia to Saudi Arabia. But, of course, that region is a setting quite different from where almost all studies on the impact of season of birth had been conducted before. In MENA countries, it is *winter* that offers a mostly still very sunny, but more pleasant, season. So, newborn babies can, for instance, be outside their homes more frequently than in the often unbearable summer heat—and thus profit from both more sunlight and social contacts. Typically, doctors in the Gulf countries prescribe vitamin D in the summer, taking into account that people often do not get enough sun because they stay inside. This is why the 2018 analysis assumed that being born in the MENA spring or early summer should be related to that lower level of cheerfulness and liveliness found among people born later in the year of more northern countries.

The MENA study used the number of summer months (April to September) in one's first half year after birth as an indicator of the extent to which a baby had to cope with often extremely hot weather. Experiencing more of these months showed the expected relationships with one's preference for hedonic audio-visual media genres ("Comedy," "Drama," "Films on DVD") and with a slight but significant rejection of "Religious/spiritual" content, but interestingly also of "Daytime talk shows."

The present study, as a secondary analysis, replicates and refines the MENA one by exploring the impact of one's birth climate on preferences not only on specific audio-visual media genres—as in the MENA analysis. Now also a number of *music* styles are included. And like almost all studies on the effects of season of birth so far, this one looks again at the north of the northern hemisphere. It uses data from *Germany*—a country with relatively moderate summers and often "real" winters, i.e., with freezing temperatures and snow on the ground. So, the first, and general, hypothesis of this study reads:

H1. The more winter months in the first half year of their life individuals have experienced, the more they prefer hedonic media genres.

Also, as in the MENA analysis, age and gender will be looked at again as possible moderators of the impact of one's birth month. As to *age*, Oliver and Raney (2011, p. 999) suggest that *older* people may generally become more eudaimonic and thus not need hedonic media content that much anymore to compensate for a lack of cheerfulness. Quite consequently, eudaimonic genres may also be suitable for this purpose. But even *any* effect of the climate of one's birth on media-content preferences—whatever they are—could *fade* with becoming older, just because one's first half year after birth is longer ago: one of the results of the MENA study (Schoenbach, 2018, see also Cordova-Palomera et al., 2015; Harada et al., 2011; Peiser & Schoenbach, 1994).

In his review of the impact of winter months after birth on *depression*, Schnittker (2018) goes even further. He suggests that among today's younger cohorts this relationship may actually be weaker from the start—because conditions of life have significantly improved during the last 50 years,

Klaus Schönbach

making differences between lives of newborn babies in winter and in summer less important. Schnittker's example of those better conditions is food preservation, including refrigeration and distribution. But one could also think of more widespread central heating, better hygiene and, above all, the progress in medical (but also psychiatric) diagnosis and therapy.

All three assumptions seem plausible—i.e., older winter-borns do not need hedonic media content anymore, or any notable impact of one's birth date may only last as long as one is young, or this effect may be weak even for newborns already. A fourth possibility, of course, could still be that the impact of season of birth on hedonic media-content preferences at least somewhat stays as long as we live. This is why we do not test a hypothesis for the role of age, but will try to answer the following research question:

RQ1. How does age influence the relationships between the number of winter months right after birth and media-genre preferences?

Our second research question concerns *gender* as a moderator variable. Previous studies have shown that the impact of season of birth sometimes differs between women and men—albeit inconclusively (e.g., Lee, Lee & Lee, 2021; Blanch & Solé, 2021; Chotai et al, 2009; Kamata et al., 2009; Weber et al., 1998). More often, however, the role of gender has not been investigated at all. But women or men may be differently sensitive to darker months after birth and thus also show a different need to alleviate a lack of cheerfulness or liveliness by more entertaining media content. In the 2018 MENA study, gender did not matter (Schoenbach, 2018). Just to be safe, however, the following analysis includes gender again. But we do not dare formulate a hypothesis at this stage of our exploration, but instead ask:

RQ2. How does gender influence the relationships between the number of winter months right after birth and media-genre preferences?

A second hypothesis adds *education* as a third possible moderator to our analysis. Education has been shown to be an important determinant of one's media-genre preferences (see, e.g., the overview in Wonneberger, Schoenbach & Meurs, 2009). But so far, it has not been taken into account systematically in season-of-birth research of all kinds. Plausible, however, that somebody born with fewer summer months, but with a higher education, commands a wider range of possibilities to compensate for a lack of cheerfulness and of feeling lucky—and consequently does not have to rely on hedonic media use that much (see already Rosengren & Windahl, 1972). This could not only be due to a wider intellectual range by more education but also to factors that often correlate with it—one's social class, for instance, and one's family socialization (see, e.g., Bourdieu, 1984). If so, the higher educated may actually need more sophisticated media content to be pleased (see, e.g., Knobloch-Westerwick, 2006). So, the according hypothesis reads:

H2. The lower one's education and the more winter months in the first half year of their life individuals have experienced, the more they prefer hedonic media genres.

Method

Our secondary analysis uses a large and representative survey of the German adult population: the so-called "German General Social Survey," in short "ALLBUS." The ALLBUS is a trend study, supervised by *GESIS— Leibniz Institute for the Social Sciences* and repeated every other year to observe attitudes, behaviors and social change in Germany. Its focus shifts, but it always carries an extensive demography, including one's month and country of birth. In 2014, and as an exception, the questionnaire contained also two item batteries about media-genre preferences. The ALLBUS sample is supposed to represent all adults (18 years and older) living in Germany and sufficiently capable to be interviewed in German.

The survey used face-to-face interviews via *Computer-Assisted Personal Interviewing (CAPI)* and was in the field between March 24 and September 13, 2014. In total, 3,471 persons participated, with a reasonable response rate of 35 percent. The data were weighted to represent the population as closely as possible. Weighting criteria were the number of East and West Germans as well as the size and composition of the household the respondent belonged to (see a detailed description of the questionnaire, the sampling and weighting procedures in Baumann & Schulz, 2015).

For the purpose of this analysis, those 2,991 respondents are used who did not only live in Germany in 2014 but were also *born* there. The reason is simple: To investigate the potential impact of the season of birth, we have to make sure that the climate conditions for all of respondents, when they were newborns, were as comparable as possible. Unfortunately, the dataset does not contain the respondents' exact *birthplaces*—for more precision of the weather conditions right after birth. But although Germans often perceive Hamburg in the north and Munich in the south of the country (a little more than 600 kilometers apart) as having almost opposite climates, this difference has actually not been that dramatic, at least as a long-term average. Between 1981 and 2010 and in July, the height of summer, Hamburg reached 7.0 sunshine hours per day, Munich 7.7. In January, Munich had an average of 2.6 hours of sunshine a day, Hamburg

followed with 1.6 hours. (see, e.g., https://www.dwd.de/DE/leistungen/k
limadatendeutschland/mittelwerte/sonne_8110_fest_html.html?view=n
asPublication). And the average meteorological summer temperature in
Munich, again from 1981 to 2010, was 18.3 degrees Celsius, in Hamburg
17.1. During meteorological winter, it was an average 1.9 degrees in Hamburg and 1.0 in Munich (https://www.wetterkontor.de/de/wetter/deutsch-
land/monatswerte-station.asp).

Even if these rather small climate differences could be regarded as serious, we should keep in mind that a little fewer or more sun hours and a
little higher or lower temperature in one's first half year represent only one
potential cause for more joy of life and vividness. As discussed above, we
assume that one's *experience* of summer or winter is at least as important:
the baby's social environment, e.g., how "summery" or "wintery" parents
and other people behave. It could be possible, for instance, that the short
and often not very warm summers in northern Sweden are experienced
as exciting and pleasant as the much longer and mostly warmer ones in
southern Germany.

Measurement

Our independent variable is the number of winter months in the first half
year of one's life. It was based on the responses to:

"Please tell me in which month and year you were born."

The English wording of this question and of the other ones used in this
analysis are retrieved from the extensive description of the 2014 ALLBUS
survey by Baumann and Schulz (2015).

We defined winter months in Germany as October to March—so, their
number could range from zero (born in April) to six (born in October).
For the 2,940 respondents in the survey who were born in Germany and
whose month of birth we know, the mean of this number is 3.0, with a
standard deviation of 1.8.

For our dependent variables, the attractiveness of specific media genres,
the survey used here contained two batteries of items for a secondary
analysis: (a) interest in specific genres on television and (b) liking specific
kinds of music.

(a) Interest in specific *television genres* was measured by the question: "Now, I will name you different television programs. Please tell me by means of this list how strongly you are interested in programs such as this one."

The responses listed were: "Very strongly," "Strongly," "Medium," "A little" and "Not at all." For our analysis, the five answers were coded from 5 to 1, with "Very strongly" interested as 5 and "Not at all" interested as 1.

These were the types of television programs the respondents had to react to—with an N of 2,876 (in parentheses their average interest score between 1 and 5, and its standard deviation, separated by a comma): "Entertainment shows, quiz programs" (2.5, 1.1), "Sports programs" (3.0, 1.3), "News" (4.2, .9), "Political magazine programs" (3.0, 1.1), "Art and culture programs" (2.7, 1.1), "Detective movies, crime series" (3.2, 1.2) and "Family and entertainment series" (2.6, 1.1).

(b) To find out about their *taste of music*, the respondents were asked: "Now, I will name you different kinds of music. Please tell me by means of this list how much you like listening to this music."

On the list the possible responses were: "I like listening to... very much," "I like listening to...," "I neither like nor dislike listening to...," I dislike listening to..." and "I dislike listening to... very much." For our analysis the five answers were coded from 5 to 1, with "I like listening to... very much" as 5 and "I dislike listening to... very much" as 1.

These were the music styles the respondents had to react to—with an N between 2,934 and 2,949 (in parentheses their average liking score between 1 and 5, and its standard deviation, separated by a comma): "German folk music" (2.6, 1.3), "Folk music of other cultures" (2.6, 1.1), "German 'Schlager' music"—i.e., a Barry-Manilow type of popular German music (3.1, 1.2), "Pop music and today's charts" (3.6, 1.2), "Rock music" (3.4, 1.3), "Heavy Metal" (2.1, 1.3), "Electronic music—such as House, Techno, Electro" (2.3, 1.3), "Hip Hop, Soul, Reggae" (2.7, 1.3), "Classical music" (3.2, 1.2), "Opera" (2.5, 1.2), "Musical" (3.2, 1.2) and "Jazz" (2.8, 1.2).

Of course, one could assume that the items of the two batteries available for our analysis are connected, representing *styles* of liking music and of being interested in types of television programs. But a factor analysis (principal component) of all these genres together only reveals two—fairly weak—factors, with an explained variance of as low as 16 percent each. And only *music styles* considerably load on them—i.e., there is neither a

Klaus Schönbach

really close relationship *between* TV genres alone nor between TV and kinds of music.

One music factor is represented by "Classical music," "Opera", "Jazz" and "Folk music of other cultures"—with loadings (after rotation) of at least .48. Cronbach's alpha for these four items is a satisfactory .75. This is why we create an additive index of them and call it "High-culture music." The index ranges from 4 to 20, and its mean is 14.3 with a standard deviation of 4.3.

The second music factor is represented by "German folk music" and "German 'Schlager' music," with loadings (after rotation) of .80 and .77, respectively. Their additive index is called "'Schlagers' & German folk." Its range is 2 to 10 and its mean is 5.7 with a standard deviation of 2.2.

Finally, two more kinds of music are at least fairly strongly correlated (Pearson's r = .53**): "Hip Hop, Soul, Reggae" and "Electronic music—such as House, Techno, Electro." We name their additive index "Hip Hop & Electronic." It ranges from 2 to 10, and its mean is 5.0 with a standard deviation of 2.3.

In a preliminary attempt to categorize the media genres of the survey into hedonistic and non-hedonistic ones, we assume that the following types of television programming are mostly pleasant and "fun"—and thus, at least in principle, providing enough hedonic benefits to distract from one's lack of an outgoing temperament and also to allow identification with the protagonists of these genres as exemplars of cheerfulness (see above, Zillmann, 1988): "Entertainment shows, quiz programs," "Sports programs," "Family and entertainment series" and "Detective movies, crime series." As not primarily hedonic genres we consider "News," "Political magazine programs" and "Art and culture programs" (see a similar classification of media genres by Carpentier et. al., 2008).

As to music, and in terms of hedonism, we assume—again preliminarily—that most kinds of *popular* music are experienced as generally more pleasurable and as more fun than, e.g., classical music, opera, jazz, and folk music of other cultures (the components of our index "high-culture music"). If we accept this, at least *more* compensatory types of music for those with more darker months after birth would be: "'Schlagers' & German folk," "Pop music and today's charts," "Rock music" and "Musical." In contrast, "High-culture music," but also "Hip Hop & Electronic" and "Heavy Metal" might be experienced as more challenging and strenuous by most Germans.

This categorization is not to imply that the genres we classified as less suited for a hedonic compensation of less cheerful- and liveliness are also less popular—they are not, as the means of their scores above document: At least on average, "Classical music" is just as attractive as "German 'Schlager' music"—with their mean scores of liking them: 3.2 and 3.1, respectively (see above). We still do assume, though, that, e.g., "High-culture music" is not used that often to alleviate the consequences of fewer summer months after birth for one's temperament.

However, any unobjectionable classification of genres is difficult, of course. So far we have used a kind of "popular taste" approach to hedonic well-being—we expect that most people regard, e. g., "Entertainment shows, quiz programs" as more fun than "Art and culture programs." But we cannot ignore that there may be individuals that do not only *use* the latter more often than the former, but who also *enjoy* them hedonically: for instance the higher educated (see above)—something to be explored in our analysis.

For RQ1, the *age* of the respondent was calculated in years, based on the question about one's year of birth (see above). The average age of our sample members was 49.0 years, its standard deviation 17.5 years (N = 2,949).

Gender (RQ2) was determined by the interviewers of the survey. Forty-nine percent of 2,951 respondents were assigned "female" and 51 percent "male."

Finally, for our hypothesis H2, *education* as a proxy for one's intellectual, but also social, capital (see above) was gauged by the question:

"Which school-leaving certificate do you have?"

On a list, possible answers began with "A I'm still a high school student" and "B No school leaving certificate." The other items on the list mirror (in ascending order) the German educational system—this is why we have to quote the responses literally (in parentheses the rough equivalent in the U.S., again retrieved from Baumann & Schulz, 2015): "C Volks-/ Hauptschulabschluss bzw. Polytechnische Oberschule mit Abschluss 8. oder 9. Klasse" (= approximately a certificate of secondary education), „D Mittlere Reife, Realschulabschluss bzw. Polytechnische Oberschule mit Abschluss 10. Klasse" (= approximately high school), „E Fachhochschulreife (Abschluss einer Fachoberschule etc.)" (= approximately high school, but additionally qualifying for a vocational university), „F Abitur bzw. Erweiterte Oberschule mit Abschluss 12. Klasse" (= approximately college) and "G A different leaving certificate."

We excluded the 39 cases of still being a high-school student and of "A different leaving certificate" and constructed a scale of one's formal education by assigning scores to the five levels B to F of schooling, ascending

Klaus Schönbach

from 1 to 5. The mean of this scale, then, was 3.3 with a standard deviation of 1.3 (N = 2,916).

Analyses

In a fairly rigid fashion, *multiple linear regressions* serve as the statistical tool to determine the relationship between the number of winter months soon after birth and a specific media-genre preference: In a first step, for every genre and our sample as a whole, age, education and gender are simultaneous control variables, but also all the other media-genre preferences measured in our survey. The next step of the analysis, then, explores how the three demographics may *moderate* this impact (RQ1, RQ2, H2). For this purpose, the respondents are segmented: To investigate the role of *age*, we divide the sample into three almost equal portions and repeat our analyses for each subsample. The three age categories consist of those 41 years and younger, 42 to 57 years and, finally, 58 years and older.

For *gender*, we analyze men and women separately. For *education* as a moderating variable, its five levels are collapsed into two categories and also looked at separately. The two categories represent a *lower* formal education, i.e., levels B, C and D (ending with „approximately high school"), and a *higher* one, i.e. levels E and F (starting with „approximately high school, but additionally qualifying for a vocational university").

In these subgroups of the survey, multiple regressions still control for all the other media-genre preferences but also for the two demographic variables *not* used for segmentation, respectively—i.e., for age and education when the sample is split into men and women; for age and gender when formal education is analyzed; and for gender and education when the three categories of age are investigated separately.

To answer our RQs and to test H2 about the roles of age, gender and education, we apply two statistical conditions to determine whether they moderate the relationships between season of birth and TV or music genres: (a) the beta weight for at least one of the categories of these demographics should be significant at least on the five-percent level, and (b) the difference between it and the beta of at least one of the other respective categories should be statistically significant as well (again p smaller or equal .05). To compare these betas we use Fisher's z, as suggested, e. g., by Hemmerich (2017).

Results

The number of winter months in the first half year after one's birth is significantly related to half of the 14 media genres and their indices that could be investigated in this secondary analysis—to four of them for *all* respondents and three for at least one of our demographic subgroups. As suggested by the general hypothesis H1, "Entertainment programs, quiz shows," "Sports programs" and "Family and entertainment series" on television are a little more preferred by respondents with more darker months soon after birth—in other words, media content that one might generally regard as hedonic. And one of the music styles that we assumed to be less useful for alleviating a lack of cheerfulness, "Heavy Metal," is actually *disliked* somewhat, but fairly universally, the more winter months there were after birth (Table 1).

Table 1: Relationships Between the Number of Winter Months Right After Birth and Preferences for Television and Music Genres

	All	Age (in years)			Gender		Formal education	
		18 - 41	42 - 57	58+	Female	Male	Lower	Higher
Television genres:								
Entertainment shows, quiz programs	.04*	.06	.02	.02	.04	.03	.05*	.02
Sports programs	.05**	-.00	.06*	.08**	.04	.05*	.03	.06*
Family and entertainment series	.04*	.07*	.03	-.01	.06*	.01	.04	.04
Detective movies, crime series	-.01	-.03	.02	-.01	.02	-.03	-.01	.01
News	.03	-.03	.03	.09**	.02	.04	.04	.01
Political magazine programs	.01	-.02	-.03	.07*	.01	.01	.01	-.01
Art and culture programs	.01	-.01	-.03	.06*	.03	-.01	.03	-.02
Music genres:								
'Schlagers' & German folk	.02	.00	.04	.01	.04	.01	.02	.03

	All	Age (in years)			Gender		Formal education	
		18 - 41	42 - 57	58+	Female	Male	Lower	Higher
Pop music and today's charts	.02	.04	.04	.03	.00	.04	.02	.05
Rock music	.00	.01	-.00	.03	.01	-.01	-.02	.04
Musical	.02	-.02	.05	.03	.04	.01	.03	.00
Hip Hop & Electronic	.00	.04	-.02	.02	-.01	.01	.00	-.00
High-culture music	.02	-.01	.01	.04	.02	.02	.00	.05
Heavy Metal	-.06**	-.07*	-.06	-.03	-.06*	-.06*	-.06*	-.04
Minimal N	2,904	958	993	951	1,419	1,484	1,831	1,103

Note: Standardized betas from multiple regressions, controlled for all other genre preferences, age, gender and formal education, and also segmented by age, gender and formal education.

* betas, significant at the 5-percent level

** betas, significant at the 1-percent level.

These relationships are also confirmed in the smaller samples of one or the other of our demographic subgroups: "Entertainment shows, quiz programs" among the lower educated, "Sports programs" in the oldest group, "Family and entertainment series" in the youngest one, and finally the dislike of "Heavy Metal" also in this age category, but separately among women and men as well. The six other music styles of our analysis, however, simply do not matter significantly, neither as liked or disliked in connection with one's month of birth—although we had expected four of them as entertaining in a hedonic sense: "'Schlagers' & German folk," "Pop music and today's charts," "Rock music" and "Musical." In one of the age categories—the oldest one—we find even positive relationships of being winter-born with three media genres not considered to be particularly hedonic: "News" on television, "Political magazine programs" and "Art and cultural programs."

So, age indeed seems to be a relevant moderator (RQ1), but gender and education (RQ2 and H2) are not: Once the two statistical conditions described in our analyses section are applied, neither gender nor education significantly discriminate the relationships between TV- or music-genre preferences and the number of winter months soon after birth. In other

How Does One's Season of Birth Influence Television- and Music-Genre Preferences?

words, women and men do not really differ regarding the role played by their season of birth for media genre preferences, nor do higher or lower educated respondents. So, H2 is rejected.

In sum, however, our general hypothesis H1 is supported: The patterns in our data indicate that the fall/winter borns have a higher likelihood to prefer what we had called hedonic media genres.

Summary, Conclusions and Discussion

Does season of birth influence the attractiveness of media content? In this explorative analysis, a 2018 study in six MENA countries (Schoenbach, 2018) was both replicated and refined—now not in an often extremely hot region of the world but in Germany. This is why we expected that those with more *winter* months in their first half year should alleviate a lack of liveliness and cheerfulness by preferring hedonic media offerings. In sum, this seems to be the case—and even more universally than in the MENA study. An explanation could be that German summers, compared to its winters, are more impressive for newborns than the mild winters are in North Africa and the Middle East. In other words, Germans may simply "make more" of their summers than the MENA population does of their "summery" winters.

There is one subgroup in our analysis, however, that presents us with an interesting exception to this general result in Germany: the oldest one. Surprisingly, compared to at least the youngest respondents, those 58+ years old and with longer winters after birth are somewhat more interested in "News," "Political magazine programs" and "Arts and culture programs" on TV—even after the preferences for all the other genres as well as education and gender are controlled for. We had assumed that these types of TV programming should actually be less compensatory for a deficit in cheerful- and liveliness than "Family and entertainment series," for instance.

The MENA study (Schoenbach, 2018) had found similar evidence for older individuals—even more strikingly: In that region, older people preferred entertaining media content of *all* kinds less often, the more—in that case—hot *summer* months they had to endure soon after birth. The results of our analyses in Germany do not go that far—the oldest group of our sample is not systematically less interested in or dislikes hedonic genres more than other people. But, all in all, in Germany as well, and as suggested by Oliver and Raney (2011, p. 999—see above), older people

Klaus Schönbach

may indeed become more *eudaimonic*, also in their preferences of which media content they find compensatory.

As in the MENA study (Schoenbach, 2018), *gender* did not show as an important moderating variable in our analysis—i.e., women with more winter months soon after birth do not prefer more and/or different media content for mood management than males, at least not among the 14 genres we could investigate here. Also, one's *formal education* was not relevant as a moderator either. This makes our null results for liking or disliking specific *music* styles still puzzling. Sure, in the MENA study, both "Listen to music" as its only—and very general—variable for the *use* of music had not emerged as significant either. Nor had "Music videos" as the only measure of one's *preference* for musical media content (Schoenbach, 2018). But although our German data discerned specific kinds of music, only one of them, "Heavy Metal," shows up significantly in our analyses at all.

It is still surprising, though, that higher educated people with more winter months after birth do not like "High-culture music" significantly more than the low educated. And should *younger* respondents with longer winters as newborns not differ more strongly from the older ones in their preference for "Pop music and today's charts" and "Hip Hop & Electronic"?

What could be the reasons for this generally feeble role of music in our study? On the one hand, music as such may not be regarded as *absorbing* enough when it comes to the management of long-term emotional *traits*, as opposed to temporary bad moods (see above—Knobloch, 2003). Stronger stimuli than music may be needed, in this case audio-visual ones. This is probably why several television genres showed results as expected by our general hypothesis whereas music styles simply were treated indifferently.

On the other hand, some genres that our analyses did not reveal as significant as well may be too *strenuous* to be entertaining, too hermetic, not pleasant enough, again even for younger or higher educated people. This definitely seems to apply to "Heavy Metal," rejected by most of our respondents with more winter months soon after birth. And when it comes to "High-culture music" and "Hip Hop & Electronic," all of our respondents with a darker first half year tendentially shy back from liking them.

A cautious conclusion: What many people with more winter months soon after birth instead seem to be interested in is genres that are not only stimulating audio-visually, but also "mainstream," "middle-of-the-road," i.e., accessible—without being too bland, though: The effect of season of birth in one of our segmentations underscores such a compromise. To older winter-borns, "Sports programs" were more attractive than for the youngest respondents, whereas "Family and entertainment series" were less popular among them—not exciting enough anymore after all these years?

To be sure, as in the MENA study (Schoenbach, 2018) replicated here, all relationships we have found are weak in statistical terms. But actually, one should not expect *strong* effects of the climate following one's birth date (see Schoenbach, 2018, and Peiser & Schoenbach, as early as in 1994). First of all, even for the youngest of our respondents, 18 years old, it is long ago. Second, season of birth, of course, is just *one* of the influence factors for our temperament and may be buried under a lot of "noise": for instance, and quite naturally, one's upbringing and education, material life conditions, but also sometimes dramatic turning points in life.

But our analyses could actually also *underestimate* the impact of season of birth—because the study certainly suffers from the typical constraints of a secondary analysis. First of all, we could investigate *indirect* effects of one's climate after birth only. But based on a number of previous studies (see above), season of birth quite plausibly influences one's temperament. Plausible as well is that temperament, in a next step, could have consequences for one's media-content preferences—serving as mood management, even many years later. Second, the impact of one's birth date might show greater effects once its climate conditions could be defined more precisely—e.g., by not only counting the summer or winter months right after birth, but also by using the exact weather of these months at one's exact birthplace.

Of course, one could also think of refining the *dependent* variables of our analysis: For instance, more media genres—and more fine-grained ones—would be useful: Maybe there were no significant effects of season of birth on liking a very general genre such as "Rock music." Respondents may simply be split about what it means: For instance, some of them may call the music of *Deep Purple* not "rock," but suffer from it as already too much "Heavy Metal"—and may therefore not like it. Or "jazz" could mean either its lively and energetic form or a more laid-back and sublime one. Also, other *moderating* conditions could be explored that might strengthen or weaken the relationships between season of birth and interest in specific media offerings: one's media socialization at home, for instance.

Finally, what do our results mean for uses-and-gratifications research in communication studies—i.e., for explaining the purposes people use media content for? First of all, the extension of mood-management theory that was suggested in the MENA study (Schoenbach, 2018) seems to work again: Entertaining media content seems to be preferred not only to compensate for situational and temporary bad moods, but also for more

Klaus Schönbach

structural deficits in cheerfulness and liveliness. For many people, this compensation may need middle-of-the-road media offerings—absorbing, but not too challenging. Lastly, it should be mentioned once again that the relationships investigated here were not intended to finally incorporate notions of astrology—the planets of one's sign of the zodiac—in media-audience research, but to suggest that the impact of one's first experiences in life can shape media preferences.

References

Antonsen, J. H., Gonda, X., Dome, P., & Rihmer, Z. (2013). Associations between seasons of birth and suicide: A brief review. *Neurospsychopharmacologia Hungarica, 14,* 177-187.

Aristotle (about 340 BC/2000). *Nicomachean ethics.* Cambridge, England: Cambridge University Press.

Asano, R. et al., 2016). Season of birth predicts emotional and behavioral regulation in 18-month-old infants: Hamamatsu Birth Cohort for Mothers and Children (HBC study). *Frontiers in Public Health, 4*(152), doi: 10.3389/fpubh.2016.00152

Axt, P., & Axt-Gadermann, M. (2004). *Mai-Frau sucht Dezember-Mann: Wie unser Geburtsmonat Gesundheit, Karriere und Partnerschaft beeinflusst und wie wir diese Chancen nutzen koennen* [May woman in quest of December man: How our month of birth influences health, career and partnership, and how we can use these opportunities]. Munich, Germany: Herbig.

Baumann, H., & Schulz, D. (2015). *ALLBUS 2014: Variable report.* Cologne, Germany: GESIS.

Blanch, A., & Solé, S. (2021). Performance in male and female elite tennis across season of birth. *Chronobiology International, 38,* 851-857.

Bourdieu, P. (1984). *Distinction: A critique of the judgment of taste.* Cambridge, MA: Harvard University Press.

Boxer, A. (2020). *A scheme of heaven: Astrology and the birth of science.* London: Profile Books.

Carpentier, F. R. D. et al. (2008). Sad kids, sad media? Applying mood management theory to depressed adolescents' use of media. *Media Psychology, 11,* 143-166.

Chodick, G. et al. (2009). Seasonality in birth weight: Review of global patterns and potential causes. *Human Biology, 81,* 463-477.

Chotai, J., Joukamaa, M., Taanila, A., Lichtermann, D., & Miettunen, J. (2009). Novelty seeking among adult women is lower for the winter borns compared to the summer borns: Replication in a large Finnish birth cohort. *Comprehensive Psychiatry, 50,* 562-566.

Chotai, J., & Wiseman, R. (2005). Born lucky? The relationship of feeling lucky and month of birth. *Personality and Individual Differences, 39*, 1451-1460.

Cordova-Palomera, A. et al. (2015). Season of birth and subclinical psychosis: Systematic review and meta-analysis of new and existing data. *Psychiatry Research*, DOI:10.1016/j.psychres.2014.11.072

Cortmaker, S. L., Kagan, J., Caspi, A. & Silva, P. (1997). Daylength during pregnancy and shyness in Children: Results from northern and southern hemispheres. *Developmental Psychology, 31*, 107-114.

Day, F. R. et al. (2015). Season of birth is associated with birth weight, pubertal timing, adult body size and educational attainment: A UK Biobank study. *Heliyon, 1*, https://doi.org/10.1016/j.heliyon.2015.e00031

Dhuey, E. et al. (2017). *School starting age and cognitive development. NBER Working Paper* No. 23660. Cambridge, MA: the National Bureau of Economic Research.

Harada, T. et al. (2011). Effect of birth season on circadian typology appearing in Japanese young children aged 2 to 12 years disappears in older students aged 18 to 25 years. *Chronobiology International, 28*, 638-642.

Hemmerich, W. (2017). StatistikGuru: Korrelationen statistisch vergleichen [StatistikGuru: Comparing correlations statistically], https://statistikguru.de/rechner/korrelationen-vergleichen.html

Hori, H., Sasayama, D., Matsuo, J., Kawamoto, Y., Kinoshita, Y., & Kunugi, H. (2012). Relationships between season of birth, schizotypy, temperament, character and neurocognition in a non-clinical population. *Psychiatry Research, 195*, 69-75.

Kahneman, D., Diener, E., & Schwarz, N. (1999). *Well-being: The foundations of hedonic psychology*. New York: Russell Sage Foundation.

Kamata, M., Suzuki, A., Matsumoto, Y., Togashi, H., & Otani, K. (2009). Effect of month of birth on personality traits of healthy Japanese. *European Psychiatry, 24*, 86-90.

Knobloch, S. (2003). Mood adjustment via mass communication. *Journal of Communication, 53*, 233-250.

Knobloch-Westerwick, S. (2006). Mood management theory: Evidence and advancements. In J. Bryant & P. Vorderer (Eds.), *Psychology of entertainment* (pp. 239-254). Mahwah, NJ: Lawrence Erlbaum Associates.

Lee, H., Lee, H-K., & Lee, K. (2021). Is personality linked to season of birth? *PlosOne*, https://doi.org/10.1371/journal.pone.0253815

Lewis, P. et al. (2021). Perinatal photoperiod associations with diabetes and chronotype prevalence in a cross-sectional study of the UK Biobank. *Chronobiology International, 38*, 33-359.

Longo, A. et al. (2017). Association of neovascular age-related macular degeneration with month and season of birth in Italy. *Aging, 9*, 133-141.

Martinez-Bakker, M., Bakker, K. M., King, A. A., & Rohani, P. (2014). Human birth seasonality: Latitudinal gradient and interplay with childhood disease dynamics. *Proceedings of the Royal Society B, 282*, 20132438.

Klaus Schönbach

McMahan, E. A., & Estes, D. (2011). Hedonic versus eudaimonic conceptions of well-being: Evidence of differential associations with experienced well-being. *Social Indicators Research, 103,* 93-108.

Namatovu, F. et al. (2017). Season and region of birth as risk factors for coeliac disease a key to the aetiology? *Archives of Disease in Childhood, 101,* 1114–1118.

Natale, V., & Di Milia, L. (2011). Season of birth and morningness: Comparison between northern and southern hemispheres. *Chronobiology International, 28,* 727-730.

Oliver, M. B., & Raney, A. A. (2011). Entertainment as pleasurable and meaningful: Identifying hedonic and eudaimonic motivations for entertainment consumption. *Journal of Communication, 61,* 984-1004.

Pazderska, A. et al. (2016). Impact of month of birth on the risk of development of autoimmune Adisson's Disease. *The Journal of Clinical Endocrinology & Metabolism, 101,* 4214-4218.

Peiser, W., & Schoenbach, K. (1994). Die Sterne luegen nicht: Sternzeichen und Gemuet [The stars don't lie: Signs of the zodiac and temperament]. *Bild der Wissenschaft,* (6), 70-73.

Roseboom, T. (2018). *De eerste 1000 dagen: Het fundamentele belang van een goed begin vanuit biologisch, medisch en maatschappelijk perspectief* [The first 1000 days: The fundamental importance of a good start from a biological, medical and societal perspective]. Utrecht, The Netherlands: De Tijdstroom.

Rosengren, K. E., & Windahl, S. (1972). Mass media consumption as a functional alternative. In D. McQuail (Ed.), *Sociology of mass communication* (pp. 166-194). Harmondsworth, England: Penguin.

Schnittker, J. (2018). Season of birth and depression in adulthood: Revisiting historical forerunner evidence for in-utero effects. *SSM—Population Health, 4,* 307-316.

Schoenbach, K. (2018). Season of birth and media use. *Communications: The European Journal of Communication, 43,* 535-560.

Uji, T. et al. (2021). Birth month and mortality in Japan: A population based prospective cohort study. *Chronobiology International, 38,* 1023-1031.

Waterman, A. S. (1993). Two conceptions of happiness: Contrasts of personal expressiveness (eudaimonia) and hedonic enjoyment. *Journal of Personality and Social Psychology, 64,* 678-691.

Weber, G. W., Prossinger, H., & Seidler, H. (1998). Height depends on months of birth. *Nature, 391,* 754-755.

Whitaker, J., Velez, J. A., & Knobloch-Westerwick, S. (2012). Mood Management und Selective Exposure in interaktiven Unterhaltungsmedien [Mood management and selective exposure in interactive entertainment media]. In L. Reinecke & S. Trepte (Eds.), *Unterhaltung in neuen Medien [Entertainment in new media]* (pp. 30-47). Cologne, Germany: Halem.

Wonneberger, A., Schoenbach, K, & Meurs, L. van (2009). Dynamics of individual television viewing behavior: Models, empirical evidence, and a research program. *Communication Studies, 60,* 235-252.

How Does One's Season of Birth Influence Television- and Music-Genre Preferences?

Zillmann, D. (1988). Mood management through communication choices. *American Behavioral Scientist, 31*, 327-340.

Zhang, Y. et al. (2019). Birth month, birth season, and overall and cardiovascular disease mortality in US women: Prospective cohort study. *British Medical Journal, 367*, 16058.

***Klaus Schönbach** (Dr. phil, Mainz, 1975) is an Honorary Professor of Zeppelin University, Friedrichshafen, Germany, and an Honorary Fellow of the Amsterdam School of Communication Research, University of Amsterdam, The Netherlands. His research deals with political communication, media audiences, persuasive communication and journalism. He was Wolfram Peiser's doctoral advisor at the Department of Journalism and Communication Research, University of Music, Theater and Media, Hanover, Germany.*

Modes of Authentication

Realism Cues and Media Users' Assessment of Realism Across Media and Genres

Felix Frey, Benjamin Krämer & Wolfram Peiser[1]

Abstract

Media users' perception of the correspondence of media content to reality has significant consequences for media use and effects. At the same time, new media environments have been complicating the users' task of judging the realism of media information. Against that background, our study addresses the cues and criteria on which media users base their realism assessments using an online survey of a diverse population. Based on our respondents' assessments of a broad spectrum of realism cues, we first identify fundamental criteria underlying users' realism judgments across media and media genres. Second, using cluster analysis, we identify homogenous groups of users based on the criteria they perceive as enhancing or reducing media realism. And third, we investigate how these perception

---

1 This article aims to reconstruct what was, to our knowledge, the only presentation at a major conference that Wolfram Peiser submitted and prepared together with researchers at his chair at LMU Munich. The study was presented on 29 May 2017 at the annual conference of the International Communication Association in San Diego by Felix Frey and Benjamin Krämer and is based on a study conducted in a master seminar the authors taught in 2015 to 2016 (we would like to thank the students for their contributions to the conceptual discussion, the development of the measurements, and the realization of the study). We planned to publish the contribution in the form of a journal article but unfortunately never elaborated a full text before Wolfram Peiser passed away.

The present contribution is based on an extended abstract submitted for review for the conference as well as the slides and notes for the presentation. It therefore mostly reflects the state of research and of our scholarship at that time. However, we think that the theoretical framework and empirical findings are more relevant than ever today. In the main text, we mostly rely on literature that had been published before the study was conducted. Where it seems necessary or interesting, we add remarks based on more current developments in our footnotes. We present the results in a more elaborate way than it had been possible in the original presentation and have therefore conducted further analyses.

Modes of Authentication

patterns relate to users' realism assessments and use of various media and genres, media skepticism, and sociodemographic variables.

Media trust recently has reached a new low in the U.S. (Swift, 2016); and in Europe, media skeptics are voicing their hostility towards 'mainstream media' more aggressively than before (Haller, 2015).[2] One of the reasons for this "credibility crisis" (Carr, Barnidge, Lee, & Tsang, 2014, p. 453) is the perception among a part of the population that reality is not reflected accurately by ('mainstream') media portrayals. The perceived relationship of media content to reality has been the object of communication research under various terms and in various contexts, such as perceived media bias (e.g., Eveland & Shah, 2003), perceived realism (e.g., Busselle & Greenberg, 2000; Hall, 2009), (media) authenticity (e.g., Duffy, 2013; Enli, 2015), source, message, or media credibility (e.g., Metzger, Flanagin, Eyal, Lemus, & McCann, 2003; Self, 1996), media trust (e.g., Gunther, 1988), media skepticism (e.g., Tsfati & Peri, 2006), and the hostile media phenomenon (e.g., Vallone, Ross, & Lepper, 1995).[3] Integrating some of these terms, Austin defines "apparent reality assessments" of media users as the "degree to which an individual believes media portrayals of issues or people reflect reality" (Austin & Dong, 1994, p. 974). These apparent reality or realism assessments of media users can be assumed to have significant consequences for media use and media effects (Tsfati & Ariely, 2014;

---

2 Since the time of the presentation, trends in media trust in different countries have been discussed extensively, sometimes complicating the picture with regard to the conceptual and empirical aspects of media trust, but mostly leading to the same diagnosis that a substantial but not overwhelming part of the population in Western democracies distrusts the media (see Fawzi et al., 2021, for a recent overview of research on media trust). Since then, skepticism or hostility toward the media has also often been treated in the context of populism (e.g., Fazwi, 2019). However, we think that it would still be wise to broaden the perspective and to consider a multitude of judgments concerning the realism of media content and a wide variety of potential factors.

3 Today, we would add that research often refers to the catchwords of "fake news" or "disinformation" not only as labels for substantial phenomena but also as categories with which politicians, other communicators, and users express their skepticism or radical distrust toward certain categories of media outlets (not always clearly with regard to the correctness of claims proper but all kinds of concerns and accusations regarding alleged biases and manipulations); for example, see Egelhofer and Lecheler (2018) on these two perspectives on "fake news" as genre and label. However, again, we think that the analysis of such discourses or attitudes should be complemented by studies with a wider focus on different kinds of perceptions of media content in terms of their realism.

Carr et al., 2014, p. 455). At the same time, the task of judging the realism of media information has become more challenging for users, since new media environments with new types of information providers outside of professional journalism, the convergence of media and hybridization of genres, and digital editing technologies have been complicating the users' task of judging the realism of media information (Metzger, Flanagin, Eyal, Lemus, & McCann, 2003). Against that background, one important question concerns the cues and criteria on which media users base their realism assessments. Building on existing research in this field, our study aims at, first, empirically investigating how various established or proposed "authenticity markers" (Dickerson, 2012) and realism criteria across various media and genres relate to each other and, second, whether media users can be differentiated based on to their preference and reliance on certain realism criteria and disregard of others. We thus investigate the diversity of realism assessments and criteria, going beyond the most ideology-driven and hostile distrust and thereby aim to contribute to a broader picture of judgments of realism that is relevant to media practitioners and audience researchers alike and that can inform public debates that often focus on the most extreme accusations of untruthfulness toward the media.

Conceptions of Media Realism

How media content relates to reality can be captured by a number of concepts that are not always clearly defined and demarcated, such as truth, truthfulness, realism, plausibility, credibility, authenticity, and others.

There is of course no scholarly consensus on what constitutes truth (see, e.g., Glanzberg, 2018, for different theories). We may assume that for most media users, truth will probably mean that individual factual claims are correct or correspond to reality or that one has good reasons (such as arguments or evidence) to believe them. However, we prefer the broader concept of realism over that of truth proper.[4] Realism can encompass a wider variety of judgements that we assume recipients do not always

---

4 Of course, like truth, "realism" has various meanings. We do not refer to the meaning usually implied in philosophy, i.e., the existence of certain entities, properties, or facts independently of statements or the mind (see, e.g., Brock & Mares, 2007). What we have in mind is closer to the everyday understanding of something being realistic or to artistic or literary realism: a fit with reality that does not necessarily amount to factual truth proper in every aspect (see, e.g., Morris, 2004, for a discussion of different meanings and literary realism in particular).

clearly distinguish or that, taken together, contribute to their overall idea of how media content relates to reality.

To begin with, something can be "realistic" in someone's eye even if they are not sure whether the claim is literally and positively true. It may be plausible or credible based on certain preexisting knowledge or certain cues, or because a communicator is sufficiently trustworthy. It may be somewhat speculative or difficult to verify but reasonable. "Realistic" representations may also paint the broader picture recipients expect them to, i.e., select or highlight the aspects that they consider most relevant, reflect a broader worldview of "how things really are," or strike the right sober tone. All of these types of criteria and judgements matter in particular with regard to media reception because users are most often unable to establish the correctness of a claim in a way that they would consider necessary in other contexts to judge something as true in the strictest sense (such as direct observation, personal expertise or experience, or access to reliable primary data or documents). This is one of the aspects where relying on the media is most often a matter of trust, not independent verification.[5]

Certain aspects of our conception of realism are also often captured by different understandings of authenticity. First, it sometimes stands for the uncompromised transmission of information or meaning. Here, the focus is less on the representation of certain facts but on the absence of manipulation or compromising influences along a chain of communication that usually originates with an authoritative source (Lethen, 1995).[6] Second, authenticity is often understood as the preservation, realization, or expression of some positive essence, either of an aspect of culture or a person (although such essentialism has often been deconstructed and criticized, see, e.g., Ferrara, 2009; Handler, 1986). In this sense, the media

---

5 This is a point in our argument where it is or used to be customary in parts of German communication research to cite Luhmann's (2000, p. 1) dictum "Whatever we know about our society, or indeed about the world in which we live, we know through the mass media. [...] On the other hand, we know so much about the mass media that we are not able to trust these sources."

6 While many today are still concerned with the faithful transmission of the statements by political or epistemic authorities, citing, for example, ideological biases, sensationalism, foreign propaganda, or digital manipulation of source material as dangers to authentic news, this is exactly what others fear: the media as a mouthpiece of the elites, not of ordinary people with their everyday experience and concerns. While the discussion of the second, "populist" criticism of the media's authenticity has received increasing attention over time, we should not underestimate the demand in the population for what people consider "reliable" media (whatever this sometimes naive realism implies in each case).

Felix Frey, Benjamin Krämer & Wolfram Peiser

can "keep it real" in the eyes of their audience with its cultural standards of authenticity, for example, by focusing on ordinary life and people instead of things or people that are seen as fake, staged, corrupted, or out of touch. Third, authenticity can be defined as truthfulness or sincerity in communication. What is expressed is actually believed or felt, and presented without any hidden motives or agenda.[7]

Based on these general ideas of realism as plausibility or authenticity, we can then turn to the more specific criteria recipients may to determine how "real" media content is and review previous findings on the effects of such cues.

Realism Assessments by Users

Several characteristics of the source or the message have been proposed or empirically demonstrated to affect users' realism assessments. One group of 'immanent' factors are characteristics of the source or the media message, which also can be employed strategically by communicators. First, professional news journalism traditionally features figures and statistics (Koetsenruijter, 2011), experts as sources (Steele, 1995), or direct quotes (Sundar, 1998) to authenticate news reports. These cues convey the impression that a report is based on solid evidence or close observation of events. Second, rendering content production more transparent by disclosing sources and detailing the process of information acquisition has been suggested to further credibility (e.g., Chadha & Koliska, 2015; Gilpin, Palazzolo, & Brody, 2010; Karlsson, Clerwall, & Nord, 2014). The idea behind such attempts is to counter the idea of compromising influences or manipulation, and to convey an idea that the process of content production is thorough and reliable. Similarly, live on-the-scene reporting (Scannell, 1996), undercover reporting, and no or only limited editing of footage attests to the immediacy and fidelity of a media representation to reality and therefore might result in assessments of content as more rea-

---

7   However, some authors differentiate between sincerity or truthfulness and authenticity (Trilling, 1971). Habermas (1987) defines truthfulness as one aspect of his concept of communicative action—the claim implied in many utterances that one expresses what one actually thinks, feels, believes to be true or morally right etc., and that one does not pursue different, hidden aims other than the one to make others understand and rationally accept one's explicit claims. Relatedly, but with an emphasis on form instead of content, he reserves "authenticity" for the accomplished expression of experiences that makes them relatable.

Modes of Authentication

listic (Enli, 2015). Third, media skeptics ascribe more credibility to citizen journalism than to professional journalism (Carr et al., 2014). Therefore, contributions from 'ordinary people' could also enhance perceived social realism of media content. Similarly, reducing social distance between the media and its public by featuring 'real', 'ordinary' people in the media, or allowing reporters, presenters, journalists or hosts to present themselves as ordinary, feeling human beings might also further realism (Coleman & Moss, 2008; Coupland, 2001; Duffy, 2013; Enli, 2015, p. 137).

In addition, users draw on external information to judge the realism of a message. First, messages diverging from the user's own opinion are perceived to be less credible and biased against the user's opinion (Metzger et al., 2003). Second, discrepancies between media portrayals and information from friends or acquaintances perceived as similar (Eveland & Shah, 2003) or from other users' online comments (Lee, 2012) might impair perceived realism. Third, the consonance of a message with 'mainstream' or 'alternative' media, respectively, influences realism assessments (Tsfati & Peri, 2006). Whereas certain media users trust established institutions such as legacy media outlets, others are receptive to the claims of alternative media as a corrective, supplement, or substitute to these outlets. Both sides can then distinguish themselves by being "critical" and thus more "realist" because they are not gullible either to the disinformation of fringe outlets or the affirmative portrayals by the naive or corrupt mainstream media.

Whereas the effects of many of these realism cues—examined in isolation—are empirically established, their relationship to each other remains unclear since most of the relevant studies used experimental designs and included only a small number of factors at a time. Also, the question of whether and how users differ in the criteria on which they base their realism assessments on has received little scholarly attention. Finally, important strands of empirical research (e.g., research on perceived realism) focus on fictional content, hampering the generalizability of their results to media as a whole, and to nonfictional, journalistic information in particular.

We therefore lack an inter-individual, cross-category (in terms of the types of cues), cross-media, cross-genre perspective on realism judgements. Our study therefore aims to fill these gaps using an online survey to investigate three research questions:

> RQ1: Which fundamental criteria underlying users' realism judgments across media and media genres can be identified based on their assessments of realism cues?

Felix Frey, Benjamin Krämer & Wolfram Peiser

RQ2a: Are there groups of users differing in the criteria they perceive as enhancing or reducing media realism?

RQ2b: How do these perception patterns relate to the respective users' realism assessments and use of various media and genres, their media skepticism, and sociodemographic and personality variables?

Method

Data was collected from a quota sample among members of a convenience online access panel (Leiner, 2012) using a standardized online questionnaire. For 17 message characteristics and external cues discussed above, participants were asked how much they perceive them to enhance the realism of media content, answering two questions („Please indicate whether the following features enhance or reduce a media portrayal's realism [German: "Wirklichkeitsnähe"] in your personal view" for 10 cues, and „To what extent do the following situations make you skeptical with regard to the accuracy of a media report's portrayal of reality?" for 7 cues). In addition, data on perceived realism of the media in general, specific media, and media genres (question: „How close do media portrayals in general/in genre XY approximate reality in your personal view?"), news media skepticism (4 items, α = .81, e. g., „News coverage serves the interests of the Big Boys and the powerful in politics, economy and society"), participants' media use (print newspapers, TV in general and various genres, Internet in general and online newspapers, social media, and blogs), the personality traits neuroticism (Satow, 2012; 4 items, α = .81), conscientiousness (Satow, 2012; 4 items, α = .73), and ambiguity tolerance (Radant & Dalbert, 2003; 4 items, α = .69), and sociodemographic variables (age, education, gender) was collected. A quota sample was used to ensure sufficient demographic heterogeneity. A total of 928 German, Austrian and Swiss respondents completed the survey at least partially (response rate: 24.4 %). 53 cases were removed due to implausibly short completion times (< 5 minutes total), high overall item non-response rate (> 15%), missing data in the realism cue variables used for factor and cluster analyses or because they were detected to be multivariate outliers (n = 4). The resulting sample used in the following analyses (N = 875) was 50,1 percent female with age ranging from 18 to 86 (M = 42.4, SD = 14.6). 57.1 percent of the respondents had a university entrance diploma.

Table 1: Factor Analysis of Realism Cue Items

Items	Evidence	Coherence	Common sense	Intra-media congruence	No human interference
Enhances realism (ER), when information is substantiated with figures and statistics.	**.70**				
ER when sources & information acquisition process are indicated.	**.57**				.23
ER when direct quotations are used.	**.54**				
ER when expert sources are cited/shown.	**.52**				
ER when reporters/journalists are reporting directly from the scene.	**.44**		.29	− .23	
Become skeptical (BS), when friends evaluate the topic differently than the report.		**.64**			
BS when user comments on the Internet contradict the report.		**.48**			
BS when voices outside established media (e.g., activists, bloggers, advocacy groups) advocate otherwise.		**.46**			
BS when media content contradicts my personal opinion.		**.46**			− .20
ER when photos or video footage created by ordinary citizens is used (e.g., cell phone camera).			**.61**		
ER when those affected or ordinary citizens have their say.			**.60**		
BS when created not by professional journalists but by ordinary citizens.	.32	.29	**− .44**		
ER when media content relies on undercover research.	.28		**.29**		
BS when the media content deviates from what many other media report.		.37		**.35**	
BS when topic is presented in much the same way by most of the media.		.23		**− .64**	
ER when media content is recognizably edited (e.g., background comments, cuts) or are prerecorded (not live).					**− .54**
ER when reporters/journalists react emotionally to extraordinary events.			.28		**− .39**
Variance explained:	13.6 %	8.7 %	6.4 %	3.6 %	3.5 %

Notes. Pattern coefficients for PFA w. direct oblimin rotation. Total variance explained: 35.8 %. KMO = .73, N = 875.

Results

To identify broader criteria underlying users' realism assessments (RQ1), a principal factor analysis with direct oblimin rotation on the 17 realism factor evaluations was used (see Table 1 for detailed results).

Horn's parallel analysis, Kaiser criterion and scree plot suggested a solution with five factors explaining 36.0 percent of total variance. The first factor, 'Evidence', comprises five items measuring users' perceived contribution of figures and statistics, quotes, expert sources, disclosure of sources and the information acquisition process, and on-the-scene-reporting. The second factor, 'Coherence', includes four items concerning the consistency of media content with the users' own opinion, knowledge and experiences, and with opinions expressed by friends and acquaintances, in online user comments, and alternative media (blogs, activists, interest groups). The third factor, 'common sense', is described by items measuring the perceived authenticating impact of including footage, statements or entire reports authored by 'ordinary people'. Two items measuring the impact of perceived consonance of a media message with messages from other media characterize the fourth factor, labeled 'inter-media congruency'. And the fifth factor, labeled 'No human interference', includes two items measuring the effect of noticeable editing and emotional commenting (by journalists) on perceived realism of media content. This factor and the factor 'Evidence' are the only two factors correlated more strongly than $r = .20$.

To identify groups of users using similar criteria for assessing realism (RQ2a), we applied k-means clustering using squared Euclidean distances to the same set of 17 items. Indices for determining the optimal number of clusters implemented in the R-Package NbClust (Charrad, Ghazzali, Boiteau & Niknafs, 2014) suggested optimal cluster numbers of 3 (proposed by 9 indices), 5 (4), 6 (4) or 3 (3) clusters; we selected the 6 cluster solution because it allowed the most plausible and productive interpretation of the groups (see Figure 1 for an overview).

Fig. 1 Average z-scores for cluster items per cluster

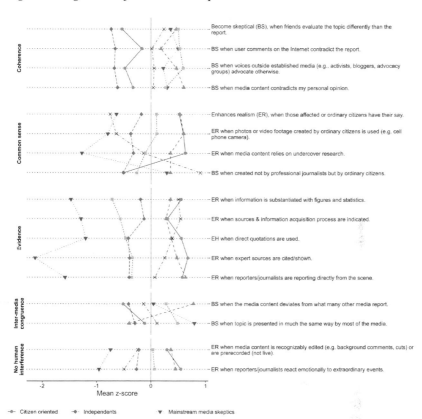

Then, we explored whether these six clusters differed in various other respects, most importantly their realism assessments and use of various media and genres, media skepticism, and sociodemographic and personality variables (RQ2b). In the following, we describe the six clusters based on results of both analyses combined; in the case of the context variables, only variables significantly differing between the clusters (see Table 2) are discussed.

Table 2: Significant Differences Between Clusters in Socio-Demographic and Personality Characteristics, Realism Assessments, and Media Use

	MMA		PJO		CO		MMS		CS		IN		χ^2	df	p	N	V
Socio-demographics & traits	%		%		%		%		%		%						
Gender (percentage female)	59.5		49.1		49.0		32.6		48.3		49.4		20.88	10	.020	874	.11
	M	SD	M	SD	M	SD	M	SD	M	SD	M	SD	F^1	df_2	p	N	ω^2
Media skepticism	3.3	0.8	3.0	0.8	3.3	0.8	4.0	0.8	3.7	0.7	3.2	0.8	21.87	280.2	<.001	875	.107
Education (years)	12.1	3.1	14.4	2.7	13.0	3.2	11.6	2.8	12.0	2.9	13.5	3.2	18.37	276.5	<.001	856	.092
Positive attitude asylum & refugees	4.5	1.7	5.3	1.6	4.8	1.7	3.4	2.0	4.1	1.8	4.6	1.7	13.01	277.7	<.001	873	.064
Age (years)	45.9	16.3	39.7	14.5	45.8	14.7	39.1	13.8	42.1	13.6	40.0	12.8	5.95	281.0	<.001	871	.028
Ambiguity tolerance	-0.2	0.9	0.2	0.8	0.1	0.8	0.3	0.9	-0.2	0.8	0.1	0.9	5.88	265.8	<.001	858	.028
Involvement creation of media content	1.9	1.1	2.1	1.2	2.2	1.4	2.3	1.3	1.8	1.1	1.9	1.2	2.79	275.0	.018	874	.010
Media realism assessments & expectations																	
Realism: news public TV	4.1	0.8	4.0	0.8	4.0	0.8	2.5	0.9	3.3	0.8	3.8	0.8	34.08	279.2	<.001	875	.159
Realism: informational content general	3.6	0.7	3.6	0.7	3.6	0.6	2.6	0.8	3.0	0.6	3.4	0.7	26.95	277.9	<.001	874	.129
Realism: political TV news magazines	3.8	0.8	3.6	0.8	3.9	0.7	2.5	1.0	3.2	0.8	3.5	0.8	25.09	276.7	<.001	871	.121
Realism: online quality newspapers	3.5	1.0	3.5	0.8	3.6	0.9	2.3	0.8	2.9	0.8	3.4	0.7	24.01	274.9	<.001	865	.117
Realism: political TV features & documentaries	3.8	0.7	3.7	0.7	3.8	0.7	2.6	0.9	3.2	0.8	3.5	0.8	23.94	273.5	<.001	868	.117
Realism: media content (general)	3.2	0.7	3.0	0.8	3.3	0.8	2.3	0.8	2.7	0.7	2.9	0.7	22.05	279.4	<.001	874	.107
Realism: print newspapers	3.7	0.8	3.6	0.7	3.6	0.7	2.7	0.9	3.1	0.8	3.5	0.7	21.65	278.0	<.001	871	.106
Realism: news commercial TV	3.3	0.8	2.7	0.9	3.1	1.0	2.0	0.8	2.8	0.8	2.9	0.8	19.58	281.4	<.001	874	.096
Realism: TV (general)	3.2	0.8	2.8	0.7	3.1	0.8	2.1	0.8	2.6	0.7	2.8	0.8	18.50	274.4	<.001	867	.092
Realism: TV crime drama/series	2.2	0.8	1.9	0.7	2.3	0.8	1.7	0.9	1.9	0.8	1.8	0.6	10.34	276.5	<.001	874	.051
Realism: TV casting shows	1.5	0.7	1.2	0.5	1.5	0.7	1.1	0.4	1.5	0.7	1.3	0.6	8.46	297.9	<.001	870	.041

Modes of Authentication

	MMA		PJO		CO		MMS		CS		IN						
Realism: online tabloid newspapers	2.3	0.9	1.9	0.8	2.2	0.8	1.7	0.8	2.1	0.8	2.0	0.7	7.05	280.0	<.001	869	.034
Realism: social networks	2.3	0.9	1.9	0.7	2.4	0.9	2.0	0.9	2.3	0.8	2.1	0.8	6.39	272.6	<.001	859	.030
Realism: TV soap operas	1.6	0.8	1.3	0.5	1.6	0.9	1.2	0.5	1.4	0.8	1.4	0.6	6.40	285.2	<.001	871	.030
Realism: reality TV	1.4	0.7	1.2	0.4	1.4	0.7	1.1	0.4	1.4	0.7	1.2	0.5	5.60	289.0	<.001	871	.026
Expectations realism of informational content	4.4	0.6	4.5	0.6	4.4	0.6	4.4	0.6	4.3	0.7	4.2	0.7	4.38	283.3	.001	873	.019
Realism: TV news satire/comedy	2.9	1.1	3.1	1.1	3.0	1.1	2.7	1.4	2.6	1.0	2.8	1.0	4.34	276.2	.001	872	.019
Expectations realism of media content (general)	4.1	0.8	4.2	0.8	4.3	0.7	4.3	0.8	4.1	0.8	4.0	0.8	3.32	282.8	.006	875	.013
Realism: blogs	2.6	1.0	2.5	0.8	2.7	1.0	2.2	1.0	2.6	0.9	2.6	0.8	2.48	270.4	.032	851	.009
Media consumption (days/week)																	
Commercial news broadcasts	2.4	2.3	1.3	1.5	1.8	2.0	2.2	2.3	2.3	2.2	1.7	1.9	8.01	276.5	<.001	869	.039
Online quality newspaper	1.8	2.5	2.6	2.6	2.2	2.7	2.1	2.7	1.3	2.2	2.2	2.7	5.73	275.3	.001	871	.026
TV casting shows	0.8	0.8	0.6	0.3	0.7	0.4	0.6	0.4	0.7	0.5	0.7	0.5	4.09	281.8	.001	868	.017
TV soap operas	1.4	1.8	0.8	1.0	0.9	1.1	0.8	0.8	0.8	0.9	0.9	1.2	3.65	289.9	.003	871	.015
TV crime drama/series	2.2	1.8	1.5	1.2	1.7	1.5	1.9	1.9	1.7	1.6	1.7	1.4	3.31	272.3	.006	870	.013
Public news broadcast	4.1	2.4	4.0	2.4	3.8	2.4	3.0	2.4	3.3	2.4	3.6	2.5	3.09	282.3	.010	874	.012
Print newspapers	3.1	2.8	2.0	2.6	2.8	2.8	2.2	2.3	2.4	2.6	2.4	2.7	2.80	276.6	.017	869	.010
TV general	5.2	2.4	4.2	2.8	4.7	2.6	4.9	2.7	4.6	2.6	4.5	2.6	2.75	280.5	.019	872	.010
Internet general	6.2	1.7	6.7	1.0	6.7	1.1	6.7	1.1	6.5	1.4	6.6	1.0	2.71	281.3	.021	874	.010
Reality TV	0.7	0.8	0.5	0.2	0.6	0.6	0.7	0.9	0.7	0.7	0.6	0.5	2.55	259.8	.028	868	.009
Online tabloid newspapers	1.1	1.9	0.7	1.7	1.0	2.0	1.3	2.2	1.3	2.2	1.1	2.0	2.44	278.7	.035	871	.008

Notes. [1] Welch tests, $df_1 = 5$, variables sorted by effect size. Results for 13 variables with no significant group differences are not reported.

Felix Frey, Benjamin Krämer & Wolfram Peiser

Mainstream Media Audience (MMA, 18.6 %)

A first group of users, representing 18.6 percent of the sample, is overall characterized by a rather favorable evaluation of most of the realism criteria surveyed and a lack of extreme preferences or aversions. These people become somewhat, but not too skeptical about the realism of a media message when friends, user comments on the Internet, voices outside the media and, above all, they themselves evaluate or present a topic differently than the message (factor "Coherence"). Also, they perceive realism to increase to a certain degree, when persons affected by the respective issue or ordinary citizens have their say, when picture or video footage created by citizens is used, and when undercover research was involved; however, they perceive it as a risk to realism if content was produced entirely by laypeople, not by professional journalists (factor "Common sense"). In addition, the traditional means of verification and authentication in journalism, i.e., the presentation of statistics and figures, quotes and experts, the transparency of sources and the research process, or (most clearly) reporting directly from the scene of an event (factor "Evidence"), also increase the realism of an article; other user groups, however, attribute a stronger influence on their realism assessment to these means. They rate editing contributions as less damaging to realism than all other groups and emotional reactions from reporters as more enhancing to realism than most other groups except for the citizen oriented (see below, factor "No human interference"). The most marked difference compared to the other groups is the perceived detrimental effect of incongruent presentations across different media on the realism assessment of these persons: If a message presents a topic differently than many or most other media, this group of people becomes more skeptical with regard to the realism of this message than all other groups. In sum, individuals in this group are (mildly) sympathetic to both the established means of authentication in journalism and the representation and participation of lay people in the creation of media content; the greatest threat to the assessment of a media message as "realistic" comes from incongruence—in different media or between the media representation and one's own opinion. Both because of their favorable and non-extreme assessments of realism criteria and their compatibility with the conventional means of presentation in traditional mass media, we propose to call this group the mainstream media users.

Apart from the realism criteria used for clustering, this group is characterized by the highest percentage of female users (59.5%), the highest average age (M = 45.9 years) and a medium education (M = 12.1 years). In terms of media skepticism, this group ranks in the middle between the other groups, but in comparison gives the highest realism ratings for many categories of media content surveyed. Specifically, this applies to the realism of media content in general and informational content in general, to TV in general, news broadcasts in public and commercial TV, political TV features/documentaries, TV casting shows, TV soap operas, reality TV, print newspapers, and online tabloid newspapers, the latter few categories suggesting overall a certain leaning toward popular media and especially television formats. This leaning also manifests itself in the pattern of media consumption of the mainstream media users: They are the most frequent users of TV in general, commercial news broadcasts, TV casting shows, reality TV, TV soap operas, TV crime dramas/series, and print newspapers, but second to last in the frequency of online quality newspaper consumption. In general, across genres and groups, we can observe significant weak or moderate positive correlations between realism ratings and frequency of consumption. Finally, this group is on average the least ambiguity-tolerant among the six clusters, explaining the negative effect of incongruent representations on realism judgments.

Professional Journalism Objectivists (PJO, 18.6%)

A second group, similar to the mainstream media audience, is characterized by a favorable assessment of the classic authentication strategies of journalism ("Evidence"); unlike the MMA, however, this applies in particular to "hard" evidence in the form of figures/statistics and the transparency of sources and the research process. Regarding the perceived effect of congruence in representations and evaluations on the realism assessment, this group lies in the average of the six groups: The congruence of a media portrayal with the portrayal or evaluation of the same topic by friends, user comments on the Internet, voices outside the media and one's own opinion, as well as with other media, are neither perceived as particularly beneficial nor particularly detrimental to realism. The most distinguishing characteristic of this group of people, however, is their high regard for professionalism in the production of "realistic" media content: Compared to the other groups, the participation or contributions of lay people in the production of media content are perceived as most clearly detrimental to realism. This is matched by the second most pronounced disapproval of human intervention in the form of recognizable editing of material or emotional involvement on the part of reporters or moderators. Due to the emphasis on professionalism and objectivity in ensuring the realism of media content, we refer to this group as *professional journalism objectivists*.

Felix Frey, Benjamin Krämer & Wolfram Peiser

In terms of contextual variables, PJOs are on average the least media-skeptical among the six groups, have the highest level of education (*M* = 14.4 years), the second lowest average age (*M* = 39.7 years), and the most positive attitudes toward asylum and refugees. While they have the highest expectations for the realism of informational content among the six clusters, they make a clear distinction between informative and pseudo-informative content and between high-quality and lower-quality outlets when evaluating the realism of different genres: PJOs rate the realism of informational content in general, online quality newspapers, print newspapers, political TV features, public news broadcasts, and TV news satire shows higher than all or most of the other groups, but have fairly low or even the lowest ratings of the realism of news in commercial TV, TV casting shows, online tabloids, social networks, TV soap operas, and reality TV shows. Their media repertoire reflects these evaluations in conjunction with a greater openness to online media compared to the MMA: PJOs use online quality newspapers, public television newscasts, and the internet in general more frequently than most or all of the other groups, but are generally well below all or most other groups in the mean frequency of commercial television newscast, online tabloid, general TV, TV casting show, TV soap opera, TV crime drama show, reality TV, and also print newspaper use.

Citizen Oriented (CO, 17.7 %)

Like the two groups described above, a third group of media users perceives traditional journalistic means of authentication as enhancing realism, in the case of the use of direct quotations and the inclusion of experts even to the greatest extent compared to the other groups ("Evidence"). In contrast, this group rates discrepancies in the portrayal or evaluations of a topic between some media representation and other sources (including other media representations) as significantly less damaging to the perceived realism of that representation than MMAs, PJOs and indeed all but one group ("Coherence", "Inter-media congruence"). Even more clearly positive than MMAs (and all six groups on average) and in marked contrast to PJOs, this group of people evaluates the contribution of laypersons to media content: Contributions like viewpoints, opinions, pictures and videos, but also the production of entire articles by non-professional persons, increase their assessed realism significantly more in the perception of these persons than in the perception of the other groups ("Common sense"). In line with this appreciation of non-professional contributions, this group of people also shows the most positive assessment of the effect of subsequent editing and emotional reactions by moderators or reporters on realism. Because of these perceived positive effects of the "human factor" and especially contributions by "ordinary" citizens on the realism of media portrayals, we refer to this group as the *citizen oriented*.

In terms of sociodemographic variables and realism assessments, citizen-oriented users are very similar to MMAs: they are on average the oldest (M = 45.8 years), slightly more educated, but more balanced in gender than the MMA group. They are neither particularly media skeptical nor particularly trusting compared to the other groups, and have very favorable and sometimes the highest realism ratings for media in general and many genres. In terms of media use, however, the citizen oriented fall between the MMA and the PJO groups: Apart from a more frequent use of online quality newspapers and the Internet in general, they use media less overall and with a somewhat greater distance from television in general and popular TV formats in particular than the MMA.

Mainstream Media Skeptics (MMS, 4.9%)

While the three groups of media users just described rate the classic journalistic means of authentication above average, the other three groups believe that these means do not increase the realism of media content. One group in particular even sees them as reducing realism, with the role of experts being rated as the most detrimental to realism. Statistics, transparency of the research process, quotes and live reporting from the crime scene are also most clearly rejected in a comparison of all groups ("Evidence"). Although less extreme, but in comparison still most strongly among the six groups, this group regards both the presence of human actors ("No human interference") and contributions by laypersons ("Common sense"), as reducing realism. Finally, this group of media users also evaluates it more critically than average if a media representation deviates from representations and evaluations in other sources, including the personal views of friends, comments by Internet users and the users themselves ("Coherence", "Intermedia congruence"). However, with the exception of the most critical attitude toward uniform portrayals of an issue in most media, these ratings are not the most negative among the six groups. Because of the extremely skeptical attitude towards the means of authentication used by traditional news journalism, we refer to this group as the *mainstream media skeptics* (MMS).

Felix Frey, Benjamin Krämer & Wolfram Peiser

The mainstream media skeptics are on average the least educated (M = 11.6 years), youngest (M = 39.1 years), most male (67.4 %), and most media skeptic among the six groups and also report the least positive attitude towards asylum and refugees. This group consistently has lowest average realism ratings of all groups, not only for media content and information content in general, but also for virtually all more specific media genres surveyed. Only the content of social networks is perceived as slightly less realistic by the PJOs. Tellingly, MMSs rate TV satire/comedy shows as the most realistic among all genres surveyed, on par with print newspapers.

However, the media use of the MMS seems to be decoupled from their realism ratings to some extent: While the lowest realism scores of all six groups go hand in hand with the lowest usage frequencies for public news broadcasts and print newspapers (PJOs use print newspapers even less frequently but use them online instead), and low consumption of TV casting shows and soap operas is on par with other groups, MMS do not use commercial news programs, online quality newspapers, TV crime shows and reality TV shows the least frequently of the six groups. Online tabloids and TV in general, which MMS also perceive as very unrealistic, are even used more frequently than by almost all other groups.

Coherence-Seekers (CS, 19.8%)

Like the MMSs, a fifth group of media users also considers the classic journalistic means of authentication to be below average in terms of realism compared to the other groups ("Evidence") and is in the average of all six groups when evaluating the effect of human intervention and non-professional contributions ("Common sense") on the realism of media content. However, this group attributes clearly above-average positive effects on realism to the congruence of media portrayals with portrayals and evaluations by other sources such as friends, user comments on the Internet, voices outside the established media, other media and their own opinions ("Coherence", "Inter-media congruence"). Therefore, we refer to this group of media users as *coherence seekers* (CS).

In terms of their sociodemographic and personality characteristics as well as realism assessments, Coherence Seekers are the less extreme neighbors of MMSs: They are second to last when it comes to education (M = 12.0 years), share of women (48.3 %), media skepticism and (positive) attitude towards asylum and refugees. Also, their negative assessment of the realism of media content in general, informational content in general, TV in general, and print newspapers, political TV documentaries, political TV news magazines, online quality newspapers, and public news broadcasts is exceeded only by MMS, commercial news broadcasts are also rated more negatively only by one group, the PJOs. And their realism ratings of TV news satire programs are actually the lowest of all six groups. In contrast, the CS's realism ratings of TV casting shows and reality TV shows are (among) the highest of all six groups. The coherence seekers' media use is quite average, with a few exceptions: They are (among) the most avid users of commercial news broadcasts, reality TV shows, and online tabloids. And consistent with their respective realism ratings, they use public newscasts only slightly more often than the MMSs and online quality newspapers least often of all groups.

Independents (IN, 20.3%)

Finally, a sixth group of media users shows below-average appreciation for all of the realism criteria examined, acting as a negative counterbalance to the MMAs' mildly benevolent ratings. However, this group particularly clearly rejects being negatively impressed in their realism judgment by a media portrayal not matching other portrayals and opinions—those of friends, user comments, other media or voices outside established media, or their own opinion ("Coherence", "Inter-media congruence"). Especially in view of the further characteristics of the cluster members (see below) it seems plausible to interpret this cluster as a group of people who do not believe or want their realism assessments to be dependent on some rather superficial characteristics of the report. A more far-reaching interpretation could be that these people are generally skeptical of the idea of the "one" reality or truth, which is why they are not particularly impressed by contradictory portrayals or evaluations of the same topic. This is why we refer to this group as the *independents*; somewhat more boldly, we could also call them constructivists or (epistemic) relativists.

In their other characteristics, Independents are very similar to the group of PJOs: They are among the least skeptical of the media, the second most educated, relatively positive about asylum and refugees, and comparatively young (M = 40.0 years). The pattern of reality assessments is also quite similar to that of the PJOs, but somewhat less pronounced: Their realism ratings are medium to high, with positive assessments especially for quality journalistic offerings and rather negative ones for popular entertainment formats. Interestingly, they have the lowest realism expectations for media content in general and information content, which supports our interpretation of their realism criteria above. The pattern of their media use is

Felix Frey, Benjamin Krämer & Wolfram Peiser

also similar to that of the PJO, but with less extreme swings: They keep a certain distance from commercial news broadcasts and television in general and are relatively Internet-savvy. For example, they use printed newspapers comparatively rarely, but online quality newspapers second most frequently among the six groups.

Conclusion

In sum, our study's original contribution to the field are the identification of (a) five rather independent criteria which media users apply to assess the apparent realism of media content (Coherence, Common sense, Evidence, Inter-media congruence and No human interference), and (b) six groups of users who differ in their relative (self-reported) reliance on these five criteria as well as socio-demographic and personality characteristics, realism assessments and media repertoire: Mainstream media audience, Professional journalism objectivists, Citizen oriented, Mainstream media skeptics, Coherence-seekers, and Independents. These results are based on a field study with a heterogeneous quota-based sample surveying a set of items covering a wide array of potential message and social realism cues instead of focusing on a single or a few realism factors. These findings may help contextualize or explain diverging reality assessments of the same media content by different (groups of) individuals. Regression models predicting the realism assessments in our study by the factor scores of the five realism criterion factors explained between 26 percent (public newscasts) and 13 percent (online quality newspapers) of the respective realism ratings in the case of (quality) journalism or rather broad content categories such as media content in general, informational content or TV content in general, and between 3 and 6 percent (online tabloids) in the case of popular media categories or online content like blogs and social networks.

One limitation of our study is the use of single item self-report measures for the realism criteria—a methodological concession that allowed us to cover the widest possible range of criteria and context variables. Thus, reliability cannot be adequately demonstrated, and our results are confined to the *perceived* impact of message factors and external cues on realism judgments. A second limitation is the use of a non-representative online access panel for sampling. The mostly correlational analyses we conducted are less affected by sample characteristics; however, the cluster structure and sizes obtained in our analysis should be replicated and possibly extended in further studies. Other possible next steps would be to develop the items used in our study into a proper scale for preferred modes of authentication as a trait, thereby expanding it to include items and criteria more relevant to realism judgments in online media, and to further explore the implications of preferred realism criteria for media effects and media selection.

References

Austin, E. W., & Dong, Q. (1994). Source v. content effects on judgments of news believability. *Journalism & Mass Communication Quarterly, 71*(4), 973–983. doi:10.1177/107769909407100420

Busselle, R. W., & Greenberg, B. S. (2000). The nature of television realism judgments: A reevaluation of their conceptualization and measurement. *Mass Communication & Society, 3*(2-3), 249–268. doi:10.1207/S15327825MCS0323_05

Brock, S., & Mares, E. (2007). *Realism and anti-realism.* Checham: Acumen.

Carr, D. J., Barnidge, M., Lee, B. G., & Tsang, S. J. (2014). Cynics and skeptics: Evaluating the credibility of mainstream and citizen journalism. *Journalism & Mass Communication Quarterly, 91*, 452–470. doi:10.1177/1077699014538828

Chadha, K., & Koliska, M. (2014). Newsrooms and transparency in the digital age. *Journalism Practice, 9*(2), 215–229. doi:10.1080/17512786.2014.924737

Charrad, M., Ghazzali, N., Boiteau, V., Niknafs, A. (2014). NbClust: An R package for determining the relevant number of clusters in a data set. *Journal of Statistical Software, 61*(6), 1–36.

Coleman, S., & Moss, G. (2008). Governing at a distance - politicians in the blogosphere. *Information Polity, 13*, 7–20.

Coupland, N. (2001). Stylization, authenticity and TV news review. *Discourse Studies, 3*(4), 413–442.

Dickerson, A. V. (2012). *Nothing but the truth and the whole truthiness: Examining markers of authenticity in the modern documentary* (Master's Thesis). San Jose State Univ., San Jose, CA.

Duffy, B. E. (2013). Manufacturing authenticity: The rhetoric of "real" in women's magazines. *The Communication Review, 16*(3), 132–154. doi:10.1080/10714421.2013.807110

Egelhofer, J. L., & Lecheler, S. (2019). Fake news as a two-dimensional phenomenon: A framework and research agenda. *Annals of the International Communication Association, 43*(2), 97-116. doi:10.1080/23808985.2019.1602782

Enli, G. (2015). *Mediated authenticity: How the media constructs reality.* New York: Lang.

Eveland, W. P., & Shah, D. V. (2003). The impact of individual and interpersonal factors on perceived news media bias. *Political Psychology, 24*, 101–117. doi:10.1111/0162-895X.00318

Fawzi, N. (2019). Untrustworthy news and the media as "enemy of the people?" How a populist worldview shapes recipients' attitudes toward the media. *The International Journal of Press/Politics, 24*(2), 146-164. doi:10.1177/1940161218811981

Fawzi, N., Steindl, N., Obermaier, M., Prochazka, F., Arlt, D., Blöbaum, B., ... & Ziegele, M. (2021). Concepts, causes and consequences of trust in news media–a literature review and framework. *Annals of the International Communication Association, 45*(2), 154-174. doi:0.1080/23808985.2021.1960181

Ferrara, A. (2009). Authenticity without a true self. In P. Vannini, & J. P. Williams (Eds.), *Authenticity in culture, self, and society* (pp. 21-35). Farnham: Ashgate.

Gilpin, D. R., Palazzolo, E. T., & Brody, N. (2010). Socially mediated authenticity. *Journal of Communication Management, 14*(3), 258–278. doi:10.1108/13632541011064526

Glanzberg, M. (2018) (Ed.). *The Oxford handbook of truth.* Oxford: Oxford University Press.

Gunther, A. (1988). Attitude extremity and trust in media. *Journalism Quarterly, 65,* 279–287.

Hall, A. (2009). Perceptions of media realism and reality TV. In R. L. Nabi & M. B. Oliver (Eds.), *The Sage handbook of media processes and effects* (pp. 423–438). Los Angeles: Sage.

Haller, M. (2015, October 27). *Who to believe? European media's credibility crisis.* European Journalism Observatory. Retrieved from http://en.ejo.ch/ethics-quality/who-to-believe-european-medias-credibility-crisis

Handler, R. (1986). Authenticity. *Anthropology Today, 2,* 2-4. doi:10.2307/3032899

Karlsson, M., Clerwall, C., & Nord, L. (2014). You ain't seen nothing yet: Transparency's (lack of) effect on source and message credibility. *Journalism Studies, 15,* 668–678. doi:10.1080/1461670X.2014.886837

Koetsenruijter, A. W. M. (2011). Using numbers in news increases story credibility. *Newspaper Research Journal, 32*(2), 74–82.

Lee, E.-J. (2012). That's not the way it is: How user-generated comments on the news affect perceived media bias. *Journal of Computer-Mediated Communication, 18*(1), 32–45. doi:10.1111/j.1083-6101.2012.01597.x

Leiner, D. J. (2012). *SoSci Panel: The noncommercial online access panel.* Poster presented at the GOR 2012, 6th March, Mannheim. Retrieved from https://www.so scisurvey.de/panel/download/SoSciPanel.GOR2012.pdf

Lethen, H. (1995). Versionen des Authentischen: sechs Gemeinplätze. In H. Böhme & K. R. Scherpe (Eds.), *Literatur und Kulturwissenschaften. Positionen, Theorien, Modelle* (pp. 205–231). Reinbek bei Hamburg: Rowohlt.

Luhmann, N. (2000). *The reality of the mass media.* Stanford: Stanford University Press.

Metzger, M. J., Flanagin, A. J., Eyal, K., Lemus, D. R., & McCann, R. M. (2003). Credibility for the 21st century: Integrating perspectives on source, message, and media credibility in the contemporary media environment. *Communication Yearbook, 27,* 293–335.

Morris, P. (2004). *Realism.* London: Routledge.

Radant, M., & Dalbert, C. (2003). *Zur Dimensionalität der Ambiguitätstoleranz* [Regarding the dimensionality of the construct ‚ambiguity tolerance']. Poster presentation, 7th DPPD Conference of the Deutsche Gesellschaft für Psychologie, Halle, Germany.

Satow, L. (2012). *Big Five Persönlichkeitstest (B5T). Test und Skalendokumentation.* [Big Five Inventory (B5T): Documentation of test and scale]. https://www.psych archives.org/bitstream/20.500.12034/423.2/1/PT_9006357_B5T_Forschungsberic ht.pdf

Scannell, P. (1996). *Radio, television and modern life: A phenomenological approach.* Oxford: Blackwell.

Self, C. C. (1996). Credibility. In M. B. Salwen & D. W. Stacks (Eds.), *An integrated approach to communication theory and research* (pp. 421-441). Mahwah, NJ: Lawrence Erlbaum Assoc.

Steele, J. E. (1995). Experts and the operational bias of television news: The case of the Persian Gulf War. *Journalism & Mass Communication Quarterly, 72,* 799–812.

Sundar, S. S. (1998). Effect of source attribution on perception of online news stories. *Journalism & Mass Communication Quarterly, 75,* 55–68.

Swift, A. (2016, September 14). *Americans' trust in mass media sinks to new low.* Gallup. Retrieved from www.gallup.com/poll/195542/americans-trust-mass-med ia-sinks-new-low.aspx

Trilling, L. (1971). *Sincerity and authenticity.* Cambridge: Harvard University Press.

Tsfati, Y., & Ariely, G. (2014). Individual and contextual correlates of trust in media across 44 countries. *Communication Research, 41*(6), 760–782. doi:10.1177/0093650213485972

Tsfati, Y., & Peri, Y. (2006). Mainstream media skepticism and exposure to sectorial and extranational news media: The case of Israel. *Mass Communication & Society, 9*(2), 165–187.

Vallone, R. P., Ross, L., & Lepper, M. R. (1985). The hostile media phenomenon: Biased perception and perceptions of media bias in coverage of the Beirut Massacre. *Journal of Personality and Social Psychology, 49*(3), 577–585.

Felix Frey (Dr. phil., Leipzig University, 2015) is a Research Fellow at the Institute of Communication and Media Studies at Leipzig University. His research focuses on modes and strategies of media reception and use, communicative practices and struggles of media users in changing media environments, and methodological issues, especially in theory development. From 2014 to 2017, Felix was a research and teaching associate in Wolfram Peiser's team.

Felix Frey, Benjamin Krämer & Wolfram Peiser

Benjamin Krämer *(Dr. rer. pol., LMU Munich, 2012) is Akademischer Rat auf Zeit and Privatdozent at LMU Munich's Department of Media Communication. His research focuses on political communication (with an emphasis on populist communication), media use and reception, and online communication as well as on the development and adaptation of new empirical methods and strategies of systematic theory building. Wolfram Peiser supervised his PhD and was a member of the supervision committee of his habilitation in Munich. Benjamin worked as research and teaching associate at his chair from 2006 to 2021.*